9 T H - Edition

CELEBRITY DIRECTORY™

9TH - Edition

CELEBRITY DIRECTORY™

 Axiom Information Resources

ISSN 1083-1614

ISBN 0-943213-31-2

Printed in the United States of America

SPECIAL SALES

The Celebrity Directory™ is available at special quantity discounts. For information, write:

Axiom Information Resources Inc., P.O. Box 8015-T, Ann Arbor, Michigan 48107 U.S.A.

Introduction

Welcome to the new and expanded ninth edition of the Celebrity Directory™. This new edition incorporates many changes suggested by our readers' enthusiastic response to previous editions. As always, our aim is to provide the reference librarian, speaking engagement coordinator, general researcher or fan with the easiest-to-use, most accurate and comprehensive collection of celebrity names and addresses available anywhere.

The editors have researched and arranged data on thousands of prominent persons engaged in all fields of human accomplishment throughout the world. If a person is famous and worth locating, it's almost certain that his or her name and address is listed in the convenient, alphabetically-arranged Celebrity Directory™.

Most of the celebrities listed in this directory welcome correspondence concerning their lives and work. Please remember when writing to a celebrity, as well as writing to Axiom Information Resources Inc., it is always best to enclose a stamped, self-addressed envelope. Of course, the editorial staff and publisher cannot guarantee that listed celebrities will respond to correspondence.

We have made every effort to ensure that the information contained in the Celebrity Directory™ is up-to-date and accurate. We cannot accept responsibility for inaccuracies created by a celebrity's moving or changing his or her mail arrangements after the directory went to press.

We welcome any suggestions or inquiries concerning the Celebrity Directory™, and we sincerely hope this new edition will provide our readers with even more entertainment and information. All inquiries concerning this book should be sent to Axiom Information Resources Inc., P.O. Box 8015-X, Ann Arbor, Michigan 48107 U.S.A.

Beverly Aadland
27617 Ennismore Avenue
Canyon Country, CA 91351
"Actress"

Aaliyah
9255 Sunset Blvd. #804
West Hollywood, CA 90069
"Singer"

Henry Aaron
1611 Adams Drive S.W.
Atlanta, GA 30311
"Ex-Baseball Player"

Bruce Abbott
4526 Wilshire Blvd.
Los Angeles, CA 90010
"Actor"

Dihanne Abbott
460 West Avenue #46
Los Angeles, CA 90065
"Actress"

Gregory Abbott
P.O. Box 68
Bergenfield, NY 07621
"Singer"

Paula Abdul
771 Teakwood Road
Los Angeles, CA 90049
"Singer"

Kareem Abdul-Jabbar
1436 Summitridge Drive
Beverly Hills, CA 90210
"Basketball Player"

Abdullah The Butcher
1000 S. Industrial Blvd.
Dallas, TX 75207
"Wrestler"

Akeem Abdul Olajuwon
10 Greenway Plaza E.
Houston, TX 77046
"Basketball Player"

Ian Abercrombie
1040 North Gardner
Los Angeles, CA 90046
"Actor"

F. Murray Abraham
40 Fifth Avenue #2C
New York, NY 10011
"Actor"

Leslie Abramson
4929 Wilshire Blvd.
Los Angeles, CA 90010
"Attorney"

Victoria Abril
11 rue Chanez
F-75016 Paris FRANCE
"Actress"

Ray Abruzzo
20334 Pacific Coast Hwy.
Malibu, CA 90265
"Actor"

AC/DC
46 Kensington Ct. St.
London W8 5DP ENGLAND
"Rock & Roll Group"

Bettye Ackerman
302 North Alpine Drive
Beverly Hills, CA 90210
"Actress"

Forrest Ackerman
2495 Glendower
Los Angeles, CA 90027
"Author"

Leslie Ackerman
4439 Worster Avenue
Studio City, CA 91604
"Actress"

Joss Ackland
76 Oxford Street
London W1N OAX ENGLAND
"Actor"

David Ackroyd
273 N. Many Lakes Drive
Kalispell, MT 59901
"Actor"

Timothy Ackroyd
33 Chepstone Road
London W2 5BP ENGLAND
"Actor"

Jay Acovone
3811 Multiview Drive
Los Angeles, CA 90068
"Actor"

Deborah Adair
P.O. Box 1980
Studio City, CA 91614
"Actress"

Red Adair
P.O. Box 747
Bellville, TX 77418
"Fire Extinguishing Expert"

Theo Adam
Schillerstr. 14
01326 Dresden GERMANY
"Basso-Baritone"

Brooke Adams
248 S. Van Ness Avenue
Los Angeles, CA 90004
"Actress"

Bryan Adams
406-68 Water Street
Vancouver BC V6B 1A4 CANADA
"Singer"

Cindy Adams
1050 Fifth Avenue
New York, NY 10028
"Actress"

Don Adams
2160 Century Park East #110
Los Angeles, CA 90067
"Actor, Writer, Director"

Edie Adams
8040 Okean Terrace
Los Angeles, CA 90046
"Singer, Actor"

Gerry Adams
51/55 Falls Road
Belfast BT 12
NORTHERN IRELAND
"Political Leader

Joey Adams
1050 Fifth Avenue
New York, NY 10028
"Actor, Writer, Director"

Julie Adams
4605 Lankershire Blvd. #305
North Hollywood, CA 91602
"Actress"

Maria Adams
247 S. Beverly Drive #102
Beverly Hills, CA 90212
"Actress"

Mason Adams
900 Fifth Avenue
New York, NY 10021
Actor"

Maud Adams
11901 Sunset Blvd. #214
Los Angeles, CA 90049
"Actress, Model"

Richard Adams
26 Church Street
Whitechurch, Hants. ENGLAND
"Author"

Tom Adams
29-31 Kings Road
London SW3 ENGLAND
"Actor"

ADC Band
17397 Santa Barbara
Detroit, MI 48221
"Rock & Roll Group"

Herb Adderly
8 Pelham Road
Philadelphia, PA 19119
"Musician"

Merv Adelson
600 Sarbonne Road
Los Angeles, CA 90077
"TV Producer"

Isabelle Adjani
2 rue Lord Byron
F-75008 Paris, FRANCE
"Actress"

Tracee Adkins
1250-6th Avenue #401
Santa Monica, CA 90401
"Singer"

Lou Adler
3969 Villa Costera
Malibu, CA 90265
"Director, Producer"

King Bhumibol Adulyadey
Villa Chiralada
Bangkok, THAILAND
"King Of Thailand"

Aerosmith
584 Broadway #1009
New York, NY 10012
"Rock & Roll Group"

Ben Affleck
405 S. Beverly Drive #500
Beverly Hills, CA 90212
"Actor"

John Agar
639 North Hollywood Way
Burbank, CA 91505
"Actor"

Andre Agassi
8921 Andre Drive
Las Vegas, NV 89113
"Tennis Player"

Martin Agronsky
4001 Brandywine Street
Washington, DC 20016
"TV Producer"

Jenny Agutter
1026 Montana Avenue
Santa Monica, CA 90403
"Actress"

Danny Aiello
4 Thornhill Drive
Ramsey, NJ 07446
"Actor"

Troy Aikman
P.O. Box 630227
Irving, TX 75063
"Football Player"

Roger Ailes
440 Park Avenue South
New York, NY 10016
"Producer, Director"

Anouk Aimee
201 rue du Faubourg St. Honore
F-75008 Paris, FRANCE
"Actress"

Danny Ainge
2910 North Central
Phoenix, AZ 95012
"Basketball Player"

Air Supply
14755 Ventura Blvd. #1-710
Sherman Oaks, CA 91403
"Rock & Roll Group"

Franklin Ajaye
1312 South Orange Drive
Los Angeles, CA 90019
"Comedian, Actor"

Emperor Akihoto
The Imperial Palace
1-1 Chiyoda - Chiyoda-Ku
Tokyo, JAPAN
"Emperor of Japan"

Alabama
P.O. Box 529
Ft. Payne, AL 35967
"C&W Group"

Brick Alan
976 Murfreesboro Road #93
Nashville, TN 37217
"Singer"

Buddy Alan
600 East Gilbert
Tempe, AZ 85281
"Singer"

Alarm
47 Bernard Street
St. Albans, Herts ENGLAND
"Rock & Roll Group"

President Hafez Al-Assad
Presidential Office
Damascus, SYRIA
"President of Syria"

Edward Albee
P.O. Box 697
Montauk, NY 11954
"Writer, Producer"

Anna Marie Alberghetti
10333 Chrysanthemum Lane
Los Angeles, CA 90077
"Actress, Singer"

Eddie Albert
719 Amalfi Drive
Pacific Palisades, CA 90272
"Actor"

Edward Albert
27320 Winding Way
Malibu, CA 90265
"Actor"

Prince Albert
Palais De Monaco
Boite Postal 158
98015 Monte Carlo Monaco
"Prince of Monaco"

Dolores Albin
23388 Mulholland Drive
Woodland Hills, CA 91364
"Actress"

Medeleine Albright
1318 34th Street NW
Washington, DC 20007
"Secretary of State"

Dr. Tenley Albright
2 Commonwealth Avenue
Boston, MA 02117
"Skater"

Amy Alcott
1411 Fifth Street #306
Santa Monica, CA 90401
"Golfer"

Alan Alda
641 Lexington Avenue #1400
New York, NY 10022
"Actor"

Antony Alda
15 Seaview Drive North
Rolling Hills, CA 90274
"Actor"

Ginger Alden
6554 Whitetail Lane
Memphis, TN 38115
"Model"

Norman Alden
106 North Croft Avenue
Los Angeles, CA 90048
"Actor"

Dr. Ed "Buzz" Aldrin, Jr.
838 N. Doheny Drive #1407
W. Hollywood, CA 90069
"Astronaut"

Frank Aletter
5430 Corbin Avenue
Tarzana, CA 91356
"Actor"

Kyle Aletter
5430 Corbin Avenue
Tarzana, CA 91356
"Actress"

Denise Alexander
270 N. Canon Drive
Beverly Hills, CA 90210
"Actress"

Doyle Alexander
5416 Hunter Park Court
Arlington Park, TX 76017
"Ex-Baseball Player"

Jane Alexander
The Lansburgh
1100 Pennsylvania Ave. NW 520
Washington, DC 20506
"Actress"

Lamar Alexander
1109 Owen Place NE
Washington, DC 20008
"Ex-Governor"

Jason Alexander
405 S. Beverly Drive #500
Beverly Hills, CA 90212
"Actor"

Shana Alexander
156 Fifth Avenue #617
New York, NY 10010
"News Correspondent"

Kim Alexis
345 North Maple Drive #185
Beverly Hills, CA 90210
"Model"

Kristian Alfonso
P.O. Box 557
Brockton, MA 02403
"Actress"

Muhammad Ali
P.O. Box 187
Berrien Springs, MI 49103
"Former Boxing Champion"

Tatyana Ali
4924 Balboa Blvd. #377
Encino, CA 91316
"Actress"

Mehmet Ali Agca
Rebibbia Prison
Rome ITALY
"Attempted to Kill Pope"

Alicia-Ana
3511 Sea Ledge Lane
Santa Barbara, CA 93109
"Actress"

Alice in Chains
207 1/2 First Avenue South, #300
Seattle, WA 98104
"Grunge Band"

Jed Allan
P.O. Box 5302
Blue Jay, CA 92317
"Actor"

Betty Allen
645 St. Nicholas Avenue
New York, NY 10030
"Mezzo-Soprano"

Chad Allen
6489 Cavalleri Road #204
Mailbu, CA 90265
"Actor"

Elizabeth Allen
P.O. Box 243
Lake Peekskill, NY 10537
"Actress"

Joan Allen
40 W. 57th Street
New York, NY 10019
"Actress"

Jonelle Allen
8730 Sunset Blvd. #480
Los Angeles, CA 90069
"Actress, Singer"

Karen Allen
P.O. Box 237
Monterey, MA 01245
"Actress"

Marcus Allen
433 Ward Parkway #29
Kansas City, MO 64112
"Football Player"

Marty Allen
1991 Pago Court
Las Vegas, NV 89117
"Actor, Comedian"

Nancy Allen
8154 Mulholland Terrace
Los Angeles, CA 90046
"Actress"

Rex Allen, Jr.
128 Pine Oak Drive
Hendersonville, TN 37075
"Singer"

Sean Barbara Allen
1622 Sierra Bonita Avenue
Los Angeles, CA 90046
"Actress, Writer"

Steve Allen
15201-B Burbank Blvd.
Van Nuys, CA 91411
"Actor, Writer, Comedian"

Tim Allen
1122 S. Robertson Blvd. #15
Los Angeles, CA 90035
"Actor"

Woody Allen
930 Fifth Avenue
New York, NY 10018
"Actor, Director, Comedian"

Kirstie Alley
132 S. Rodeo Drive #300
Beverly Hills, CA 90212
"Actress"

Michael Allinson
112 Knollwood Drive
Larchmont, NY 10538
"Actor"

Mose Allison
34 Dogwood Street
Smithtown, NY 11787
"Pianist, Composer"

Greg Allman
650 California Street #900
San Francisco, CA 94108
"Musician"

Christopher Allport
121 North San Vicente Blvd.
Beverly Hills, CA 90211
"Actor"

Gloria Allred
6300 Wilshire Blvd. #1500
Los Angeles, CA 90048
"Attorney, Feminist"

June Allyson
1651 Foothill Road
Ojai, CA 93023
"Actress"

Maria Conchita Alonso
P.O. Box 537
Beverly Hills, CA 90213
"Actress"

Felipe Alou
7263 Davit Circle
Lake Worth, FL 33467
"Ex-Baseball Player"

Hollis Alpert
P.O. Box 142
Shelter Island, NY 11964
"Writer"

Carol Alt
111 East 22nd Street #200
New York, NY 10010
"Actress"

Jeff Altman
4345-C Freedom Drive
Calabasas, CA 91302
"Comedian, Actor"

Robert Altman
502 Park Avenue #15G
New York, NY 10022
"Writer, Producer, Director"

Robert Altman
9200 Harrington Drive
Potomac, MD 20854
"Financier"

Luigi Alva
via Moscova 46/3
20121 Mailand ITALY
"Tenor"

Trini Alvarado
233 Park Avenue South
10th Floor
New York, NY 10003
"Actress"

Lance Alworth
990 Highland Drive #300
Solana Beach, CA 92075
"Ex-Football Player"

Christiane Amanpour
25 rue de Ponthieu
75008 Paris, France
"Broadcast Journalist"

Rodney Amateau
133 1/2 South Linden Drive
Beverly Hills, CA 90212
"Film Writer, Producer

Nicolas Amer
14 Great Russell Street
London WC1 ENGLAND
"Actor"

America
345 N. Maple Drive #300
Beverly Hills, CA 90210
"Rock & Roll Group"

Aldrich Ames
P.O. Box 3000
White Deer, PA 17887
"Alledged Spy"

Ed Ames
1457 Claridge
Beverly Hills, CA 90210
"Singer"

Rachel Ames
303 South Crescent Heights
Los Angeles, CA 90048
"Author"

Madchen Amick
P.O. Box 48107
Los Angeles, CA 90048
"Actress"

Idi Amin
Box 8948
Jidda 21492 SAUDI ARABIA
"Deposed Ruler"

Suzy Amis
8942 Wilshire Blvd.
Beverly Hills, CA 90211
"Actress"

Clevland Amory
200 West 57th Street
New York, NY 10019
"Writer"

Deborah Amos
c/o National Public Radio
2025 "M" Street N.W.
Washington, DC 20036
"News Correspondent"

John Amos
P.O. Box 587
Califon, NJ 07830
"Actor"

Tori Amos
P.O. Box 8456
Clearwater, FL 34618
"Singer"

Bill Anderson
P.O. Box 888
Hermitage, TN 37076
"Singer"

Brad Anderson
13022 Wood Harbour Drive
Montgomery, TX 77356
"Cartoonist"

Daryl Anderson
5923 Wilbur Avenue
Tarzana, CA 91356
"Actor"

Gillian Anderson
110-555 Brooks Bank Avenue #10
No. Vancouver BC V7J 3S5
CANADA
"Actress"

Harry Anderson
422-292nd Avenue, N.E.
Fall City, WA 98024
"Actor, Comedian"

Jack Anderson
7810 Kachina Lane
Potomac, MD 20854
"News Correspondent"

John Anderson
Nova University
Center for Law
Ft. Lauderdale, FL 33314
"Politician"

Loni Anderson
3355 Clerendon Road
Beverly Hills, CA 90210
"Actress"

Louie Anderson
8033 Sunset Blvd. #605
Los Angeles, CA90046
"Comedian"

Lynn Anderson
514 Fairlane Drive
Nashville, TN 37211
"Singer"

Mary Anderson
1127 Norman Place
Los Angeles, CA 90049
"Actress"

Melissa Sue Anderson
1558 Will Geer Road
Topanga, CA 90290
"Actress"

Melody Anderson
P.O. Box 6919
New York, NY 10128
"Actress"

Michael Anderson
483 Southbank House
Black Prince Road
London SE1 7SJ ENGLAND
"Film Director"

Michael J. Anderson
3838 Vinton Avenue #302
Culver City, CA 90232
"Actor"

Pamela Anderson-Lee
9255 Sunset Blvd. #920
Los Angeles CA 90069
"Actress"

Paul Anderson
1603 McIntosh Street
Vidalia, GA 30474
"Weightlifter"

Richard Anderson
10120 Cielo Drive
Beverly Hills, CA 90210
"Actor"

Richard Dean Anderson
8942 Wilshire Blvd.
Beverly Hills, CA 90211
"Actor"

Sheri Anderson
3633 Willowcrest Avenue
Studio City, CA 91604
"TV Writer"

George "Sparky" Anderson
P.O. Box 6415
Thousand Oaks, CA 91359
"Ex-Baseball Manager"

Terry Anderson
50 Rockefeller Plaza
New York, NY 10020
"News Correspondent"

Bibi Andersson
P.O. Box 5037
S-10241 Stockholm SWEDEN
"Actress"

Ursula Andress
Via Francesco Siacci 38
I-00197 Rome ITALY
"Actress"

John Andretti
2416 Music Valley Drive
Nashville, TN 37214
"Race Car Driver"

Mario Andretti
53 Victory Lane
Nazareth, PA 18064
"Race Car Driver"

Michael Andretti
3310 Airport Road
Allentown, PA 18103
"Race Car Driver"

Prince Andrew
Sunninghill Park
Windsor, ENGLAND
"England Royalty"

Anthony Andrews
Unit 5/3-4
The Chambers
Chelsea Harbour
London SW10 0FX ENGLAND
"Actor"

Julie Andrews
P.O. Box 491668
Los Angeles, CA 90049
"Singer"

Patti Andrews
9823 Aldea Avenue
Northridge, CA 91354
"Singer"

Tige Andrews
4914 Encino Terrace
Encino, CA 91316
"Actor, Writer"

Vanessa Angel
9000 Sunset Blvd. #1000
Los Angeles, CA 90069
"Actress"

Maya Angelou
3240 Valley Road
Winston-Salem, NC 28106
"Writer, Poet"

The Angels
P.O. Box 3864
Beverly Hills, CA 90212
"Rock & Roll Group"

Kenneth Anger
354 East 91st Street #9
New York, NY 10128
"Film Director"

Jean-Hughes Anglade
151 El Camino Drive
Beverly Hills, CA 90212
"Actress"

Philip Anglim
2404 Grand Canal
Venice, CA 90291
"Actor"

Edward Anhalt
500 Amalfi Drive
Pacific Palisades, CA 90272
"Writer, Producer"

Jennifer Aniston
5750 Wilshire Blvd. #580
Los Angeles, CA 90036
"Actress"

John Aniston
4872 Topanga Canyon Blvd. #311
Woodland Hills, CA 91364
"Actor"

Paul Anka
10573 West Pico Blvd. #159
Los Angeles, CA 90064
"Singer"

Ann-Margaret
5664 Cahuenga Blvd. #336
North Hollywood, CA 91601
"Actress"

Kofi Annan
799 United Nations Plaza
New York, NY 10017
"United Nations Secretary"

Princess Anne
Gatcombe Park
Glouchestershire, ENGLAND
"England Royalty"

Wallis Annenberg
10273 Century Woods Place
Los Angeles, CA 90067
"Magazine Executive"

Francesca Annis
2 Vicarage Court
London W8 ENGLAND
"Actress"

Michael Ansara
4624 Park Mirasol
Calabasas, CA 91302
"Actor"

Susan Anspach
473 16th Street
Santa Monica, CA 90402
"Actress"

Adam Ant
503 The Chambers
Chelsea Harbour, Lots Road
London SW10 0XF ENGLAND
"Singer"

Lysette Anthony
25-22 Marshall Street #300
London W1V 1LL ENGLAND
"Actress"

Ray Anthony
9288 Kinglet Drive
Los Angeles, CA 90069
"Orchestra Leader"

Susan Anton
16830 Ventura Blvd. #300
Encino, CA 91436
"Actress"

Lou Antonio
530 Gaylord Drive
Burbank, CA 91505
"Actor, Writer, Director"

Michelangelo Antonioni
Via Vincenzo Tiberio 18
Rome, ITALY
"Film Director"

Gabrielle Anwar
253 - 26th Street #A-203
Santa Monica, CA 90402
"Actress"

Rocky Aoki
8685 N.W. 53rd Terrace
Miami, FL 33155
"Food Entrepreneur"

Luis Aparicio
P.O. Box 590
Cooperstown, NY 13325
"Ex-Baseball Player"

Fiona Apple
509 Hartnell Street
Monterey, CA 93940
"Singer"

Christina Applegate
9055 Hollywood Hills Road
Los Angeles, CA 90046
"Actress"

John Aprea
727 North Martel Avenue
Los Angeles, CA 90046
"Actor"

Corazon Aquino
c/o Pius XVI Center, UN
Manila PHILIPPINES
"Politician"

Yassir Arafat
Gaza City, Gaza Strio
Palestine ISRAEL
"Politician"

Alan Arbus
2208 North Beverly Glen
Los Angeles, CA 90077
"Actor"

Loreen Arbus
8841 Appian Way
Los Angeles, CA 90046
"Writer"

Anne Archer
13201 Old Oak Lane
Los Angeles, CA 90049
"Actress"

Bernard Archer
Holt Barton
Witham Frairy
Somerset ENGLAND
"Actor"

Beverly Archer
606 North Larchmont Blvd. #309
Los Angeles, CA 90004
"Actress"

Dennis Archer
2 Woodward Avenue
Detroit, MI 48226
"Mayor"

Jeffrey Archer
93 Albert Embankment
London SE1 ENGLAND
"Author"

Army Archerd
442 Hilgard Avenue
Los Angeles, CA 90024
"Columnist"

Toni Arden
34-34 75th Street
Jackson Heights, NY 11372
"Singer"

Moshe Arens
49 Hagderat
Savyon, ISRAEL
"Politician"

Oscar Arias
Apdo 8-6410-1000
San Jose, COSTA RICA
"Politician"

Ben Aris
47 West Square
London SE11 4SP ENGLAND
"Actor"

Adam Arkin
2372 Veteran Avenue #102
Los Angeles, CA 90064
"Actor, Director"

Alan Arkin
21 E. 40th Street #1705
New York, NY 10016-0501
"Actor"

Samuel Z. Arkoff
3205 Oakdell Lane
Studio City, CA 91604
"Film Producer"

Roone Arledge
1330 Avenue of the Americas
New York, NY 10019
"TV Producer"

Giorgio Armani
Palazzo Durini 24
1-20122 Milan ITALY
"Fashion Designer"

Joan Armatrading
27 Queensdale Place
London W11 ENGLAND
"Singer, Guitarist"

Rep. Dick Armey (TX)
House Cannon Bldg. #301
Washington, DC 20515
"Politician"

Russell Arms
2918 Davis Way
Palm Springs, CA 92262
"Actor, Singer"

Anne Armstrong
Armstrong Ranch
Armstrong, TX 78338
"Politician"

Bess Armstrong
151 El Camino Drive
Beverly Hills, CA 90212
"Actress"

Curtis Armstrong
3867 Shannon Road
Los Angeles, CA 90027
"Actor"

Garner Ted Armstrong
P.O. Box 2525
Tyler, TX 75710
"Evangelist, Author"

Neil Armstrong
777 Columbus Avenue
Lebanon, OH 45036
"Astronaut"

R.G. Armstrong
3856 Reklaw Drive
North Hollywood, CA 91604
"Actor"

John Arnatt
3 Warren Cottage
Woodland Way
Surrey KT10 6NN ENGLAND
"Actor"

Lucie Arnaz
P.O. Box 636
Cross River, NY 10518
"Actress"

James Arness
P.O. Box 49003
Los Angeles, CA 90049
"Actor"

Jeanetta Arnette
840 N. Huntley Drive #3
Los Angeles, CA 90069
"Actress"

Alison Arngrim
P.O. Box 46891
Los Angeles, CA 90046
"Actress"

Eddy Arnold
P.O. Box 97
Brentwood, TN 37027
"Singer"

Tom Arnold
638 Lindero Canyon Road #367
Agoura Hills, CA 91301
"Actor"

Francois Arnoul
53 rue Censier
F-75005 Paris FRANCE
"Actress"

Stefan Arnsten
1017 Laurel Way
Beverly Hills, CA 90210
"Actor"

Alexis Arquette
1999 Avenue of the Stars #2850
Los Angeles, CA 90067
"Actor"

David Arquette
8942 Wilshire Blvd.
Beverly Hills, CA 90211
"Actor"

Patricia Arquette
9560 Wilshire Blvd. #516
Beverly Hills, CA 90212
"Actress"

Rosanna Arquette
7704 Woodrow Wilson Drive
Los Angeles, CA 90046
"Actress"

Rod Arrants
260 S. Beverly Drive #308
Beverly Hills, CA 90212
"Actor"

Arrested Development
9380 SW 72nd Street #B-220
Miami, FL 33174
"Music Group"

Gus Arriola
P.O. Box 3275
Carmel, CA 93921
"Cartoonist"

Beatrice Arthur
2000 Old Ranch Road
Los Angeles, CA 90049
"Actress"

Maureen Arthur
9200 Sunset Blvd. #1130
Los Angeles, CA 90069
"Actress"

Robert Arthur
1711 Kings Way
Los Angeles, CA 90069
"Producer"

Mary Kay Ash
16251 Dallas Parkway
Dallas, TX 75248
"Cosmetic Executive"

Dana Ashbrook
924 Westwood Blvd. #900
Los Angeles, CA 90024
"Actress"

Daphne Ashbrook
10683 Santa Monica Blvd.
Los Angeles, CA 90025
"Actress"

Linden Ashby
12424 Wilshire Blvd.#840
Los Angeles, CA 90025
"Actor"

Jane Asher
Coventry Street
London, W1 ENGLAND
"Actress"

Peter Asher
644 North Doheny Drive
Los Angeles, CA 90069
"Record Producer"

William Asher
54-337 Oak Hill Blvd.
La Quinta, CA 92253
"Writer, Producer"

Renee Asherson
28 Elsworth Road
London NW3 ENGLAND
"Actress"

David Ashford
53 Moat Drive
Harrow, Middlesex ENGLAND
"Actor"

Evelyn Ashford
818 Plantation Lane
Walnut, CA 91789
"Athlete"

Ashford & Simpson
254 West 72nd Street #1-A
New York, NY 10023
"Vocal Duo"

Vladimir Ashkenazy
Sonnenhof 4
6004 Lucerne, SWITZERLAND
"Pianist"

Edward Ashley
4054 Pylon Way
Oceanside, CA 92056
"Actor"

Elizabeth Ashley
1223 North Ogden Drive
Los Angeles, CA 90046
"Actress"

Jennifer Ashley
11130 Huston St. #6 .
North Hollywood, CA 91601
"Actress"

John Ashton
700 Hinsdale Drive
Ft. Collins, CO 80526
"Actor"

Luke Askew
8383 Wilshire Blvd., #954
Beverly Hills, CA 90211
"Actor"

Asleep At The Wheel
P.O. Box 463
Austin, TX 75767
"Rock & Roll Group"

Edward Asner
12400 Ventura Blvd. #371
Studio City, CA 91604
"Actor"

Jennifer Aspen
10390 Santa Monica Blvd. #300
Los Angeles, CA 90025
"Actress"

Armand Assante
367 Windsor Highway
New Windsor, NY 12553
"Actor"

Pat Ast
1412 1/4 North Hayworth Avenue
Los Angeles, CA 90046
"Actress"

Robyn Astaire
1155 San Ysidro Drive
Beverly Hills, CA 90210
"Widower of Fred Astaire"

John Astin
P.O. Box 49698
Los Angeles, CA 90049
"Actor, Director, Writer"

Mackenzie Astin
4526 Wilshire Blvd.
Los Angeles, CA 90010
"Actor"

Sean Astin
5438 Norwich Avenue
Van Nuys, CA 91411
"Actor"

William Atherton
5102 San Feliciano Drive
Woodland Hills, CA 91364
"Actor"

Chet Atkins
1096 Lynwood Blvd.
Nashville, TN 37215
"Guitarist"

Christopher Atkins
6934 Bevis Avenue
Van Nuys 91405
"Actor"

Tom Atkins
10100 Santa Monica Blvd. #2500
Los Angeles, CA 90067
"Actor"

Rowan Atkinson
5 Soho Square
London W1V 5DE ENGLAND
"Actor, Comedian"

David Attenborough
5 Park Road
Richmond Green
Surrey ENGLAND
"TV Producer"

Sir Richard Attenborough
Old Friars
Richard Green, Surrey
ENGLAND
"Writer, Producer"

Margaret Atwood
70 Wynford Drive
Don Mills, Ontario
M3C 1J9 CANADA
"Authoress"

Rene Auberjonois
8428-C Melrose Place
Los Angeles, CA 90069
"Actor"

Jacques Aubuchon
20978 Rios Street
Woodland Hills, CA 91364
"Actor"

Louis Auchincloss
1111 Park Avenue
New York, NY 10028
"Author, Critic"

Stephanie Audran
95 Bis rue de Chezy
92200 Neuilly-sur-seine
FRANCE
"Actor"

Red Auerbach
780 Boylston Street
Boston, MA 02199
"Basketball Executive"

Nadja Auermann
Via San Vittore 40
I-20123 Milan ITALY
"Actress"

Claudine Auger
151 El Camino Drive
Beverly Hills, CA 90212
"Actress"

Ira Augustain
3900 Ramboz Drive
Los Angeles, CA 90063
"Actor"

Jean Pierre Aumont
4 Allee des Brouillards
F-65018 Paris FRANCE
"Author"

Jean Aurel
40 rue Lauriston
F-7016 Paris, FRANCE
"Writer"

Karen Austin
3356 Rowena Avenue
Los Angeles, CA 90027
"Actress"

Teri Austin
4245 Laurel Grove
Studio City, CA 91604
"Actress"

Tracy Austin
1751 Pinnacle Drive #1500
McLean, VA 22102
"Tennis Player"

Alan Autry
15301 Ventura Blvd. #345
Sherman Oaks, CA 91403
"Actor"

Frankie Avalon
4303 Spring Forest Lane
Westlake Village, CA 91362
"Singer"

MichaelAngelo Avallone
80 Hilltop Blvd.
East Brunswick, NJ 08816
"Author"

Richard Avedon
407 East 75th Street
New York, NY 10021
"Photographer"

James Avery
8075 West 3rd Street #303
Los Angeles, CA 90048
"Actor"

Margaret Avery
P.O. Box 3493
Hollywood, CA 90078
"Actress"

Val Avery
84 Grove Street #19
New York, NY 10014
"Actor"

Hoyt Axton
102 Bedford Street #102
Hamilton, MT 59840
"Singer, Songwriter"

Dan Aykroyd
1180 S. Beverly Drive#618
Los Angeles, CA 90035
"Actor"

Leah Ayres
15718 Milbank
Encino, CA 91436
"Actress"

Hank Azaria
2211 Corinth #210
Los Angeles, CA 90064
"Actor"

Paul Azinger
7847 Chick Evans Place
Sarasota, FL 34240
"Golfer"

Charles Aznavour
76-78 ave. des Champs Elysses
F-75008 Paris FRANCE
"Singer"

Candice Azzara
8899 Beverly Blvd. #510
Los Angeles, CA 90048
"Actress"

B-52
P.O. Box 60468
Rochester, NY 14606
"Rock & Roll Group"

Shirley Babashoff
16260 Mercury Drive
Westminster, CA 92683
"Swimmer"

Sec. Bruce Babbitt
Department of Interior
"C" St. Between 18th & 19th NW
Washington, DC 20240
"Secretary of Interior"

Harry Babbitt
7 Rue St. Cloud
Newport Beach, CA 91660
"Conductor"

Barbara Babcock
530 West California Blvd.
Pasadena, CA 91105
"Actress"

Tai Babilonia
13889 Valley Vista Blvd.
Sherman Oaks, CA 91423
"Ice Skater"

Baby's
1545 Archer Road
Bronx, NY 10462
"Music Group"

Babyface
8436 West 3rd Street #650
Los Angeles, CA 90048
"Singer"

Lauren Bacall
1 West 72nd Street #43
New York, NY 10023
"Actress"

Barbara Bach
1541 Ocean Avenue #200
Santa Monica, CA 90401
"Actress"

Catherine Bach
15930 Woodvale Road
Encino, CA 91436
"Actress"

Burt Bacharach
10 Ocean Park Blvd #4
Santa Monica, CA 90405
"Composer, Pianist"

Don Bachardy
145 Adelaide Drive
Santa Monica, CA 90402
"Writer"

Bachman-Turner-Overdrive
1505 West 2nd Avenue, #200
Vancouver BC V6H 3Y4 Canada
"Rock and Roll Group"

Wally Backman
160 S.E. 39th Street
Hillsboro, OR 97123
"Baseball Player"

Henny Backus
10914 Bellagio Road
Los Angeles, CA 90077
"Actress"

James Bacon
10982 Topeka Drive
Northridge, CA 91324
"Actor"

Kevin Bacon
P.O. Box 668
Sharon, CT 06069
"Actor"

Sarah Badel
4 Ovington Gardens
London SW3 1LS ENGLAND
"Actress"

Jane Badler
10000 Santa Monica Blvd. #315
Los Angeles, CA 90067
"Actress"

John Badham
288 Hot Springs Road
Montecito, CA 93108
"Film Director"

Max Baer, Jr.
3455 Eastern Avenue
Las Vegas, NV 89109
"Film Director"

Parley Baer
4967 Bilmoor Avenue
Tarzana, CA 91356
"Actor"

Joan Baez
P.O. Box 1026
Menlo Park, CA 94025
"Singer"

Vince Bagetta
3928 Madelia Avenue
Sherman Oak, CA 91403
"Actor"

Donovan Bailey
625 Hales Chapel Road
Gray, TN 37615
"Sprinter"

F. Lee Bailey
1400 Centre Park Blvd. #909
West Palm Beach, FL 33401
"Attorney"

G.W. Bailey
4972 Calvin
Tarzana, CA 91356
"Actor"

Jim Bailey
5909 West Colgate Avenue
Los Angeles, CA 90036
"Actor"

Joel Bailey
6550 Murietta Road
Van Nuys, CA 91401
"Actor"

Razzy Bailey
P.O. Box 62
Geneva, NE 68361
"Singer"

Barbara Bain
1501 Skylark Lane West
West Hollywood, CA 90069
"Actress"

Conrad Bain
1230 Chickory Lane
Los Angeles, CA 90049
"Actress"

Beryl Bainbridge
42 Albert Street
London NW1 7NU ENGLAND
"Author"

Scott Baio
4333 Forman Avenue
Toluca Lake, CA 91602
"Actor"

Scott Bairstow
9701 Wilshire Blvd., 10th Flr.
Beverly Hills, CA 90212
"Actor"

Oksana Baiul
P.O. Box 719
Simsbury, CT 06070
"Ice Skater"

Anita Baker
8216 Tivoli Cove Drive
Las Vegas, NV 89128
"Singer"

Carroll Baker
P.O. Box 480589
Los Angeles, CA 90048
"Actress"

Colin Baker
2-3 Golden Square #42-43
London W1R 3AD ENGLAND
"Actor"

Diane Baker
2733 Outpost Drive
Los Angeles, CA 90068
"Actress, Director"

Dusty Baker
40 Livingston Terrace Drive
San Bruno, CA 94066
"Ex-Baseball Player"

Graham Baker
232 North Canon Drive
Beverly Hills, CA 90210
"Film Director"

Howard Baker
P.O. Box 8
Huntsville, TN 37756
"Former Senator"

Joe Don Baker
23339 Hatteras
Woodland Hills, CA 91364
"Actor"

Raymond Baker
254-A 26th Street #312
Santa Monica, CA 90402
"Actor"

Roy Ward Baker
125 Gloucester Road
London SW7 4TE ENGLAND
"Film Director"

Tyler Baker
4731 Laurel Canyon Blvd. #5
North Hollywood, CA 91607
"Actor"

Brenda Bakke
21838 Encina Road
Topanga, CA 90290

James (Jim) Bakker
P.O. Box 1007
Hendersonville, NC 28793
"TV Evangelist"

Tammy Faye Bakker-Messner
72727 Country Club Drive
Rancho Mirage, CA 92270
"TV Evangelist"

Scott Bakula
15300 Ventura Blvd. #315
Sherman Oaks, CA 91403
"Actor"

Bob Balaban
390 West End Avenue
New York, NY 10024
"Actor"

Belinda Balaski
1434 1/2 N. Curson Ave.
Los Angeles, CA 90046
"Actress"

Adam Baldwin
1301 Carlyle Avenue
Santa Monica, CA 90402
"Actor"

Alec Baldwin
132 S. Rodeo Drive #300
Beverly Hills, CA 90212
"Actor"

Daniel Baldwin
1144 17th Street #9
Santa Monica, CA 90403
"Actor"

Stephen Baldwin
8730 Sunset Blvd. #490
Los Angeles, CA 90069
"Actor"

William Baldwin
955 S. Carrillo Drive #200
Los Angeles, CA 90048
"Actor"

Christian Bale
685 McCowan Road
Box 66534
Toronto, Ontario M1J 3N8
CANADA
"Actor"

Darla Balenda
15848 Woodvale
Encino, CA 91316
"Actress"

Marty Balin
436 Belvedere Street
San Francisco, CA 94117
"Singer, Songwriter"

Fairuza Balk
9100 Wilshire Blvd., #1000W
Beverly Hills, CA 90212
"Actress"

Carl Ballantine
2575 N. Beachwood Drive
Los Angeles, CA 90068
"Actor, Comedian"

Christine Ballard
11501 Chandler Blvd.
North Hollywood, CA 91601
"TV Writer, Director"

Hank Ballard
P.O. Box 3125
Beverly Hills, CA 90212
"Singer"

Kaye Ballard
P.O. Box 922
Rancho Mirage, CA 92270
"Actress, Singer"

Lucinda Ballard
180 East End Avenue
New York, NY 10028
"Costume Designer"

Mark Ballou
9300 Wilshire Blvd. #555
Beverly Hills, CA 90212
"Actor"

Talia Balsam
1999 Avenue of the Stars #2850
Los Angeles, CA 90067
"Actress"

Anne Bancroft
2301 La Mesa Drive
Santa Monica, CA 90405
"Actress, Writer, Director"

Prince Bandar al-Saud
601 New Hampshire Avenue N.W.
Washington, DC 20037
"Royalty"

Antonio Banderas
3110 Main Street #205
Santa Monica, CA 90405
"Actor"

Sal Bando
104 West Juniper Lane
Mequon, WI 52092
"Ex-Baseball Player"

Moe Bandy
909 Meadowlark Lane
Goodlettsville, TN 37072
"Singer"

Victor Banerjee
10 East Harrington
Calcutta 700071 INDIA
"Actor"

Abolhassan Bani Sadr
Auvers-Sur-Oise
FRANCE
"Politician"

Ernie Banks
613 W. Serano Drive
Gilbert, AZ 85233
"Ex-Baseball Player"

Jonathan Banks
909 Euclid Street #8
Santa Monica, CA 90403
"Actor"

Tyra Banks
9800 S. 2nd Avenue
Inglewood, CA 90305
"Model"

Ian Bannen
1999 Avenue of the Stars #2850
Los Angeles, CA 90067
"Actor"

Sir Roger Bannister
21 Bardwell Road
Oxford OX2 6SV ENGLAND
"Actor"

Jack Bannon
9255 Sunset Blvd. #515
Los Angeles, CA 90069
"Actor"

Christine Baranski
Woodcreek Road
Bethlehem, CT 06751
"Actress"

Adrienne Barbeau
9255 Sunset Blvd. #515
Los Angeles, CA 90069
"Actress"

Glynis Barber
19 Denmark Street
London, WC2H 8NA ENGLAND
"Actress"

Joseph Barbera
12003 Briarvale Lane
Studio City, CA 91604
"Film Producer"

Paula Barbieri
P.O. Box 20483
Panama City, FL 32411
"Actress"

John Barbour
4254 Forman Avenue
Toluca Lake, CA 91602
"Writer, Comedian"

Brigitte Bardot
La Madrigue F-83990
St. Tropez, FRANCE
"Actress"

Bobby Bare
1183 West Main Street
Hendersonville, TN 37075
"Singer, Songwriter"

Bob Barker
1851 Outpost Drive
Los Angeles, CA 90068
"TV Show Host"

Ellen Barkin
9830 Wilshire Blvd.
Beverly Hills, CA 90212
"Actress"

Charles Barkley
10 Greenway Plaza E.
Houston, TX 77046
"Basketball Player"

Roger Barkley
5435 Burning Tree Drive
La Canada, CA 91011
"Actor"

Carl Barks
P.O. Box 524
Grants Pass, OR 97526
"Cartoonist"

Peter Barkworth
47 Flask Walk
London NW3 ENGLAND
"Actor, Comedian"

Randy Barlow
5514 Kelly Road
Brentwood, TN 37027
"Singer"

Dr. Christian Barnard
Box 6143, Welgemoed 7538
Capetown SOUTH AFRICA
"Heart Surgeon"

Binnie Barnes
838 North Doheny Drive #B
Los Angeles, CA 90069
"Actress"

Joanna Barnes
267 Middle Road
Santa Barbara CA 93108
"TV Writer"

Priscilla Barnes
8428-C Melrose Place
W. Hollywood, CA 90069
"Actress"

Barney
300 E. Bethany Road # 8000
Allen, TX 75002
"Cartoon Personality"

Doug Barr
P.O. Box 63
Rutherford, CA 94573
"Actor"

Julia Barr
420 Madison Avenue #1400
New York, NY 10017
"Actress"

Steve Barr
P.O. Box 395
Mt. Laurel, NJ 08054
"Cartoonist"

Marie-Christine Barrault
2429 Beverly Avenue
Santa Monica, CA 90406
"Actress"

Majel Barrett
P.O. Box 691370
W. Hollywood, CA 90069
"Actress"

Barbara Barrie
15 W. 72nd Street #2A
New York, NY 10023
"Actress"

Maurice Barrier
201 rue du Fg. St. Honore
F-75008 Paris FRANCE
"Actor"

Chuck Barris
17 East 76th Street
New York, NY 10021
"TV Host, Producer"

Dana Barron
151 El Camino Drive
Beverly Hills, CA 90212
"Actress"

Sydney Biddle Barrows
210 West 70th Street
New York, NY 10023
"Alleged Madam, Socialite"

Dave Barry
1 Herald Plaza
Miami, FL 33101
"Comedian"

Gene Barry
10100 Santa Monica Blvd. #2490
Los Angeles, CA 90067
"Actor"

John Barry
540 Centre Island Road
Oyster Bay, NY 11771
"Composer"

Len Barry
3096 Janice Circle
Chamblee, GA 30341
"Singer"

Marion Barry
161 Raleigh Street SE
Washington, DC 20032
"Mayor"

Patricia Barry
P.O. Box 49895
Los Angeles, CA 90049
"Actress"

Philip Barry, Jr.
12742 Highwood Street
Los Angeles, CA 90049
"Writer, Producer"

Raymond Barry
4526 Wilshire Blvd.
Los Angeles, CA 90010
"Actor"

Sy Barry
34 Saratoga Drive
Jericho, NY 11753
"Cartoonist"

Drew Barrymore
1122 S. Robertson Blvd. #15
Los Angeles, CA 90035
"Actress"

John Blyth Barrymore
144 South Peck Drive
Beverly Hills, CA 90212
"Actor"

Lionel Bart
8-10 Bulstrode Street
London W1M 6AM ENGLAND
"Lyricist, Composer"

Jean Bartel
229 Bronwood Avenue
Los Angeles, CA 90049
"Actress"

Paul Bartel
7860 Fareholm Drive
Los Angeles, CA 90046
"Actor, Director"

Steve Bartkowski
10745 Bell Road
Duluth, GA 30136
"Ex-Football Player"

Bonnie Bartlett
3500 West Olive #1400
Burbank, CA 91505
"Actress"

Peter Barton
10417 Eastbourne #3
Los Angeles, CA 90025
"Actor"

Billy Barty
4502 Farmdale Avenue
North Hollywood, CA 91602
"Actor"

Mikhail Baryshnikov
157 W. 57th St.#502
New York, NY 10019
"Ballet Dancer"

Harry Basch
920 1/2 So. Serrano Avenue
Los Angeles, CA 90006
"Actor"

Basia
2100 Colorado Ave.
Santa Monica, CA 90404
"Rock & Roll Group"

Carmen Basilio
67 Boxwood Drive
Rochester, NY 14617
"Boxer"

Kim Basinger
4833 Don Juan Place
Woodland Hills, CA 91367
"Actress"

Angela Bassett
9911 West Pico Blvd. PH#1
Los Angeles, CA 90035
"Actress"

Jennifer Bassey
9229 Sunset Blvd. #315
Los Angeles, CA 90069
"Actress"

Shirley Bassey
24 Avenue Princess Grace #1200
Monte Carlo MONACO
"Singer"

William Bast
6691 Whitley Terrace
Los Angeles, CA 90068
"Screenwriter"

Amelia Batchelor
14811 Mulholland Drive
Los Angeles, CA 90024
"Actress"

Charles Bateman
303 South Crescent Heights
Los Angeles, CA 90048
"Actor"

Jason Bateman
2623-2nd Street
Santa Monica, CA 90405
"Actor"

Justine Bateman
11288 Ventura Blvd. #190
Studio City, CA 91604
"Actress"

Alan Bates
122 Hamilton Terrace
London NW8 ENGLAND
"Actor"

Kathy Bates
6220 Del Valle
Los Angeles, CA 90048
"Actress"

Randall Batinkoff
P.O. Box 555
Ferndale, NY 12734
"Actor"

Kathleen Battle
165 West 57th Street
New York, NY 10019
"Opera Singer"

Belinda Bauder
6401 West 6th Street
Los Angeles, CA 90048
"Actress"

Bruce Bauer
12456 Ventura Blvd. #1
Studio City, CA 91604
"Actor"

Hank Bauer
11150 Alejo Place
San Diego, CA 92124
"Ex-Baseball Player"

Jamie Lyn Bauer
10643 Riverside Drive
Toluca Lake 91602
"Actress"

Sammy Baugh
c/o General Delivery
Rotan, Texas 79546
"Ex-Football Player"

Jon "Bowzer" Bauman
3168 Oakshire Drive
Los Angeles, CA 90068
"Actor, Singer"

Meredith Baxter
151 El Camino Drive
Beverly Hills, CA 90212
"Actress"

Stanley Baxter
2 Ormond Road, Richmond
Surrey TW10 6TH ENGLAND
"Actor, Comedian"

Bay City Rollers
27 Preston Grange Road
Lothian, SCOTLAND
"Rock & Roll Group"

Birch Bayh
1575 "I" Street #1025
Washington, DC 20005
"Ex-Senator"

Don Baylor
56325 Riviera
La Quinta, CA 92253
"Manager & Baseball Player"

Elgin Baylor
3939 South Figueroa
Los Angeles, CA 90037
"Ex-Basketball Player"

Beach Boys
4860 San Jacinto Circle #F
Fallbrook, CA 92028
"Rock & Roll Group"

Michael Beach
10100 Santa Monica Blvd., #2500
Los Angeles, CA 90067
"Actor"

Stephanie Beacham
79 High Ridge Road
Easton, CT 06612
"Actress"

Jennifer Beals
14755 Ventura Blvd. #710
Sherman Oaks, CA 91403
"Actress"

Abe Beame
1111-20 Street N.W.
Washington, DC 20575
"Ex-Politician"

Bob Beamon
7355 NW 41st Street
Miami, FL 33166
"Long Jump Record Holder"

Alan Bean
9173 Briar Forest Drive
Houston, TX 77024
"Astronaut, Painter"

Orsen Bean
444 Carol Canal
Venice, CA 90291
"Actor, Comedian"

Sean Bean
76 Oxford Street
London W1N OAX ENGLAND
"Actor"

Amanda Bearse
15332 Antioch Street #143
Pacific Palisades, CA 90272
"Actress"

Emmanuelle Beart
40 rue Francois ler
F-75008 Paris FRANCE
"Actress"

Allyce Beasley
147 N. Windsor Blvd.
Los Angeles, CA 90004
"Actress"

Beastie Boys
c/o William Morris
1325 Avenue of the Americas
New York, NY 10019
"Rap Group"

Queen Beatrix
Kasteel Drakesteijn
Lage Vuursche 3744 BA
HOLLAND
"Royalty"

Ned Beatty
2706 North Beachwood Drive
Los Angeles, CA 90028
"Actor"

Warren Beatty
13671 Mulholland Drive
Beverly Hills, CA 90210
"Actor, Director, Writer"

Beavis & Butt-Head
1515 Broadway #400
New York, NY 10036
"Music Group"

Gilbert Becaud
4 place de la Bourse
F-75002 Paris FRANCE
"Singer, Songwriter"

Jeff Beck
11 Old South Lincolns Inn
London WC2 ENGLAND
"Singer, Guitarist"

John Beck
12424 Wilshire Blvd. #840
Los Angeles, CA 90025
"Actor"

Marilyn Beck
P.O. Box 11079
Beverly Hills, CA 90213
"Columnist, Critic"

Michael Beck
15301 Ventura Blvd. #345
Sherman Oaks, CA 91403
"Actor"

Noelle Beck
P.O. Box 5617
Beverly Hills, CA 90210
"Actress"

Boris Becker
Nusslocher Str. 51
6906 Leiman, GERMANY
"Tennis Player"

Sidney Beckerman
10490 Wilshire Blvd. #906
Los Angeles, CA 90024
"Film Producer"

Brian Bedford
10100 Santa Monica Blvd. #2500
Los Angeles, CA 90067
"Actor"

Kabir Bedi
8271 Melrose Avenue #202
Los Angeles, CA 90046
"Actor"

The Bee Gees
20505 US 19 N. #12-290
Clearwater, FL 34624
"Rock & Roll Group"

David Beecroft
4558 Longridge Avenue
Sherman Oaks, CA 91423
"Actor"

Geoffrey Beene
550-7th Avenue
New York, NY 10018
"Fashion Designer"

Leslie Bega
9229 Sunset Blvd. #710
Los Angeles, CA 90069
"Actress"

Jason Beghe
7473 Mulholland Drive
Los Angeles, CA 90046
"Actor"

Ed Begley, Jr.
1900 Avenue of the Stars #1640
Los Angeles, CA 90067
"Actor"

Sam Behrens
3546 Longridge Avenue
Sherman Oaks, CA 91423
"Actor"

Nina Beilina
400 West 43rd Street #7D
New York, NY 10036
"Violinist"

David Belafonte
1350 Avenue of the Americas
New York, NY 10019
"Actor"

Harry Belafonte
300 West End Avenue #5A
New York, NY 10023
"Singer, Actor"

Shari Belafonte
3546 Longridge Avenue
Sherman Oaks, CA 91423
"Actress, Model"

Christine Belford
12747 Riverside Drive #208
North Hollywood, CA 91607
"Actress"

Belita
Rose Cottage
44 Crabtress Lane
London SW6 6LW ENGLAND
"Actress, Ballerina"

Albert Bell
324 W. 35th Street
Chicago, IL 60616
"Baseball Player"

Archie Bell
P.O. Box 11669
Knoxville, TN 37939
"Singer"

Bell Biv Devoe
P.O. Box 604
San Francisco, CA 94101
"R&B Group"

George Bell
324 West 35th Street
Chicago, IL 60616
"Baseball Player"

Griffin Bell
206 Townsend Place NW
Atlanta, GA 30327
"Ex-Government Official"

Laura Lee Bell
7800 Beverly Blvd. #3305
Los Angeles, CA 90036
"Actress"

Tom Bell
108 Torriano Avenue
London NW5 ENGLAND
"Actor"

Bellamy Brothers
13917 Restless Lane
Dade City, FL 33525
"Vocal Duo"

Bruce Belland
6226 Elisa Place
Encino, CA 91436
"TV Writer"

Kathleen Beller
11288 Ventura Blvd. #304
Studio City, CA 91604
"Actress"

Maria Bello
7920 Sunset Blvd. #400
Los Angeles, CA 90046
"Actress"

Marco Bellocchio
Viale Mazzini 117
00195 Rome, ITALY
"Film Director"

Saul Bellow
1126 E. 59th Street
Chicago, IL 60637
"Writer"

Louie Bellson
12804 Raymer Street
North Hollywood, CA 91605
"Drummer"

Pamela Bellwood
7444 Woodrow Wilson Drive
Los Angeles, CA 90046
"Actress, Photographer"

Jean-Paul Belmondo
9 rue des St. Peres
F-75007 Paris FRANCE
"Actor"

Robert Beltran
2210 Talmadge Street
Los Angeles, CA 90027
"Actor"

James Belushi
8033 Sunset Blvd. #88
Los Angeles, CA 90046
"Actor"

Pat Benatar
2644-30th Street
Santa Monica, CA 90403
"Singer"

Brian Benben
3854 Ventura Canyon Ave.
Sherman Oaks, CA 91423
"Actor"

Johnny Bench
324 Bishopsbridge Drive
Cincinnati, OH 45255
"Ex-Baseball Player"

Peter Benchley
35 Boudinot Street
Princeton, NJ 08540
"Author"

Billy Benedict
1347 N. Orange Grove Avenue
Los Angeles, CA 90046
"Actor"

Dirk Benedict
4605 Lankershim Blvd. #305
North Hollywood, CA 91602
"Actor"

Nick Benedict
10637 Burbank Blvd.
No. Hollywood, CA 91601
"Actor"

Paul Benedict
84 Rockland Place
Newton, MA 02164
"Actor"

Tex Beneke
11761 E. Speedway Blvd.
Tucson, AZ 85748
"Orchestra Leader"

Annette Bening
13671 Mulholland Drive
Beverly Hills, CA 90210
"Actress"

Richard Benjamin
719 North Foothill Road
Beverly Hills, CA 90210
"Actor, Director"

Bruce Bennett
2702 Forester Road
Los Angeles, CA 90064
"Actor"

Hywell Bennett
15 Golden Square #300
London W1R 3AG ENGLAND
"Actor"

Tony Bennett
130 West 57th Street #9D
New York, NY 10019
"Singer"

William Bennet
20 W. Lenox Street
Chevy Chase, MD 20815
"Ex-Government Official"

Joan Benny
1131 Coldwater Canyon
Beverly Hills, CA 90210
"Wife of Jack Benny"

Joan Benoit
R.R. #1 - Box 1455AA
Freeport, ME 04302
"Track Athlete"

George Benson
519 Next Day Hill Drive
Englewood, NJ 07631
"Singer, Guitarist"

Robby Benson
P.O. Box 1305
Woodland Hills, CA 91364
"Actor, Writer"

John Bentley
Wedgewood House
Peterworth
Sussex ENGLAND
"Actor"

Barbi Benton
40 North 4th Street
Carbondale, CO 81623
"Actress, Model"

Daniel Benzali
9016 Wilshire Blvd. #363
Beverly Hills, CA 90211
"Actor"

Tom Berenger
P.O. Box 1842
Beaufort, SC 29901
"Actor"

Berry Berenson
2840 Seattle Drive
Los Angeles, CA 90046
"Mrs. Anthony Perkins"

Patty Berg
P.O. Box 1607
Ft. Meyers, FL 33902
"Golfer"

Peter Berg
433 North Camden Drive #500
Beverly Hills, CA 90210
"Actor"

Candice Bergen
955 South Carrillo Drive #200
Los Angeles, CA 90048
"Actress"

Mrs. Edgar Bergen
1485 Carla Ridge Drive
Beverly Hills, CA 90210
"Actress"

Polly Bergen
11342 Dona Lisa Drive
Studio City, CA 91604
"Actress"

Senta Berger
Robert-Koch-Stasse 10
D-82031 Grunwald, GERMANY
"Actress"

Lee Bergere
32 Beach Plum Way
Hampton, NH 03842
"Actor"

Alan Bergman
714 North Maple Drive
Beverly Hills, CA 90210
"Lyricist"

Ingmar Bergman
P.O. Box 27127
S-10252 Stockholm SWEDEN
"Film Director"

Marilyn Bergman
714 North Maple Drive
Beverly Hills, CA 90210
"Lyricist"

Peter Bergman
4799 White Oak Avenue
Encino, CA 91316
"Actor"

Luciano Berio
11 Colombaig Radiocobdoli
53100 Siena, ITALY
"Composer, Conductor"

Elizabeth Berkeley
12401 Ventura Blvd. #122
Studio City, CA 91604
"Actress"

Steven Berkhoff
9255 Sunset Blvd. #515
Los Angeles, CA 90069
"Actor"

David Berkowitz #78A1976
Sullivan Corr. Fac., Box AG
Fallsburg, NY 12733
"Prisoner"

Milton Berle
10490 Wilshire Blvd. #1603
Los Angeles, CA 90024
"Actor, Comedian"

Warren Berlinger
10642 Arnel Place
Chatsworth, CA 91311
"Actor"

Shelley Berman
268 Bell Canyon Road
Bell Canyon, CA 91307
"Comedian"

Crystal Bernard
10866 Wilshire Blvd. #1200
Los Angeles, CA 90024
"Actress"

Ed Bernard
P.O. Box 7965
Northridge, CA 91326
"Actor"

James Bernard
#1 Oakley Gardens
Chelsea
London SW3 5QH ENGLAND
"Composer"

Edward L. Bernds
6455 Woodman Avenue
Van Nuys, CA 91401
"Writer"

Sandra Bernhard
11233 Blix Street
North Hollywood, CA 91602
"Comedianne, Actress"

Kevin Bernhardt
9300 Wilshire Blvd. #410
Beverly Hills, CA 90212
"Actor"

Collin Bernsen
401 North Poinsettia Place
Los Angeles, CA 90036
"Actor"

Corbin Bernsen
3541 N. Knoll Drive
Los Angeles, CA 90068
"Actor"

Elmer Bernstein
2715 Pearl Street
Santa Monica, CA 90405
"Composer, Conductor"

Jay Bernstein
9360 Beverly Crest Drive
Beverly Hills, CA 90210
"Talent Agent"

Kenny Bernstein
1105 Seminole
Richardson, TX 75080
"Race Car Driver"

Yogi Berra
P.O. Box 462
Caldwell, NJ 07006
"Ex-Baseball Player & Manager"

Chuck Berry
Buckner Road
Wentzville, MO 63386
"Singer, Songwriter"

Fred "Rerun" Berry
424 West 33rd Street PH
New York, NY 10019
"Actor"

Halle Berry
1122 S. Robertson Blvd. #15
Los Angeles, CA 90035
"Actress"

John Berry
1102 18th Avenue So.
Nashville, TN 37212
"Singer"

Ken Berry
15831 Foothill Blvd.
Sylmar, CA 91342
"Actor, Dancer"

Michael Berryman
P.O. Box 90054
Palmdale, CA 93590
"Actor"

HRH Prince Bertil
Hertigens av Halland
Hungl Slottet
11130 Stockholm, SWEDEN
"Royalty"

Valerie Bertinelli
P.O. Box 1984
Studio City, CA 91614
"Actress"

Luc Besson
24 rue Ives Toudic
F-75010 Paris FRANCE
"Director"

James Best
433 Pine Hill Blvd.
Geneva, FL 32732
"Actor"

Kevin Best
P.O. Box 1164
Hesperia, CA 92345
"Actor"

Martine Bestwicke
1810 Santa Monica Road
Carpinteria, CA 93013
"Actress"

Ivy Bethune
8033 Sunset Blvd. #221
Los Angeles, CA 90046
"Actress"

Zina Bethune
8033 Sunset Blvd. #221
Los Angeles, CA 90046
"Actress"

Gary Bettenhausen
2550 Tree Farm Road
Martinsville, IN 46151
"Race Car Driver"

Tony Bettenhausen
109-B Gasoline Alley
Speedway, IN 46222
"Race Car Driver"

Lyle Bettger
P.O. Box 1076
Pai, HI 96779
"Actor"

Jerome Bettis
300 Stadium Circle
Pittsburgh, PA 15212
"Football Player"

Richard Bey
445 Park Avenue #600
New York, NY 10022
"TV Show Host"

Turhan Bey
1443 North Doheny Drive
Los Angeles, CA 90069
"Actor"

Troy Beyer
9229 Sunset Blvd. #710
Los Angeles, CA 90069
"Actress"

Richard Beymer
924 Westwood Blvd. #900
Los Angeles, CA 90024
"Actor"

Benazir Bhutto
70 Clifton Road
Karachi, PAKISTAN
"Politician"

Mayim Bialik
8942 Wilshire Blvd.
Beverly Hills, CA 90211
"Actress"

Sen. Joseph Biden, Jr.
5201 Kennett Pike
Wilmington, DE 19807
"Politician"

Michael Biehn
11220 Valley Spring Lane
No. Hollywood, CA 91602
"Actor"

Thom Bierdz
1888 N. Crescent Heights Blvd.
Los Angeles, CA 90069
"Actor"

Ramon Bieri
19963 Arce Street
Northridge, CA 91324
"Actor"

Ronald Biggs
201 rua Monte Alegre
Santa Teresa
Rio de Janiero, BRAZIL
"Train Robber"

Rozann Biggs-Dawson
1630 Ft. Campbell Blvd. #9143
Clarksville, TN 37042
"Actress"

Theodore Bikel
1131 Alta Loma Road #523
Los Angeles, CA 90069
"Actor, Singer"

Tony Bill
73 Market Street
Venice, CA 90291
"Actor, Director"

Barbara Billingsley
P.O. Box 1588
Pacific Palisades, CA 90272
"Actress"

Traci Bingham
5433 Beethoven Street
Los Angeles, CA 90066
"Actress"

Juliette Binoche
10 Avenue George V.
F-75008 Paris FRANCE
"Actress"

Matt Biondi
1404 Rimer Drive
Moraga, CA 94556
"Swimmer"

Thora Birch
9560 Wilshire Blvd., #500
Beverly Hills, CA 90212
"Actress"

Billie Bird
9255 Sunset Blvd. #515
Los Angeles, CA 90069
"Actress"

Larry Bird
RR #1-Box 77A
West Baden Springs, IN 47469
"Basketball Player"

Jane Birkin
28 rue de la Tour
F-75016 Paris, FRANCE
"Actress"

David Birney
20 Ocean Park Blvd. #11
Sanata Monica, CA 90405
"Actor"

Elvin Bishop
390 Allegan Circle
San Jose, CA 95123
"Singer, Guitarist"

Joey Bishop
534 Via Lido Nord
Newport Beach, CA 92660
"Actor, Comedian"

Stephen Bishop
7400 Yarmouth Avenue
Reseda, CA 91335
"Singer, Composer"

Jacqueline Bisset
1815 Benedict Canyon Drive
Beverly Hills, CA 90210
"Actress"

Josie Bissett
1836 Courtney Terrace
Los Angeles, CA 90046
"Actress"

Yannick Bisson
55A Sumuch Street
Toronto, Ontario
M5A 3J6 Canada
"Actor"

Clint Black
6255 Sunset Blvd. #1111
Hollywood, CA 90028
"Singer"

Jay Black
360 Central Avenue
Lawrence, NY 11559
"Musician"

Karen Black
3500 W. Olive Avenue #1400
Burbank, CA 91505
"Actress"

Blackjack
35 Brentwood
Farmingville, NY 11738
"Rock & Roll Group"

Black Oak Arkansas
1487 Red Fox Run
Lilburn, GA 30247
"C&W Group"

Honor Blackman
11 Southwick Mews
London W2 1JG ENGLAND
"Actress"

Mr. Blackwell
531 South Windsor Blvd.
Los Angeles, CA 90005
"Designer, Publisher"

Nina Blackwood
22968 Victory Blvd. #158
Woodland Hills, CA 91367
"Music Correspondent"

Taurean Blacque
5049 Rock Springs Road
Lithonia, GA 30038
"Actor"

Ruben Blades
1187 Coast Village Road #1
Montecito, CA 93108
"Singer, Actor, Songwriter"

Nell Walden Blaine
3 Ledge Road
Gloucester, MA 01930
"Painter"

Betsy Blair
11 Chalcot Gardens
England's Lane
London NW3 ENGLAND
"Actress"

Bonnie Blair
306 White Pine Road
Delafield, WI 53018
"Skater"

Janet Blair
21650 Burbank Blvd. #107
Woodland Hills, CA 91367
"Actress"

Linda Blair
8033 Sunset Blvd. #204
Los Angeles, CA 90046
"Actress"

Lionel Blair
68 Old Brompton Road #200
London SW7 3LQ ENGLAND
"TV Personality, Dancer"

Prime Minister Tony Blair
10 Downing Street
London, SWI, ENGLAND
"Politician"

Bud Blake
P.O. Box 146
Darariscotta, ME 04543
"Cartoonist"

Robert Blake
11604 Dilling Street
North Hollywood, CA 91608
"Actor"

Stephanie Blake
14332 Dickens Street #8
Sherman Oaks, CA 91423
"Actress"

Whitney Blake
30918 Broad Beach Road
Malibu, CA 90265
"Actress"

Susan Blakely
421 North Rodeo Drive #15-111
Berverly Hills, CA 90210
"Actress"

Michael Blakemore
11A St. Martin's Almhousees
Bayham
London NW1 ENGLAND
"Film Director"

Ronee Blakley
8033 Sunset Blvd. #693
Los Angeles, CA 90046
"Singer, Actress"

Noel Blanc
8306 Wilshire Blvd. #8075
Beverly Hills, CA 90211
"Writer"

Nina Blanchard
3610 Wrightwood Drive
Studio City, CA 91604
"Talent Agent"

George Blanda
P.O. Box 1153
La Quinta, CA 92253
"Football Player"

Mark Blankfield
141 South El Camino Drive #205
Beverly Hills, CA 90212
"Actor"

Bill Blass
550 - 7th Avenue
New York, NY 10019
"Fashion Designer"

Freddie Blassie
215 W. Hartdale Avenue
Hartdale, NY 10530
"Wrestler, Manager"

The Blasters
555 Choro Street #A-1
San Luis Obispo, CA 93401
"Rock & Roll Group"

Richard Blasucci
353 1/2 North Gardner
Los Angeles, CA 90036
"Actor, Writer"

Jeff Blatnick
848 Whitney Drive
Schenectady, NY 12309
"Wrestler"

Drew Bledsoe
Sullivan Stadium-Route 1
Foxboro, MA 02035
"Football Player"

Tempestt Bledsoe
10100 Santa Monica Blvd. #3490
Los Angeles, CA 90067
"Actress"

Yasmine Bleeth
9595 Wilshire Blvd. #502
Beverly Hills, CA 90212
"Actress"

Rocky Bleier
605 Ivy Street #2
Pittsburgh, PA 15232
"Ex-Football Player"

Brenda Blethyn
5 Spring Street
London W2 3RA ENGLAND
"Actress"

Brian Blessed
82 Broom Park, Teddington
Middlesex TW11 9RR ENGLAND
"Actor"

Wolf Blitzer
8929 Holly Leaf Lane
Bethesda, MD 20817
"News Correspondent"

Mary J. Blige
40 W. 57th Street
New York, NY 10019
"Singer"

Andrew Bloch
718 N. King Road #105
Los Angeles, CA 90069
"Actor"

Herb Block
1150 - 15th Street NW
Washington, DC 20071
"Cartoonist"

Hunt Block
P.O. Box 674
Pacific Palisades, CA 90272
"Actor"

Dirk Blocker
5063 La Ramada Drive
Santa Barbara, CA 93111
"Actor"

Michael Blodgett
10485 National Blvd. #22
Los Angeles, CA 90034
"Actor"

Linda Bloodworth-Thomason
4000 Warner Blvd., Bldg. #147
Burbank, CA 91505
"Film Producer"

Brian Bloom
11 Croydon Court
Dix Hills, NY 11746
"Actor"

Lindsay Bloom
P.O. Box 412
Weldon, CA 93263
"Actress"

Verna Bloom
327 East 82nd Street
New York, NY 10028
"Actress"

Betsy Bloomingdale
131 Delfern Drive
Los Angeles, CA 90077
"Business Executive"

Lisa Blount
5750 Wilshire Blvd. #580
Los Angeles, CA 90036
"Actress"

Mel Blount
R.D. 1, Box 91
Claysville, PA 15323
"Ex-Football Player"

Kurtis Blow
201 Eastern Parkway #3K
Brooklyn, NY 11238
"Singer"

Vida Blue
P.O. Box 1449
Pleasanton, CA 94566
"Ex-Baseball Player"

Judy Blume
40 E. 48th Street #1001
New York, NY 10017
"Writer"

Ann Blyth
P.O. Box 9754
Rancho Santa Fe, CA 92067
"Actress"

True Boardman
2951 Paisano Road
Pebble Beach, CA 93593
"Actor"

Michael Boatman
1571 South Kiowa Crest Drive
Diamond Bar, CA 91765
"Actor"

John Wayne Bobbit
7226 Westpark Avenue
Las Vegas, NV 89117
"Personality"

Lorena Bobbitt
709 Gray Avenue
Durham, NC 27701
"Cut off Husband's Penis"

Steven Bochco
694 Amalfi Drive
Pacific Palisades, CA 90272
"Writer, Producer"

Hart Bochner
42 Halderman Road
Santa Monica, CA 90402
"Actor"

Lloyd Bochner
42 Haldeman Road
Santa Monica, CA 90402
"Actor"

Budd Boetticher
P.O. Box 1137
Ramona, CA 92065
"Film Director"

Peter Bogdanovich
151 El Camino Drive
Beverly Hills, CA 90212
"Film Writer, Director"

Wade Boggs
6006 Windham Place
Tampa, FL 33647
"Baseball Player"

Suzy Bogguss
33 Music Sq. W. #110
Nashville, TN 37203
"Singer"

Heidi Bohay
48 Main Street
South Bound Brook, NJ 08880
"Actress"

Corinne Bohrer
4526 Wilshire Blvd.
Los Angeles, CA 90010
"Actress"

Richard Bohringer
14 Avenue Duquesne
95160 Dewil-la-Barre FRANCE
"Actor"

Brian Boitano
101 First Street #370
Los Altos, CA 94022
"Ice Skater"

Tiffany Bolling
12483 Braddock Drive
Los Angeles, CA 90066
"Actress"

Joseph Bologna
16830 Ventura Blvd. #326
Encino, CA 91436
"Actor, Writer, Director"

Henry Boltinoff
7518A English Ct.
Lake Worth, FL 33467
"Cartoonist"

Michael Bolton
P.O. Box 679
Branford, CT 06516
"Singer"

Danny Bonaduce
5740 Sunnycrest Drive
West Bloomfield, MI 48423
"Actor"

Julian Bond
4805 Mt. Hope Drive
Baltimore, MD 20215
"Politician"

Philip Bond
50 High Street
Abergwynfi
W. Gamorgan SA13 3YW
ENGLAND
"Actor"

Tommy "Butch" Bond
P.O. Box 588
Selma, CA 93662
"Actor"

Barry Bonds
9595 Wilshire Blvd. #711
Beverly Hills, CA 90212
"Baseball Player"

Steve Bond
3500 West Olive Avenue #920
Burbank, CA 91505
"Actor"

Gary U.S. Bonds
2011 Ferry Avenue U-19
Camden, NJ 08104
"Singer"

Peter Bonerz
3637 Lowry Road
Los Angeles, CA 90027
"Actor, Director"

Lisa Bonet
1551 Will Geer Road
Topanga, CA 90290
"Actress"

Jon Bon Jovi
250 West 57th Street #603
New York, NY 10107
"Rock & Roll Group"

Bobby Bonilla
390 Round Hill Road
Greenwich, CT 06831
"Baseball Player"

Rep. David E. Bonior (MI)
House Rayburn Bldg. #2207
Washington, DC 20515
"Politician"

Elayna Bonner
Uliza Tschakalowa 48
Moscow, RUSSIA
"Politician"

Frank Bonner
10100 Santa Monica Blvd. #700
Los Angeles, CA 90067
"Actor, Director"

Chastity Bono
8968 Vista Granda
West Hollywood, CA 90069
"Cher's Daughter"

Booker T & the MGs
59 Parsons Street
Newtonville, MA 02160
"R&B Group"

Debby Boone
4334 Kester Avenue
Sherman Oaks, CA 91403
"Singer"

Pat Boone
904 North Beverly Drive
Beverly Hills, CA 90210
"Actor, Singer"

Randy Boone
14250 Califa Street
Van Nuys, CA 91401
"Actor"

Charley Boorman
"The Glebe"
Annanoe County Wicklow
IRELAND
"Film Director"

John Boorman
21 Thurlue Square
London W1 ENGLAND
"Film Director"

Elayne Boosler
584 N. Larchmont Blvd.
Los Angeles, CA 90004
"Comedienne"

Debra Boostrum
700 Starkey Road #412
Largo, FL 34641
"Model"

Adrian Booth
3922 Glenridge Drive
Sherman Oaks, CA 91423
"Actor"

Connie Booth
Prince of Wales Theatre
Coventry Street
London W1V 7FE ENGLAND
"Actress"

Powers Boothe
23629 Long Valley Road
Hidden Hills, CA 91302
"Actor"

Lynn Borden
6399 Wilshire Blvd. #211
Los Angeles, CA 90048
"Actress"

David Boreanaz
400 S. Beverly Drive #216
Beverly Hills, CA 90212
"Actor"

Bjorn Borg
One Erieview Plaza #1300
Cleveland, OH 44114
"Tennis Player"

Victor Borge
Fieldpoint Park
Greenwich, CT 06830
"Pianist, Comedian"

Jim Borgman
617 Vine Street
Cincinnati, OH 45201
"Cartoonist"

Ernest Borgnine
3055 Lake Glen Drive
Beverly Hills, CA 90210
"Actor"

Tova Borgnine
3055 Lake Glen Drive
Beverly Hills, CA 90210
"Actress"

Robert Bork
5171 Palisade Lane
Washington, DC 20016
"Judge"

Matt Borlenghi
10100 Santa Monica Blvd. #2500
Los Angeles, CA 90067
"Actor"

Major Frank Borman
250-A Cotarro Court
Las Cruces, NM 88005
"Astronaut"

Philip Bosco
337 West 43rd Street #1B
New York, NY 10036
"Actor"

Tom Bosley
2822 Royston Place
Beverly Hills, CA 90210
"Actor"

Barbara Bosson
694 Amalfi Drive
Pacific Palisades, CA 90272
"Actress"

Boston
P.O. Box 6191
Lincoln Center, MA 01773
"Rock & Roll Group"

Ralph Boston
3301 Woodbine Avenue
Knoxville, TN 37914
"Track Athlete"

Barry Bostwick
1640 S. Sepulveda Blvd. #218
Los Angeles, CA 90025
"Actor"

Brian Bosworth
6331 Ramirez Mesa Drive
Malibu, CA 90265
"Actor, Football Player"

Joe Bottoms
1015 Gayley Avenue #300
Los Angeles, CA 90024
"Actor"

Sam Bottoms
4719 Willowcrest Avenue
Toluca Lake, CA 91602
"Actor"

Timothy Bottoms
532 Hot Springs Road
Santa Barbara, CA 93108
"Actor"

Lou Boudreau
415 Cedar Lane
Frankfort, IL 60423
"Ex-Baseball Player"

Pierre Boulez
Postfach 22
Baden-Baden GERMANY
"Composer, Conductor"

Jim Bouton
P.O. Box 188
North Edremont, MA 01252
"Ex-Baseball Player"

John Bowab
2598 Green Valley
Los Angeles, CA 90046
"TV Director"

Riddick Bowe
1025 Vermont Avenue NW #1025
Washington, DC 20005
"Boxer"

Antoinette Bower
1529 N. Beverly Glen
Los Angeles, CA 90077
"Actress"

David Bowie
55 Fulham High Street
London SW6 3JJ ENGLAND
"Singer, Actor"

Judi Bowker
31 Soho Square
London W1V 5DG ENGLAND
"Actress"

Peter Bowles
125 Gloucester Road
London SW7 ENGLAND
"Actor"

Christopher Bowman
5653 Kester Avenue
Van Nuys, CA 91405
"Skater"

Boxcar Willie
199 E. Garfield Road
Aurora, OH 44202
"Singer"

Sen. Barbara Boxer (CA)
112 Hart Office Bldg.
Washington, DC 20510
"Politician"

Bruce Boxleitner
P.O. Box 5513
Sherman Oaks, CA 91403
"Actor"

Lara Flynn Boyle
12190 1/2 Ventura Blvd. #304
Studio City, CA 91604
"Actress"

Peter Boyle
130 East End Avenue
New York, NY 10024
"Actor"

Boyz II Men
5750 Wilshire Blvd. #300
Los Angeles, CA 90036
"R&B Group"

Lorraine Bracco
130 W. 57th Street #5E
New York, NY 10019
"Actress"

Eddie Bracken
69 Douglas Road
Glen Ridge, NJ 07028
"Actor"

Ray Bradbury
10265 Cheviot Drive
Los Angeles, CA 90064
"Author"

Barbara Taylor Bradford
425 East 58 Street
New York, NY 10022
"Writer"

Richard Bradford
121 N. San Vicente Blvd.
Beverly Hills, CA 90211
"Actor"

Benjamin Bradlee
3014 "N" Street NW
Washington, DC 20007
"Journalist"

Bill Bradley
4 Hawthorn Avenue
Princeton, NJ 08540
"Ex-Senator"

Ed Bradley
285 Central Park West
New York, NY 10024
"Newscaster"

Kathleen Bradley
5154 Cimarron Street
Los Angeles, CA 90062
"Actress"

Owen Bradley
P.O. Box 120838
Nashville, TN 37212
"Pianist"

Tom Bradley
3631 Mt. Vernon Drive
Los Angeles, CA 90008
"Ex-Mayor of Los Angeles"

Terry Bradshaw
1925 N. Pearson Lane
Roanoke, TX 76262
"Ex-Football Player"

James Brady
1255 "I" Street #1100
Washington, DC 20005
"Ex-White House Press Sec."

Eric Braeden
13723 Romany Drive
Pacific Palisades, CA 90272
"Actor"

Sonia Braga
295 Greenwich Street #11B
New York, NY 10007
"Actress"

Don Bragg
P.O. Box 171
New Gretna, NJ 08224
"Track Athlete"

Kenneth Branagh
Studios Road
Shepperton
Middlesex TW17 0QD ENGLAND
"Actor, Director"

Klaus Maria Brandauer
Fischernforf 76
8992 Alta-Ausse, AUSTRIA
"Actor/Director"

Jonathan Brandis
11684 Ventura Blvd. #909
Studio City, CA 91604
"Actor"

Marlon Brando
13828 Weddington
Van Nuys, CA 91401
"Actor"

Michael Brandon
11664 National Blvd. #108
Los Angeles, CA 90064
"Actor"

Brand X
17171 Roscoe Blvd. #104
Northridge, CA 91325
"Actor"

Brandy
536 East 169th Street
Carson, CA 90746
"Singer"

Laura Branigan
250 W. 57th Street#821
New York, NY 10107
"Singer, Songwriter"

Benjamin Bratt
8969 Sunset Blvd.
Los Angeles, CA 90069
"Actor"

Andre Braugher
9830 Wilshire Blvd.
Beverly Hills, CA 90212
"Actor"

Asher Brauner
190 North Canon Drive #201
Beverly Hills, CA 90210
"Actor"

Toni Braxton
3350 Peachtree Road #1500
Atlanta, GA 30326
"Singer"

Julian Bream
122 Wigmore Street
London W1 ENGLAND
"Guitarist"

Peter Breck
6310 San Vicente Blvd. #520
Los Angeles, CA 90048
"Actor"

Buddy Bregman
11288 Ventura Blvd. #700
Studio City, CA 91604
"Director, Producer"

Tracey E. Bregman
7800 Beverly Blvd. #3371
Los Angeles, CA 90036
"Actress"

Eileen Brennan
974 Mission Terrace
Camarillo, CA 91310
"Actress"

Melissa Brennan
6520 Platt Avenue #634
West Hills, CA 90307
"Actress"

Amy Brenneman
9150 Wilshire Blvd. #175
Beverly Hills, CA 90212
"Actress"

David Brenner
1575 Silver King Drive
Aspen, CO 81611
"Comedian, Talk Show Host"

Dori Brenner
2106 Canyon Drive
Los Angeles, CA 90068
"Actress"

Bobbie Bresee
P.O. Box 1222
Hollywood, CA 90078
"Actress, Model"

Jimmy Breslin
75 Central Park West
New York, NY 10023
"Author, Columnist"

Martin Brest
831 Paseo Miramar
Pacific Palisades, CA 90272
"Film Writer, Director"

George Brett
P.O. Box 419969
Kansas City, MO 64141
"Baseball Player"

Teresa Brewer
384 Pinebrook Blvd.
New Rochelle, NY 10803
"Singer"

Mary Brian
4107 Troost Avenue
North Hollywood, CA 90212
"Actress"

Beth Brickell
P.O. Box 26
Paron, AR 72122
"Writer, Director"

Beau Bridges
5525 North Jed Smith Road
Hidden Hills, CA 91302
"Actor, Director"

Jeff Bridges
985 Hot Springs Road
Montecito, CA 93108
"Actor"

Todd Bridges
3518 Cahuenga Blvd. W. #216
Los Angeles, CA 90068
"Actor"

Charlie Brill
3635 Wrightwood Drive
Studio City, CA 91604
"Actor"

Bernie Brillstein
9150 Wilshire Blvd. #350
Beverly Hills, CA 90212
"Talent Agent"

Wilfred Brimley
415 North Camden Drive #121
Beverly Hills, CA 90210
"Actor"

Christie Brinkley
344 East 59th Street
New York, NY 10022
"Model"

David Brinkley
111 E. Melrose Street
Chevy Chase, MD 20815
"Ex-TV Show Host"

Valerie Brisco-Hooks
1 Hoosier Dome
Indianapolis, IN 46225
"Actress"

Danielle Brisebois
341 Madison Avenue
14th Floor
New York, NY 10017
"Actress"

May Britt
P.O. Box 525
Zephyr Cove, NV 89448
"Actress"

Morgan Brittany
3434 Cornell Road
Agoura Hills, CA 91301
"Actress, Model"

Tony Britton
76 Oxford Street
London W1N 0AX ENGLAND
"Actor"

Lou Brock
P.O. Box 28398
St. Louis, MO 63146
"Ex-Baseball Player"

Beth Broderick
1999 Avenue of the Stars #2850
Los Angeles, CA 90067
"Actress"

Matthew Broderick
P.O. Box 69646
Los Angeles, CA 90069
"Actor"

Kevin Brodie
4292 Elmer Avenue
North Hollywood, CA 91602
"Actor"

Lane Brody
P.O. Box 24775
Nashville, TN 37202
"Singer"

Ronnie Brody
21 Bartle Road
London W11 ENGLAND
"Actor"

Tom Brokaw
941 Park Avenue #14C
New York, NY 10025
"Newscaster"

James Brolin
6838 Zumirez Drive
Malibu, CA 90265
"Actor"

Josh Brolin
8200 Dover Canyon Road
Paso Robles, CA 93446
"Actor"

John Bromfield
P.O. Box 2655
Lake Havau City, AZ 86405
"Actor"

Edgar M. Bronfman
375 Park Avenue
New York, NY 10152
"Distillery Executive"

Charles Bronson
P.O. Box 2644
Malibu, CA 90265
"Actor"

Faith Brook
109 Jermyn Street
London SW1Y 6A5 ENGLAND
"Actress"

Jayne Brook
9150 Wilshire Blvd. #350
Beverly Hills, CA 90212
"Actress"

Hilary Brooke
40 Via Casitas
Bonsall, CA 92003
"Actress"

Gary Brooker
5 Cranley Gardens
London SW7 ENGLAND
"Singer, Composer"

Brooklyn Bridge
P.O. Box 63
Cliffwood, NJ 07721
"Rock & Roll Group"

Brooks & Dunn
P.O. Box 120669
Nashville, TN 37212
"Country Music Duo"

Albert Brooks
1880 Century Park E. #900
Los Angeles, CA 90067
"Actor, Writer, Director"

Avery Brooks
360 Christopher Drive
Princeton, NJ 08540
"Actor"

Donnie Brooks
359-B East Magnolia Blvd.
Burbank, NJ 91502
"Comedian"

Foster Brooks
315 South Beverly Drive #216
Beverly Hills, CA 90212
"Comedian"

Garth Brooks
3322 West End Avenue #1100
Nashville, TN 37203
"Singer"

James L. Brooks
8942 Wilshire Blvd.
Beverly Hills, CA 90211
"TV Writer, Producer"

Mel Brooks
2301 La Mesa Drive
Santa Monica, CA 90405
"Actor, Writer, Director"

Rand Brooks
1701 Capistrano Circle
Glendale, CA 91207
"Actress"

Kevin Brophy
15010 Hamlin Street
Van Nuys, CA 91411
"Actor"

Pierce Brosnan
23715 West Malibu Road
Malibu, CA 90265
"Actor, Model"

Dr. Joyce Brothers
235 E. 45th Street
New York, NY 10017
"Psychologist"

Louise Brough
1808 Voluntary Road
Vista, CA 92083
"Tennis Player"

Haywood Hale Broun
189 Plochman
Woodstock, NY 12498
"Sportswriter, Sportscaster"

Rebecca Broussard
9911 West Pico Blvd. PH A
Los Angeles, CA 90035
"Actress"

Bobby Brown
1324 Thomas Place
Ft. Worth, TX 76107
"Singer"

Bryan Brown
110 Queen Street
Woollahra NSW 2025
AUSTRALIA
"Actor"

Clarence "Gatemouth" Brown
434 Avenue U.
Bogalusa, LA 70427
"Singer, Guitarist"

Dee Brown
150 Causeway Street
Boston, MA 02114
"Basketball Player"

Denise Brown
P.O. Box 380
Monarch Bay, CA 92629
"Nicole Brown-Simpson's Sister"

Dwier Brown
749 1/2 N. Lafayette Park Pl.
Los Angeles, CA 90026
"Actor"

Edmund "Jerry" Brown, Jr.
295 Third Street
Oakland, CA 94607
"Ex-Governor"

Georg Stanford Brown
2565 Greenvalley Road
Los Angeles, CA 90046
"Actor, Director"

Helen Gurley Brown
1 West 81st Street #220
New York, NY 10024
"Author, Editor"

Hubie Brown
6 Cobblewood Road
Livingston, NJ 07039
"Basketball Coach"

James Brown
1217 West Medical Park Road
Augusta, GA 30909
"Singer

Ex-Gov. Jerry Brown
200 Harrison Street
Oakland, CA 94607
"Politician"

Jim Brown
1851 Sunset Plaza Drive
Los Angeles, CA 90069
"Ex-Football Player, Actor"

Jim Ed Brown
P.O. Box 121089
Nashville, TN 37212
"Singer"

Johnny Brown
2732 Woodhaven Drive
Los Angeles, CA 90068
"Performer"

Julie Brown
8912 Burton Way
Beverly Hills, CA 90211
"Comedienne"

Kimberlin Brown
4439 Worster Avenue
Studio City, CA 91604
"Singer"

Lisa Brown
448 West 44th Street
New York, NY 10036
"Actress"

Nacio Herb Brown, Jr.
1739 DeCamp Drive
Beverly Hills, CA 90210
"Actor"

Peter Brown
854 Cypress Avenue
Hermosa Beach, CA 90254
"Actor"

Ruth Brown
1852 Vista Del Mar
Hollywood, CA 90028
"Singer"

Susan Brown
11931 Addison Street
North Hollywood, CA 91607
"Actress"

T. Graham Brown
P.O. Box 50337
Nashville, TN 37205
"Singer"

Thomas Wilson Brown
5918 Van Nuys Blvd.
Van Nuys, CA 91401
"Actor"

Vanessa Brown
5914 Coldwater Canyon Avenue
North Hollywood, CA 91607
"Actress"

Willie L. Brown, Jr.
401 Van Ness Avenue #336
San Francisco, CA 94102
"Politician"

Woody Brown
6548 Colbath Avenue
Van Nuys, CA 91401
"Actor"

Jackson Browne
3746 Kling Street
Studio City, CA 91604
"Singer, Composer"

Kathy Browne
P.O. Box 2939
Beverly Hills, CA 90213
"Actress"

Roscoe Lee Browne
3531 Wonderview Drive
Los Angeles, CA 90068
"Actor, Writer, Director

Kurt Browning
11160 River Valley Road #3180
Edmondton, Alberto
T5J 2G7 CANADA
"Ice Skater"

Ricou Browning
5221 SW 196th Lane
Ft. Lauderdale, FL 33332
"Writer, Producer"

Dave Brubeck
221 Millstone Road
Wilton, CT 06807
"Pianist"

Carol Bruce
1361 North Laurel #9
Los Angeles, CA 90046
"Actress"

Kitty Bruce
31 Harrison Street
New York, NY 10019
"Singer"

Jerry Bruckheimer
13822 Highwood Street
Los Angeles, CA 90049
"Film Producer"

Bo Brundin
1716 Clybourn Avenue
Burbank, CA 91505
"Actor"

Carla Bruni
62, Bd. de Sebastopol
75003 Paris FRANCE
"Model"

Frank Bruno
Box 2266
Brentwood
Essex CM1S 0AQ ENGLAND
"Boxer"

Ellen Bry
2401 Main Street
Santa Monica, CA 90405
"Actress"

Dora Bryan
11 Marine Parade
Brighton Sussex ENGLAND
"Actress"

Zachary Ty Bryan
1999 Avenue of the Star #2850
Los Angeles, CA 90067
"Actor"

Anita Bryant
P.O. Box 7300
Branson, MO 65615
"Singer"

Michael Bryant
Willow Cottage
Kington Magna
Dorset SP8 5EW ENGLAND
"Actor"

Scott Bryce
10100 Santa Monica Blvd. #2500
Los Angeles, CA 90067
"Actor"

Zbigniew Brzezinski
1800 "K" St. NW #400
Washington, DC 20006
"Politician"

Sergei Bubka
Kuibisheva St. 42
252023 Kiev UKRAINE
"Pole-Vaulter"

Angela "Bay" Buchanan
909 11th Street NE
Washington, D.C. 20002
"Pat Buchanan's Sister"

Ian Buchanan
3500 W. Olive #1400
Burbank, CA 91505
"Actor"

Patrick J. Buchanan
1017 Savile Lane North
McLean, VA 22101
"Politician, Columnist"

Horst Buchholz
232 rue du Fbg. South
St. Honore
F. 75008 Paris FRANCE
"Actor"

Art Buchwald
4327 Hawthorne Street NW
Washington, DC 20016
"Columnist"

Betty Buckner
10643 Riverside Drive
Toluca Lake, CA 91602
"Actress"

Bill Buckner
2425 W. Victory Road
Meridian, ID 83642
"Ex-Baseball Player"

Lindsay Buckingham
900 Airole Way
Los Angleles, CA 90077
"Singer, Songwriter"

The Buckinghams
620 - 16th Avenue South
Hopkins, MN 55343
"Rock & Roll Group"

Betty Buckley
420 Madison Avenue #1400
New York, NY 10017
"Actress"

William F. Buckley, Jr.
150 East 35th Street
New York, NY 10016
"Author, Editor"

Julie Budd
180 West End Avenue
New York, NY 10023
"Actress"

Terence Budd
29 Rylette Road
London W12 ENGLANG
"Actor"

Zola Budd
1 Church Row
Wandsworth Plain
London SW18 ENGLAND
"Runner"

Don Budge
P.O. Box 789
Dingman's Ferry, PA 18328
"Tennis Player"

Maria Bueno
Rua Consolagao 3414 #10
1001 Edificio Augustus
Sao Paulo, BRAZIL
"Tennis Player"

Jimmy Buffet
424A Fleming Street
Key West, FL 33040
"Singer, Songwriter"

Warren Buffett
3555 Farnam Street
Omana, NE 68131
"Business Executive"

The Buggles
22 St. Peters Square
London W69 NW ENGLAND
"Rock & Roll Group"

Vincent T. Bugliosi
1926 W. Mountain Street
Glendale, CA 91201
"Attorney, Author"

Genevieve Bujold
27258 Pacific Coast Hwy.
Malibu, CA 90265
"Actress"

Donald Buka
1501 Beacon Street #1802
Brookline, MA 02146
"Actor"

Ray Buktenica
2057 N. Beverly Glen Blvd.
Los Angeles, CA 90077
"Actor"

Joyce Bulifant
P.O. Box 5006
Snowmass Village, CO 81615
"Actress"

Richard Bull
200 E. Delware Place #20F
Chicago, IL 60611
"Actor"

Jim J. Bullock
11617 Laurelwood Drive
Studio City, CA 91604
"Actor"

Sandra Bullock
291 S. La Cienega Blvd. #616
Beverly Hills, CA 90211
"Actress"

Grace Bumbry
165 West 57th Street
New York, NY 10019
"Opera Singer"

Brooke Bundy
833 N. Martel Avenue
Los Angeles, CA 90046
"Actress"

Jim Bunning
7410 New LaGrange Road #130
Louisville, KY 40222
"Politician, Ex-Baseball Player"

Lou Burdette
2019 Beveva Road
Sarasota, FL 34232
"Ex-Baseball Player"

Gregg Burge
420 Madison Avenue #1400
New York, NY 10017
"Singer"

Richard Burgi
2622 Victoria Blvd.
Laguna Beach, CA 92651
"Actor"

Delta Burke
1012 Royal Street
New Orleans, LA 70116
"Actress"

Paul Burke
2217 Avenida Caballeros
Palm Springs, CA 92262
"Actor"

Soloman Burke
1048 Tatnall Street
Macon, GA 31201
"Singer"

Dennis Burkley
5145 Costello Avenue
Sherman Oaks, CA 91423
"Actor"

Tom Burleson
c/o General Delivery
Newland, NC 28657
"Actor"

Carol Burnett
7800 Beverly Blvd.
Los Angeles, CA 90036
"Actress, Comedienne"

Nancy Burnett
7800 Beverity Blvd. #3305
Los Angeles, CA 90036
"Actress"

Edward Burns
588 Broadway #210
New York, NY 10012
"Actor, Screenwriter"

Eileen Burns
4000 West 43rd Street
New York, NY 10036
"Actress"

Eric Burns
448 1/2 N. Stanley Avenue
Los Angeles, CA 90046
"News Correspondent"

James MacGregor Burns
Bee Hill Road
Williamstown, MA 01267
"Political Scientist, Historian"

Jere Burns
P.O. Box 3596
Mammoth Lakes, CA 93546
"Actor"

Ken Burns
Maple Grove Road
Walpole, NH 03608
"Documentary Producer"

Kenny Burrell
163 Third Avenue #206
New York, NY 10003
"Jazz Musician"

Leroy Burrell
1801 Ocean Park Blvd. #112
Santa Monica, CA 90405
"Track & Field"

James Burrows
5555 Melrose Avenue #D-228
Los Angeles, CA 90038
"Writer, Producer"

Ellen Burstyn
P.O. Box 217
Palisades, NY 10964
"Actress"

Kate Burton
1530 Broadway
New York, NY 10036
"Actress"

Lance Burton
3770 S. Las Vegas Blvd.
Las Vegas, NV 89109
"Magician"

Levar Burton
13601 Ventura Blvd. #209
Sherman Oaks, CA 91423
"Actor"

Mrs. Sally Burton
Pays de Galles
Coligny, SWITZERLAND
"Widow of Richard Burton"

Tim Burton
445 Redondo Avenue, #7
Long Beach, CA 90814
"Actor, Director, Producer"

Tony Burton
3500 W. Olive Avenue #1400
Burbank, CA 91505
"Actor"

Warren Burton
280 S. Beverly Drive #400
Beverly Hills, CA 90212
"Actor"

Wendell Burton
6526 Costello Drive
Van Nuys, CA 91401
"Actor"

Gary Busey
18424 Coastline Drive
Malibu, CA 90265
"Actor"

Jake Busey
18424 Coastline Drive
Malibu, CA 90265
"Actor"

Timothy Busfield
39-100 Z-Line Road
Clarksburg, CA 95613
"Actor"

Barbara Bush
9 West Oak Drive
Houston, TX 77056
"Ex-First Lady"

Dick Bush
8 Grande Parade, #16
Plymouth
Devon PL1 3DF ENGLAND
"Cinematographer"

George Bush
9 West Oak Drive
Houston, TX 77056
"Ex-President of United States"

George Bush, Jr.
P.O. Box 12428
Austin, TX 78711
"Governor"

Kate Bush
P.O. Box 120, Welling
Kent DA16 3DS ENGLAND
"Singer, Songwriter"

Joe Bushkin
435 East 52nd Street
New York, NY 10022
"Pianist, Composer"

Dr. Jerry Buss
P.O. Box 10
Inglewood, CA 90306
"Basketball Team Owner"

Mangosutho Buthelezi
Union Bldg.
Pretoria 0001
South Africa
"Zulu Chief"

Brett Butler
4370 Tujunga Avenue #150
Studio City, CA 91604
"Actress"

Brett Butler
3248 Strathmore Drive
Duluth, GA 30136
"Baseball Player"

Dean Butler
1310 Westholme Avenue
Los Angeles, CA 90024
"Actor"

Jerry Butler
164 Woodstone Drive
Buffalo Grove, IL 60089
"Singer"

Yancy Butler
6154 Glen Tower
Los Angeles, CA 90068
"Actor"

Joey Buttafuoco
P.O. Box 335
Agoura Hills, CA 91376
"Sex with Amy Fisher"

Mary Jo Buttafuoco
P.O. Box 335
Agoura Hills, CA 91376
"Joey's wife"

Dick Button
250 West 57th Street #818
New York, NY 10107
"TV Producer"

Red Buttons
778 Tortuoso Way
Los Angeles, CA 90077
"Actor"

Ruth Buzzi
6310 San Vicente Blvd. #401
Los Angeles, CA 90048
"Actress"

Gabriel Byrne
9560 Wilshire Blvd. #516
Beverly Hills, CA 90212
"Actor"

Charlie Byrd Trio
11806 North 56th Street #B
Tampa, FL 33617
"Jazz Trio"

Tom Byrd
121 North San Vincente Blvd.
Beverly Hills, CA 90211
"Actor"

Tracy Byrd
8245 Gladys #201
Beaumont, TX 77706
"Singer"

David Byrne
110 W. 57th Street
New York, NY 10019
"Singer, Songwriter"

Edd Byrnes
P.O. Box 1623
Beverly Hills, CA 90213
"Actor"

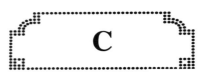

James Caan
P.O. Box 6646
Denver, CO 80206
"Actor"

Montserrat Caballe
Caball, Via Augusta 59
Barcelona, E-08006 SPAIN
"Opera Singer"

Ava Cadell
8033 Sunset Blvd. #661
Los Angeles, CA 90046
"Actress, Model"

Frank Cady
110 East 9th Street #C-1005
Los Angeles, CA 90210
"Actor"

Sid Caesar
1910 Loma Vista
Beverly Hills, CA 90210
"Actor, Comedian"

Stephen Caffrey
12338 Cantura Street
Studio City, CA 91604
"Actor"

Nicholas Cage
363 Copa de Oro
Los Angeles, CA 90077
"Actor"

Dean Cain
11718 Barrington Court #513
Los Angeles, CA 90049
"Actor"

Michael Caine
Rectory Farm House
North Stoke
Oxfordshire ENGLAND
"Actor"

Rory Calhoun
P.O. Box 689
Morongo Valley, CA 92256
"Actor"

Joseph Cali
247 South Beverly Drive #102
Beverly Hills, CA 90212
"Actor"

Anthony Call
305 Madison Avenue #4419
New York, NY 10165
"Actor"

Brandon Call
5918 Van Nuys Blvd.
Van Nuys, CA 91401
"Actor"

James Callahan
8271 Melrose Avenue #202
Los Angeles, CA 90046
"Actor"

John Callahan
342 North Alfred Street
Los Angeles, CA 90048
"Actor"

K. Callan
4957 Matilija Avenue
Sherman Oaks, CA 91423
"Actress"

Michael (Mickey) Callan
1730 Camden Avenue #201
Los Angeles, CA 90025
"Actor"

Thomas Callaway
6360 Wilshire Blvd. #1707
Los Angeles, CA 90048
"Actor"

Charlie Callas
P.O. Box 67-B-69
Los Angeles, CA 90067
"Comedian, Actor"

Lt. William Calley
V.V. Vicks Jewelry
Cross Country Plaza
Columbus, GA 31906
"Ex-Military"

Simon Callow
60 Finborough Road
London SW10 ENGLAND
"Actor"

Corinne Calvet
1431 Ocean Avenue #109
Santa Monica, CA 90401
"Actress"

John Calvin
3639 Regel Place
Los Angeles, CA 90068
"Actor"

Hector Camacho
4751 Yardarm Lane
Boynton Beach, FL 33436
"Boxer"

Candace Cameron-Bure
8369-A Sausalito Avenue
West Hills, CA 91304
"Actress"

Dean Cameron
3500 W. Olive Ave. #1400
Burbank, CA 91505
"Actor"

James Cameron
919 Santa Monica Blvd.
Santa Monica, CA 90401
"Director"

Joanna Cameron
P.O. Box 1400
Pebble Beach, CA 93953
"Actress, Director"

John Cameron
35 Ragged Hall Lane
St. Albans
Herts. AL2 3LB ENGLAND
"Composer, Conductor"

Kirk Cameron
P.O. Box 8665
Calabasas, CA 91372
"Actor"

Colleen Camp
473 North Tigertail Road
Los Angeles, CA 90049
"Actress"

Joseph Campanella
4647 Arcola Avenue
North Hollywood, CA 91602
"Actor"

Bert Campaneria
P.O. Box 5096
Scottsdale, AZ 85261
"Ex-Baseball Player"

Alan Campbell
130 West 42nd Street #2400
New York, NY 10036
"Actor"

Bill Campbell
8942 Wilshire Blvd.
Beverly Hills, CA 90211
"Actor"

Bruce Campbell
14431 Ventura Blvd. #120
Sherman Oaks, CA 91423
"Actor"

Cheryl Campbell
5 Milner Place
London N1 ENGLAND
"Actress"

Earl Campbell
P.O. Box 909
Austin, TX 78767
"Football Player"

Glen Campbell
28 Biltmore Estate
Phoenix, AZ 85016
"Singer, Actor, Composer"

Julia Campbell
1925 Century Park E. #2320
Los Angeles, CA 90067
"Actress"

Ken Campbell
74 Watermint Quay
London N16 England
"Actor"

Kim Campbell
Canadian Consulate
550 S. Hope Street
Los Angeles, CA 90071
"Ex-Prime Minister"

Luther Campbell
8400 N.E. 2nd Avenue
Miami, FL 33138
"Rap Singer"

Naomi Campbell
107 Greene Street
New York, NY 10012
"Model"

Neve Campbell
101-1184 Denman Street
Box 119, Vancouver
BC V7G 2M9 CANADA
"Actress"

Nicholas Campbell
1206 N. Orange Grove
Los Angeles, CA 90046
"Actor"

Tevin Campbell
9830 Wilshire Blvd.
Beverly Hills, CA 90212
"Singer"

Tisha Campbell
5750 Wilshire Blvd. #640
Los Angeles, CA 90036
"Actress"

William Campbell
21502 Velicata Street
Woodland Hills, CA 91364
"Actor"

Jane Campion
500 Oxford Street
Level 18 #11
Bondi Junction
NSW 2022-AUSTRALIA
"Actress"

David Canary
903 South Mansfield Avenue
Los Angeles, CA 90036
"Actor"

Vincent Canby
215 West 88th Street
New York, NY 10024
"Film Critic"

John Candelaria
6361 Stoneridge Court
Riverdale, GA 30274
"Ex-Baseball Player"

Stephen J. Cannell
1220 Hillcrest
Pasadena, CA 91106
"TV Writer, Producer"

Billy Cannon
656 Lobdell Avenue
Baton Rouge, LA 70806
"Football Player"

Dyan Cannon
8033 Sunset Blvd. #254
Los Angeles, CA 90046
"Actress, Writer"

Freddie Cannon
18641 Cassandra Street
Tarzana, CA 91356
"Singer, Songwriter"

J. D. Cannon
45 W. 60th Street #10J
New York, NY 10023
"Actor"

Katherine Cannon
1310 Westholme Avenue
Los Angeles, CA 90024
"Actress"

Diana Canova
5670 Old Highway 395 N.
Carson City, NV 89707
"Actress"

Jose Canseco
3025 Meadow Lane
Ft. Lauderdale, FL 33331
"Baseball Player"

Lana Cantrell
300 East 71st Street
New York, NY 10021
"Singer, Actress"

Virginia Capers
4317 Canoga Drive
Woodland Hills, CA 91364
"Actress"

John Cappelletti
28791 Brant Lane
Laguna Niguel, CA 92677
"Ex-Football Player"

Ahna Capri
8227 Fountain Avenue #2
Los Angeles, CA 90046
"Actress"

Jennifer Capriatti
5435 Blue Heron Lane
Wesley Chapel, FL 33543
"Tennis Player"

Kate Capshaw
P.O. Box 869
Pacific Palisades, CA 90272
"Actress"

Captain & Tennille
(Toni & Daryl Dragon)
P.O. Box 608
Zephyr Cove, NV 89448
"Music Duo"

Irene Cara
8033 Sunset Blvd. #735
Los Angeles, CA 90046
"Actress, Singer"

Roger Caras
22108 Slab Bridge Road
Freeland, MD 21053
"News Correspondent"

Jack Cardiff
Lluca 4, E-03730 Javea
Provence (Alicante) SPAIN
"Film Director"

Pierre Cardin
59 rue du Faubourg
St-Honore
F-75008 Paris, FRANCE
"Fashion Designer"

Claudia Cardinale
Via Flaminia KW77
Prima Porta
00188 Rome, ITALY
"Actress"

Rod Carew
5144 East Crescent Drive
Anaheim, CA 92807
"Ex-Baseball Player"

Drew Carey
955 S. Carrillo Drive, #100
Los Angeles, CA 90048
"Actor"

Harry Carey, Jr.
P.O. Box 3256
Durango, CO 81302
"Actor"

Jim Carey
47 Kingman Street
Weymouth, MA 02188
"Hockey Player"

Mariah Carey
P.O. Box 4450
New York, NY 10101
"Singer"

Rick Carey
119 Rockland Avenue
Larchmont, NY 10538
"Swimmer"

419 N. Larchmont Blvd.
Los Angeles, CA 90004
"Actor"

Len Cariou
100 West 57th Street #149
New York, NY 10019
"Actor"

Frankie Carle
P.O. Box 7415
Mesa, AZ 85216
"Band Leader"

George Carlin
11911 San Vicente Blvd. #348
Los Angeles, CA 90049
"Comedian"

Lynn Carlin
15301 Ventura Blvd. #345
Sherman Oaks, CA 91403
"Actress"

Belinda Carlisle
21A Noel Street
London W1V 3PD ENGLAND
"Singer, Songwriter"

Kitty Carlisle-Hart
32 East 64th Street
New York, NY 10021
"Actress"

Mary Carlisle
517 North Rodeo Drive
Beverly Hills, CA 90210
"Actress"

King Juan Carlos
Palacio de La Carcuela
Madrid, SPAIN
"Royalty"

Larry Carlton
10130 Hegel Street
Bellflower, CA 90212
"Guitarist"

Rebekah Carlton-Luff
9300 Wilshire Blvd.#410
Beverly Hills, CA 90212
"Actress"

Steve Carlton
555 S. Camino Del Rio #B2
Durango, CO 81301
"Ex-Baseball Player"

Eric Carmen
1015 N. Doheny Drive #1
Los Angeles, CA 90069
"Singer, Songwriter"

Julie Carmen
4526 Wilshire Blvd.
Los Angeles, CA 90010
"Actress"

Ian Carmichael
The Priory, Grosmont
Whitby, Yorks. YO22 SQT
ENGLAND
"Actor, Producer"

Judy Carne
2 Horatio Street #10N
New York, NY 10014
"Actress"

Kim Carnes
2031 Old Natchez Terrace
Franklin, TN 37064
"Singer, Songwriter"

Art Carney
RR 20, Box 911
Westbrook, CT 06498
"Actor"

Princess Caroline
Villa Le Clos St. Pierre
Avenue Saint Martin
Monte Carlo MONACO
"Royalty"

Leslie Caron
10 av. George V
F-75116 Paris FRANCE
"Actress"

A.J. Carothers
2110 The Terrace
Los Angeles, CA 90049
"Screenwriter"

Carleton Carpenter
R.D. #2 Chardavoyne Road
Warwick, NY 10990
"Actor"

Charisma Carpenter
9300 Wilshire Blvd. #410
Beverly Hills, CA 90212
"Actress"

John Carpenter
8532 Hollywood Blvd.
Los Angeles, CA 90046
"Actor, Director"

Mary-Chapin Carpenter
1250 6th Street #401
Santa Monica, CA 90401
"Singer"

Richard Capenter
9386 Raviller Drive
Downey, CA 90240
"Pianist, Composer"

Scott Carpenter
P.O. Box 3161
Vail, CO 81658
"Astronaut"

Allan Carr
1203 N. Sweezer #101
West Hollywood, CA 90069
"Film Writer, Producer"

Caleb Carr
8899 Beverly Blvd. #102
Los Angeles, CA 90048
"Author"

Darlene Carr
1604 North Vista Avenue
Los Angeles, CA 90046
"Actress"

Jane Carr
121 N. San Vicente Blvd.
Beverly Hills, CA 90211
"Actress"

Vikki Carr
P.O. Box 780968
San Antonio, TX 78278
"Singer, Songwriter"

David Carradine
628C S. San Fernando Blvd.
Burbank, CA 91502
"Actor"

Keith Carradine
P.O. Box 460
Placeville, CO 81430
"Actor, Singer"

Robert Carradine
355 So. Grand Ave. #4150
Los Angeles, CA 90071
"Actor"

Barbara Carrera
P.O. Box 7876
Beverly Hills, CA 90212
"Actress, Model"

Tia Carrere
8228 Sunset Blvd. #300
Los Angeles, CA 90046
"Actress"

Jim Carrey
P.O. Box 57593
Sherman Oaks, CA 91403
"Comedian, Actor"

Mathieu Carriere
26 rue Vavin
F-75006 Paris FRANCE
"Actor"

Lord Carrington
Manor House
Bledlow, Aylesbury
Buckinghamshire HP17 9PE
ENGLAND
"Politician"

Diahann Carroll
9255 Doheny Road
Los Angeles, CA 90069
"Actress, Singer"

Pat Carroll
14 Old Tavern Lane
Harwich Port, MA 02646
"Actress"

Kitty Carruthers
22 East 71st Street
New York, NY 10021
"Ice Skater"

Peter Carruthers
22 East 71st Street
New York, NY 10021
"Ice Skater"

Marcey Carsey
4024 Radford Ave. #3
Studio City, CA 91604
"TV Producer"

Joanna Carson
400 St. Cloud Road
Los Angeles, CA 90024
"Ex-Wife of Johnny Carson"

Johnny Carson
6962 Wildlife
Malibu, CA 90265
"Ex- TV Show Host, Comedian"

Amy Carter
1 Woodland Drive
Plains, GA 31780
"Ex-President's Daughter"

Benny Carter
8321 Skyline Drive
Los Angeles, CA 90046
"Saxophonist"

Betty Carter
307 Lake Street
San Francisco, CA 94118
"Singer"

Carlene Carter
50 W. Main Street
Ventura, CA 93001
"Singer"

Chris Carter
9242 Beverly Blvd. #200
Beverly Hills, CA 90210
"Writer, Producer"

Deana Carter
9830 Wilshire Blvd.
Beverly Hills, CA 90212
"Singer"

Dixie Carter
10635 Santa Monica Blvd. #130
Los Angeles, CA 90025
"Actress"

Carter Family
P.O. Box 508
Hendersonville, TN 37075
"Music Group"

Helena Bonham Carter
7 W. Health Avenue
London NW11 7S ENGLAND
"Actress"

Hodding Carter III
211 South St. Asaph
Alexandria, VA 22314
"News Correspondent"

Jack Carter
1023 Chevy Chase Drive
Beverly Hills, CA 90210
"Comedian, Actor"

Jimmy Carter
1 Woodland Drive
Plains, GA 31780
"Former President of USA"

John Carter
11846 Ventura Blvd. #100
Studio City, CA 91604
"Actor"

Lynda Carter
9200 Harrington Drive
Potomac, MD 20854
"Actress, Singer"

Mel Carter
504 W. 168th Street
New York, NY 10032
"Singer, Actor"

Nell Carter
8484 Wilhire Blvd. #500
Beverly Hills, CA 90211
"Actress, Singer"

Ralph Carter
21 St. James Place
Brooklyn, NY 11205
"Actor"

Rosalyn Carter
1 Woodland Drive
Plains, GA 31780
"Former First Lady"

Rubin "Hurricane" Carter
1313 Brookedge Drive
Hamlin, NY 14464
"Boxer, Ex-Convict"

Terry Carter
244 Madison Avenue #332
New York, NY 10016
"Actor"

Thomas Carter
10958 Strathmore Drive
Los Angeles, CA 90024
"Actor, Director"

Gabrielle Carteris
1925 Century Park E. #2320
Los Angeles, CA 90067
"Actress"

Barbara Cartland
Camfield Place, Hatfield
Hertfordshire AL9 6JE ENGLAND
"Novelist"

Angela Cartwright
10143 Riverside Drive
Toluca Lake, CA 91602
"Actress"

Veronica Cartwright
12754 Sarah Street
Studio City, CA 91604
"Actress"

Anthony Caruso
1706 Mandeville Lane
Los Angeles, CA 90049
"Actor"

David Caruso
270 N. Canon Drive #1058
Beverly Hills, CA 90210
"Actor"

Dana Carvey
775 E. Blythdale Avenue
Mill Valley, CA 94941
"Comedian, Actor"

James Carville
209 Pennsylvania Avenue. SE #800
Washington, DC 20003
"Political Consultant"

Rosie Casals
P.O. Box 537
Sausalito, CA 94966
"Tennis Player"

Harold Case
34 Cunningham Park
Harrow, Middlesex
HA1 4AL ENGLAND
"Cinematographer"

Bernie Casey
6145 Flight Avenue
Los Angeles, CA 90056
"Actor, Ex-Football Player"

Lawrence Casey
4139 Vanette Place
North Hollywood, CA 91604
"Actor"

Johnny Cash
700 E. Main Street
Hendersonville, TN 37075
"Singer"

June Carter Cash
700 E. Main Street
Hendersonville, TN 37075
"Singer"

Pat Cash
281 Clarence Street
Sydney NSW 2000 AUSTRALIA
"Tennis Player"

Rosanne Cash
326 Carlton Avenue #3
Brooklyn, NY 11205
"Singer, Songwriter"

Philip Casnoff
216 S. Plymouth Blvd.
Los Angeles, CA 90004
"Actor"

Tina Caspary
11350 Ventura Blvd. #206
Studio City, CA 91604
"Actress"

Billy Casper
P.O. Box 210010
Chula Vista, CA 91921
"Golfer"

Peggy Cass
200 East 62nd Street
New York, NY 10021
"Actress"

Nick Cassavetes
22223 Buena Ventura Street
Woodland Hills, CA 91364
"Actor"

Jean-Pierre Cassel
76 Oxford Street
London W1N OAX ENGLAND
"Actor"

Seymour Cassell
2800 Neilson Way #1610
Santa Monica, CA 90405
"Actor"

David Cassidy
3799 Las Vegas Blvd. So.
Las Vegas, NV 89109
"Actor, Singer"

Joanna Cassidy
133 N. Irving Blvd.
Los Angeles, CA 90004
"Actress"

Patrick Cassidy
10433 Wilshire Blvd. #605
Los Angeles, CA 90024
"Actor"

Ryan Cassidy
4949 Strohm Avenue
North Hollywood, CA 91601
"Actor"

Shaun Cassidy
8484 Wilshire Blvd. #500
Beverly Hills, CA 90212
"Actor, Singer"

Oleg Cassini
3 West 57th Street
New York, NY 10019
"Fashion Designer"

Tricia Cast
20 Georgeff Road
Rolling Hills Estates, CA 90274
"Actress"

John Castle
126 Kennington Park Road
London W1 ENGLAND
"Mezzo-Soprano"

Fidel Castro
Palacio del Gobierno
Havana, CUBA
"Politician"

Darlene Cates
P.O. Box 39
Forney, TX 75126
"Actress"

Gilbert Cates
936 Hilts Avenue
Los Angeles, CA 90024
"Film Director"

Phoebe Cates
1636 3rd Avenue #309
New York, NY 10128
"Actress"

Mary Jo Catlett
4375 Farmdale Avenue
Studio City, CA 91604
"Actress"

Kim Cattrell
151 El Camino Drive
Beverly Hills, CA 90212
"Actress"

Maxwell Caufield
340 East 64th Street #25
New York, NY 10021
"Actor"

Steve Cauthen
c/o Cauthen Ranch
Boone County
Walton, KY 41094
"Horse Racer"

Carrie Cavalier
3200 Wyoming Avenue
Burbank, CA 91505
"Actress"

Michael Cavanaugh
P.O. Box 16758
Beverly Hills, CA 90209
"Actor"

Dick Cavett
109 East 79th Street #2C
New York, NY 10021
"TV Show Host, Comedian"

Evonne Goolagong Cawley
1 Erieview Plaza #1300
Cleveland, OH 44114
"Tennis Player"

Christopher Cazenove
9300 Wilshire Blvd. #555
Beverly Hills, CA 90212
"Actor"

Orlando Cepeda
331 Brazelton Court
Suison City, CA 94505
"Ex-Baseball Player"

Eugene Cernan
7 Windemere
Houston, TX 77063
"Astronaut"

Rick Cerrone
63 Eisenhower
Cresskill, NJ 07626
"Ex-Baseball Player"

Don Cervantez
1830 North Mariposa #2
Los Angeles, CA 90027
"Actor"

Peter Cetera
1880 Century Park East #900
Los Angeles, CA 90067
"Singer, Musician"

Ron Cey
22714 Creole Road
Woodland Hills, CA 91364
"Ex-Baseball Player"

Alex Chadwick
c/o National Public Radio
2025 "M" Street N.W.
Washington, DC 20036
"News Correspondent"

Mme. Chaing Kai-Shek
Locust Valley
Lattingtown, NY 11560
"Politician"

Chairman of the Board
2300 East Independence Blvd.
Charlotte, NC 28205
"Music Group"

George Chakiris
7266 Clinton Street
Los Angeles, CA 90036
"Actor"

Richard Chamberlain
3711 Round Top Drive
Honolulu, HI 96822
"Actor, Producer"

Wilt Chamberlain
11111 Santa Monica Blvd. #1000
Los Angeles, CA 90025
"Ex-Basketball Player"

Marilyn Chambers
3230 E. Flamingo Road #202
Las Vegas, NV 89121
"Actress"

Tom Chambers
P.O. Box 1369
Phoenix, AZ 85001
"Basketball Player"

Violetta Chamorro
Presidential Palace
Managua, NICARAGUA
"Politician"

Marge Champion
484 West 43rd Street
New York, NY 10036
"Actress, Dancer"

Charles Champlin
2169 Linda Flora Drive
Los Angeles, CA 90024
"Film Critic"

Jackie Chan
145 Waterloo Road, Kowloon
Hong Kong, Republic of China
"Actor"

Kyle Chandler
606 N. Larchmont Blvd. #309
Los Angeles, CA 90004
"Actor"

Otis Chandler
1421 Emerson
Oxnard, CA 93033
"Publisher"

Patrice Chanel
19216 Andmark Avenue
Carson, CA 90746
"Actress"

Michael Chang
2657 Windmill Parkway #348
Henderson, NV 89014
"Tennis Player"

Carol Channing
9301 Flicker Way
Los Angeles, CA 90069
"Actress"

Stockard Channing
2801 Hutton Drive
Beverly Hills, CA 90210
"Actress"

Rosalind Chao
10100 Santa Monica Blvd. #2500
Los Angeles, CA 90067
"Actress"

Doug Chapin
9911 W. Pico Blvd. PH 1
Los Angeles CA 90035
"Film Producer"

Tom Chapin
57 Piermont Place
Piermont, NY 10968
"Singer"

Geraldine Chaplin
Caios del Peral 314 Piso
E-28013 Madrid SPAIN
"Actress"

Judith Chapman
247 South Beverly Drive #102
Beverly Hills, CA 90212
"Actress"

Lonny Chapman
3973 Goodland Avenue
Studio City, CA 91604
"Actor"

Marguerite Chapman
11558 Riverside Drive #304
Hollywood, CA 91602
"Actress"

Mark David Chapman
#81 A 3860
Attica State Prison, Box 149
Attica, NY 14011
"John Lennon's Killer"

Mark Lindsay Chapman
P.O. Box 16758
Beverly Hills, CA 90209
"Actor"

David Chappelle
9560 Wilshire Blvd. #500
Beverly Hills, CA 90210
"Actor"

Patricia Charbonneau
749 1/2 N. Lafayette Park Pl.
Los Angeles, CA 90026
"Actress"

Cyd Charisse
10724 Wilshire Blvd. #1406
Los Angeles, CA 90024
"Actress, Dancer"

Josh Charles
8942 Wilshire Blvd.
Beverly Hills, CA 90211
"Actor"

HRH Prince Charles
Highgrove House
Gloucestershire ENGLAND
"Royalty"

Ray Charles
2107 W. Washington Blvd. #200
Los Angeles, CA 90018
"Singer, Pianist"

Suzette Charles
3680 Madrid Street
Las Vegas, NV 89121
"Former Miss America"

Leslie Charleson
2314 Live Oak Drive East
Los Angeles, CA 90068
"Actress"

Tony Charmoli
1271 Sunset Plaza Drive
Los Angeles, CA 90069
"Director, Choreography"

Charo
532 Portlock Road
Honolulu, HI 96825
"Singer"

Melanie Chartoff
10380 Tennessee Avenue
Los Angeles, CA 90064
"Actress"

David Charvet
8969 Sunset Blvd.
Los Angeles, CA 90069
"Actor"

Julio Ceasar Chavez
539 Telegraph Canyon Road #253
Chula Vista, CA 91910
"Boxer"

Barrie Chase
3750 Beverly Ridge Drive
Sherman Oaks, CA 91423
"Actress, Dancer"

Chevy Chase
955 S. Carrillo Drive #200
Los Angeles, CA 90048
"Actor, Writer"

Lorraine Chase
68 Old Brompton Road
London SW7 ENGLAND
"Actress"

Benjamin Chavis
P.O. Box 1661
Ellicott City, MD 21041
"Ex-N.A.A.C.P. Director"

Don Cheadle
2454 Glyndon Avenue
Venice, CA 90291
"Actor"

Cheap Trick
3805 County Road
Middleton, WI 53262
"Rock & Roll Group"

Maree Cheatham
8391 Beverly Blvd. #244
Los Angeles, CA 90048
"Actress"

Chubby Checker
320 Fayette Street #200
Conshohocken, PA 19426
"Singer, Songwriter"

Molly Cheek
13038 Landale Street
Studio City, CA 91604
"Actress"

Joan Chen
2601 Filbert Street
San Francisco, CA 94123
"Actress"

Mrs. Anna Chenault
2510 Virgina Avenue NW #1404
Washington, DC 20005
"Author, Journalist"

Dick Cheney
500 North Akard Street #3600
Dallas, TX 75201
"EX-Secretary of Defense"

Cher
P.O. Box 960
Beverly Hills, CA 90213
"Actress, Singer"

Colby Chester
5750 Wilshire Blvd. #512
Burbank, CA 91506
"Actor"

Mark Chestnut
P.O. Box 128031
Nashville, TN 37212
"Singer"

Morris Chestnut
1800 Avenue of the Stars #400
Los Angeles, CA 90067
"Actor"

Sam Chew, Jr.
8075 West 3rd Street #303
Los Angeles, CA 90048
"Actor"

Hank Cheyne
12304 Santa Monica Blvd. #104
Los Angeles, CA 90025
"Actor"

Michael Chiklis
4310 Sutton Place
Sherman Oaks, CA 91413
"Actor"

Julia Child
103 Irving Street
Cambridge, MA 02138
"TV Personality"

Linden Chiles
2521 Skyline
Topanga, CA 90290
"Actor"

Lois Chiles
644 San Lorenzo
Santa Monica, CA 90402
"Actress"

Jacques Chirac
Palais de l'Elysses
55 rue du Faubourg-St.-Honore
F-75008 Paris FRANCE
"President of France"

Shirley Chisholm
80 Wentworth Lane
Palm Coast, FL 32137
"Politician"

Joey Chitwood
4410 West Alva Street
Tampa, FL 33614
"Race Car Driver"

Anna Chlumsky
70 West Hubbard #200
Chicago, IL 60610
"Actress"

Margaret Cho
151 El Camino Drive
Beverly Hills, CA 90212
"Actress"

Chocolate Milk
P.O. Box 82
Great Neck, NY 11021
"R&B Group"

David Chokachi
11685 Gorham Avenue #5
Los Angeles, CA 90024
"Actor"

Rae Dawn Chong
4526 Wilshire Blvd.
Los Angeles, CA 90010
"Actress"

Thomas Chong
1625 Casale Road
Pacific Palisades, CA 90272
"Actor, Writer, Director"

Deepak Chopra
948 Granvis Altamira
Palos Verdes, CA 90274
"Author"

Raymond Chow
23 Barker Road
Craigside Mansion #5B
HONG KONG (BCC)
"Film Director"

Jean Chretien
24 Sussex Drive
Ottawa, Ontario
K1M OMS CANADA
"Prime Minister"

Todd Christensen
991 Sunburst Lane
Alpine, UT 84004
"Football Player"

Claudia Christian
148A Queensway, Bayswater
London W2 6LT ENGLAND
"Actress"

Julie Christie
23 Linden Gardens
London W2 ENGLAND
"Actress"

Lou Christie
228 W. 71st Street #1E
New York, NY 10023
"Singer"

Dennis Christopher
175 Fifth Avenue #2413
New York, NY 10010
"Actor"

Warren Christopher
400 S. Hope Street #1060
Los Angeles, CA 90071
"Ex-Secretary of State"

William Christopher
P.O. Box 50698
Pasadena, CA 91105
"Actor"

Connie Chung
1 W. 72nd Street
New York, NY 10023
"Newscaster"

Thomas Haden Church
8969 Sunset Blvd.
Los Angeles, CA 90069
"Actor"

"Cicciolina"
Via Cassia 1818
I-00123 Rome ITALY
"Actress"

Joseph Cicippio
2107 - 3rd Street
Norristown, PA 19401
"Ex-Hostage"

Michael Cimino
9015 Alta Cedro
Beverly Hills, CA 90210
"Writer, Producer"

Cinderella
P.O. Box 543
Drexel Hill, PA 19026
"Rock & Roll Group"

Charles Cioffi
10100 Santa Monica Blvd. #2500
Los Angeles, CA 90067
"Actor"

Henry Cisneros
2478 Devonport Lane
Los Angeles, CA 90077
"Ex-Secretary of H.U.D."

Liz Claiborne
650 Fifth Avenue
New York, NY 10019
"Fashion Designer"

Clancy Brothers
11806 N. 56th Street, #B
Tampa, FL 33617
"Folk Group"

Tom Clancy
P.O. Box 800
Huntington, MD 20639
"Novelist"

Gordon Clapp
9300 Wilshire Blvd. #555
Beverly Hills, CA 90212
"Actor"

Eric Clapton
46 Kensington Court
London WE8 5DT ENGLAND
"Singer, Guitarist"

Candy Clark
5 Briarhill Road
Montclair, NJ 07042
"Actress"

Dane Clark
1680 Old Oak Road
Los Angeles, CA 90049
"Actor, Director"

Dick Clark
3003 West Olive Avenue
Burbank, CA 91505
"Ex-TV Show Host, Producer"

Doran Clark
10100 Santa Monica Blvd. #2500
Los Angeles, CA 90067
"Actress"

Joe Clark
707-7th Avenue SW #1300
Calgary, Alb. T2P 3H6 CANADA
"Ex-Prime Minister"

Lynn Clark
247 South Beverly Drive #102
Beverly Hills, CA 90212
"Actress"

Marcia Clark
151 El Camino Drive
Beverly Hills, CA 90212
"Attorney"

Marsha Clark
335 N. Maple Drive #360
Beverly Hills, CA 90210
"Actress"

Mary Higgins Clark
210 Central Park South
New York, NY 10019
"Writer"

Oliver Clark
2781 La Castana Drive
Los Angeles, CA 90046
"Actor"

Petula Clark
15 Chemin Rieu, CH-1208
Geneva SWITZERLAND
"Singer, Actress"

Ramsey Clark
36 East 12th Street
New York, NY 10003
"Politician"

Roy Clark
1800 Forrest Blvd.
Tulsa, OK 74114
"Singer, Guitarist"

Susan Clark
7943 Woodrow Wilson Drive
Los Angeles, CA 90046
"Actress"

Will Clark
1000 Papworth Avenue
Metairie, LA 70005
"Baseball Player"

Angela Clarke
7557 Mulholland Drive
Los Angeles, CA 90046
"Actress"

Arthur C. Clarke
4715 Gregory's Road
Colombo SIR LANKA
"Author"

Bob Clarke
127 Rivershore Drive
Seaford, DE 19973
"Cartoonist"

Brian Patrick Clarke
333-D Kenwood
Burbank, CA 91505
"Actor"

Jordan Clarke
121 N. San Vicente Blvd.
Beverly Hills, CA 90211
"Actor"

Robert Clarke
4841 Gentry Avenue
North Hollywood, CA 91607
"Actor"

Stanley Clarke
1807 Benedict Canyon
Beverly Hills, CA 90210
"Guitarist, Composer"

Robert Clary
10001 Sun Dial Lane
Beverly Hills, CA 90210
"Actor"

The Clash
268 Camden Road
London NW1 ENGLAND
"Rock & Roll Group"

Andrew Dice Clay
836 North La Cienega Blvd. #202
Los Angeles, CA 90069
"Comedian, Actor"

Nicholas Clay
15 Golden Square #315
London W1R 3AG ENGLAND
"Actor"

Jill Clayburgh
P.O. Box 18
Lakeville, CT 06039
"Actress"

John Cleese
82 Ladbroke Road
London W11 3NU ENGLAND
"Actor, Writer"

Roger Clemens
11535 Quall Hollow
Houston, TX 77024
"Baseball Player"

David Clennon
954 - 20th Street #B
Santa Monica, CA 90403
"Actor"

Van Cliburn
455 Wilder Place
Shreveport, LA 71104
"Pianist"

Jimmy Cliff
51 Lady Musgrove Road
Kingston JAMAICA
"Singer"

Clark Clifford
9421 Rockville Pike
Bethesda, MD 20814
"Attorney"

Linda Clifford
1560 Broadway #1308
New York, NY 10036
"Singer"

Eleanor Clift
1750 Pennsylvania Ave. N.W.
Suite #1220
Washington, DC 20001
"News Correspondent"

Debra Clinger
1206 Chickasaw Drive
Brentwood, TN 37027
"Actress"

President Bill Clinton
1600 Pennsylvania Avenue
Washington, DC 20500
"President of United States"

Chelsea Clinton
Stanford University
Wilbur Hall
Palo Alto, CA 94305
"Daughter of the President"

Hillary Rodham-Clinton
1600 Pennsylvania Avenue
Washington, DC 20500
"First Lady, Attorney"

John Clive
4 Court Lodge, Chelsea
London SW3 AJA ENGLAND
"Actor, Writer"

George Clooney
4000 Warner Blvd. #B81-117
Burbank, CA 91522
"Actor"

Rosemary Clooney
1019 North Roxbury Drive
Beverly Hills, CA 90210
"Singer"

Glenn Close
9830 Wilshire Blvd.
Beverly Hills, CA 90212
"Actress"

Jerry Clower
P.O. Box 121089
Nashville, TN 37212
"Comedian"

The Coasters
4905 S. Atlantic Avenue
Daytona Beach, FL 32127
"Vocal Group"

Phyllis Coates
P.O. Box 1969
Boyes Hot Springs, CA 95416
"Actress"

Dan Coats
1300 South Harrison Street #3158
Ft. Wayne, IN 46802
"Politician"

Julie Cobb
10110 Empyrean Way #304
Los Angeles, CA 90067
"Actress"

James Coburn
1607 Schuyler Road
Beverly Hills, CA 90210
"Actor, Director"

Imogene Coca
P.O. Box 5151
Westport, CT 06881
"Actress"

Hank Cochran
Rt. 2, Box 438
Hunter Lane
Hendersonville, TN 37075
"Singer, Songwriter"

Johnnie Cochran, Jr.
2373 Hobart Blvd.
Los Angeles, CA 90027
"Attorney"

Bruce Cockburn
1775 Broadway #433
New York, NY 10019
"Singer, Songwriter"

Joe Cocker
9830 Wilshire Blvd.
Beverly Hills, CA 90212
"Singer"

Iron Eyes Cody
2013 Griffith Park Blvd.
Los Angeles, CA 90039
"Actor"

David Allan Coe
P.O. Box 270188
Nashville, TN 37227
"Singer, Songwriter"

Sebastian Coe
Starsgood
High Barn Road
Effingham
Surrey KT24 SPW ENGLAND
"Runner"

Susie Coelho
3500 West Olive Avenue #1440
Burbank, CA 91505
"Actress, Model"

Joel Coen
9560 Wilshire Blvd. #516
Beverly Hills, CA 90212
"Film Director"

Paul Coffey
633 Hawthorne Street
Birmingham, MI 48009
"Hockey Player"

Frank "Junior" Coghlan
12522 Argyle Avenue
Los Alamitos, CA 90720
"Actor"

Alexander Cohen
25 West 54th Street #5-F
New York, NY 10019
"TV/Theater Producer"

Larry Cohen
2111 Coldwater Canyon
Beverly Hills, CA 90210
"Writer, Producer"

Leonard Cohen
121 Leslie Street
No. York, Ontario
M3C 2J9 CANADA
"Singer, Songwriter"

William Cohen
The Pentagon
Room 2E777 #1400
Washington, DC 20201
"Secretary of Defense"

Mindy Cohn
9300 Wilshire Blvd. #400
Beverly Hills, CA 90212
"Actress"

Robert Colbert
10000 Riverside Drive #6
Toluca Lake, CA 91602
"Actor"

Dennis Cole
3518 Cahuenga Blvd. W. #216
Los Angeles, CA 90068
"Actor"

Gary Cole
10390 Santa Monica Blvd. #300
Los Angeles, CA 90025
"Actor"

George Cole
Donnelly
Newham Hill Bottom
Nettleford Oxon, ENGLAND
"Actor"

Michael Cole
6332 Costello Avenue
Van Nuys, CA 91401
"Actor"

Mrs. Marie Cole
South House
Tyringham, MA 01264
"Widow of Nat Cole"

Natalie Cole
955 S. Carrillo Drive #200
Los Angeles, CA 90048
"Singer"

Tina Cole
3340 Sierra Oaks Drive
Sacramento, CA 95864
"Actress"

Dabney Coleman
360 North Kenter Avenue
Los Angeles, CA 90049
"Actor"

Durell Coleman
800 S. Robertson Blvd. #5
Los Angeles, CA 90035
"Actor"

Gary Coleman
4710 Don Miguel Drive
Los Angeles, CA 90008
"Actor"

Jack Coleman
4230 Colfax Avenue #304
Studio City, CA 91604
"Actor"

Lisa Coleman
3105 Ledgewood
Los Angels, CA 90068
"Actress"

Nancy Coleman
484 West 43rd Street #42-G
New York, NY 10036
"Actress"

John Colicos
615 Yonge Street #401
Toronto Ontario
M4Y 1Z5 CANADA
"Actor"

Margaret Colin
41 Bradford Avenue
Montclair, NJ 07043
"Actress"

Mark Collie
3322 West End Avenue #520
Nashville, TN 37203
"Guitarist"

Gary Collins
2751 Hutton Drive
Beverly Hills, CA 90210
"Actor, TV Show Host"

Jackie Collins
616 N. Beverly Drive
Beverly Hills, CA 90210
"TV Show Host, Author"

Joan Collins
9255 Doheny Road
Los Angeles, CA 90069
"Actress, Producer"

Judy Collins
450 7th Avenue #603
New York, NY 10123
"Singer, Songwriter"

Kate Collins
1410 York Avenue #4-D
New York, NY 10021
"Actress"

Lewis Collins
22 Westbere Road
London NW2 3SR ENGLAND
"Actor"

Marva Collins
4146 West Chicago Avenue
Chicago, IL 60651
"Educator"

Michael Collins
P.O. Box 600
Avon, NC 27915
"Writer"

Phil Collins
30 Ives Street
London SW3 2ND ENGLAND
"Singer, Drummer"

Stephen Collins
10390 Santa Monica Blvd. #300
Los Angeles, CA 90025
"Actor"

Scott Colomby
1425 N. Queens Road
Los Angeles, CA 90069
"Actor"

Color Me Badd
P.O. Box 552113
Carol City, FL 33055
"Music Group"

Charles Colson
P.O. Box 97103
Washington, DC 20090
"Author"

Marshall Colt
923 Ocean Avenue #5
Santa Monica, CA 90403
"Actor"

Jessie Colter
1117-17th Avenue South
Nashville, TN 37212
"Singer"

Chi Coltrane
5955 Tuxedo Terrace
Los Angeles, CA 90068
"Singer"

Robbie Coltrane
47 Courtfield Road #9
London SW7 4DB ENGLAND
"Actor"

Franco Columbu
2947 South Sepulveda Blvd.
Los Angeles, CA 90064
"Actor, Bodybuilder"

Chris Columbus
847 North Franklin Avenue
River Forest, IL 60305
"Screenwriter"

Nadia Comaneci
4421 Hidden Hills Road
Norman, OK 73072
"Gymnast"

Jeffrey Combs
13601 Ventura Blvd. #349
Sherman Oaks, CA 91423
"Actor"

Sean "Puff Daddy" Combs
8436 West 3rd St. #650
Los Angeles, CA 90048
"Rap Singer"

Betty Comden
117 East 95th Street
New York, NY 10128
"Writer"

Paul Comi
1665 Oak Knoll Avenue
San Marino, CA 91108
"Actor"

Perry Como
305 Northern Blvd. #3-A
Great Neck, NY 11021
"Singer"

Cristi Conaway
P.O. Box 46515
Los Angeles CA 90046
"Actress"

Jeff Conaway
3162 Durand Drive
Los Angeles, CA 90068
"Actor"

Dave Conception
Urb. Los Caobos Botalon 5d
Piso-Maracay 5 VENEZUELA
"Ex-Baseball Player"

Gino Conforti
1440 Veteran Avenue #603
Los Angeles, CA 90024
"Actor"

Ray Coniff
2154 Hercules Drive
Los Angeles, CA 90046
"Composer"

John Conlee
38 Music Square East #117
Nashville, TN 37203
"Singer, Songwriter"

Darlene Conley
9200 Sunset Blvd. #1201
Los Angeles, CA 90069
"Actress"

Earl Thomas Conley
657 Baker Road
Smyrna, TN 37167
"Singer, Songwriter"

Joe Conley
P.O. Box 6487
Thousand Oaks, CA 91359
"Actor"

Didi Conn
14820 Valley Vista Blvd.
Sherman Oaks, CA 91403
"Actress"

Jennifer Connelly
8942 Wilshire Blvd.
Beverly Hills, CA 90211
"Actress"

Bart Conner
4421 Hidden Hills Road
Norman, OK 73072
"Athlete"

Dennis Conner
720 Gateway Center Drive
San Diego, CA 92102
"Yachtsman"

Jason Connery
535 Kings Road #19
London SW10 0SZ ENGLAND
"Actor"

Sean Connery
9830 Wilshire Blvd.
Beverly Hills, 90212
"Actor"

Harry Connick, Jr.
323 Broadway
Cambridge, MA 02139
"Pianist, Singer"

Billy Connolly
7424 Woodrow Wilson Drive
Los Angeles, CA 90046
"Actor"

Norma Connolly
4411 Los Feliz Blvd. #1201
Los Angeles, CA 90027
"Actress"

Patrick Connor
3 Spring Bank
New Mills nr. Stockport
SK12 4AS ENGLAND
"Actor"

Carol Connors
1709 Ferrari Drive
Beverly Hills, CA 90210
"Songwriter"

Jimmy Connors
200 South Refugio Road
Santa Ynez, CA 93460
"Tennis Player"

Mike Connors
4810 Louise Avenue
Encino, CA 91316
"Actor"

Barnaby Conrad
3530 Pine Valley Drive
Sarasota, FL 34239
"Author, Painter"

Charles Conrad, Jr.
6301 Princeville Circle
Huntington Beach, CA 92648
"Astronaut"

Christian Conrad
21006 Dumetz Road
West Hills, CA 91364
"Actor"

Kimberly Conrad
10236 Charing Cross Road
Los Angeles, CA 90077
"Mrs. Hugh Hefner"

Paul Conrad
28649 Crestridge Road
Palos Verdes, CA 90274
"Cartoonist"

Robert Conrad
11300 W. Olympic Blvd. #610
Los Angeles, CA 90064
"Actor, Writer"

Shane Conrad
1999 Avenue of the Star #2850
Los Angeles, CA 90067
"Actor"

Kevin Conroy
10100 Santa Monica Blvd. #2500
Los Angeles, CA 90067
"Actor"

John Considine
10100 Santa Monica Blvd. #2490
Los Angeles, CA 90067
"Actor, Writer"

Tim Considine
3708 Mountain View Avenue
Los Angeles, CA 90066
"Actor, Writer, Director"

Michel Constantin
17 Blvd. Bartole Beauvallon
8321 Sainte Maxime, FRANCE
"Actor"

Ex-King Constantine
4 Linnell Drive
Hampstead Way
London NW11 ENGLAND
"Royalty"

Michael Constantine
513 W. 54th Street
New York, NY 10019
"Actor"

John Conte
72-920 Parkview Drive
Palm Desert, CA 92260
"Actor"

Bill Conti
117 Fremont Place
Los Angeles, CA 90005
"Composer, Arranger"

Tom Conti
Chatto & Linnet
Shaftesbury Avenue
London W1 ENGLAND
"Actor"

Frank Converse
10100 Santa Monica Blvd. #2490
Los Angeles, CA 90067
"Actor"

Peggy Converse
2049 Century Park E. #2500
Los Angeles, CA 90067
"Actress"

Gary Conway
11240 Chimney Rock Road
Paso Robles, CA 93446
"Actor"

Kevin Conway
1999 Ave. of the Stars #2850
Los Angeles, CA 90067
"Actor"

Tim Conway
P.O. Box 17047
Encino, CA 91416
"Actor, Director"

Rep. John Conyers (MI)
House Rayburn Bldg. #2426
Washington, DC 20515
"Politician"

Ry Cooder
326 Entrada Drive
Santa Monica, CA 90402
"Guitarist, Songwriter"

Keith Coogan
1640 S. Sepulveda Blvd. #218
Los Angeles, CA 90025
"Actor"

Carole Cook
8829 Ashcroft Avenue
Los Angeles, CA 90048
"Actress"

Fielder Cook
180 Central Park South
New York, NY 10019
"TV Writer, Producer"

Robin Cook
4601 Gulf Shore Blvd. #P4
Naples, FL 33940
"Screenwriter"

Alistair Cook
Nassau Point
Cutchogue, NY 11935
"Journalist, TV Announcer"

Danny Cooksey
9300 Wilshire Blvd. #410
Beverly Hills, CA 90212
"Singer"

Catherine Cookson
23 Glastonbury Grove
Newcastle-Upton-Tyne
NE2 2HB ENGLAND
"Authoress"

Peter Cookson
30 Norfolk Road
Southfield, MA 01259
"Actor"

Dr. Denton Cooley
3014 Del Monte Drive
Houston, TX 77019
"Heart Surgeon"

Martha Coolidge
2129 Coldwater Canyon
Beverly Hills, CA 90210
"Director"

Rita Coolidge
560 Hilbert Drive
Fallbrook, CA 92028
"Singer, Actress"

Coolio
11 Lorraine Street #58
Brooklyn, NY 11231
"Singer"

Pat Coombs
5 Wendela Court
Harrow-On-The-Hill
Middlesex ENGLAND
"Actress"

Gerry Cooney
22501 Linden Blvd.
Jamaica, NY 11411
"Boxer"

Alice Cooper
4135 East Keim Drive
Paradise Valley, AZ 85253
"Singer, Songwriter"

Ben Cooper
733 N. Seward Street PH
Los Angeles, CA 90038
"Actor"

Chris Cooper
955 S. Carrillo Dr. #300
Los Angeles, CA 90048
"Actor"

Henry Cooper
5 Ledway Drive
Webley
Middlesex ENGLAND
"TV Personality"

Jackie Cooper
9621 Royalton
Beverly Hills, CA 90210
"Actor, Director"

Jeanne Cooper
8401 Edwin Drive
Los Angeles, CA 90046
"Actress"

7813 Sunset Blvd.
Los Angeles, CA 90046
"Actor"

L. Gordon Cooper
5011 Woodley Avenue
Encino, CA 91436
"Astronaut"

Marc Copage
P.O. Box 461677
Los Angeles, CA 90046
"Actor"

Joan Copeland
88 Central Park West
New York, NY 10023
"Actress"

Stewart Copeland
9000 Sunset Blvd. #515
West Hollywood, CA 90069
"Drummer"

Teri Copley
5003 Coldwater Canyon Avenue
Sherman Oaks, CA 91423
"Actress"

David Copperfield
515 Post Oak Blvd. #300
Houston, TX 77027
"Magician"

Francis Coppola
916 Kearny Street
San Francisco, CA 94133
"Writer, Producer"

Sophia Coppola
781-5th Avenue
New York, NY 10022
"Actress"

Gretchen Corbett
1801 Avenue of the Stars #902
Los Angeles, CA 90067
"Actress"

John Corbett
1327 Brinkley Avenue
Los Angeles, CA 90049
"Actor"

Michael Corbett
1503 W. Morningside Drive
Burbank, CA 91506
"Actor"

Ronnie Corbett
57 Gt. Cumberland Place
London W1H 7LJ ENGLAND
"Comedian"

Barry Corbin
2113 Greta Lane
Ft. Worth, TX 76120
"Actor"

Ellen Corby
9026 Harratt
Los Angeles, CA 90069
"Actress"

Kevin Corcoran
8617 Balcom
Northridge, CA 91325
"Actor"

Barbara Corday
532 South Windsor Blvd.
Los Angeles, CA 90020
"TV Writer, Producer"

Mara Corday
P.O. Box 800393
Valencia, CA 91355
"Actress"

Angel Cordero
P.O. Box 90
Jamaica, NY 11411
"Horse Jockey"

Chick Corea
2635 Griffith Park Blvd.
Los Angeles, CA 90039
"Musician"

Prof. Irwin Corey
58 Nassau Drive
Great Neck, NY 11022
"Comedian"

Jeff Corey
29445 Bluewater Road
Malibu, CA 90265
"Actor, Director"

Ann Corio
721 E. Grinnell Drive
Burbank, CA 91501
"Burlesque"

Al Corley
10000 Santa Monica Blvd. #305
Los Angles, CA 90067
"Singer"

Pat Corley
1317 - 5th Street #200
Santa Monica, CA 90401
"Actor"

Roger Corman
2501 La Mesa Drive
Santa Monica, CA 90402
"Writer, Producer"

Cornelius Bros. & Sister Rose
2 Professional Drive, #240
Gaithersburg, TN 30879
"R&B Group"

Helen Cornelius
1906 Chet Atkins Place #502
Nashville, TN 37212
"Singer"

Don Cornell
100 Bayview Drive #1521
North Miami, FL 33160
"Singer"

Lydia Cornell
142 South Bedford Drive
Beverly Hills, CA 90212
"Actress, Model"

Leanza Cornett
P.O. Box 119
Atlantic City, NJ 08404
"TV Show Host"

Georges Corraface
1 rue Gueneguard
F-75006 Paris ENGLAND
"Actor"

Adrienne Corri
2-4 Noel Street
London W1V 3RB ENGLAND
"Actress"

Bud Cort
955 South Carrillo Drive, #300
Los Angeles, CA 90048
"Actor"

Dan Cortese
16698 Calle Arbolada
Pacific Palisades, CA 90272
"Actor"

Joe Cortese
4724 Poe Avenue
Woodland Hills, CA 91364
"Actor"

Valentina Cortese
Piazza Sant' Erasmo 9
I-20121 Milan, ITALY
"Actress"

Norman Corwin
1840 Fairburn Avenue #302
Los Angeles, CA 90025
"Writer, Producer"

Bill Cosby
P.O. Box 4049
Santa Monica, CA 90411
"Actor, Comedian"

Pierre Cossette
8899 Beverly Blvd. #100
Los Angeles, CA 90048
"Film Producer"

Mary Costa
3340 Kingston Pike, Unit 1
Knoxville, TN 37919
"Soprano"

Constantin Costa-Gavras
244 rue Saint-Jacques
75005 Paris, FRANCE
"Filmwriter, Director"

Midge Costanza
11811 West Olympic Blvd.
Los Angeles, CA 90264
"Ex-President Aide"

Bob Costas
30 Rockefeller Plaza
New York, NY 10112
"Sportscaster"

Elvis Costello
9028 Great West Road
Middlesex TW8 9EW ENGLAND
"Singer"

Mariclare Costello
8271 Melrose Avenue #110
Los Angeles, CA 90046
"Actress"

Nicholas Coster
1624 North Gardner
Los Angeles, CA 90046
"Actor"

Kevin Costner
P.O. Box 275
Montrose, CA 91021
"Actor"

David Coulier
9150 Wilshire Blvd. #350
Beverly Hills, CA 90212
"Actor"

Fred Couples
5609 Cradlerock Circle
Plano, TX 75093
"Golfer"

Katherine Couric
1100 Park Avenue #15A
New York, NY 10128
"TV Show Host"

Jim Courier
1 Erieview Plaza #1300
Cleveland, OH 44114
"Tennis Player"

Hazel Court
1111 San Vicent Blvd.
Santa Monica, CA 90402
"Actress"

Tom Courtenay
30 Charlywood Road
London SW15 ENGLAND
"Actor"

Jerome Courtland
1064 Spruce Street
Winnetka, IL 60093
"Film Director"

Robin Cousins
2887 Hollyridge Drive
Los Angeles, CA 90068
"Ice Skater"

Bob Cousy
427 Salisbury Street
Worchester, MA 01609
"Basketball Player"

Franklin Cover
1422 North Sweetzer #402
Los Angeles, CA 90069
"Actor"

Archibald Cox
34 Old Connecticut Path
Wayland, MA 01778
"Politician"

Bobby Cox
P.O. Box 4064
Atlanta, GA 30302
"Baseball Manager"

Courteney Cox
1122 S. Robertson Blvd. #15
Los Angeles, CA 90035
"Actress"

1010 Hammond Street #102
Los Angeles, CA 90069
"Actor"

Ronny Cox
13948 Magnolia Blvd.
Sherman Oaks, CA 91423
"Actor, Film Producer"

Peter Coyote
774 Marin Drive
Mill Valley, CA 94941
"Actor"

Cuffy Crabbe
11216 North 74th Street
Scottsdale, AZ 85260
"Actor"

Billy "Crash" Craddock
3007 Old Martinsville Road
Greensboro, NC 27455
"Singer, Songwriter"

Jenny Craig
P.O. Box 387190
La Jolla, CA 92038
"Physical Fitness Director"

Jim Craig
15 Jyre Lane
North Easton, MA 02356
"Hockey Player"

Wendy Craig
29 Roehampton Gate
London SW15 5JR ENGLAND
"Actress"

Yvonne Craig
P.O. Box 827
Pacific Palisades, CA 90272
"Actress"

Jeanne Crain
1029 Arbolado Road
Santa Barbara, CA 93103
"Actress"

Douglass Cramer
738 Sarbonne Road
Los Angeles, CA 90077
"TV Writer, Producer"

Floyd Cramer
110 Glancy Street #201
Goodettsville, TN 37072
"Pianist"

Grant Cramer
9911 W. Pico Blvd. #1060
Los Angeles, CA 90035
"Actor"

Barbara Crampton
501 South Beverly Drive 3rd Floor
Beverly Hills, CA 90212
"Actress"

Bruce Crampton
80472 Pebble Beach
La Quinta, CA 92253
"Golfer"

Gemma Craven
42 Hazelburg Road
London SW6 ENGLAND
"Actress"

Matt Craven
5033 Campo Road
Woodland Hills, CA 91364
"Actor"

Wes Craven
8491 Sunset Blvd. #375
Los Angeles, CA 90069
"Writer, Producer"

Christina Crawford
7 Springs Farm Sanders Road
Tensed, ID 83870
"Authoress"

Cindy Crawford
132 South Rodeo Drive #300
Beverly Hills, CA 90212
"Model"

Johnny Crawford
2440 El Contento Drive
Los Angeles, CA 90068
"Actor"

Michael Crawford
10 Argyle Street
London W1V 1AB ENGLAND
"Actor"

Randy Crawford
911 Park Street S.W.
Grand Rapids, MI 49504
"Singer"

Bettino Craxi
Palazzo Chigi
Piazza Colonna
1-00100 Rome, ITALY
"Prime Minister"

Robert Cray
P.O. Box 170429
San Francisco, CA 94117
"Band Leader"

Richard Crenna
16030 Ventura Blvd. #380
Sherman Oaks, CA 91423
"Actor, Director"

Ben Crenshaw
2905 San Gabriel #213
Austin, TX 78705
"Golfer"

Marshall Crenshaw
110 W. 57th Street #300
New York, NY 10019
"Singer, Songwriter"

The Crew-Cuts
29 Cedar Street
Creskill, NJ 07626
"Vocal Group"

Michael Crichton
433 N. Camden Drive #500
Beverly Hills, CA 90210
"Filmwriter, Director"

The Crickets
7200 France Avenue South #330
Edina, MN 55435
"Rock & Roll Group"

Quentin Crisp
46 East 3rd Street
New York, NY 10003
"Actor"

Peter Criss
4905 S. Atlanta Avenue
Daytona Beach, FL 32127
"Drummer, Singer"

Judith Crist
180 Riverside Drive
New York, NY 10024
"Film Critic"

Linda Cristal
9129 Hazen Drive
Beverly Hills, CA 90210
"Actress"

Mary Jane Croft
2160 Century Park East #812
Los Angeles, CA 90067
"Actor"

James Cromwell
1801 Avenue of the Stars #902
Los Angeles, CA 90067
"Actor"

David Cronenberg
217 Avenue Road
Toronto, Ontario
M5R 2J3 CANADA
"Film Writer, Director"

Walter Cronkite
870 United Nations Plaza #25A
New York, NY 10017
"Broadcast Journalist"

Hume Cronyn
63-23 Carlton Street
Rego Park, NY 11374
"Actor"

Annette Crosbie
68 St. James's Street
London SW1A 1LE ENGLAND
"Actress"

Cathy Lee Crosby
1223 Wilshire Blvd. #404
Santa Monica, CA 90403
"Actress"

David Crosby
P.O. Box 9008
Solvang, CA 93464
"Singer, Songwriter"

Denise Crosby
345 North Maple Drive #300
Beverly Hills, CA 90210
"Actor"

Mrs. Kathryn Crosby
P.O. Box 85
Genda, NV 89411
"Widower of Bing Crosby"

Mary Crosby
3500 W. Olive Avenue #1400
Burbank, CA 91505
"Actress"

Norm Crosby
1400 Londonderry Place
Los Angeles, CA 90069
"Comedian, Actor"

Philip Crosby
21801 Providencia
Woodland Hills, CA 91364
"Actor"

Crosby, Stills & Nash
14930 Ventura Blvd. #206
Sherman Oaks, CA 91403
"Rock & Roll Group"

Ben Cross
Contejo la Perdiz
Barriada de Concelada
Esteponda Malaga SPAIN
"Actor"

Christopher Cross
P.O. Box 127465
Nashville, TN 37212
"Singer, Songwriter"

Marcia Cross
10100 Santa Monica Blvd. #2500
Los Angeles, CA 90067
"Actress"

Andrae Crouch
20265 Wells Drive
Woodland Hills, CA 91364
"Singer"

Lindsay Crouse
15115 1/2 Sunset Blvd. #D
Pacific Palisades, CA 90272
"Actress"

Sheryl Crow
10345 West Olympic Blvd., #200
Los Angeles, CA 90064
"Singer"

Cameron Crowe
9830 Wilshire Blvd.
Beverly Hills, CA 90212
"Filmwriter, Producer"

Tanya Crowe
8271 Melrose Avenue #110
Los Angeles, CA 90046
"Actress"

Rodney Crowell
P.O. Box 120576
Nashville, TN 37212
"Singer, Songwriter"

Mart Crowley
8955 Beverly Blvd.
Los Angeles, CA 90048
"Writer"

Tom Cruise
14775 Ventura Blvd. #1-710
Sherman Oaks, CA 91403
"Actor"

Denny Crumm
23015 Third Street
Louisville, KY 40292
"Basketball Coach"

Brandon Cruz
1178 East Lucero Court
Camarillo, CA 93010
"Actor"

Jon Cryer
9560 Wilshire Blvd. #500
Beverly Hills, CA 90212
"Actor"

Billy Crystal
9830 Wilshire Blvd.
Beverly Hills, CA 90212
"Actor, Comedian"

Melinda Culea
P.O. Box 2022
Beverly Hills, CA 90213
"Actress"

Kieran Culkin
151 El Camino Drive
Beverly Hills, CA 90212
"Actor"

Macaulay Culkin
124 West 60th Street
New York, NY 10023
"Actor"

Brett Cullen
2229 Glyndon Avenue
Venice, CA 90291
"Actor"

Robert Culp
1270 Sunset Plaza Drive
Los Angeles, CA 90069
"Actor, Writer, Director"

Michael Culver
5 Clancarty Road
London SW6 ENGLAND
"Actor"

Constance Cummings
68 Old Church Street
London SW3 6EP ENGLAND
"Actress"

Randall Cunningham
5020 Spanish Heights Drive
Las Vegas, NV 89118
"Football Player"

Secy. Andrew Cuomo
4571-7th Street SW
Washington, DC 20024
"Government Official"

Mario Cuomo
50 Sutton Place So. #11-G
New York, NY 10022
"Ex-Governor"

Mike Curb
3907 West Alameda Avenue
Burbank, CA 91505
"Record Producer"

Kevin Curren
5808 Back Court
Austin, TX 78764
"Tennis Player"

Cherie Currie
3050 North Chandelle Road
Los Angeles, CA 90046
"Singer"

Louise Currie
1317 Del Resto Drive
Beverly Hills, CA 90210
"Actress"

Mark Curry
12115 Magnolia Blvd. #134
North Hollywood, CA 91607
"Actor"

Tim Curry
9560 Wilshire Blvd. #516
Beverly Hills, CA 90212
"Actor"

Jane Curtin
10450 Revuelta Way
Los Angeles, CA 90077
"Actress"

Valerie Curtin
15622 Meadowgate Road
Encino, CA 91316
"Actress, Writer"

Dan Curtis
2500 Broadway
Santa Monica, CA 90404
"Actor"

Jamie Lee Curtis
9830 Wilshire Blvd.
Beverly Hills, CA 90212
"Actress"

Keene Curtis
6363 Ivarene Avenue
Los Angeles, CA 90068
"Actor"

Robin Curtis
9911 W. Pico Blvd. #1960
Los Angeles, CA 90035
"Actress"

Tony Curtis
11831 Folkstone Lane
Los Angeles, CA 90077
"Actor, Director"

Joan Cusack
540 N. Lakeshore Dr. #521
Chicago, IL 60611
"Actress"

John Cusack
838 Sheridan
Evanston, IL 60202
"Actor"

Clive Cussier
5539 E. Sanna
Paradise Valley, AZ 85253
"Novelist"

Lise Cutter
4526 Wilshire Blvd.
Beverly Hills, CA 90210
"Actress"

Jon Cypher
424 Manzanita Avenue
Ventura, CA 93003
"Actor"

Billy Ray Cyrus
1225-B - 16th Avenue
Nashville, TN 38212
"Singer"

Larry Czonka
37256 Hunter Camp Road
Lisbon, OH 44432
"Ex-Football Player"

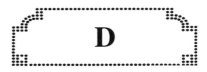

Augusta Dabney
North Mountain Road
Dobbs Ferry, NY 10522
"Actress"

Maryan d'Abo
8391 Beverly Blvd. #200
Los Angeles, CA 90048
"Actress"

Olivia d'Abo
1122 S. Robertson Blvd. #15
Los Angeles, CA 90035
"Actress"

Mark Dacascos
4703 Coldwater Canyon #101
Studio City, CA 91604
"Actor"

Willem Dafoe
33 Wooster Street #200
New York, NY 10013
"Actor"

Tim Daggett
1750 East Boulder Street
Colorado Springs, CO 80909
"Gymnast"

Arlene Dahl
P.O. Box 116
Sparkill, NY 10976
"Actress"

Bill Dailey
1331 Park Avenue SW.
Albuquerque, NM 87104
"Actor"

Janet Dailey
1947 Lakeshore Drive
Branson, MO 65616
"Author"

John Dalancie
1313 Brunswick Avenue
South Pasadena, CA 91030
"Actor"

Dick Dale
P.O. Box 1713
Twenty Nine Palms, CA 92277
"Singer, Guitarist"

Jim Dale
28 Berkeley Square
London W1X 6HD ENGLAND
"Actor"

The Dalai Lama
Thekchen Choling
McLeod Gunji, Hangra Dist.
Himachal Pradesh, INDIA
"Religious Leader"

Richard M. Daley
121 North Main Street
Chicago, IL 60602
"Mayor of Chicago"

Dallas Cowboys Cheerleaders
1 Cowboy Parkway
Irving, TX 75063
"Cheerleading Team"

Abby Dalton
P.O. Box 100
Mammoth Lakes, CA 93546
"Actress"

Audrey Dalton
22461 Labrusca
Mission Viejo, CA 92692
"Actress"

Lacy J. Dalton
909 Meadowlark Lane
Goodlettsville, TN 37027
"Singer"

Timothy Dalton
21 Golden Square
London W1R 3PA ENGLAND
"Actor"

Roger Daltry
18/21 Jermyn Street #300
London SW1Y 6HP ENGLAND
"Singer, Actor"

John Daly
P.O. Box 109601
Palm Beach Gardens, FL 33418
"Golfer"

Rad Daly
5750 Wilshire Blvd. #512
Los Angeles, CA 90036
"Actor"

Timothy Daly
11718 Barrington Court #252
Los Angeles, CA 90049
"Actor"

Tyne Daly
515 Ocean Avenue #601
Santa Monica, CA 90402
"Actress"

Sen. Alfonse D'Amato (NY)
520 Hart Senate Office Building
Washington, DC 20510
"Politician"

Jacques D'Amboise
244 West 71st Street
New York, NY 10023
"Choreographer"

Leo Damian
25366 Malibu Road
Malibu, CA 90265
"Conductor"

Michael Damian
P.O. Box 25573
Los Angeles, CA 90025
"Actor"

Mark Damon
2781 Benedict Canyon
Beverly Hills, CA 90210
"Actor"

Stuart Damon
367 North Van Ness Avenue
Los Angeles, CA 90004
"Actor"

Vic Damone
21700 Oxnard Street #400
Woodland Hills, CA 91367
"Singer"

Bill Dana
P.O. Box 1792
Santa Monica, CA 90406
"Actor, Comedian"

Justin Dana
16830 Ventura Blvd. #300
Encino, CA 91436
"Actor"

Charles Dance
47 Courtfield Road #17
London SW7 ENGLAND
"Actor"

Ruby Dandridge
3737 Don Felipe Drive
Los Angeles, CA 90008
"Actress"

Claire Danes
9830 Wilshire Blvd.
Beverly Hills, CA 90212
"Actress"

Shera Danese
1801 Avenue of the Stars #902
Los Angeles, CA 90067
"Actress"

Beverly D'Angelo
8033 Sunset Blvd. #247
Los Angeles, CA 90046
"Actress"

Rodney Dangerfield
530 East 76th Street
New York, NY 10021
"Comedian, Actor"

Charlie Daniels Band
17060 Central Pike
Lebanon, TN 37087
"C&W Group"

Jeff Daniels
137 Park Street
Chelsea, MI 48118
"Actor"

William Daniels
11766 Wilshire Blvd. #760
Los Angeles, CA 90025
"Actor"

Nicholas Daniloff
2400 "N" Street NW
Washington, DC 20037
"News Correspondent"

Alexandra Danilov
100 West 57th Street
New York, NY 10019
"Ballerina"

Blythe Danner
8942 Wilshire Blvd.
Beverly Hills, CA 90211
"Actress"

Sybil Danning
8578 Walnut Drive
Los Angeles, CA 90046
"Actress"

Danny & The Juniors
P.O. Box 1017
Turnersville, NJ 08012
"Vocal Group"

Linda Dano
8827 Beverly Blvd.
Los Angeles, CA 90048
"Actress"

Ted Danson
165 Copper Cliff Lane
Sedona, AZ 86336
"Actor"

Joe Dante
3176 Lindo Street
Los Angeles, CA 90068
"Film Director"

Nikki Dantine
9744 Wilshire Blvd. #308
Beverly Hills, CA 90212
"Actress"

Tony Danza
10202 W. Washington Blvd.
#DLEANBL
Culver City, CA 90232
"Actor"

Patti D'Arbanville
125 Main Avenue
Sea Cliff, NY 11579
"Actress"

Patrika Darbo
346 North Avon Street
Burbank, CA 91505
"Actress"

Terence Trent D'Arby
10 Great Marlborough Street
London W1V 2LP ENGLAND
"Singer"

Mireille Darc
78 Blvd. Malesherbes
75008 Paris FRANCE
"Actress"

Christopher Darden
675 S. Westmoreland Avenue
Los Angeles, CA 90005
"Attorney"

Severn Darden
RR #4, Box 251-S
Santa Fe, NM 87501
"Actor"

Alvin Dark
103 Cranberry Way
Easley, SC 29640
"Ex-Baseball Player"

Johnny Dark
1100 North Alta Loma #707
Los Angeles, CA 90069
"Comedian"

Jennifer Darling
P.O. Box 57593
Sherman Oaks, CA 91403
"Actress"

Joan Darling
P.O. Box 6700
Tesuque, NM 87574
"Writer, Director"

Ron Darling
19 Woodland Street
Millbury, MA 01527
"Baseball Player"

James Darren
P.O. Box 1088
Beverly Hills, CA 90213
"Actor, Singer"

Danielle Darrieux
1 Rue Alfred de Vingnu
F-75008 Paris, FRANCE
"Actress"

Henry Darrow
9300 Wilshire Blvd. #555
Beverly Hills, CA 90212
"Actor"

Sen. Tom Daschle (SD)
615 South Main
Aberdeen, SD 57401
"Politician"

Sam Dash
110 Newlands
Chevy Chase, MD 20815
"Watergate Participate"

Stacey Dash
8730 Sunset Blvd. #220 W
Los Angeles, CA 90069
"Actress"

Jules Dassin
8 Athinalon Efivon St.
Athens 11521 GREECE
"Actor, Director"

Brad Daugherty
2923 Streetsboro Road
Richfield, OH 44286
"Basketball Player"

Elyssa Davalos
2934 1/2 Beverly Glen Circle #53
Los Angeles, CA 90077
"Actress"

Richard Davalos
852 S. Spruce Street
Montebello, CA 90640
"Actor, Director"

Nigel Davenport
5 Annis Close
Kinnerton Street
London SW1 ENGLAND
"Actor"

Robert Davi
1907 Vallecito Drive
San Pedro, CA 90732
"Actor"

Marty Davich
1044 Armada Drive
Pasadena, CA 91103
"Actor"

Hal David
10430 Wilshire Blvd.
Los Angeles, CA 90024
"Lyricist"

Joanna David
25 Maida Avenue
London W2 ENGLAND
"Actress"

Keith David
1134 West 105th St.
Los Angeles, CA 90044
"Actor"

Mack David
1575 Toledo Circle
Palm Springs, CA 92262
"Composer"

Lolita Davidovich
3220 East Ojal Avenue
Ojai, CA 93023
"Actress"

Doug Davidson
P.O. Box 5608
Santa Barbara, CA 93150
"Actor"

Eileen Davidson
13340 Galewood Drive
Sherman Oaks, CA 91423
"Actress"

Gordon Davidson
165 Mabery Road
Santa Monica, CA 90406
"Film Director"

John Davidson
6051 Spring Valley Road
Hidden Hills, CA 91302
"Singer, Actor"

Tommy Davidson
3800 Weslin Avenue
Sherman Oaks, CA 91423
"Actor"

Embeth Davidtz
151 El Camino Drive
Beverly Hills, CA 90212
"Actor"

Lane Davies
P.O. Box 2053
Thousand Oaks, CA 91358
"Actor"

Al Davis
1220 Harbor Bay Parkway
Alameda, CA 94502
"Football Team Owner"

Angela Davis
4400 Keller Avenue #260
Oakland, CA 94506
"Author, Politician"

Ann B. Davis
23315 Eagle Gap
San Antonio, TX 78255
"Actress"

Benjamin Davis
1001 Wilson Blvd. #906
Arlington, VA 22209
"Black Military General"

Billy Davis, Jr.
2639 Laverty Court #5
Newbury Park, CA 91320
"Singer"

Clifton Davis
141 Janine Drive
La Habra Heights, CA 90631
"Actor, Clergyman"

Geena Davis
420 S. Spalding Drive
Beverly Hills, CA 90212
"Actress"

Glenn Davis
5241 Vantage Avenue #102
North Hollywood, CA 91607
"Actor"

Jim Davis
450 Country Road
New Albany, IN 47320
"Cartoonist"

Jimmie Davis
P.O. Box 15826
Baton Rouge, LA 70895
"Ex-Govenor, Singer"

Judy Davis
129 Bourke Street
Woollomooloo
Sydney NSW 2011 AUSTRALIA
"Actress"

Mac Davis
10960 Wilshire Blvd.
Los Angeles, CA 90024
"Singer, Actor"

Martha Davis
4777 Firmament
Sherman Oaks, CA 91423
"Singer"

Marvin Davis
1120 Schuyler Road
Beverly Hills, CA 90210
"Film Executive"

Ossie Davis
44 Cortland Avenue
New Rochelle, NY 10801
"Actor, Writer, Director"

Phyllis Davis
18319 Hart Street #11
Reseda, CA 91335
"Actress"

Skeeter Davis
309 Seward Road
Brentwood, TN 37027
"Singer"

Todd Davis
245 South Keystone Street
Burbank, CA 91506
"Actor"

Tyrone Davis
1048 Tatnall Street
Macoa, GA 31201
"Singer"

Willie Davis
7532 Vista Del Mar
Venice, CA 90291
"Ex-Baseball Player"

Bruce Davison
P.O. Box 57593
Sherman Oaks, CA 91403
"Musician"

Peter Davison
18-21 Jermyn Street #300
London SW1Y 6HP ENGLAND
"Actor"

Pam Dawber
2236-A Encinitas Blvd
Encinitas, CA 92024
"Actress"

Dominique Dawes
P.O. Box 8400
Silver Spring, MD 20907
"Gymnast"

Pete Dawkins
178 Rumson Road
Rumson, NJ 07760
"Former Politician"

Andre Dawson
5715 S.W. 130th Street
Miami, FL 33156
"Baseball Player"

Len Dawson
121 W. 48th Street #1906
Kansas City, MO 64112
"Sportscaster"

Richard Dawson
1117 Angelo Drive
Beverly Hills, CA 90210
"Ex-TV Show Host, Actor"

Doris Day
P.O. Box 223163
Carmel, CA 93922
"Actress"

Laraine Day
10313 Lauriston Avenue
Los Angeles, CA 90025
"Actress"

Daniel Day-Lewis
46 Albermarle Street
London W1X 4PP ENGLAND
"Actor"

Taylor Dayne
1401 University Drive #305
Coral Springs, FL 33071
"Singer"

Billy Dean
P.O. Box 870689
Stone Mountain, GA 30087
"Singer"

Eddie Dean
32161 Sailview Lane
Westlake Village, CA 91360
"Actor, Singer"

Isabel Dean
43-A Princess Road
Regent's Park
London NW1 8JS ENGLAND
"Actress"

Jimmy Dean
8000 Centerview Parkway #400
Cordova, TN 38018
"Singer"

John Dean
9496 Rembert Lane
Beverly Hills, CA 90210
"Author"

Robin Deardan
4659 Ethel Avenue
Sherman Oaks, CA 91423
"Actress"

Blossom Dearie
P.O. Box 21
East Durham, NY 12423
"Singer"

Justin Deas
10100 Santa Monica Blvd. #2500
Los Angeles, CA 90067
"Actor"

Michael K. Deaver
4 Chaparrel Lane
Palos Verdes, CA 90274
"Ex-Government Official"

Dr. Michael De Bakey
Baylor College of Medicine
1200 Moursund Avenue
Houston, TX 77030
"Heart Surgeon"

Burr De Benning
4235 Kingfisher Road
Calabasas, CA 91302
"Actor"

Dorothy DeBorba
1810 Montecito Avenue
Livermore, CA 94550
"Actress"

Chris De Burge
Bargy Castle, Tonhaggard
Wesxord, IRELAND
"Singer, Guitarist"

Rosemary De Camp
317 Camino de Los Colinas
Redondo Beach, CA 90277
"Actress"

Yvonne DeCarlo
13834 Magnolia Blvd.
Sherman Oaks, CA 91423
"Actress"

Mary Decker Slaney
2923 Flintlock Street
Eugene, OR 97401
"Track Athlete"

Fred de Cordova
1875 Carla Ridge Drive
Beverly Hills, CA 90210
"Film-TV Director"

Joey Dee
141 Dunbar Avenue
Fords, NJ 08863
"Singer"

Ruby Dee
44 Cortland Avenue
New Rochelle, NY 10801
"Actress"

Sandra Dee
880 Hilldale Avenue #15
Los Angeles, CA 90069
"Actress"

Dee-Lite
428 Cedar Street NW
Washington, DC 20012
"Singer"

Mickey Deems
13114 Weddington Street
Van Nuys, CA 90401
"Actor, Director"

Deep Pruple
P.O. Box 254
Sheffield S6 IDF ENGLAND
"Rock & Roll Group"

Morris Dees
Rolling Hills Ranch
Route #1
Mathews, AL 36052
"Attorney"

Rick Dees
3400 Riverside Drive #800
Burbank, CA 91505
"Radio-TV Personality"

Eddie Deezen
8205 Santa Monica Blvd. #1-316
West Hollywood, CA 90046
"Actor"

Def Leppard
72 Chancellor's Road
London W6 9QB ENGLAND
"Rock & Roll Group"

Ellen DeGeneres
1122 S. Roxbury Drive
Los Angeles, CA 90035
"Actress"

Hubert De Givenchy
3 Avenue George V
75008 Paris, FRANCE
"Fashion Designer"

Gloria DeHaven
73 Devonshire Road
Cedar Grove, NJ 07009
"Actress"

Penny DeHaven
P.O. Box 83
Brentwood, TN 37027
"Singer"

Olivia DeHavilland
Boite Postale 156-16
Paris, Cedex 16-75764
FRANCE
"Actress"

Deja Vu
1 Touchstone Lane
Chard, Somerset
TA20 IRF ENGLAND
"Rock & Roll Group"

Frederick deKlerk
Box 1692, Groenkloof
0027 Pretoria SOUTH AFRICA
"Politician"

Oscar De La Hoya
2401 S. Atlantic Blvd.
Monterey Park, CA 91754
"Boxer"

Kim Delaney
2515 Benedict Canyon Drive
Beverly Hills, CA 90210
"Actress"

Raven De La Croix
11130 Huston Street #8
North Hollywood, CA 91601
"Actress, Model"

John deLancie
1313 Brunswick Avenue
South Pasadena, CA 91030
"Actor"

Dana Delany
3435 Ocean Park Blvd. #201-N
Santa Monica, CA 90405
"Actress"

Oscar de la Renta
Brook Hill Farm
Skiff Mountain Road
Kent, CT 06757
"Fashion Designer"

De La Soul
2697 Heath Avenue
Bronx, NY 10463
"Music Group"

Frances De La Tour
15 Golden Square #315
London S1R 3AG ENGLAND
"Actress"

Dino De Laurentis
Via Poutina Ku 23270
Rome, ITALY
"Motion Picture Producer"

Myrna Dell
12958 Valley Heart Drive #4
Studio City, CA 91604
"Actress"

Rep. Ronald V. Dellums (CA)
House Rayburn Bldg. #2108
Washington, DC 20515
"Politician"

Ken Delo
844 South Masselin
Los Angeles, CA 90048
"Singer"

Alan Delon
Rt. de Malagnous 170
CH-1224 Chene-Bougeries
SWITZERLAND
"Actor"

Nathalie Delon
3 Qual Malaquais
75006 Paris, FRANCE
"Actor"

John Z. DeLorean
567 Larnington Road
Bedminister, NJ 07921
"Automobile Builder"

Michael DeLorenzo
8271 Melrose Avenue, #110
Los Angeles, CA 90046
"Actor"

Daniele Delorme
16 rue de Marignan
75008 Paris, FRANCE
"Actor"

Victoria De Los Angeles
East Magnini, Paseo de Gracia
87-7-D Barcelona SPAIN
"Soprano"

George Deloy
11460 Amanda Drive
Studio City, CA 91604
"Actor"

Vanessa Del Rio
285 Fifth Avenue#224
Brooklyn, NY 11215
"Actress"

Milton De Lugg
2740 Claray Drive
Los Angeles, CA 90024
"Composer, Conductor"

Benicio Del Toro
8730 Sunset Blvd. #490
Los Angeles, CA 90069
"Actor"

Dom Deluise
1186 Corsica Drive
Pacific Palisades, CA 90272
"Actor, Director"

Michael Deluise
1186 Corsica Drive
Pacific Palisades, CA 90272
"Actor"

Peter Deluise
1223 Wilshire Blvd. #411
Santa Monica, CA 90403
"Actor"

The Del Vikings
6400 Pleasant Park Drive
Chanhassen, MN 55317
"Music Group"

Jonathan Demme
c/o Clinica Estetico
127 W. 24th St., 7th Fl.
New York, NY 10011
"Director"

Rebecca De Mornay
760 North La Cienega Blvd. #200
Los Angeles, CA 90069
"Actress"

Patrick Dempsey
2644 N. Beachwood Drive
Los Angeles, CA 90068
"Actor"

Nigel Dempster
10 Buckingham Street
London WC2 ENGLAND
"Writer"

Dame Judi Dench
46 Albermarle Street
London W1X 4PP ENGLAND
"Actress"

Catherine Deneuve
76 rue Bonaparte
F-75006 Paris FRANCE
"Actress"

Maurice Denham
44 Brunswick Gardens #2
London W8 ENGLAND
"Actor"

Lydie Denier
5350 Sepulveda Blvd. #9
Sherman Oaks, CA 91411
"Actress"

Robert DeNiro
375 Greenwich Street
New York, NY 10013
"Actor"

Anthony John Denison
7920 Sunset Blvd. #400
Los Angeles, CA 90046
"Actor"

Michael Denison
76 Oxford Street
London W1N OAX ENGLAND
"Actor"

Brian Dennehy
121 North San Vincente Blvd.
Beverly Hills, CA 90211
"Actor"

Martin Denny
6770 Hawaii Kai Drive #402
Honolulu, HI 96825
"Composer"

Reginald Denny
844 N. Vernon Avenue
Azusa, CA 91702
"L.A. Riot Beating Victim"

John Densmore
49 Halderman Road
Santa Monica, CA 90402
"Musician"

Bucky Dent
2606 Varandah Lane #816
Arlington, TX 76006
"Ex-Baseball Player"

Bob Denver
P.O. Box 269
Princeton, WV 24740
"Actor"

Brian De Palma
5555 Melrose Avenue
Ernst Lubitch Annex #119
Los Angeles,.CA 90038
"Writer, Producer"

Gerard Depardieu
4 Place de la Chapelle
F-75800 Bougival, FRANCE
"Actor"

Suzanne De Passe
1100 North Altal Loma #805
Los Angeles, CA 90069
"TV Writer"

Depeche Mode
P.O. Box 1281
London N1 9UX ENGLAND
"Rock & Roll Group"

Johnny Depp
500 S. Sepulveda Blvd. #500
Los Angeles, CA 90049
"Actor"

Bo Derek
3625 Roblar
Santa Ynez, CA 93460
"Actress, Model"

Bruce Dern
23430 Malibu Colony Road
Malibu, CA 90265
"Actor"

Laura Dern
2401 Main Street
Santa Monica, CA 90405
"Actress"

Cleavant Derricks
121 N. San Vicente Blvd. #1204
Beverly Hills, CA 90211
"Actor"

Alan Dershowitz
1563 Massachusetts Avenue
Cambridge, MA 02138
"Attorney, Professor"

Jean Desailly
53 quai des Grand Augistina
F-75006 Paris, FRANCE
"Actor"

Robert Desiderio
1475 Sierra Vista Drive
Aspen, CO 81611
"Actor"

George Deukmejian
555 W. 5th Street
Los Angeles, CA 90013
"Ex-Governor"

Donna Devarona
77 West 66th Street
New York, NY 10023
"Ice Skater"

Gail Devers
20214 Leadwell
Canoga Park, CA 91304
"Track & Field"

Loretta Devine
5816 Ernest Avenue
Los Angeles, CA 90034
"Actress"

Danny Devito
P.O. Box 491246
Los Angeles, CA 90049
"Actor"

Devo
P.O. Box 6868
Burbank, CA 91510
"Rock & Roll Group"

Duchess of Devonshire
Chatsworth, Bakewell
Derbyshire ENGLAND
"Royalty"

Duke of Devonshire
Chatsworth, Bakewell
Derbyshire ENGLAND
"Royalty"

Peter DeVries
170 Cross Highway
Westport, CT 06880
"Author, Editor"

Jacqueline Dewit
436 South Alandele Avenue
Los Angeles, CA 90036
"Actress"

Joyce De Witt
1250 6th Street #403
Santa Monica, CA 90401
"Actress"

Susan Dey
10390 Santa Monica Blvd. #300
Los Angeles, CA 90025
"Actress"

Cliff DeYoung
2143 Colby Avenue
Los Angeles, CA 90025
"Actor"

Diamond Rio
242 W. Main Street #236
Hendersonville, TN 37075
"Music Group"

Bobby Diamond
5309 Comercio Way
Woodland Hills, CA 91364
"Actor"

Neil Diamond
10345 W. Olympic Blvd. #200
Los Angeles, CA 90064
"Singer, Songwriter"

Don Diamont
8485E Melrose Place
Los Angeles, CA 90069
"Actor"

John Diaquino
151 El Camino Drive
Beverly Hills, CA 90212
"Actor"

Cameron Diaz
345 N. Maple Drive #397
Beverly Hills, CA 90210
"Actress"

Rob Dibbie
54 Summit Farms Road
Southington, CT 06489
"Baseball Player"

Vincent Di Bona
1912 Thayer Avenue
Los Angeles, CA 90025
"Director, Producer"

Leonardo DiCaprio
4325 Edenhurst Avenue
Los Angeles, CA 90039
"Actor"

George Di Cenzo
247 Cherry Lane
Doylestown, PA 18901
"Actor"

Douglas Dick
604 Gretna Green Way
Los Angeles, CA 90049
"Actor"

Dick & Dee Dee
1650 Broadway #508
New York, NY 10019
"Vocal Duo"

Jimmy Dickens
1030 N. Woodland Drive
Kansas City, MO 64118
"Singer"

Angie Dickinson
1715 Carla Ridge Drive
Beverly Hills, CA 90210
"Actress"

Brenda Dickson
2160 Century Park E. #412
Los Angeles, CA 90067
"Actress"

Bo Diddley
1560 Broadway #1308
New York, NY 10036
"Singer, Guitarist"

John Diehl
10100 Santa Monica Blvd. #2500
Los Angeles, CA 90025
"Actor"

Charles Dierkop
733 N. Seward Street PH
Los Angeles, CA 90038
"Actor"

Dena Dietrich
1155 North La Cienega Blvd. #302
Los Angeles, CA 90069
"Actress"

Joe Diffle
1009 - 16th Avenue South
Nashville, TN 37212
"Singer"

Barry Diller
1365 Enterprise Drive
West Chester, PA 19280
"Business Executive"

Phyllis Diller
163 South Rockingham Avenue
Los Angeles, CA 90049
"Actress, Comedienne"

Bradford Dillman
770 Hot Springs Road
Santa Barbara, CA 93103
"Actor"

C. Douglas Dillon
169 S. Beach Road
Hobe Sound, FL 33455
"Banker, Diplomat"

Denny Dillon
350 West 57th Street #16A
New York, NY 10019
"Actress"

Kevin Dillon
49 West 9th Street #5B
New York, NY 10011
"Actor"

Matt Dillon
40 West 57th Street
New York, NY 10019
"Actor"

Melinda Dillon
1999 Ave. of the Stars #2850
Los Angeles, CA 90067
"Actress"

Dom DiMaggio
162 Point Road
Marion, MA 02738
"Ex-Baseball Player"

Joe DiMaggio
3230 Stirling Road
Hollywood, FL 33021
"Ex-Baseball Player"

Dion Di Mucci
8803 Mayne Street
Bellflower, CA 90706
"Singer"

Rep. John D. Dingell (MI)
House Rayburn Bldg. #2328
Washington, DC 20515
"Politician"

David Dinkins
625 Madison Avenue
New York, NY 10022
"Ex-Mayor"

Celine Dion
4, Place Laval #500
Laval, PQ H7N 5Y3 CANADA
"Singer"

Christian Dior
St. Anna-Platz 2
80538 Munich, GERMANY
"Fashion Designer"

Dire Straits
509 Hartnell Street
Monterey, CA 93940
"Rock & Roll Group"

The Dirt Band
P.O. Box 1915
Aspen, CO 81611
"Music Group"

Bob Dishy
20 East 9th Street
New York, NY 10003
"Actor, Writer"

Roy Disney
500 South Buena Vista Street
Burbank, CA 91521
"Writer, Producer"

Sacha Distal
3, Quai Malaquais
75006 Paris FRANCE
"Singer"

Mike Ditka
29 English Turn Drive
New Orleans, LA 70131
"Football Coach"

Andrew Divoff
10637 Burbank Blvd.
North Hollywood, CA 91601
"Actor"

Donna Dixon
8955 Norma Place
Los Angeles, CA 90069
"Actress"

Ivan Dixon
8431 Compatible Way #103
Charlotte, NC 28263
"Actor, Director"

Jesse Dizon
6427 Gloria Avenue
Van Nuys, CA 91406
"Actor, Writer"

Edward Dmytryk
3945 Westfall Drive
Encino, CA 91436
"Director"

Alan Dobie
Pontus, Molash
Kent CT4 8HW ENGLAND
"Actor"

Lawrence Dobkin
1787 Old Ranch Road
Los Angeles, CA 90049
"Actor, Writer, Director"

Kevin Dobson
3511 Sea Ledge Lane
Santa Barbara, CA 93109
"Actor"

Peter Dobson
1351 N. Crescent Heights #318
Los Angeles, CA 90046
"Actor"

Larry Doby
1884 Bellmore Avenue
Bellmore, NY 11710
"Baseball Manager"

E. L. Doctorow
170 Broadview Avenue
New Rochelle, NY 10804
"Writer"

Carol Doda
P.O. Box 387
Fremont, CA 94537
"Dancer"

Bobby Doerr
94449 Territorial Road
Junction City, OR 97448
"Ex-Baseball Player"

Shannon Doherty
133 South Rodeo Drive #300
Beverly Hills, CA 90212
"Actress"

Don Dolan
14228 Emelita Street
Van Nuys, CA 91401
"Actor"

Thomas Dolby
20 Manchester Square
London W1 ENGLAND
"Singer, Songwriter"

Elizabeth Dole
9909 Collins Avenue
Bal Harbour, FL 33154
"Ex- Govt. & Red Cross Official"

Robert J. Dole
9909 Collins Avenue
Bal Harbour, FL 33154
"Ex-Senator"

Ami Dolenz
6058 St. Clair Avenue
North Hollywood, CA 91606
"Actress"

Mickey Dolenz
9000 Sunset Blvd. #1200
Los Angeles, CA 90069
"Musician, Actor"

Arielle Dombasle
201 rue du Faubourg St. Honore
F-75008 Paris FRANCE
"Actress"

Pete Domenici
625 Silver SW #130
Albuquerque, NM 87102
"Politician"

Placido Domingo
150 Central Park South
New York, NY 10019
"Tenor"

Fats Domino
5515 Marais Street
New Orleans, LA 70117
"Singer, Pianist"

Elinor Donahue
4525 Lemp Avenue
North Hollywood, CA 91602
"Actress"

Phil Donahue
420 East 54th St. #22-F
New York, NY 10022
"TV Show Host"

Troy Donahue
1022 Euclid Avenue #1
Santa Monica, CA 90403
"Actor"

Elyse Donaldson
5330 Lankershim Blvd. #210
North Hollywood, CA 91610
"Actress"

Sam Donaldson
1125 Crest Lane
McLean, VA 22101
"Broadcast Journalist"

Peter Donat
Box 441
Wolfville
Nova Scotia B0P 1Z0 CANADA
"Actor"

Stanley Donen
11828 La Grange Avenue
Los Angeles, CA 90025
"Film Director"

Donfeld
2900 Hutton Drive
Beverly Hills, CA 90210
"Costume Designer"

Yolande Donlan
2-4 Noel Street
London W1V 3RB ENGLAND
"Actress, Writer"

Clive Donner
1466 North Kings Road
Los Angeles, CA 90069
"Film Director"

Jorn Donner
Pohjoisranta 12
00170 Helsinki 17
FINLAND
"Film Director"

Richard Donner
4000 Warner Blvd., #102
Burbank, CA 91522
"Film Director"

Robert Donner
3828 Glenridge Drive
Sherman Oaks, CA 91423
"Actor"

Mary Agnes Donoghue
427 Alta Avenue
Santa Monica, CA 90402
"Writer"

Amanda Donohue
151 El Camino Drive
Beverly Hills, CA 90212
"Actress"

Terry Donohue
11918 Laurelwood
Studio City, CA 91604
"Football Coach"

Donovan
8794 Lookout Mountain Road
Los Angeles, CA 90069
"Singer, Songwriter"

Art Donovan
1512 Jeffers Road
Baltimore, MD 21204
"Ex-Football Player"

Elysa Donovan
8730 Sunset Blvd. #480
Los Angeles, CA 90069
"Actress"

Tate Donovan
368 N. Gardner Street
Los Angeles, CA 90036
"Actor"

Doobie Brother
15140 Sonoma Highway
Glen Ellen, CA 95442
"Rock & Roll Group"

James Doohan
P.O. Box 2800
Redmond, WA 98073
"Actor"

Vince Dooley
P.O. Box 1472
Athens, GA 30603
"Football Coach"

The Doors
144 South Elm Drive #5
Beverly Hills, CA 90212
"Rock & Roll Group"

Karin Dor
Nordliche Munchner Street 43
0-82031 Grunwald GERMANY
"Actress"

Ann Doran
3939 Walnut Avenue
Carmichael, CA 95608
"Actress"

Stephen Dorff
9701 Wilshire Blvd., 10th Flr.
Beverly Hills, CA 90212
"Actor"

Dolores Dorn
7461 Beverly Blvd. #400
Los Angeles, CA 90036
"Actress"

Michael Dorn
3751 Multiview Drive
Los Angeles, CA 90068
"Actor"

Tony Dorsett
6005 Kettering Court
Dallas, TX 75248
"Ex-Football Player"

David Dortort
133 Udine Way
Los Angeles, CA 90024
"Writer, Producer"

Roy Dotrice
6 Meadow Lane
Leasingham, Seaford
Lincs. NB34 8L2 ENGLAND
"Actor"

Jeff Doucette
970 Palm Avenue #308
W. Hollywood, CA 90069
"Actor"

Doug E. Doug
4024 Radford Avenue #3
Studio City, CA 91604
"Rap Singer"

Brandon Douglas
10683 Santa Monica Blvd.
Los Angeles, CA 90025
"Actor"

Donna Douglas
P.O. Box 49455
Los Angeles, CA 90049
"Actress, Singer"

Eric Douglas
9000 Sunset Blvd. #405
Los Angeles, CA 90069
"Actor"

Illena Douglas
1640 S. Sepulveda Blvd. #218
Los Angeles, CA 90025
"Actress"

James "Buster" Douglas
465 Waterbury Court #A
Gahanna, OH 43230
"Boxer"

Jerry Douglas
181 N. Canyon View
Los Angeles, CA 90049
"Actor"

Kirk Douglas
805 North Rexford Drive
Beverly Hills, CA 90210
"Actor, Director"

Michael Douglas
151 Central Park West
New York, NY 10023
"Actor, Producer"

Mike Douglas
1876 Chartley Road
Gates Mill, OH 44040
"TV Show Host, Singer"

Robert Douglas
1810 Parliament Road
Leucadia, CA 92024
"Actor, Director"

Robyn Douglass
10 Canterbury Court
Wilmette, IL 60091
"Actress"

Sarah Douglas
8485-E Melrose Place
Los Angeles, CA 90069
"Actress"

Brad Dourif
125 S. Robertson Blvd. #126
Beverly Hills, CA 90211
"Actress"

Billie Dove
P.O. Box 5005
Rancho Mirage, CA 92270
"Actress"

Peggy Dow
2121 S. Yorkstown Avenue
Tulsa, OK 74114
"Actress"

Doris Dowling
9026 Elevado Avenue
Los Angeles, CA 90069
"Actress"

Lesley-Anne Down
6252 Paseo Canyon
Malibu, CA 90265
"Actress"

Morton Downey, Jr.
2049 Century Park E. #2750
Los Angeles, CA 90067
"Ex-TV Show Host"

Robert Downey, Jr.
1350 1/2 N. Harper Avenue
Los Angeles, CA 90046
"Actor"

Roma Downey
55 W. 900 South
Salt Lake City, UT 84101
"Actress"

Big Al Downing
10 Luanita Lane
Newport News, VA 23606
"Singer"

Hugh Downs
157 Columbus Avenue
New York, NY 10023
"TV Journalist"

Stan Dragoti
755 Stradella Road
Los Angeles, CA 90024
"Writer, Producer"

Victor Drai
70-447 Pecos Road
Rancho Mirage, CA 92270
"Film Producer"

Frances Drake
1511 Summit Ridge Drive
Beverly Hills, CA 90210
"Actress"

Larry Drake
1901 Avenue of the Stars #620
Los Angeles, CA 90067
"Actor"

Polly Draper
1324 North Orange Grove
Los Angeles, CA 90046
"Actress"

Dave Dravecky
13840 Gleneagle Drive
Colorado Springs, CO 80921
"Ex-Baseball Player"

Dr. Dre
10900 Wilshire Blvd. #1230
Los Angeles, CA 90024
"Rap Singer"

Tom Dreesen
14570 Benefit Street #201
Sherman Oaks, CA 91403
"Comedian"

Fran Drescher
9336 West Washington Blvd. #R
Culver City, CA 90232
"Actress"

Griffen Drew
P.O. Box 16753
Beverly Hills, CA 90209
"Actress"

Clyde Drexler
University of Houston Basketball
Houston, TX 77277
"Ex-Basketball Player"

Richard Dreyfuss
14820 Valley Vista Blvd.
Sherman Oaks, CA 91403
"Actor"

The Drifter
10 Chelsea Court
Neptune, NJ 07753
"Vocal Group"

Minnie Driver
37 Berwick Street
London W1 ENGLAND
"Actress"

Allen Drury
P.O. Box 647
Tiburon, CA 94920
"Author"

James Drury
P.O. Box 899
Cypress, TX 77429
"Actor"

Roy Drusky
131 Trivett Drive
Portland, TN 37148
"Singer, Songwriter"

Fred Dryer
4117 Radford Avenue
Studio City, CA 91604
"Actor, Football Player"

Ja'Net DuBois
8306 Wilshire Blvd. #189
Beverly Hills, CA 90211
"Actress"

Peter Duchin
305 Madison Avenue #956
New York, NY 10165
"Pianist"

David Duchovny
110-555 Brooks Bank Blvd. #10
North Vancouver BC V7J 3S5
CANADA
"Actor"

Rick Ducommun
7967 Woodrow Wilson Drive
Los Angeles, CA 90046
"Comedian"

Michael Dudikoff
3037 Danalda Drive
Los Angeles, CA 90064
"Actor"

Peter Duffell
29 Roehampton Gate
London SW15 5JR ENGLAN
"TV Writer, Director"

Julia Duffy
9255 Sunset Blvd. #1010
Los Angeles, CA 90069
"Actress, Director"

Patrick Duffy
P.O. Box "D"
Tarzana, CA 91356
"Actor, Director"

Dennis Dugan
15611 Royal Oak Drive
Encino, CA 91436
"Actor"

Kitty Dukakis
85 Perry Street
Brookline, MA 02146
"Author, Wife of Michael"

Michael Dukakis
85 Perry Street
Brookline, MA 02146
"Ex-Govornor"

Olympia Dukakis
222 Upper Mountain Road
Montclair, NJ 07043
"Actress"

Bill Duke
8306 Wilshire Blvd. #438
Beverly Hills, CA 90211
"Actor"

David Duke
P.O. Box 577
Metairie, LA 70004
"White Supremacist, Politician"

Patty Duke
5110 E. Dodd Road
Hayden, ID 83835
"Actress"

David Dukes
255 South Lorraine Blvd.
Los Angeles, CA 90004
"Actor"

The Dukes
11 Chartfield Square
London SW15 ENGLAND
"Rock & Roll Group"

Keir Dullea
320 Fleming Lane
Fairfield, CT 06430
"Actor"

Melvin Dummar
Dummar's Restaurant
Gabbs, NV 89409
"Alleged in Howard Hughes' Will"

Faye Dunaway
P.O. Box 15778
Beverly Hills, CA 90209
"Actress"

Sandy Duncan
61 West 90th Street
New York, NY 10024
"Actress"

Angelo Dundee
450 N. Park Road #800
Hollywood, FL 33021
"Boxing Trainer"

Holly Dunn
209 10th Avenue South #347
Nashville, TN 37203
"C&W Singer"

Dominick Dunne
155 East 49th Street
New York, NY 10017
"Author, Producer"

Griffin Dunne
1501 Broadway #2600
New York, NY 10036
"Actor, Producer"

Murphy Dunne
4400 Encinal Canyon Road
Malibu, CA 90265
"Actor"

Debbie Dunning
8740 Oland Avenue
Sun Valley, CA 91352
"Actress"

Jerry Dunphy
5515 Melrose Avenue
Los Angeles, CA 90038
"Actor"

Kirsten Dunst
P.O. Box 15036
Beverly Hills, CA 90209
"Actress"

Pierre duPont
Patterns
Rockland, DE 19732
"Ex-Govenor"

Duran Duran
P.O. Box 21
London W10 6XA ENGLAND
"Rock & Roll Group"

Margie Durante
511 North Beverly Drive
Beverly Hills, CA 90210
"Mrs. Jimmy Durante"

Deanna Durbin-David
B.P. 3315
75123 Paris Cedex 03
FRANCE
"Actress"

Charles Durning
10590 Wilshire Blvd. #506
Los Angeles, CA 90024
"Actor"

Marj Dusay
1964 Westwood Blvd. #400
Los Angeles, CA 90025
"Actress"

Nancy Dussault
12211 Iredell Street
Studio City, CA 91604
"Actress"

Deborah Dutch
850 N. Kings Road #109
W. Hollywood, CA 90069
"Actress"

Charles Dutton
1201 Alta Loma Road
Los Angeles, CA 90069
"Actor"

Robert Duvall
P.O. Box 520
The Plains, VA 22171
"Actor"

Shelley Duvall
Rt. 1, Box, 377-A
Blanco, TX 78606
"Actress"

Lenny Dykstra
236 Chester Road
Devon, PA 19333
"Baseball Player"

Bob Dylan
P.O. Box 870
Cooper Station
New York, NY 10276
"Singer, Songwriter"

Richard Dysart
654 Copeland Court
Santa Monica, CA 90405
"Actor"

George Dzundza
19320 Wells Drive
Tarzana, CA 91356
"Actor"

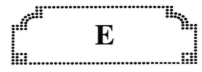

Lawrence Eagleburger
350 Park Avenue #2600
New York, NY 10022
"Ex-Government Official"

The Eagles
8900 Wilshire Blvd. #300
Beverly Hills, CA 90211
"Rock & Roll Group"

Thomas F. Eagleton
1 Mercantitle Center
St. Louis, MO 63101
"Former Senator"

Dale Earnhardt
Box 595-B, Rt. #10
Mooresville, NC 28115
"Race Car Driver"

Earth Wind & Fire
9169 Sunset Blvd.
Los Angeles, CA 90069
"R&B Group"

Tony Eason
1000 Fulton Road
Hempstead, NY 11550
"Football Player"

Jeff East
99 Spindrift Driev
Rancho Palos Verdes, CA 90275
"Actor"

Leslie Easterbrook
5218 Bellingham Avenue
Valley Village, CA 91607
"Actress"

Richard Eastham
1529 Oriole Lane
Los Angeles, CA 90069
"Actor"

Michael Easton
8730 Sunset Blvd. #220W
Los Angeles, CA 90069
"Actor"

Robert Easton
9169 Sunset Blvd.
Los Angeles, CA 90069
"Actor"

Sheena Easton
7095 Hollywood Blvd. #469
Hollywood, CA 90028
"Singer, Songwriter"

Alison Eastwood
62 bd. de Sepastopol
F-75003 Paris FRANCE
"Actress"

Clint Eastwood
4000 Warner Blvd. #16
Burbank, CA 91522
"Actor"

Kyle Eastwood
2049 Century Park East #3500
Los Angeles, CA 90067
"Actor"

Fred Ebb
146 Central Park West #14D
New York, NY 10023
"Lyricist"

Jose Eber
9465 Santa Monica Blvd. #606
Beverly Hills, CA 90212
"Hair Stylist"

Christine Ebersole
1244-A 11th Street
Santa Monica, CA 90401
"Actress"

Roger Ebert
P.O. Box 146366
Chicago, Il 60614
"Film Critic"

Bonnie Ebsen
P.O. Box 356
Agoura, CA 91301
"Actress"

Buddy Ebsen
P.O. Box 2069
Polos Verdes Estates, CA 90274
"Actor"

Dennis Eckersley
39 Plympton Road
Sudbury, MA 01776
"Baseball Player"

Steven Eckholdt
137 N. Larchmont Blvd. #138
Los Angeles, CA 90004
"Actor"

James Eckhouse
4222 Murietta Avenue
Sherman Oaks, CA 91423
"Actor"

Stefan Edberg
Spinnaregaten 6
S-59352 Vastervik SWEDEN
"Tennis Player"

Duane Eddy
1906 Chet Atkins Place #502
Nashville, TN 37212
"Singer, Guitarist"

Barbara Eden
P.O. Box 5556
Sherman Oaks, CA 91403
"Actress"

Gertrude Ederle
4465 S.W. 37th Avenue
Ft. Lauderdale, FL 33312
"Swimmer"

Richard Edlund
13335 Maxella Avenue
Marina del Rey, CA 90292
"Actor"

Louis Edmonds
250 West 57th Street #2317
New York, NY 10107
"Actor"

HRH The Prince Edward
Buckingham Palace
London SW1 ENGLAND
"Royalty"

Anthony Edwards
15260 Ventura Blvd. #1420
Sherman Oaks, CA 91403
"Actor"

Blake Edwards
P.O. Box 491668
Los Angeles, CA 90049
"Writer, Producer, Director"

Gail Edwards
232 N. Canon Drive
Beverly Hills, CA 90210
"Actress"

Jennifer Edwards
309 S. Glenroy Avenue
Los Angeles, CA 90049
"Actress"

Luke Edwards
6212 Banner
Los Angeles, CA 90038
"Actor"

Paddi Edwards
1800 Avenue of the Stars #400
Los Angeles, CA 90067
"Actress"

Ralph Edwards
610 Arkell Drive
Beverly Hills, CA 90210
"TV Show Host, Producer"

Ronnie Claire Edwards
4900 Los Feliz Blvd.
Los Angeles, CA 90027
"Actress"

Steve Edwards
3980 Royal Oaks Place
Encino, CA 91436
"TV Show Host"

Julie Ege
3300 Hokksund
NORWAY
"Actress, Model"

Samantha Eggar
12304 Santa Monica Blvd. #104
Los Angeles, CA 90025
"Actress"

Nicole Eggert
20591 Queens Park
Huntington Beach, CA 92646
"Actress"

Marta Eggerth
Park Drive North
Rye, NY 10508
"Actress, Singer"

Lisa Eichorn
19 West 44th Street #1000
New York, NY 10036
"Actress"

Jill Eikenberry
197 Oakdale Avenue
Mill Valley, CA 94941
"Actress"

Cynthia Eilbacher
P.O. Box 8920
Universal City, CA 91608
"Actress"

Lisa Eilbacher
4600 Petit Avenue
Encino, CA 91436
"Actress"

Michael Eisner
500 South Buena Vista
Burbank, CA 91521
"Disney Executive"

Britt Ekland
1888 N. Crescent Heights Blvd.
West Hollywood, CA 90069
"Actress"

Jack Elam
1257 Siskiyou Blvd. #222
Ashland, OR 97520
"Actor"

Dana Elcar
10000 Santa Monica Blvd. #350
Los Angeles, CA 90067
"Actor, Director"

Lee Elder
4130 Palm Aire Dr. W. #302B
Pompano Beach, FL 33096
"Golfer"

Dr. Joycelyn Elders
800 Marshall Street
Little Rock, AR 72202
"Ex-Surgeon General"

Carmen Electra
1515 Broadway
New York, NY 10036
"Actress"

Electric Light Orchestra
9850 Sandalfoot Blvd. #458
Boca Raton, FL 33428
"Rock & Roll Group"

Erika Eleniak
1640 S. Sepulvede Blvd. #218
Los Angeles, CA 90025
"Actress"

Danny Elfman
345 N. Maple Drive #385
Beverly Hills, CA 90210
"Actor"

Jenna Elfman
7920 Sunset Blvd. #400
Los Angeles, CA 90046
"Actress"

Larry Elgart
2065 Gulf of Mexico Drive
Longboat Key, FL 34228
"Composer"

Christine Elise
400 S. Beverly Drive #216
Beverly Hills, CA 90212
"Actress"

HRH Elizabeth II
Buckingham Palace
London SW1 ENGLAND
"Royalty

HM Queen Elizabeth
Clarence House
London SW1 ENGLAND
"The Queen's Mother"

Hector Elizando
15030 Ventura Blvd. #751
Sherman Oaks, CA 91403
"Actor"

Robert Ellenstein
5215 Sepulveda Blvd. #23-F
Culver City, CA 90230
"Actor, Director"

Linda Ellerbee
96 Morton Street
New York, NY 10014
"Journalist"

Jane Elliot
606 N. Larchmont Blvd. #309
Los Angeles, CA 90004
"Actress"

David James Elliott
9560 Wilshire Blvd. #516
Beverly Hills, CA 90212
"Actor"

Gordon Elliott
555 West 57th Street
New York, NY 10019
"TV Show Host"

Ross Elliott
5702 Graves Avenue
Encino, CA 91316
"Actor"

Sam Elliott
33050 Pacific Coast Hwy.
Malibu, CA 90265
"Actor"

Sean Elliott
P.O. Box 530
San Antonio, TX 78292
"Basketball Player"

Stephen Elliott
3948 Woodfield Drive
Sherman Oaks, CA 91403
"Actor"

Harlan Ellison
P.O. Box 55548
Sherman Oaks, CA 91423
"Actor"

Daniel Ellsberg
90 Norwood Avenue
Kensington, CA 94707
"Author"

Michael Elphick
37 Dennington Park Road
London SW6 ENGLAND
"Actor"

Ernie Els
P.O. Box 2255
Parklands 2121 SOUTH AFRICA
"Golfer"

Elvira (Cassandra Peterson)
P.O. Box 38246
Los Angeles, CA 90038
"Actress"

John Elway
10030 E. Arapahoe Road
Englewood, CO 80112
"Football Player"

Cary Elwes
1901 Avenue of the Stars #1245
Los Angeles, CA 90067
"Actor"

Joe Ely
7101 Hwy. 71 W. #A9
Austin, TX 78735
"Singer, Songwriter"

Ron Ely
151 El Camino Drive
Beverly Hills, CA 90212
"Actor"

Kelly Emberg
1608 North Poinsettia
Manhattan Beach, CA 90266
"Model"

Ethan Embry
9560 Wilshire Blvd. #516
Beverly Hills, CA 90212
"Actor"

Douglas Emerson
1450 Belfast Drive
Los Angeles, CA 90069
"Actor"

Emir of Bahrain
721 Fifth Avenue, 60th Floor
New York, NY 10022
"Royalty"

Emir of Kuwait
Banyan Palace
Kuwait City Kuwait
"Royalty"

Emmanuel
1406 Georgette Street
Santurce PUERTO RICO 00910
"Fashion Designer"

Noah Emmerich
121 N. San Vicente Blvd.
Beverly Hills, CA 90211
"Actor"

Dick Enberg
Box 710
Rancho Santa Fe, CA 92067
"Sportscaster"

Georgia Engel
350 West 57th Street #10E
New York, NY 10019
"Actress"

Susan Engel
43A Princess Road
Regent's Park
London NW1 8JS ENGLAND
"Actress"

England Dan
P.O. Box 82
Great Neck, NY 11021
"Singer, Songwriter"

Robert Englund
1616 Santa Cruz Street
Laguna Beach, CA 93651
"Actor"

Bill Engvall
8380 Melrose Avenue #310
Los Angeles, CA 90069
"Actor"

Brian Eno
330 Harrow Road
London W9 ENGLAND
"Singer, Producer"

Russell Enoch
43A Princess Road
Regent's Park
London NW1 8JS ENGLAND
"Actor"

John Enos
12424 Wilshire Blvd. #840
Los Angeles, CA 90025
"Actor"

Philippe Entremont
Schwarzenbergplatz 10/7
A-1040 Vienna, AUSTRIA
"Pianist"

John Entwhistle
1705 Queen Court
Los Angeles, CA 90068
"Musician, Singer"

En Vogue
151 El Camino Drive
Beverly Hills, CA 90212
"Music Group"

Nora Ephron
390 West End Avenue
New York, NY 10024
"Screenwriter"

Omar Epps
P.O. Box 5617
Beverly Hills, CA 90210
"Actor"

Richard Erdman
5655 Greenbush Avenue
Van Nuys, CA 91401
"Actor, Director"

John Ericson
933 Camino De Chelly
Santa Fe, NM 89501
"Actor"

Carl Erskine
6214 South Madison Avenue
Anderson, IN 46013
"Ex-Baseball Player"

Julius Erving
P.O. Box 8269
Cherry Hill, NJ 08002
"Ex-Basketball Player"

Bill Erwin
12324 Moorpark Street
Studio City, CA 91604
"Actor"

Christoph Eschenbach
2 Avenue d'Alena
75016 Paris, FRANCE
"Pianist"

"Boomer" Esiason
1 Falcon's Place
Suwanee, GA 30174
"Football Player"

Carl Esmond
576 Tigertail Road
Los Angeles, CA 90049
"Actor"

Giancarlo Esposito
25 Sea Colony Drive
Santa Monica, CA 90405
"Actor"

William Grey Espy
205 West 54th Street #3D
New York, NY 10019
"Actor"

David Essex
109 Eastbourne Mews
London W2 ENGLAND
"Singer, Actor"

Gloria Estefan
555 Jefferson Avenue
Miami Beach, FL 33139
"Singer"

Billie Sol Estes
1004 South College
Brady, TX 76825
"Financier, Ex-Convict"

Rob Estes
910 Idaho Avenue
Santa Monica, CA 90403
"Actor"

Simon Estes
Hoschstr. 43
8706 Feldmeilen SWITZERLAND
"Basso-Baritone"

Emilio Estevez
P.O. Box 4041
Malibu, CA 90264
"Actor, Writer"

Ramon Estevez
837 Ocean Avenue #101
Santa Monica, CA 90402
"Actor"

Erik Estrada
3768 Eureka Drive
Studio City, CA 91604
"Actor"

Susan Estrich
124 So. Las Palmas Avenue
Los Angeles, CA 90004
"Actress"

Joe Eszterhas
8942 Wilshire Blvd.
Beverly Hills, CA 90211
"Screenwriter"

Melissa Etheridge
P.O. Box 884563
San Francisc, CA 91488
"Singer"

Bob Eubanks
5900 Highridge Road
Hidden Hills, CA 91302
"TV Show Host"

Kevin Eubanks
173 Brighton Avenue
Boston, MA 02134
"Band leader"

Wesley Eure
P.O. Box 69405
Los Angeles, CA 90069
"Actor"

Europe
Box 22036
S-10422 Stockholm SWEDEN
"Rock & Roll Group"

Eurythmics
P.O. Box 245
London N8 Q0G ENGLAND
"Rock & Roll Group"

Linda Evangelista
2640 Carmen Crest Drive
Los Angeles, CA 90068
"Model"

Andrea Evans
310 West 72nd Street #7G
New York, NY 10023
"Actress"

Dale Evans Rogers
19838 Tomahawk Road
Apple Valley, CA 92307
"Actress"

Evans Evans
3114 Abington Drive
Beverly Hills, CA 90210
"Actress"

Greg Evans
660 Elm Tree Lane
San Marcos, CA 92069
"Cartoonist"

Janet Evans
8 Barneburg
Dove Canyon, CA 92679
"Swimmer"

Linda Evans
6714 Villa Madera Drive
Tacoma, WA 98499
"Actress"

Mary Beth Evans
P.O. Box 50105
Pasadena, CA 91115
"Actress"

Mike Evans
12530 Collins Street
North Hollywood, CA 91605
"Actor"

Robert Evans
10033 Woodlawn Drive
Beverly Hills, CA 90210
"Producer, Actor"

Roland Evans
3125 "O" Street. NW
Washington, DC 20007
"Columnist"

Trevor Eve
60 St. James's Street
London W1 ENGLAND
"Actor"

Chad Everett
5472 Island Forest Place
Westlake Village, CA 91362
"Actor"

Rupert Everett
76 Oxford Street
London, W1N 0AX ENGLAND
"Actor"

Angie Everhart
23 Watts Street #600
New York, NY 10013
"Model"

Don Everly
277 Comroe Road
Nashville, TN 37213
"Singer"

Phil Everly
277 Comroe road
Nashville, TN 37213
"Singer"

Charles Evers
416 W. County Line Road
Tougaloo, MS 39174
"Civil Rights Worker"

Jason Evers
232 North Crescent Drive #101
Beverly Hills, CA 90210
"Actor"

Myrlie Evers-Williams
4805 Mt. Hope Drive
Baltimore, MD 21215
"NAACP Ex-Director"

Chris Evert
500 N.E. 25th Street
Wilton Manors, FL 33305
"Tennis Player"

Greg Evigan
10433 Wilshire Blvd. #210
Los Angeles, CA 90024
"Actor, Singer"

Weeb Ewbank
4160 Steamboat Blvd. #103
Ft. Myers, FL 33919
"Ex-Football Coach"

Patrick Ewing
37 Summit Street
Englewood Cliffs, NJ 07632
"Basketball Player"

Exile
909 Meadowlark Lane
Goodlettsville, TN 37072
"Music Group"

Extreme
189 Carlton Street
Toronto, Ontario
M5A 2K7 CANADA
"Music Group"

Richard Eyer
2739 Underwood Lane
Bishop, CA 93514
"Actor"

Shelley Fabaras
P.O. Box 6010-MSC 826
Sherman Oaks, CA 91413
"Actress"

Ava Fabian
2112 Broadway
Santa Monica, CA 90404
"Actress, Model"

Fabio
P.O. Box 4
Inwood, NY 11696
"Male Model"

Nanette Fabray
14360 Sunset Blvd.
Pacific Palisades, CA 90272
"Actress"

HM King Fahd
Royal Palace
Riyadh, SAUDI ARABIA
"Royalty"

Jeff Fahey
8942 Wilshire Blvd.
Beverly Hills, CA 90211
"Actor"

Bruce Fairbairn
9744 Wilshire Blvd. #308
Beverly Hills, CA 90212
"Actor"

Douglas Fairbanks, Jr.
575 Park Avenue
New York, NY 10021
"Actor"

Barbara Fairchild
P.O. Box 158766
Nashville, TN 37215
"Singer"

Morgan Fairchild
P.O. Box 57593
Sherman Oaks, CA 91403
"Actress"

Adam Faith
76 Oxford Street
London W1N OAX ENGLAND
"Singer, Actor"

Marianne Faithfull
235 Footscray Road
New Eltham
London SE9 2EL ENGLAND
"Singer, Songwriter"

Lola Falana
1201 "N" Street NW, #A-5
Washington, DC 20005
"Singer, Actress"

Nick Faldo
Pier House
Strand on the Green
London W4 3NN ENGLAND
"Golfer"

Lee Falk
P.O. Box Z
Truro, MA 02666
"Cartoonist"

Peter Falk
100 Universal City Plaza #507 1B
Universal City, CA 91608
"Actor, Director"

Jinx Falkenburg
10 Shelter Rock Road
Manhasset, NY 11030
"Actress, Model"

Rev. Jerry Falwell
P.O. Box 6004
Forest, VA 24551
"Evangelist"

Hampton Fancher III
115 S. Topanga Canyon Blvd. #180
Topanga, CA 90290
"Screenwriter"

Stephanie Faracy
8765 Lookout Mountain Road
Los Angeles, CA 90046
"Actress"

Debrah Farentino
9460 Wilshire Blvd. #700
Beverly Hills, CA 90210
"Actress"

James Farentino
1340 Londonderry Place
Los Angeles, CA 90069
"Actor"

Linda Farentino
10683 Santa Monica Blvd.
Los Angeles, CA 90025
"Actress"

Antonio Fargas
18149 Ventura Blvd. #187
Tarzana, CA 91356
"Actor"

Donna Fargo
P.O. Box 150527
Nashville, TN 37215
"Singer"

Dennis Farina
955 S. Carrillo Drive #300
Los Angeles, CA 90048
"Actor"

Lillian Farley
84 Kenneth Avenue
Huntington, NY 11743
"Model"

Art Farmer
49 East 96th Street
New York, NY 10128
"Jazz Musician"

Shannon Farnon
12743 Milbank Street
Studio City, CA 91604
"Actress"

Richard Farnsworth
P.O. Box 215
Lincoln, NM 88338
"Actor"

Jamie Farr
53 Ranchero
Bell Canyon, CA 91307
"Actor, Director"

Louis Farrakhan
4855 So. Woodlawn Ave.
Chicago, IL 60615
"Religious Leader"

Mike Farrell
MSC 826
P.O. Box 6010
Sherman Oaks, CA 91413
"Actor, Writer, Director"

Sharon Farrell
11532 Chiquita Street
Studio City, CA 91604
"Actress"

Shea Farrell
1930 Century Park West #403
Los Angeles, CA 90067
"Actor"

Terry Farrell
9229 Sunset Blvd. #710
Los Angeles, CA 90069
"Actress"

Mia Farrow
124 Henry Sanford Road
Bridgewater, CT 06752
"Actress"

Dante Fascell
6300 SW 99th Terrace
Miami, FL 33156
"Politician"

Howard Fast
222 Berkeley Street
Boston, MA 02116
"Writer"

Fat Boys
250 W. 57th Street #1723
New York, NY 10107
"Rap Group"

David Faustino
12156 Laurel Terrace Drive
Studio City, CA 91604
"Actor"

Brett Favre
3071 Gothic Court
Green Bay, WI 54213
"Football Player"

Allen Fawcett
8091 Selma Avenue
Los Angeles, CA 90046
"Actor, TV Show Host"

Farrah Fawcett
3130 Antelo Road
Los Angeles, CA 90077
"Actress, Model"

Alice Faye
P.O. Box 1356
Rancho Mirage, CA 92270
"Actress, Singer"

Tom Fears
126 24th Street
Newport Beach, CA 92663
"Ex-Football Player"

Melinda Fee
1835 E. Michelle Street
West Covina, CA 91791
"Actress"

Dr. Feelgood
3 East 54th Street
New York, NY 10022
"Singer"

Jules Feiffner
RR #1 Box 440
Vineyard Haven, MA 02568
"Writer"

Alan Feinstein
9229 Sunset Blvd. #311
Los Angeles, CA 90069
"Actor"

Sen. Dianne Feinstein (CA)
331 Hart Office Bldg.
Washington, DC 20510
"Politician"

Michael Feinstein
2131 Cedarhurst Drive
Los Angeles, CA 90027
"Actor"

Don Felder
P.O. Box 6051
Malibu, CA 90265
"Singer, Songwriter"

Corey Feldman
3209 Tareco Drive
Los Angeles, CA 90068
"Actor"

Barbara Feldon
14 E. 74th Street
New York, NY 10021
"Actress, Model"

Tovah Feldshuh
322 Central Park West #11B
New York, NY 10025
"Actor"

Martin Feldstein
147 Clifton Street
Belmont, MA 02178
"Economist"

Jose Feliciano
266 Lyons Plain Road
Weston, CT 06883
"Singer, Guitarist"

Maria Felix
Hegel 610 Col. Polanco
Mexico D.F. MEXICO
"Actress"

Norman Fell
4240 Promenade Way #232
Marina del Rey, CA 90292
"Actor"

Bob Feller
P.O. Box 170
Novelty, OH 44072
"Ex-Baseball Player"

Edith Fellows
2016 1/2 North Vista Del Mar
Los Angeles, CA 90068
"Actress"

Narvel Felts
2005 Narvel Felts Avenue
Malden, MO 63863
"Singer"

John Femia
1650 Boradway #714
New York, NY 10019
"Singer"

Freddy Fender
P.O. Box 270540
Corpus Christi, TX 78427
"Singer, Songwriter"

Sherilyn Fenn
5530 Ventura Canyon Avenue
Van Nuys, CA 91401
"Actress"

Jay Ferguson
P.O. Box 57078
Sherman Oaks, CA 91423
"Singer"

Maynard Ferguson
P.O. Box 716
Ojai, CA 93023
"Trumpeter"

Mary Jo Fernandez
133 1st Street Northeast
St. Petersburg, FL 33701
"Tennis Player"

Ferrante & Teicher
12224 Avila Drive
Kansas City, MO 64145
"Piano Duo"

Cristina Ferrare
1280 Stone Canyon
Los Angeles, CA 90077
"Actress, Model"

Geraldine Ferraro
22 Deepdene Road
Forest Hills, NY 11375
"Ex-Congresswoman"

Conchata Ferrell
1347 North Seward Street
Los Angeles, CA 90028
"Actress"

Andrea Ferreol
10 Avenue George V
F-75008 Paris FRANCE
"Actress"

Lupita Ferrer
861 Stone Canyon Road
Los Angeles, CA 90077
"Actress"

Mel Ferrer
6590 Camino Carreta
Carpenteria, CA 93013
"Actor"

Miguel Ferrer
4334 Kester Avenue
Sherman Oaks, CA 91403
"Actor"

Lou Ferrrigno
P.O. Box 1671
Santa Monica, CA 90402
"Actor, Bodybuilder"

Brian Ferry
59A Chesson Road
London W14 9QS ENGLAND
"Singer, Songwriter"

Debra Feuer
9560 Wilshire Blvd. #500
Beverly Hills, CA 90212
"Actress"

Mark Fidrych
260 West Street
Northboro, MA 01532
"Ex-Baseball Player"

John Fiedler
225 Adams Street #10B
Brooklyn, NY 11201
"Actor"

Chelsea Field
P.O. Box 5617
Beverly Hills, CA 90210
"Actress"

Sally Field
P.O. Box 492417
Los Angeles, CA 90049
"Actress"

Shirley Anne Field
2-4 Noel Street
London W1V 2RB ENGLAND
"Actress"

Sylvia Field
3263 Via Alta Mira
Fallbrook, CA 92028
"Actress"

Freddie Fields
8899 Beverly Blvd. #918
Los Angeles, CA 90048
"Motion Picture Producer"

Mrs. Fields
462 Bearcat Drive
Salt Lake City, UT 84115
"Cookie Executive"

Kim Fields
9034 Sunset Blvd. #250
Los Angeles, CA 90069
"Actress"

Ralph Fiennes
17 Broad Circle #12
London WC2B 5QN ENGLAND
"Actor"

Harvey Fierstein
232 North Canon Drive
Beverly Hills, CA 90210
"Dramatist, Actor"

Jon Finch
18/21 Jermyn Street #300
London SW1Y 6HP ENGLAND
"Actor"

Travis Fine
12754 Sarah Street
Studio City, CA 91604
"Actor"

Rollie Fingers
4894 Eastcliff Court
San Diego, CA 92130
"Ex-Baseball Player"

Fyvush Finkel
8730 Sunset Blvd. #480
Los Angeles, CA 90069
"Actor"

Albert Finney
45 - 51 Whitfield Street
London W1 ENGLAND
"Actor"

Linda Fiorentino
9830 Wilshire Blvd.
Beverly Hills, CA 90212
"Actress"

Ann Firbank
76 Oxford Street
London W1N 0AX ENGLAND
"Actress"

Eddie Firestone
303 South Crescent Heights
Los Angeles, CA 90048
"Actor"

The Firm
57A Great Titchfield Street
London W1P 7FL ENGLAND
"Rock & Roll Group"

Colin Firth
46 Albermarle Street
London W1X 4PP ENGLAND
"Actor"

Peter Firth
4 Windmill Street
London W1 England
"Actor"

Bobby Fischer
186 Route 9-W
New Windsor, NY 12550
"Chess Player"

Dietrich Fischer-Diskau
Lindenalle 22
D-14050 Berlin 19 GERMANY
"Baritone"

Larry Fishburne
4116 W. Magnolia Blvd. #101
Burbank, CA 91505
"Actor"

Amy Fisher
3595 State School Road
Albion, NY 14411
"Statutory Rape Victim"

Carrie Fisher
1700 Coldwater Canyon
Beverly Hills, CA 90210
"Actress"

Eddie Fisher
10000 North Point Street #1802
San Francisco, CA 94109
"Actor, Singer"

Frances Fisher
8730 Sunset Blvd. #490
Los Angeles, CA 90069
"Actress"

Joely Fisher
9465 Wilshire Blvd. #430
Beverly Hills, CA 90212
"Actress"

Mary Fisher
3075 Hampton Place
Boco Raton, FL 33434
"AIDS Advocate"

Terry Louise Fisher
5314 Pacific Avenue
Marina del Rey, CA 90292
"TV Writer, Producer"

Todd Fisher
3435 Ocean Park Blvd. #206
Santa Monica, CA 90405
"Actor"

Michael Fishman
P.O. Box 827
Los Alamitos, CA 90720
"Actor"

Carlton Fisk
16612 Catawba Road
Lockport, IL 60441
"Ex-Baseball Player"

Christian Fittipaldi
282 Alphaville Baruei, 064500
Sao Paulo BRAZIL
"Race Car Driver"

Emerson Fittipaldi
950 South Miami Avenue
Miami, FL 33130
"Race Car Driver"

Rick Fitts
1903 Dracena Drive
Los Angeles, CA 90068
"Actor"

Geraldine Fitzgerald
50 East 79th Street
New York, NY 10019
"Actress"

Marlin Fitzwater
2001 Swan Terrace
Alexandria, VA 22307
"Ex Press Secretary"

Roberta Flack
1 West 72nd Street
New York, NY 10023
"Singer, Songwriter"

Fanny Flagg
1520 Willina Lane
Montecito, CA 93108
"Actress"

Rick Flair
2722 Plantation Road
Charlotte, NC 28270
"Wrestler"

The Flamingos
141 Dunbar Avenue
Fords, NJ 08863
"Vocal Group"

Fionnula Flanagan
121 N. San Vicente Blvd.
Beverly Hills, CA 90211
"Actress"

Susan Flannery
789 River Rock Road
Santa Barbara, CA 93108
"Actress"

Flash Cadillac
433 E. Cucharras Street
Colorado Springs, CO 80903
"Rock & Roll Group"

Jennifer Flavin
7271 Angela Avenue
Canoga Park, CA 91307
"Model"

Fleetwood Mac
4905 South Atlantic Avenue
Daytona Beach, FL 32127
"Rock & Roll Group"

Mick Fleetwood
4905 South Atlantic Avenue
Daytona Beach, FL 32127
"Drummer, Songwriter"

Charles Fleischer
749 North Crescent Heights Blvd.
Los Angeles, CA 90038
"Actor"

Peggy Fleming
1122 S. Robertson Blvd. #15
Los Angeles, CA 90035
"Ice Skater"

Rhonda Fleming
10281 Century Woods Way
Los Angeles, CA 90067
"Actress"

Louise Fletcher
1520 Camden Avenue #105
Los Angeles, CA 90025
"Actress"

Lucy Lee Flippin
1753 Canfield Avenue
Los Angeles, CA 90035
"Actress"

Calista Flockhart
405 S. Beverly Dr. #500
Beverly Hills, CA 90212
"Actress"

Flock of Seagulls
526 Nicollett Mall
Minneapolis, MN 55402
"Rock & Roll Group"

Myron Floran
26 Georgeff Road
Rolling Hills, CA 90274
"Composer"

Tom Flores
11220 N.E. 53rd Street
Kirkland, WA 98033
"Football Executive"

Ray Floyd
P.O. Box 545957
Surfside, FL 33154
"Golfer"

Doug Flutie
22 Robin Hood Road
Natick, MA 01760
"Football Player"

Larry Flynt
9211 Robin Drive
Los Angeles, CA 90069
"Publisher"

Nina Foch
P.O. Box 1884
Beverly Hills, CA 90213
"Actress"

Dan Fogelberg
P.O. Box 2399
Pagosa Springs, CO 81147
"Singer, Songwriter"

John Fogerty
10423 Aubrey Drive
Beverly Hills, CA 90210
"Singer, Songwriter"

Tom Foley
601 West 1st Ave. #2W
Spokane, WA 99204
"Ex-Congressman"

Ken Follett
P.O. Box 708
London SW10 0DH ENGLAND
"Author"

Meg Follows
121 North San Vicente Blvd.
Beverly Hills, CA 90211
"Actress"

Bridget Fonda
9560 Wilshire Blvd. #516
Beverly Hills, CA 90212
"Actress"

Jane Fonda
1050 Techwood Drive N.W.
Atlanta, GA 30318
"Actress, Writer"

Peter Fonda
RR#38, Box 2024
Livingston, MT 59047
"Actor, Writer, Director"

Shirlee Fonda
110 East 57th Street
New York, NY 10022
"Mrs. Henry Fonda"

Joan Fontaine
P.O. Box 222600
Carmel, CA 93922
"Actress"

D.J. Fontana
P.O. Box 262
Carteret, NJ 07008
"Drummer"

Horton Foote
95 Horatio Street #332
New York, NY 10014
"Screenwriter"

Shelby Foote
542 East Parkway South
Memphis, TN 38104
"Historian"

June Foray
22745 Erwin Street
Woodland Hills, CA 91367
"Actress"

Brian Forbes
Seven Pines
Wentworth, Surrey, ENGLAND
"Writer, Director"

Steve Forbes
60 Fifth Avenue
New York, NY 10011
"Magazine Publisher"

Mrs. Betty Ford
40365 San Dune Road
Rancho Mirage, CA 92270
"Ex-First Lady, Author"

Charlotte Ford
25 Sutton Place
New York, NY 10023
"Daughter of Henry Ford II"

Doug Ford
6241 Beaconwood Road
Lake Worth, FL 33467
"Golfer"

Eileen Ford
344 East 59th Street
New York, NY 10022
"Talent Agent"

Faith Ford
4332 Agnes Avenue
Studio City, CA 91604
"Actress, Model"

Frankie Ford
7200 France Avenue #330
Edina, MN 55435
"Singer, Songwriter"

Gerald R. Ford
40365 San Dune Road
Rancho Mirage, CA 92270
"Former President"

Glenn Ford
911 Oxford Way
Beverly Hills, CA 90210
"Actor"

Harrison Ford
3555 North Moose Wilson Road
Jackson, WY 83001
"Actor"

Maria Ford
10110 Empyrean Way #304
Los Angeles, CA 90067
"Actress"

Mick Ford
47 Courtfield Road #9
London SW7 4DB
ENGLAND
"Actor"

Ruth Ford
1 West 72nd Street
New York, NY 10023
"Actress"

Whitey Ford
38 Schoolhouse Lane
Lake Success, NY 11020
"Ex-Baseball Player"

Foreigner
9830 Wilshire Blvd.
Beverly Hills, CA 90212
"Rock & Roll Group"

George Foreman
7639 Pine Oak Drive
Humble, TX 77397
"Boxer"

Forester Sisters
P.O. Box 1456
Trenton, GA 30752
"C&W Group"

Milos Forman
Hampshire House
150 Central Park South
New York, NY 10019
"Film Director"

Frederick Forrest
513 Wilshire Blvd. #347
Santa Monica, CA 90401
"Actor"

Helen Forrest
1870 Caminito del Cielo
Glendale, CA 91208
"Singer"

Sally Forrest
1125 Angelo Drive
Beverly Hills, CA 90210
"Actress"

Steve Forrest
1605 Michael Lane
Pacific Palisades, CA 90272
"Actor"

Constance Forslund
165 West 46th Street #1214
New York, NY 10036
"Actress"

Brian Forster
16172 Flamstead Drive
Hacienda Heights, CA 91745
"Actor"

Robert Forster
1115 Pine Street
Santa Monica, CA 90405
"Actor"

Bruce Forsyth
Kent House
Upper Ground
London SE1 ENGLAND
"TV Personality"

Frederick Forsyth
61-63 Oxbridge Rd., Ealing
London W5 5SA ENGLAND
"Writer"

Bill Forsythe
20 Winton Drive
Glasgow G12 SCOTLAND
"Guitarist"

John Forsythe
3849 Roblar Avenue
Santa Ynez, CA 93460
"Actor"

Rosemary Forsythe
1591 Benedict Canyon
Beverly Hills, CA 90210
"Actress"

Fabian Forte
6671 Sunset Blvd. #1502
Los Angeles, CA 90028
"Actor, Singer"

Dick Fosbury
709 Canyon Run, Box 1791
Ketchum, ID 83340
"Track Athlete"

Gen. Joe Foss
P.O. Box 566
Scottsdale, AZ 85252
"Firearms Assoc. Executive"

Brigitte Fossey
18 rue Troyon
75017 Paris, FRANCE
"Actress"

Jodie Foster
10900 Wilshire Blvd. #511
Los Angeles, CA 90024
"Actress"

Meg Foster
10100 Santa Monica Blvd. #2500
Los Angeles, CA 90067
"Actress"

Radney Foster
1908 Wedgewood
Nashville, TN 37212
"Singer"

Pete Fountain
237 North Peters Street #400
New Orleans, LA 71030
"Clarienetist"

Four Aces
P.O. Box 519
Irvington, NJ 07111
"Vocal Group"

Four Lads
32500 Concord Drive #221
Madison Heights, MI 49071
"Vocal Group"

The Four Seasons
P.O. Box 262
Carteret, NJ 07008
"Rock & Roll Group"

Gene Fowler, Jr.
7261 Outpost Cove
Los Angeles, CA 90068
"Film Director"

John Fowles
52 Floral Street
London WC2 ENGLAND
"Author"

Douglas V. Fowley
38510 Glen Abbey Lane
Murietta, CA 92362
"Actor"

Fox Brothers
Rt. 6, Bending Chestnut
Franklin, TN 37064
"Gospel Group"

Bernard Fox
P.O. Box 270
Hartford, CT 06141
"Actor"

Edward Fox
25 Maida Avenue
London W2 1ST ENGLAND
"Actor"

James Fox
125 Gloucester Road
London SW7 4TE ENGLAND
"Actor"

Michael J. Fox
7 Peabody Court
Teaneck, NJ 07666
"Actor, Director"

Samantha Fox
110-112 Disraeli Road
London SW1S 2DX ENGLAND
"Singer, Model"

Vivica Fox
419 E. Tamarack Avenue #30
Inglewood, CA 90301
"Actress"

Jeff Foxworthy
8380 Melrose Avenue #310
Los Angeles, CA 90069
"Actor"

Robert Foxworth
1230 Benedict Canyon Drive
Beverly Hills, CA 90210
"Actor"

A.J. Foyt
6415 Toledo
Houston, TX 77008
"Race Car Driver"

Don Frabotta
5036 Riverton Avenue #2
N. Hollywood, CA 91601
"Actor"

Jonathan Frakes
9135 Hazen Drive
Beverly Hills, CA 90210
"Actor"

Peter Frampton
8927 Byron Avenue
Surfside, FL 33154
"Singer, Guitarist"

Anne Francine
24 West 40th Street #1700
New York, NY 10018
"Actress"

Tony Franciosa
567 Tigertail Road
Los Angeles, CA 90049
"Actor"

Anne Francis
P.O. Box 3282
Palm Desert, CA 92260
"Actress"

Connie Francis
50 Sullivan Drive
West Orange, NJ 07052
"Singer, Actress"

Dick Francis
P.O. Box 30866
7 Mile Beach
Grand Cayman WEST INDIES
"Author"

Freddie Francis
12 Ashley Drive
Jersey Road, Osterley
Middlesex TW7 5QA ENGLAND
"TV Director"

Genie Francis
9135 Hazen Drive
Beverly Hills, CA 90210
"Actress"

Nancy Frangione
280 S. Beverly Drive #400
Beverly Hills, CA 90212
"Actress"

Rep. Barney Frank (MA)
House Rayburn Bldg. #2210
Washington, DC 20515
"Politician"

Charles Frank
113465 Ventura Blvd. #100
Studio City, CA 91604
"Actor"

Gary Frank
11401 Ayrshire Road
Los Angeles, CA 90049
"Actor"

Joanna Frank
1274 Capri Drive
Pacific Palisades, CA 90272
"Actress"

Al Franken
9830 Wilshire Blvd.
Beverly Hills, CA 90212
"Comedian"

John Frankenheimer
3114 Abington Drive
Beverly Hills, CA 90210
"Director, Producer"

Aretha Franklin
16919 Stansbury
Detroit, MI 48235
"Singer, Songwriter"

Bonnie Franklin
10635 Santa Monica Blvd. #130
Los Angeles, CA 90025
"Actress"

Diane Franklin
2115 Topanga Skyline Drive
Topanga, CA 90290
"Actress"

Don Franklin
10101 Santa Monica Blvd. #2500
Los Angeles, CA 90067
"Actor"

Gary Franklin
7610 Beverly Blvd. #480820
Los Angeles, CA 90048
"Film Critic"

Joe Franklin
P.O. Box 1
Lynbrook, NY 11563
"TV Swow Host"

Mary Frann
10100 Santa Monica Blvd. #2490
Los Angeles, CA 90067
"Actress"

Arthur Franz
32960 Pacific Coast Hwy.
Malibu, CA 90265
"Actor"

Dennis Franz
11805 Bellagio Road
Los Angeles, CA 90049
"Actor"

Brendan Fraser
2218 Wilshire Blvd. #513
Santa Monica, CA 90403
"Actor"

Douglas Fraser
800 East Jefferson Street
Detroit, MI 48214
"Ex-Union Leader"

Linda Fratianne
P.O. Box 151
Sun Valley, ID 83353
"Skater"

Liz Frazer
29 King's Road
London SW3 ENGLAND
"Actress"

Joe Frazier
2917 North Broad Street
Philadelphia, PA 19132
"Ex-Boxer Champion"

Sheila Frazier
1179 S. Highland Avenue
Los Angeles, CA 90019
"Actress"

Walt Frazier
400 Central Park West #7W
New York, NY 10025
"Ex-Basketball Player"

Stan Freberg
10450 Wilshire Blvd. #1A
Los Angeles, CA 90024
"Actor, Director"

Peter Frechette
233 East 12th Street #2B
New York, NY 10003
"Actor"

Louis Freeh
c/o FBI
9th & Pennsylvania Avenue NW
Washington, DC 20035
"FBI Director"

Kathleen Freeman
6247 Orion Avenue
Van Nuys, CA 91406
"Actress"

Mona Freeman
608 North Alpine Drive
Beverly Hills, CA 90210
"Actor"

Morgan Freeman
c/o William Morris
1325 Avenue of the Americas
New York, NY 10019
"Actor"

Jim Fregosi
1092 Copeland Court
Tarpon Springs, FL 34689
"Ex-Baseball Player"

Phyllis Frelich
8485-E Melrose Place
Los Angeles, CA 90069
"Actress"

Leigh French
1850 North Vista Avenue
Los Angeles, CA 90046
"Actor"

Susan French
110 East 9th Street #C-1005
Los Angeles, CA 90079
"Actress"

Matt Frewer
6670 Wildlife Road
Malibu, CA 90265
"Actor"

Glen Frey
8900 Wilshire Blvd. #300
Beverly Hills, CA 90211
"Singer, Guitarist"

Janie Fricke
P.O. Box 798
Lancaster, TX 75146
"Singer"

Brenda Fricker
68 Old Brompton Road
London SW7 3LQ ENGLAND
"Actress"

Squire Fridell
7080 Hollywood Blvd. #704
Los Angeles, CA 90028
"Actor"

William Friedkin
10451 Bellagio Road
Los Angeles, CA 90077
"Film Director"

Milton Friedman
Quadrangle Office
Hoover Institute
Stanford University
Palo Alto, CA 94305
"Econominist"

Sonya Friedman
208 Harriston Road
Glen Rock, NJ 07452
"TV Show Host"

Chuck Fries
6922 Hollywood Blvd.
Los Angeles, CA 90028
"TV Executive"

Daniel Frischman
145 S. Fairfax Avenue #310
Los Angeles, CA 90036
"Actor"

David Frizzell
1010 - 16th Avenue South
Nashville, TN 37212
"Singer"

Lynette "Squeaky" Fromme
#06075180
F.C.I. Road
Marianna, FL 32446
"Prisnor"

Dominic Frontiere
280 S. Beverly Drive #411
Beverly Hills, CA 90212
"Composer, Conductor"

Georgia Frontiere
100 N. Broadway #2100
St. Louis, MO 63102
"Football Team Owner"

Sir David Frost
130 West 57th Street
New York, NY 10019
"TV Show Host"

Lindsay Frost
310 Madison Avenue #232
New York, NY 10017
"Actress"

Mark Frost
P.O. Box 1723
Studio City, CA 91604
"TV Writer"

Soleil Moon Frye
2713 North Keystone
Burbank, CA 91504
"Actress"

Leo Fuchs
609 North Kilkea Drive
Los Angeles, CA 90048
"Actor"

Alan Fudge
355 South Rexford Drive
Beverly Hills, CA 90212
"Actor"

Daisy Fuentes
2200 Fletcher Avenue
Fort Lee, NJ 07024
"MTV Host"

The Fugees
83 Riverside Drive
New York, NY 10024
"Hip-Hop Trio"

Mark Fuhrman
P.O. Box 141
Sandpoint, ID 83864
"Ex-Cop"

Penny Fuller
12428 Hesby Street
North Hollywood, CA 91607
"Actress"

Robert Fuller
5012 Auckland Avenue
North Hollywood, CA 91601
"Actor"

Eileen Fulton
25 Central Park West #2N
New York, NY 10023
"Actress"

Annette Funicello
16102 Sandy Lane
Encino, CA 91316
"Actress"

Allen Funt
P.O. Box 827
Monterey, CA 93942
"TV Show Host, Director"

John Furey
9911 West Pico Blvd. #1060
Los Angeles, CA 90035
"Actor"

Edward Furlong
9830 Wilshire Blvd.
Beverly Hills, CA 90211
"Actor"

Stephen Furst
3900 Huntercrest Court
Moopark, CA 93021
"Actor"

George Furth
3030 Durand Drive
Los Angeles, CA 90068
"Actor, Writer"

G

Kenny G
3500 W. Olive Avenue #680
Burbank, CA 91505
"Singer"

Christopher Gable
60 St. James's Street
London SW1 ENGLAND
"Actor"

Princess Zsa Zsa Gabor
1001 Bel Air Road
Los Angeles, CA 90077
"Actress"

John Gabriel
100 West 57th Street #5-Q
New York, NY 10019
"Actor"

Peter Gabriel
Box Mill
Wiltshire SN14 9PL ENGLAND
"Singer, Songwriter"

Roman Gabriel
16817 McKee Road
Charlotte, NC 28278
"Ex-Football Player"

Col. Moammar Gaddafi
State Office
Tripoli, LIBYA
"Politician"

Max Gail
P.O. Box 4160
Malibu, CA 90265
"Actor"

Courtney Gains
3300 Dabney Avenue
Altadena, CA 91001
"Actress"

John Kenneth Galbraith
30 Francis Avenue
Cambridge, MA 02138
"Economist"

Gallagher
14984 Roan Court
West Palm Beach, FL 33414
"Comedian"

Helen Gallagher
260 West End Avenue
New York, NY 10023
"Actress"

Megan Gallagher
P.O. Box 5617
Beverly Hills, CA 90210
"Actress"

Peter Gallagher
2124 Broadway #131
New York, NY 10023
"Actor"

Silvana Gallardo
10637 Burbank Blvd.
No. Hollywood, CA 91601
"Actress"

Gina Gallego
6550 Murietta Avenue
Van Nuys, CA 91401
"Actress"

Zack Galligan
9300 Wilshire Blvd. #555
Beverly Hills, CA 90212
"Actor"

Joe Gallison
13515 Magnolia Blvd. #429
Sherman Oaks, CA 91403
"Actor"

Don Galloway
1800 Century Park E. #300
Los Angeles, CA 90067
"Actor"

Rita Gam
180 West 58th Street #8B
New York, NY 10019
"Actress"

Robin Gammell
415 N. Camden Drive #121
Beverly Hills, CA 90210
"Actor"

Harvey Gantt
P.O. Box 726
Arden, NC 28704
"Politician"

Bruno Ganz
Glattalstrasse 83
8052 Zurich SWITZERLAND
"Actor"

Teresa Ganzel
9300 Wilshire Blvd. #410
Beverly Hills, CA 90212
"Actress"

Joe Garagiola
6221 East Huntress Drive
Paradise Valley, AZ 85253
"TV Show Host, Sportscaster"

Terri Garber
4526 Wilshire Blvd.
Los Angeles, CA 90010
"Actress"

Victor Garber
40 West 57th Street
New York, NY 10019
"Actor"

Gil Garcetti
139 North Cliffwood
Los Angeles, CA 90049
"District Attorney"

Andy Garcia
4323 Forman Avenue
Toulca Lake, CA 91602
"Actor"

Randy Gardner
4640 Glencove Avenue #6
Marina Del Rey, CA 90291
"Ice Skater"

Allen Garfield
289 S. Robertson Blvd. #463
Beverly Hills, CA 90211
"Actor"

Art Garfunkel
9 East 79th Street
New York, NY 10021
"Singer, Songwriter"

Beverly Garland
8014 Briar Summit Drive
Los Angeles, CA 90046
"Actress"

Jake Garn
500 Huntsman Way
Salt Lakes City, UT 84108
"Ex-Senator"

James Garner
33 Oakmont Drive
Los Angeles, CA 90049
"Actor, Director"

Janeane Garofalo
9560 Wilshire Blvd., #500
Beverly Hills, CA 90212
"Actress"

Teri Garr
9150 Wilshire Blvd. #350
Beverly Hills, CA 90212-3427
"Actress"

Betty Garrett-Parks
3231 Oakdell Road
Studio City, CA 91604
"Actress"

Brad Garrett
8370 Wilshire Blvd. #209
Beverly HIlls, CA 90211
"Comedian"

David Garrison
9229 Sunset Blvd. #710
Los Angeles, CA 90069
"Actor"

Greg Garrison
1655 Hidden Valley Road
Thousand Oaks, CA 91361
"Director"

Zina Garrison
P.O. Box 272305
Houston, TX 77277
"Tennis Player"

Jennie Garth
3500 West Olive #920
Burbank, CA 91505
"Actress"

Kathy Garver
170 Woodbridge Road
Hillsborough, CA 94010
"Actress"

Cyndy Garvey
3002-3rd Street #204
Santa Monica, CA 90405
"Talk Show Host"

Steve Garvey
11718 Barrington Court #6
Los Angeles, CA 90049
"Ex-Baseball Player"

Lorraine Gary
1158 Tower Drive
Beverly Hills, CA 90210
"Actress"

Vittorio Gassman
201 rue du Fg. St. Honors
F-75008 Paris FRANCE
"Actor"

Bill Gates
1 Microsoft Way
Redmond, WA 98052
"Microsoft Owner"

Daryl Gates
756 Portola Terrace
Los Angeles, CA 90042
"Ex-Police Chief"

Larry Gatlin
Fantacy Harbour, Waccamaw
Myrtle Beach, SC 29577
"Singer, Songwriter"

Jennifer Gatti
8383 Wilshire Blvd. #954
Beverly Hills, CA 90211
"Actress"

Willie Gault
33-26th Place
Venice, CA 90291
"Ex-Football Player"

Dick Gautier
11333 Moorpark Street #59
North Hollywood, CA 91602
"Actor, Writer"

Cassandra Gava
911 North Kings Road #301
Los Angeles, CA 90069
"Actress"

John Gavin
2100 Century Park W. #10263
Los Angeles, CA 90067
"Actor"

Rebecca Gayheart
853-7th Avenue #9A
New York, NY 10019
"Actress"

Crystal Gayle
51 Music Square East
Nashville, TN 37203
"Singer"

Jackie Gayle
2155 San Ysidro Drive
Beverly Hills, CA 90210
"Comedian"

Mitch Gaylord
7924 Hillside Avenue
Los Angeles, CA 90046
"Actor"

George Gaynes
3344 Campanil Drive
Santa Barbara, CA 93109
"Actor, Director"

Gloria Gaynor
Longford Avenue, Southall
Middlesex UB 1 3QT ENGLAND
"Singer"

Mitzi Gaynor
610 North Arden Drive
Beverly Hills, CA 90210
"Actor, Dancer"

Ben Gazzara
1080 Madison Avenue
New York, NY 10028
"Actor"

Cynthia Geary
21121 Foxtail
Mission Viejo, CA 92692
"Actress"

Tony Geary
7010 Pacific View Drive
Los Angeles, CA 90068
"Actor"

Nicolei Gedda
Valhavagen 128
S-11441 Stockholm, SWEDEN
"Tenor"

Jason Gedrick
8730 Sunset Blvd. #490
Los Angeles, CA 90069
"Actor"

Ellen Geer
21418 West Entrada Road
Topanga, CA 90290
"Actress"

Judy Geeson
Guild House
Upper St. Martin Lane
London WC2H 9EG ENGLAND
"Actress"

David Geffen
P.O. Box 8520
Universal City, CA 91608
"Record Executive"

Martha Gehman
2488 Cheremoya Avenue
Los Angeles, CA 90068
"Actress"

Larry Gelbart
807 North Alpine Drive
Beverly Hills, CA 90210
"Writer, Producer"

Sir Bob Geldof, KBE
Davington Priory
Faversham Kent, ENGLAND
"Singer"

Daniel Gelin
1 allee Pompadour
F-92190 Meudon FRANCE
"Film Director"

Sarah Michelle Gellar
11350 Ventura Blvd. #206
Studio City, CA 91604
"Actress"

Uri Geller
Sonning-on-Thames
Berkshire, ENGLAND
"Psychic"

Michael Gelman
7 Lincoln Square
New York, NY 10023
"Actor, Writer"

The X Generation
184 Glochester Place
London NW1 ENGLAND
"Rock & Roll Group"

Bryan Genesse
9000 Sunset Blvd. #1200
Los Angeles, CA 90069
"Actor"

Genesis
25 Ives Street
London SW3 ENGLAND
"Rock & Roll Group"

Peter Gennaro
115 Central Park West
New York, NY 10024
"Choreographer"

Hans-Dietrich Genscher
Am Kottenforst 16
D-53343 Wachtberg-Pech
GERMANY
"Diplomat"

Bobbie Gentry
8 Tidewater Way
Savannah, GA 31411
"Singer"

Race Gentry
2379 Mountain View Drive
Escondido, CA 92116
"Actress"

Boy George (O'Dowd)
7 Pepy's Court
84 The Chase, Clapham
London SW4 0NF ENGLAND
"Singer, Composer"

Lynda Day George
10310 Riverside Drive #104
Toluca Lake, CA 91602
"Actress"

Phyllis George
Cave Hill, Box 4308
Lexington, KY 40503
"TV Personality"

Susan George
520 Washington Blvd. #187
Marina del Rey, CA 90292
"Actress"

Wally George
14155 Magnolia Blvd. #127
Sherman Oaks, CA 91423
"TV Show Host"

Rep. Richard Gephardt (MO)
1226 Cannon House Office Building
Washington, DC 20515
"Politician"

Geraldo
17337 Ventura Blvd. #208
Encino, CA 91316
"TV Show Host"

Gil Gerard
23679 Calabasas Road #325
Calabasas, CA 91302
"Actor"

David Gerber
10800 Chalon Road
Los Angeles, CA 90077
"TV Producer"

Richard Gere
9696 Culver Blvd. #203
Culver City, CA 90232
"Actor"

David Gergen
1105 Alvord Court
McLean, VA 22102
"Journalist"

Jack Germond
1627 "K" Street NW #1100
Washington, DC 20006
"News Correspondent"

Daniel Gerroll
324 W. 83rd Street #3B
New York, NY 10024
"Actor"

Gerry & The Pacemakers
6 Ridge Road
Emerson, NJ 07630
"Music Group"

Gina Gershon
120 W. 45th Street #3601
New York, NY 10036
"Actress"

Jami Gertz
1999 Avenue of the Stars #1900
Los Angeles, CA 90067
"Actress"

Balthazar Getty
151 El Camino Drive
Beverly Hills, CA 90212
"Actor"

Estelle Getty
10960 Wilshire Blvd. #2050
Los Angeles, CA 90024
"Actress"

Gordon Getty
2880 Broadway
San Francisco, CA 94115
"Executive, Composer"

Mrs. J. Paul Getty
1535 North Beverly Drive
Beverly Hills, CA 90210
"Philanthropist"

John Getz
438 Linnie Canal
Venice, CA 90291
"Actor"

Alice Ghostley
3800 Reklaw Drive
North Hollywood, CA 91604
"Actress"

Giancarlo Giannini
Via della Giuliana 101
I-00195 Rome ITALY
"Actor"

Barry Gibb
29505 US 19 North #12-290
Clearwater, FL 34624
"Singer"

Cynthia Gibb
7920 Sunset Blvd. #400
Los Angeles, CA 90046
"Actress"

Maurice Gibb
29505 US 19 North #12-290
Clearwater, FL 34624
"Singer, Songwriter"

Robin Gibb
29505 US 19 North #12-290
Clearwater, FL 34624
"Singer, Songwriter"

Leeza Gibbons
1760 Courtney Avenue
Los Angeles, CA 90046
"TV Show Host"

Georgia Gibbs
965 Fifth Avenue
New York, NY 10021
"Singer"

Marla Gibbs
3500 W. Manchester Blvd. #267
Inglewood, CA 90305
"Actress"

Terri Gibbs
25 Cobble Creek Drive
RD 1, Box 91
Tannersville, PA 18872
"Singer, Songwriter"

Althea Gibson-Darbeu
275 Prospect Street #768
East Orange, NJ 07017
"Tennis Player"

Charles Gibson
1965 Broadway #500
New York, NY 10023
"TV Show Host"

Debbie Gibson
300 Main Street #201
Huntington, NY 11743
"Singer"

Don Gibson
P.O. Box 50474
Nashville, TN 37205
"Singer, Songwriter"

Henry Gibson
26740 Latigo Shore Drive
Malibu, CA 90265
"Actress"

Kirk Gibson
15135 Charlevois Street
Grosse Pointe, MI 48230
"Ex-Baseball Player"

Mel Gibson
4000 Warner Blvd. #P3-17
Burbank, CA 91522
"Actor, Writer"

Pamela Gidley
6161 Glen Alder Street
Los Angeles, CA 90068
"Actress"

Sir John Gielgud
South Pavillion, Wotten
Underwood Aylesbury
Buckinghamshire, ENGLAND
"Actor"

Frank Gifford
625 Madison Avenue #1200
New York, NY 10022
"Sportscaster"

Kathie Lee Gifford
625 Madison Avenue #1200
New York, NY 10022
"TV Show Host"

Elaine Giftos
1800 Avenue of the Stars #400
Los Angeles, CA 90067
"Actress"

Elsie Gilbert
1016 North Orange Grove #4
Los Angeles, CA 90046
"Actress"

Herschel Burke Gilbert
2451 Nichols Canyon
Los Angeles, CA 90046
"Composer, Conductor"

Melissa Gilbert
P.O. Box 57593
Sherman Oaks, CA 91413
"Actress"

Sara Gilbert
16254 High Valley Drive
Encino, CA 91346
"Actress"

Johnny Gill
17539 Corinthian Drive
Encino, CA 91316
"Singer, Songwriter"

Vince Gill
P.O. Box 1407
White House, TN 37188
"Singer, Songwriter"

Ann Gillespie
8899 Beverly Blvd. #705
Los Angeles, CA 90048
"Actress"

Robert Gillespie
10 Irving Road
London W14 0JS ENGLAND
"Actor, Director"

Mickey Gilley
P.O. Box 1242
Pasadena, TX 77501
"Singer, Songwriter"

Burton Gilliam
1427 Tascosa Court
Allen, TX 75013
"Actor"

Terry Gilliam
The Old Hall
South Grove Highgate
London W6 ENGLAND
"Actor, Writer, Director"

Richard Gilliland
4545 Noeline Avenue
Encino, CA 91436
"Actor"

David Gilmore
43 Portland Road
London, W11 4LJ ENGLAND
"Guitarist"

Peri Gilpin
15760 Ventura Blvd., #1730
Encino, CA 91436
"Actress"

Frank Gilroy
6 Magnin Road
Monroe, NY 10950
"Dramatist"

Clarence Gilyard Jr.
24040 Camino Del Avion #A-239
Monarch Bay, CA 92629
"Actor"

Erica Gimpel
10100 Santa Monica Blvd., #2500
Los Angeles, CA 90067
"Actress"

Jack Ging
P.O. Box 1131
La Quinta, CA 92253
"Actor"

Rep. Newt Gingrich (GA)
110 Maryland Avenue, NE
Washington, DC 20002
"Politician"

Ruth Bader Ginsbury
700 New Hampshire Avenue, NW
Washington, DC 20037
"Supreme Court Justice"

Robert Ginty
16133 Ventura Blvd. #800
Encino, CA 91436
"Actor"

Annie Girardot
10 Avenue George V
F-75008 Paris FRANCE
"Actress"

Annabeth Gish
8942 Wilshire Blvd.
Beverly Hills, CA 90211
"Actress"

Carlo Giuffre
via Massimi 45
I-00136 Rome, ITALY
"Conductor"

Rudy Giuliani
City Hall
New York, NY 10007
"Mayor"

Hubert Givenchy
3 Avenue George V
75008 Paris, FRANCE
"Fashion Designer"

Glaser Brothers
916-19th Avenue South
Nashville, TN 37212
"Music Group"

Paul Michael Glaser
317 Georgina Avenue
Santa Monica, CA 90402
"Actor, Director"

Philip Glass
231-2nd Avenue
New York, NY 10003
"Composer"

Ron Glass
2485 Wild Oak Drive
Los Angeles, CA 90068
"Actor"

Glass Tiger
238 Davenport #126
Toronto, Ontario M5R 1J6
CANADA
"Rock & Roll Group"

Paul Gleason
8091 Selma Avenue
Los Angeles, CA 90046
"Actor"

John Glenn
1000 Urlin Avenue
Columbus, OH 43212
"Ex-Senator, Astronaut"

Scott Glenn
P.O. Box 1018
Ketchum, ID 83340
"Actor"

Sharon Gless
P.O. Box 48005
Los Angeles, CA 90048
"Actress"

Bruce Glover
11449 Woodbine Street
Los Angeles, CA 90066
"Actor"

Crispin Glover
3573 Carnation Avenue
Los Angeles, CA 90026
"Actor"

Danny Glover
41 Sutter Street #1648
San Francisco, CA 94104
"Actor"

John Glover
130 W. 42nd Street #2400
New York, NY 10036
"Actor"

Julian Glover
19 Ullswater Road
London SW13 ENGLAND
"Actor"

Jean-Luc Godard
15 rue du Nord
CH-1180 Rolle
SWITZERLAND
"Film Director"

Mark Goddard
Chamberlain School
Box 778
Middleboro, MA 02346
"Actor"

Alexander Goehr
11 West Road
Cambridge, ENGLAND
"Composer"

Bob Goen
10110 Empyrean Way #304
Los Angeles, CA 90067
"TV Performer"

Bernhard Goetz
55 West 14th Street
New York, NY 10011
"Subway Shooter"

Andrew Gold
211 St. John's Road
Ridgefield, CT 06877
"Singer, Songwriter"

Ernest Gold
269 Bellino Drive
Pacific Palisades, CA 90272
"Composer"

Missy Gold
3500 West Olive Ave. #1400
Burbank, CA 91505
"Actress"

Tracey Gold
4619 Goodland Avenue
Studio City, CA 91604
"Actress"

Adam Goldberg
1925 Century Park E. #2320
Los Angeles, CA 99067
"Actor"

Gary David Goldberg
25 Oakmont Drive
Los Angeles, CA 90049
"Writer, Producer"

Leonard Goldberg
235 Ladera Drive
Beverly Hills, CA 90210
"TV-Film, Producer"

Whoopi Golberg
5555 Melrose Avenue #114
Los Angeles, CA 90038
"Actress, Comedienne"

Jeff Goldblum
2401 Main Street
Santa Monica, CA 90405
"Actor"

William Lee Golden
Rt. 2, Saundersville Road
Hendersonville, TN 37075
"Singer, Songwriter"

Ricky Paull Golin
9320 Wilshire Blvd. #300
Beverly Hills, CA 90212
"Actor"

Fred Goldman
P.O. Box 6016
Agoura Hills, CA 91376
"Ron Goldman's Father"

William Goldman
50 East 77th Street #30
New York, NY 10021
"Screenwriter"

Lelia Goldoni
15459 Wyandotte Street
Van Nuys, CA 91405
"Actress"

Bobby Goldsboro
P.O. Box 5250
Ocala, FL 32678
"Singer, Songwriter"

Bob Goldthwait
3950 Fredonia Drive
Los Angeles, CA 90068
"Actor, Comedian"

Barry Goldwater
6250 Hogahn
Paradise Valley, AZ 85253
"Ex-Senator"

Sam Goldwyn, Jr.
10203 Santa Monica Blvd. #500
Los Angeles, CA 90067
"Director, Producer"

Tony Goldwyn
940 N. Mansfield Avenue
Los Angeles, CA 90038
"Actor"

Valeria Golino
8033 Sunset Blvd. #419
Los Angeles, CA 90046
"Actress"

Arlene Golonka
515 Ocean Avenue #308N
Santa Monica, CA 90402
"Actress"

Richard Golub
42 East 64th Street
New York, NY 10021
"Attorney"

Panchito Gomez
P.O. Box 7016
Burbank, CA 91510
"Actor"

Pedro Gonzalez-Gonzalez
4154 Charles Avenue
Culver City, CA 90230
"Wrestler"

Dwight Gooden
6700 30th Street So.
St. Petersburg, FL 33712
"Baseball Player"

Grant Goodeve
21416 N.E. 68th Court
Redmond, WA 98053
"Actor"

Linda Goodfriend
5700 Etiwanda #150
Tarzana, CA 91365
"Actress"

Cuba Gooding, Jr.
5750 Wilshire Blvd. #580
Los Angeles, CA 90036
"Actor"

Dody Goodman
13834 Magnolia Blvd.
Sherman Oaks, CA 91423
"Actress"

John Goodman
619 Amalfi Drive
Pacific Palisades, CA 90272
"Actor"

Gail Goodrich
147 Byram Shore Road
Greenwich, CT 06830
"Ex-Basketball Player"

Michael Goorjian
9000 Sunset Blvd., #1200
Los Angels, CA 90069
"Actor"

Lecy Goranson
1201 Greenacre Blvd.
West Hollywood, CA 90046
"Actress"

Mikhail S. Gorbachev
49 Leningradsky Prospekt 209
Moscow, RUSSIA
"Former U.S.S.R. Chairman"

Ekaterina Gordeeva
1375 Hopmeadow Street
Simsbury, CT 06070
"Ice Skater"

Barry Gordon
1801 Avenue of the Stars #902
Los Angeles, CA 90067
"Actor"

Bruce Gordon
231-C Tano Road
Santa Fe, NM 87501
"Actor"

Don Gordon
6310 San Vicente Blvd. #520
Los Angeles, CA 90048
"Actor"

Jeff Gordon
5325 Stowe Lane
Harrisburg, NC 28075
"Race Car Driver"

Joey Gordon-Levitt
4024 Radford Avenue
Building 3
Studio City, CA 91604
"Actor"

Richard Gordon
1 Craven Hill
London W2 3EP ENGLAND
"Writer"

Robby Gordon
6300 Valley View Avenue
Buena Park, CA 90620
"Race Car Driver"

Berry Gordy
878 Stradella Road
Los Angeles, CA 90077
"Record Executive"

V.P. Albert Gore, Jr.
Admiral House
34th & Massachusetts
Washington, DC 20005
"Vice President U.S.A."

Lesley Gore
170 East 77th Street #2-A
New York, NY 10021
"Actress, Singer"

Michael Gore
15622 Royal Oak Road
Encino, CA 91436
"Composer"

Tipper Gore
Admiral House
34th & Massachusetts
Washington, DC 20005
"Wife of V.P. Albert Gore, Jr."

Cliff Gorman
333 West 57th Street
New York, NY 10019
"Actor"

Eydie Gorme
820 Greenway Drive
Beverly Hills, CA 90210
"Singer"

Karen Lynn Gorney
853-7th Avenue #7-C
New York, NY 10019
"Actress"

Frank Gorshin
P.O. Box 17731
West Haven, CT 06516
"Actor, Comedian"

Vern Gosdin
2509 Marquette Avenue
Tampa, FL 33614
"Singer, Songwriter"

Mark Paul Gosselaar
27512 Wellsley Way
Valencia, CA 91354
"Actor"

Louis Gossett, Jr.
8306 Wilshire Blvd. #438
Beverly Hills, CA 90211
"Actor, Director"

John Gotti #18261-053
Rt. 5, Box 2000
Marion, IL 62959
"Convicted Mafia Boss"

Elliott Gould
21250 Califa #201
Woodland Hills, CA 91367
"Actor"

Harold Gould
603 Ocean Avenue, 4 East
Santa Monica, CA 90402
"Actor"

Jason Gould
837 West Knoll Drive #214
Los Angeles, CA 90069
"Financier"

Sandra Gould
3219 Oakdell Lane
Studio City, CA 91604
"Actress"

Robert Goulet
3110 Monte Rosa
Las Vegas, NV 89120
"Singer"

Curt Gowdy
33 Franklin Street
Lawrence, MA 01040
"Sportscaster"

Lord Lew Grade
8 Queen Street
Embassy House
London W1X 7PH ENGLAND
"Film Executive"

Don Grady
4444 Lankershim Blvd. #207
North Hollywood, CA 91602
"Actor"

Steffi Graff
Luftschiffring 8
D-68782 Bruhl, GERMANY
"Tennis Player"

Ilene Graff
11455 Sunshine Terrace
Studio City, CA 91604
"Actress"

Sue Grafton
P.O. Box 41447
Santa Barbara, CA 93140
"Novilist"

Rev. Billy Graham
P.O. Box 779
Minneapolis, MN 55440
"Evangelist"

Sen. Bob Graham (FL)
Senate Dirksen Bldg. #241
Washington, DC 20510
"Politician"

Gary Graham
4526 Wilshire Blvd.
Los Angeles, CA 90010
"Actor"

Heather Graham
28721 Timberlane St.
Agoura Hills, CA 91301
"Actress"

Katherine Graham
2920 "R" Street N.W.
Washington, DC 20007
"Publishing Executive"

Otto Graham
2216 Riviera Drive
Saratoga, FL 34232
"Ex-Football Player"

Ronny Graham
863 Castac Place
Pacific Palisades, CA 90272
"TV Writer"

Virginia Graham
211 East 70th Street
New York, NY 10021
"TV Show Host"

Nancy Grahn
4910 Agnes Avenue
North Hollywood, CA 91607
"Actress"

Sen. Phil Gramm (TX)
Senate Russell Bldg. #370
Washington, DC 20510
"Politician"

Kelsey Grammer
3266 Cornell Road
Agoura Hills, CA 91301
"Actor"

Fred Grandy
9417 Spruce Tree Circle
Bethesda, MD 20814-1654
"Actor, Politician"

Farley Granger
1 West 72nd Street #25D
New York, NY 10023
"Actor"

Amy Grant
2910 Poston Avenue
Nashville, TN 37203
"Singer"

David Marshall Grant
2247 Vista Del Mar
Los Angeles, CA 90068
"Actor"

Eddy Grant
155-D Holland Park Drive
London W11 4UX ENGLAND
"Singer, Writer"

Gogi Grant
10323 Alamo Avenue #202
Los Angeles, CA 90064
"Singer"

Horace Grant
One Magic Place
Orlando, FL 32801
"Basketball Player"

Hugh Grant
76 Oxford Street
London W1N OAX ENGLAND
"Actor"

Johnny Grant
5800 Sunset Blvd.
Los Angeles, CA 90028
"TV Show Host"

Lee Grant
610 West End Avenue #7B
New York, NY 10024
"Actress, Director"

Rodney A. Grant
1201 Greenacre Blvd.
W. Hollywood, CA 90046
"Actor"

Dr. Tony Grant
610 South Ardmore Avenue
Los Angeles, CA 90005
"Radio Personality"

Guenther Grass
Glockenglesserstr 21
23552 Lubeck GERMANY
"Author"

Karen Grassle
3717 Edmond Lake
Louisville, KY 40207
"Actress"

Shirley Ann Grau
210 Baronne Street #1120
New Orleans, LA 70112
"Writer"

Grateful Dead
P.O. Box 1073-C
San Rafael, CA 94915
"Rock & Roll Group"

Peter Graves
9777 Wilshire Avenue #815
Beverly Hills, CA 90212
"Actor"

Teresa Graves
3437 West 78th Place
Los Angeles, CA 90043
"Actress"

Billy Gray
19612 Grandview Drive
Topanga, CA 90290
"Actor"

Colleen Gray
1432 North Kenwood Street
Burbank, CA 91505
"Actress"

Dulcie Gray
44 Brunswick Gardens
Flat #2
London W8 ENGLAND
"Actress, Author"

Erin Gray
10921 Alta View
Studio City, CA 91604
"Actress"

Linda Gray
P.O. Box 5064
Sherman Oaks, CA 91403
"Actress, Director"

Spalding Gray
22 Wooster Street
New York, NY 10013
"Writer, Actor"

William H. Gray III
500 East 62nd Street
New York, NY 10021
"U.N.C.F. President"

Kathryn Grayson
2009 La Mesa Drive
Santa Monica, CA 90402
"Actress, Singer"

Buddy Greco
9363 Wilshire Blvd. #212
Beverly Hills, CA 90210
"Singer"

Adolph Green
211 Central Park W. #19E
New York, NY 10024
"Actor, Writer"

Al Green
P.O. Box 456
Millington, TN 38083
"Singer, Clergy"

Brian Austin Green
1122 S. Robertson Blvd. #15
Los Angeles, CA 90035
"Actor"

Dallas Green
RR#1 Box 227A
West Grove, PA 19390
"Baseball Manager"

Dennis Green
9520 Viking Drive
Eden Prairie, MN 55344
"Football Coach"

Ellen Greene
36 Cranberry Street
Brooklyn, NY 11201
"Actress, Singer"

Graham Greene
121 N. San Vicente Blvd.
Beverly Hills, CA 90211
"Author"

James Greene
60 Pope's Grove, Twickenham
Middlesex ENGLAND
"Actor"

"Mean" Joe Greene
2121 George Halas Dr. NW
Canton, OH 44708
"Ex-Football Player

Michele Greene
P.O. Box 29117
Los Angeles, CA 90029
"Actress"

Shecky Greene
1642 Laverne Way
Palm Springs, CA 92264
"Comedian"

David Greenlee
1811 North Whitley #800
Los Angeles, CA 90028
"Actor"

Bud Greenspan
33 East 68th Street
New York, NY 10021
"Writer, Producer"

Alan Greenspand
20th St. & Constitution Ave. NW
Washington, DC 20551
"Federal Reserve Chairman"

Bruce Greenwood
12414 Cascade Canyon Drive
Granada Hills, CA 91344
"Actor"

Lee Greenwood
P.O. Box 6537
Sevierville, TN 37864
"Singer, Songwriter"

Michael Greenwood
14 Kingston House Prince Gate
London SW7 1LJ ENGLAND
"Actor"

Brodie Greer
300 S. Raymond Avenue #II
Pasadena, CA 91105
"Actor"

Dabs Greer
284 South Madison #102
Pasadena, CA 91101
"Actor"

Germaine Greer
29 Frenshaw Road
London SW10 0TG ENGLAND
"Feminist, Author"

(Betty) Jane Greer
966 Moraga Drive
Los Angeles, CA 90049
"Actress"

Dick Gregory
P.O. Box 3270
Plymouth, MA 02361
"Activist, Comedian"

James Gregory
55 Cathedral Rock Drive #33
Sedona, AZ 86336
"Actor"

Paul Gregory
P.O. Box 38
Palm Springs, CA 92262
"Film Producer"

Kim Greist
c/o Innovative
1999 Avenue of the Stars #2850
Los Angeles, CA 90212
"Actress"

Wayne Gretzky
9100 Wilshire Blvd. #1000W
Beverly Hills, 90212
"Hockey Player"

Jennifer Grey
7920 Sunset Blvd. #400
Los Angeles, CA 90069
"Actress"

Joel Grey
130 W. 42nd Street #1804
New York, NY 10036
"Actor, Singer"

Virginia Grey
15101 Magnolia Blvd. #54
Sherman Oaks, CA 91403
"Actress"

Richard Grieco
2934 1/2 N. Beverly Glen Circle
Suite #252
Los Angeles, CA 90077
"Actor"

Helmut Griem
Klugstr. 36
D-80638 Munich GERMANY
"Actor"

David Alan Grier
8033 Sunset Blvd. #61
Los Angeles, CA 90046
"Actor"

Pam Grier
P.O. Box 370958
Denver, CO 80237
"Actress"

Rosey Grier
P.O. Box "A"
Santa Ana, CA 92711
"Actor, Ex-Football Player"

Bob Griese
4412 Santa Maria Street
Coral Gables, FL 33146
"Ex-Football Player"

Ken Griffey, Jr.
P.O. Box 4100
Seattle, WA 98104
"Baseball Player"

Ken Griffey, Sr.
8216 Princeton Glendale Rd.#103
Westchester, OH 45069
"Ex-Baseball Player"

Archie Griffin
4965 St. Andrews Drive
Westerville, OH 43082
"Ex-Football Player"

Merv Griffin
9876 Wilshire Blvd.
Beverly Hills, CA 90210
"Singer, Producer"

Andy Griffith
P.O. Box 1968
Manteo, NC 27954
"Actor"

Melanie Griffith
3110 Main Street #205
Santa Monica, CA 90405
"Actress"

Nancy Griffith
509 Hartnell Street
Monterey, CA 93940
"Singer, Songwriter"

Thomas Ian Griffith
5444 Agnes Avenue
North Hollywood, CA 91607
"Actor"

Florence Griffith-Joyner
27758 Santa Margarita #385
Mission Viejo, CA 92691
"Track Athlete"

Gary Grimes
4578 West 165th Street
Lawndale, CA 90260
"Actor"

Tammy Grimes
10 East 44th Street #700
New York, NY 10017
"Actress"

John Grisham
P.O. Box 1156
Oxford, MS 38655
"Author"

George Grizzard
400 East 54th Street
New York, NY 10022
"Actor"

Dick Groat
320 Beach Street
Pittsburgh, PA 15218
"Ex-Baseball Player"

Charles Grodin
2200 Fletcher Avenue
Ft. Lee, NJ 07024
"Actor"

Ferde Grofe, Jr.
18139 West Coastline
Malibu, CA 90265
"Writer"

Steve Grogan
8 Country Club Drive
Foxboro, MA 02035
"Ex-Football Player"

David Groh
301 N. Canon Drive #305
Beverly Hills, CA 90210
"Actor"

Sam Groom
3708 Barham Blvd. #D-305
Los Angeles, CA 90068
"Actor"

Arye Gross
10683 Santa Monica Blvd.
Los Angeles, CA 90025
"Actor"

Michael Gross
Paul Ehlich Strasse 6
D-6000 Frankfurt 70
GERMANY
"Swimmer"

Michael Gross
P.O. Box 522
La Canada, CA 91012
"Actor"

Lou Groza
287 Parkway Drive
Berea, OH 44017
"Ex-Football Player"

Gary Grubbs
10100 Santa Monica Blvd. #2500
Los Angeles, CA 90067
"Actor"

Dave Grushin
1282 Route 376
Wappingers Falls, NY 12590
"Composer"

Peter Guber
10202 W. Washington Blvd.
Suite #1070
Culver City, CA 90232
"Film Producer"

Bob Guccione
277 Park Avenue
New York, NY 10017
"Publisher"

Pedro Guerrero
435 S. Lafayette Park Place #308
Los Angeles, CA 90057
"Ex-Baseball Player"

Christopher Guest
10573 W. Pico Blvd
Los Angeles, CA 90064
"Actor, Writer"

Lance Guest
2269 La Granada Drive
Los Angeles, CA 90068
"Actor"

Carla Gugino
151 El Camino Drive
Beverly Hills, CA 90212
"Actress"

Ron Guidry
P.O. Box 278
Scott, LA 70583
"Ex-Baseball Player"

Ann Guilbert
550 Erskine Drive
Pacific Palisades, CA 90272
"Actress"

Robert Guillaume
4709 Noeline Avenue
Encino, CA 91436
"Actor"

John Guillerman
309 S. Rockingham Avenue
Los Angeles, CA 90049
"Film Director"

Sir Alec Guiness
Kettle Brook Meadows
Petersfield, Hampshire
ENGLAND
"Actor, Director"

Professor Lani Guinier
3400 Chestnut Street
Philadelphia, PA 19104
"Attorney, Educator"

Cathy Guisewite
4900 Main Street
Kansas City, MO 64112
"Cartoonist"

Tito Guizar
Sierra Madre
640 Lomas Drive Chaupultepec
Mexico City 10 09999 MEXICO
"Actor, Guitarist"

Dorothy Gulliver
28792 Lajos Lane
Valley Center, CA 92082
"Actress"

Bryant Gumbel
524 West 57th Street
New York, NY 10019
"TV Show Host"

Greg Gumbel
347 West 57th Street
New York, NY 10019
"Sports Anchor"

Janet Gunn
9229 Sunset Blvd. #710
Los Angeles, CA 90069
"Actress"

Guns & Roses
83 Riverside Drive
New York, NY 10024
"Rock & Roll Group"

Dan Gurney
2334 South Broadway
Santa Ana, CA 92707
"Race Car Drive"

HM King Carl Gustav XVI
Kungliga Slottet
11130 Stockholm SWEDEN
"Royalty"

Arlo Guthrie
The Farm
Washington, MA 01223
"Singer, Songwriter"

Steve Guttenburg
15237 Sunset Blvd. #48
Pacific Palisades, CA 90272
"Actor"

Lucy Gutteridge
76 Oxford Street
London W1N 0AX ENGLAND
"Actress"

Jasmine Guy
21243 Ventura Blvd. #101
Woodland Hills, CA 91364
"Actress, Singer"

Tony Gwynn
15643 Boulder Ridge Lane
Poway, CA 92064
"Baseball Player"

Anne Gwynne
2388 Mulholland Drive
Woodland Hills, CA 91364
"Actress"

James "Gypsy" Haake
1256 North Flores #1
Los Angeles, CA 90069
"Actor"

Lukas Haas
10683 Santa Monica Blvd.
Los Angeles, CA 90025
"Actor"

Shelley Hack
1208 Georgina
Santa Monica, CA 90402
"Actress, Model"

Buddy Hackett
800 North Whittier Drive
Beverly Hills, CA 90210
"Comedian, Actor"

Taylor Hackford
76 Oxford Street
London W1N OAX ENGLAND
"Actor"

Gene Hackman
118 South Beverly Drive #1201
Beverly Hills, CA 90212
"Actor"

Pat Haden
8525 Wilson Avenue
San Marion, CA 91108
"Sportscaster"

Brett Hadley
5070 Woodley Avenue
Encino, CA 91436
"Actor"

Molly Hagan
8899 Beverly Blvd. #510
Los Angeles, CA 90048
"Actress"

Sammy Hagar
8502 Fathom Drive
Baldwinsville, NY 13027
"Singer"

Uta Hagen
27 Washington Square N.
New York, NY 10011
"Actress"

Merle Haggard
3009 East Street
Sevierville, TN 37862
"Singer"

Marvin Hagler
75 Presidential Drive #4
Quincy, MA 02169
"Boxer"

Larry Hagman
9950 Sulpher Mountain Road
Ojai, CA 93023
"Actor, Director"

Albert Hague
4346 Redwood Avenue #304A
Marina del Rey, CA 90292
"Actor, Composer"

Jessica Hahn
6345 Balboa Blvd. #375
Encino, CA 91316
"Radio Personality"

Charles Haid
4376 Forman Avenue
North Hollywood, CA 91602
"Actor, Producer"

Gen. Alexander Haig, Jr.
6041 Crimson Court
McLean, VA 22101
"Ex-Military Leader, Politician"

Arthur Hailey
P.O. Box N-7776
Lyford Cay
Nassau, BAHAMAS
"Writer"

Oliver Hailey
11747 Canton Place
Studio City, CA 91604
"Screenwriter"

Corey Haim
150 Carlton Street
Toronto Ontario
M5A 2K1 CANADA
"Actor"

Connie Haines
880 Mandalay Avenue #3-109
Cleanwater Beach, FL 34630
"Singer"

Randa Haines
132 S. Rodeo Drive #300
Beverly Hills, CA 90212
"TV Director"

Jester Hairston
5047 Valley Ridge Avenue
Los Angeles, CA 90043
"Actor"

Ron Hajak
17420 Ventura Blvd. #4
Encino, CA 91316
"Actor"

Khrystyne Haje
P.O. Box 8750
Universal City, CA 91608
"Actress"

Barbara Hale
13351-D Riverside Drive #261
Sherman Oaks, CA 91423
"Actress"

Georgina Hale
74A St. John's Wood
High Street
London NW8 ENGLAND
"Actress"

Jack Haley, Jr.
1443 Devlin Drive
Los Angeles, CA 90069
"Writer, Producer"

Bill Haley's Comets
9936 Majorca Place
Boca Raton, FL 33434
"Rock & Roll Group"

Anthony Michael Hall
7301 Vista Del Mar #B-101
Playa del Rey, CA 90293
"Actor"

Arsenio Hall
9560 Wilshire Blvd. #516
Beverly Hills, CA 90212
"TV Show Host, Actor"

Fawn Hall
1568 Viewsite Drive
Los Angeles, CA 90069
"Secretary, Model"

Gus Hall
235 West 23rd Street
New York, NY 10011
"Politician"

Huntz Hall
12512 Chandler Blvd. #307
North Hollywood, CA 91607
"Actor"

Jerry Hall
304 West 81st Street
New York, NY 10024
"Model"

Lani Hall
31930 Pacific Coast Highway
Malibu, CA 90265
"Singer, Songwriter"

Monty Hall
519 North Arden Drive
Beverly Hills, CA 90210
"TV Show Host"

Tom T. Hall
P.O. Box 1246
Franklin, TN 37065
"Singer, Songwriter"

Tom Hallick
13900 Tahiti Way #108
Marina del Rey, CA 90292
"Actor"

Holly Hallstrom
5750 Wilshire Blvd. #475-W
Los Angeles, CA 90036
"Model"

Brett Halsey
141 North Grand Avenue
Pasadena, CA 91103
"Actor"

Alan Hamel
8899 Beverly Blvd. #713
Los Angeles, CA 90048
"TV Personality"

Veronica Hamel
129 North Woodburn
Los Angeles, CA 90049
"Actress"

Dorothy Hamill
75490 Fairway Drive
Indian Wells, CA 92210
"Ice Skater"

Mark Hamill
P.O. Box 1051
Santa Monica, CA 90406
"Actor"

Ashley Hamilton
12824 Evanston Street
Los Angeles, CA 90049
"Actor"

Carrie Hamilton
15497 Blue Mesa Road
Gunnison, CO 81230
"Carol Burnett's Daughter"

George Hamilton
139 S. Beverly Drive #330
Beverly Hills, CA 90212
"Actor"

George Hamilton IV
203 SW Third Avenue
Gainesville, FL 32601
"Singer"

Guy Hamilton
22 Mont Port
E-07157 Port d'Andratx
Mallorca, SPAIN
"Film Director"

Josh Hamilton
151 El Camino Drive
Beverly Hills, CA 90212
"Actor"

Kim Hamilton
1229 North Horn Avenue
Los Angeles, CA 90069
"Actress"

Linda Hamilton
8955 Norman Place
West Hollywood, CA 90069
"Actress"

Scott Hamilton
4242 Van Nuys Blvd.
Sherman Oaks, CA 91403
"Ice Skater"

Harry Hamlin
612 North Sepulveda Blvd. #10
Los Angeles, CA 90049
"Actor"

Marvin Hamlisch
970 Park Avenue #501
New York, NY 10028
"Composer, Pianist"

Hammer
80 Swan Way #130
Oakland, CA 94621
"Rap Singer"

John Hammond
P.O. Box 170429
San Francisco, CA 94117
"Singer, Guitarist"

Earl Hamner
11575 Amanda Drive
Studio City, CA 91604
"TV Writer, Producer"

Susan Hampshire
Billing Road
London SW10 ENGLAND
"Actress"

James Hampton
2231 Sunset Plaza Drive
Los Angeles, CA 90069
"Actor, Writer"

Lionel Hampton
44 Rio Vista Drive
Allendale, NJ 07401
"Musician"

Herbie Hancock
3 E. 28th Street #600
New York, NY 10016
"Pianist, Composer"

Tom Hanks
P.O. Box 900
Beverly Hills, CA 90213
"Actor"

Bridget Hanley
16671 Oak View Drive
Encino, CA 91316
"Actress"

Daryl Hannah
Columbia Plaza Bldg. #8-153
Burbank, CA 91505
"Actress"

Hanson
1045 West 78th Street
Tulsa, OK 74132
"Music Trio"

Sir James Hanson
180 Brompton Road
London SW3 1HF ENGLAND
"Film Director"

Otto Harbach
3455 Congress Street
Fairfield, CT 06430
"Lyricist"

Jim Harbaugh
100 South Capital Avenue
Indianapolis, IN 46225
"Football Player"

Anfernee Hardaway
One Magic Place
Orlando, FL 32801
"Basketball Player"

Ernest Harden, Jr.
10653 Riverside Drive
Toluca Lake, CA 91602
"Actor"

Marcia Gay Harden
1358 Woodbrook Lane
Southlake, TX 76092
"Actress"

Melora Hardin
3256 Hiloak Drive
Los Angeles, CA 90068
"Actress"

Jerry Hardin
3033 Vista Crest Drive
Los Angeles, CA 90068
"Actor"

Tonya Harding
121 Morrison Street, NW #1100
Portland, OR 97204
"Ex-Ice Skater"

Kadeem Hardison
19743 Valleyview Drive
Topanga, CA 90290
"Actor"

Billy Hardwick
1576 South White Station
Memphis, TN 38117
"Bowler"

Robert Hardy
Newhall House, Carlops
Midlothian, SCOTLAND
"Actor"

Dorian Harewood
810 Prospect Blvd.
Pasadena, CA 91103
"Actress"

Billy James Hargis
Rose of Sharon Farm
Neosho, MO 64840
"Evangelist"

Mariska Hargitay
924 Westwood Blvd. #900
Los Angeles, CA 90024
"Actress"

Mickey Hargitay
1255 North Sycamore Avenue
Los Angeles, CA 90038
"Actor"

Dean Hargrove
474 Halvern Drive
Los Angeles, CA 90049
"TV Writer, Producer"

Marion Hargrove
401 Monica Avenue #6
Santa Monica, CA 90403
"TV Writer"

Susannah Harker
55 Ashburnham Grove
Greenwich, London
SW10 8UJ ENGLAND
"Actress"

Sen. Tom Harkin (IA)
880 Locust Street #125
Dubuque, IA 52001
"Politician"

John Harkins
121 N. San Vicente Blvd.
Beverly Hills, CA 90211
"Actor"

Harlem Globetrotters
1000 South Fremont Avenue
Alhambra, CA 91803
"Comedy Basketball Team"

Renny Harlin
1642 Westwood Blvd.
Los Angeles, CA 90024
"Director"

Debbie Harmon
13243 Valley Heart
Sherman Oaks, CA 91423
"Actress"

Kelly Harmon
13224 Old Oak Lane
Los Angeles, CA 90049
"Actress"

Manny Harmon
8350 Santa Monica Blvd.
Los Angeles, CA 90069
"Conductor"

Mark Harmon
2236 Encinitas Blvd. #A
Encinitas, CA 92024
"Actor"

Winsor Harmon
1900 Avenue of the Stars #1640
Los Angeles, CA 90067
"Actor"

Magda Harout
13452 Vose Street
Van Nuys, CA 91405
"Actress"

Heather Harper
20 Milverton Road
London NW67AS ENGLAND
"Actress"

Jessica Harper
3454 Glorietta Place
Sherman Oaks, CA 91423
"Actress"

Ron Harper
6767 Forest Lawn Dr. #101
Los Angeles, CA 90068
"Actor"

Tess Harper
8484 Wilshire Blvd. #500
Beverly Hills, CA 90211
"Actress"

Valerie Harper
14 East 4th Street
New York, NY 10012
"Actress"

The Harptones
55 West 119th Street
New York, NY 10026
"Vocal Group"

Woody Harrelson
2387 Kimridge Road
Beverly Hills 90210
"Actor"

Curtis Harrington
6286 Vine Way
Los Angeles, CA 90028
"Film Director"

Pat Harrington
730 Marzella Avenue
Los Angeles, CA 90049
"Actor, Writer"

Bishop Barbara Harris
138 Tremont Street
Boston, MA 02111
"Clergy"

Ed Harris
9434 East Champagne Drive
Sun Lakes, AZ 85248
"Actor"

Emmylou Harris
P.O. Box 158568
Nashville, TN 37215
"Singer, Songwriter"

Franco Harris
200 Chauser Court So.
Sewickley, PA 15143
"Ex-Football Player"

Mrs. Jean Harris
c/o General Delivery
Monroe, NH 03771
"Killed Scarsdale Diet Doctor"

Jonathan Harris
16830 Marmaduke Place
Encino, CA 91316
"Actor"

Julie Harris
132 Barn Hill Road #1267
West Chatham, MA 02669
"Actress"

Mel Harris
6300 Wilshire Blvd. #2110
Los Angeles, CA 90048
"Actress"

Neil Patrick Harris
8942 Wilshire Blvd.
Beverly Hills, CA 90211
"Actor"

Richard Harris
17 Grove Hill Road
London SE5 8DF ENGLAND
"Actor"

Sam Harris
2001 Wayne Avenue #103
San Leandro, CA 94577
"Singer"

Steve Harris
10100 Santa Monica Blvd. #2500
Los Angeles, CA 90067
"Actor"

Susan Harris
11828 La Grange #200
Los Angeles, CA 90025
"TV Producer"

George Harrison
5 Friar Park Road
Henley-On-Thames ENGLAND
"Singer, Songwriter"

Gregory Harrison
151 El Camino Drive
Beverly Hills, CA 90212
"Singer, Songwriter"

Jenilee Harrison
9744 Wilshire Blvd. #203
Beverly Hills, CA 90212
"Actress, Model"

Linda Harrison
211 North Main Street #A
Berlin, MD 21811
"Actress"

Kathryn Harrold
9255 Sunset Blvd. #901
Los Angeles, CA 90069
"Actress"

Donald Harron
P.O. Box 4700
Vancouver B.C. V6B 4A3
CANADA
"TV Show Host"

Lisa Harrow
46 Albermarle Street
London W1X 4PP ENGLAND
"Actress"

Deborah Harry
156 W. 56th Street, 5th Floor
New York, NY 10019
"Singer"

HRH Prince Harry
Highgrove House
Gloucestershire ENGLAND
"Royalty"

Ray Harryhausen
2 Ilchester Place
West Kesington
London ENGLAND
"Special Effect Technician"

Bret "Hit Man" Hart
435 Patina Place S.W.
Calgary Alberto
T3H 2P5 CANADA
"Wrestler"

Cecilia Hart
5750 Wilshire Blvd. #512
Los Angeles, CA 90036
"Actress"

Christopher Hart
6404 Hollywood Blvd. #316
Hollywood, CA 90028
"Actor"

Corey Hart
81 Hymus Blvd.
Montreal, Que. H9R 1E2
CANADA
"Singer, Songwriter"

Mother Dolores
(Dolores Hart)
Regina Laudis Convent
Bethlehem, CT 06751
"Actress, Nun"

Dorothy Hart
43 Martindale Road
Asheville, NC 28804
"Actress"

Freddie Hart
505 Canton Place
Madison, TN 37115
"Singer"

Gary Hart
1999 Broadway #2236
Denver, CO 80202
"Ex-Senator"

Jim Hart
Rt. 6, 21, Brush Hill
Carbondale, IL 62901
"Ex-Football Player"

John Hart
35109 Highway 79 #134
Warner Springs, CA 92086
"Actor"

Mary Hart
150 South El Camino Drive #303
Beverly Hills, CA 90212
"TV Show Host"

Melissa Joan Hart
10880 Wilshire Blvd. #1101
Los Angeles, CA 90024
"Actress"

Mariette Hartley
10110 Empyrean Way #304
Los Angeles, CA 90067
"Actress"

Lisa Hartman-Black
8489 West 3rd Street
Los Angeles, CA 90048
"Actress, Model"

Jim Hartz
475 L'Enfant Plaza
Washington, DC 20024
"TV Show Host"

Paul Harvey
1035 Park Avenue
River Forest, IL 60305
"News Analyst"

PJ HARVEY
193 Joralemon St.
Brooklyn, NY 11201
"Singer"

Rodney Harvey
9057A Nemo Street
West Hollywood, CA 90069
"Actor"

Ernie Harwell
2121 Trumbull Avenue
Detroit, MI 48216
"Sportscaster"

Eugene Hasenfus
c/o General Delivery
Marinette, WI 54143
"Ex-Flight Master"

Peter Haskell
19924 Acre Street
Northridge, CA 91324
"Actor"

Dennis Haskins
1735 Peyton Avenue #303
Burbank, CA 91504
"Actor"

King Hassan II
Royal Palace
Rabat, MOROCCO
"Royalty"

David Hasselhoff
5180 Louise Avenue
Encino, CA 91316
"Actor"

Marilyn Hassett
8905 Rosewood Avenue
Los Angeles, CA 90048
"Actress"

Signe Hasso
582 S. Orange Grove Avenue
Los Angeles, CA 90036
"Actress"

Bob Hastings
620 S. Sparks Street
Burbank, CA 91505
"Actor"

Sen. Orrin G. Hatch (UT)
Senate Russell Bldg. #131
Washington, DC 20510
"Politician"

Richard Hatch
3349 Cahuenga Blvd. W. #1
Los Angeles, CA 90068
"Actor"

Teri Hatcher
10100 Santa Monica Blvd. #410
Los Angeles, CA 90067
"Actress"

Bobby Hatfield
599 Camillo Street
Sierra Madre, CA 90124
"Singer"

Hurd Hatfield
Ballinterry House
Rathcormac, County Cork
IRELAND
"Actor"

Juliana Hatfield
1 Camp Street, #2
Cambridge, MA 02140
"Singer"

Noah Hathaway
144 S. Beverly Drive #405
Beverly Hills, CA 90212
"Actor"

Rutger Hauer
32 Sea Colony Drive
Santa Monica, CA 90405
"Actor"

Wings Hauser
9450 Chivers Avenue
Sun Valley, CA 91352
"Actor"

President Vaclav Havel
Hradecek
CZ-11908 Prague
CZECHOSLOVAKIA REPUBLIC
"Politician"

Richie Havens
123 West 44th Street #11A
New York, NY 10036
"Singer, Guitarist"

John Havlicek
24 Beech Road
Weston, CT 02193
"Ex-Basketball Player"

June Haver
485 Halvern Drive
Los Angeles, CA 90049
"Actress"

Nigel Havers
125 Gloucester Road
London SW7 ENGLAND
"Actor"

June Havoc
405 Old Long Ridge Road
Stamford, CT 06903
"Actress"

Ethan Hawke
1775 Broadway #701
New York, NY 10019
"Actor"

Edwin Hawkins
2041 Locust Street
Philadelphia, PA 19103
"Singer"

Sophie B. Hawkins
550 Madison Avenue, #2500
New York, NY 10022
"Singer"

John Hawksworth
24 Cottersmore Gardens #2
London W8 ENGLAND
"TV Writer, Producer"

Goldie Hawn
1491 Capri
Pacific Palisades, CA 90272
"Actress"

Nigel Hawthorne
Radwell Grange, Baldock
Hertfordshire SG7 5EU ENGLAND
"Actor"

Tom Hayden
10951 W. Pico Blvd. #202
Los Angeles, CA 90064
"Politician"

Julie Hayek
5645 Burning Tree Drive
La Canada, CA 91011
"Actress, Model"

Salma Hayek
P.O. Box 57593
Sherman Oaks, CA 91403
"Actress"

Bill Hayes
4528 Beck Avenue
North Hollywood, CA 91602
"Actor"

Bob Hayes
13901 Preston Valley Place
Dallas, TX 75240
"Ex-Football Player"

Elvin Hayes
252 Piney Point Road
Houston, TX 77024
"Ex-Basketball Player"

Isaac Hayes
504 West 168th Street
New York, NY 10032
"Singer, Songwriter"

Patricia Hayes
20 West Hill Road
London SW18 ENGLAND
"Actress"

Peter Lind Hayes
3538 Pueblo Way
Las Vegas, NV 89109
"Actor, Comedian"

Susan Seaforth Hayes
4528 Beck Avenue
North Hollywood, CA 91602
"Actress"

Jim Haynie
10519 Troon Avenue
Los Angeles, CA 90064
"Actor"

Robert Hays
6310 San Vicente Blvd. #310
Los Angeles, CA 90048
"Actor"

Dennis Haysbert
3624 Canyon Crest Road
Altadena, CA 91001
"Actor"

Brooke Hayward
305 Madison Avenue #956
New York, NY 10165
"Author, Actress"

Jonathan Haze
3636 Woodhill Canyon
Studio City, CA 91604
"Actor"

Glenne Headley
8942 Wilshire Blvd.
Beverly Hills, CA 90211
"Actress"

Mary Healy
3538 Pueblo Way
Las Vegas, NV 89109
"Actress"

George Hearn
200 West 57th Street #900
New York, NY 10019
"Actor"

Tommy Hearns
3645 Pama Lane
Las Vegas, NV 89120
"Boxer"

Patricia Hearst
110-5th Street
San Francisco, CA 94103
"Author"

Mrs. Victoria Hearst
865 Comstock Avenue #168
Los Angeles, CA 90024
"Wife of William Hearst"

Heart
151 El Camino Drive
Beverly Hills, CA 90212
"Rock & Roll Group"

Patricia Heaton
8949 Sunset Blvd. #201
Los Angeles, CA 90069
"Actress"

Ann Heche
1122 S. Roxbury Drive
Los Angeles, CA 90035
"Actress"

Jessica Hecht
9150 Wilshire Blvd. #175
Beverly Hills, CA 90212
"Actress"

Gina Hecht-Herskowitz
5930 Foothill Drive
Los Angeles, CA 90068
"Actress"

Eileen Heckart
1223 Foxboro Drive
Norwalk, CT 06851
"Actress"

Tippi Hedren
P.O. Box 189
Acton, CA 93510
"Actress"

Hee Haw
P.O. Box 140400
Nashville, TN 37214
"Comedy Show"

Howell Heflin
311 East 6th Street
Tuscumbia, AL 35674
"Politician"

Christie Hefner
680 North Lake Avenue
Chicago IL 60611
"Hugh Hefner's Daughter"

Hugh Hefner
10236 Charing Cross Road
Los Angeles, CA 90077
"Publishing Executive"

Robert Hegyes
2404 Pacific Avenue
Venice, CA 90291
"Actor"

Eric Heiden
82 Sandburg Drive
Sacramento, CA 95819
"Skater"

Katherine Heigl
924 Westwood Blvd. #900
Los Angeles, CA 90024
"Actress"

Carol Heiss
809 Lafayette Drive
Akron, OH 44303
"Actress"

Marg Helgenberger
8942 Wilshire Blvd.
Beverly Hills, CA 90211
"Actress"

Levon Helm
192 Lexington Ave. #1204
New York, NY 10016
"Actor"

Katherine Helmond
5570 Old Highway 395 N.
Carson City, NV 89701
"Actress, Director"

Sen. Jesse Helms (NC)
403 Everett Dirksen Bldg.
Washington, DC 20510
"Politician"

Leona Helmsley
Park Lane Hotel
36 Central Park South
New York, NY 10019
"Hotel Executive"

Mariel Hemingway
P.O. Box 2249
Ketchum, ID 83340
"Actress"

David Hemmings
P.O. Box 5836
Sun Valley, ID 83340
"Actor, Director"

Sherman Hemsley
15043 Valley Heart Drive
Sherman Oaks, CA 91403
"Actor"

Florence Henderson
P.O. Box 11295
Marina del Rey, CA 90295
"Singer, Actor"

Rickey Henderson
10561 Englewood Drive
Oakland, CA 94621
"Baseball Player"

Skitch Henderson
Hunt Hill Farm
RFD #3 Upland Road
New Milford, CT 06776
"Composer, Conductor"

Thomas "Hollywood" Henderson
7 Seafield Lane
Westhampton Beach, NY 11978
"Ex-Football Player"

Lauri Hendler
4034 Stone Canyon Avenue
Sherman Oaks, CA 91403
"Actress"

Heike Henkel
Tannenbergstr. 57
D-51373 Leverkusen
GERMANY
"Track Athlete"

Don Henley
8942 Wilshire Blvd.
Beverly Hills, CA 90211
"Singer, Songwriter"

Marilu Henner
2101 Castilian
Los Angeles, CA 90068
"Actress"

Linda Kaye Henning
843 N. Sycamore Avenue
Los Angeles, CA 90038
"Actress"

Tom Henrich
1547 Albino Trail
Dewey, AZ 86327
"Ex-Baseball Player"

Lance Henriksen
9540 Dale Avenue
Sunland, CA 91040
"Actor"

Clarence "Frogman" Henry
3309 Lawrence Street
New Orleans, LA 70114
"Singer, Guitarist"

Buck Henry
117 East 57th Street
New York, NY 10019
"Writer, Producer"

Gregg Henry
8956 Appian Way
Los Angeles, CA 90046
"Actor"

Justin Henry
3 Clark Lane
Rye, NY 10580
"Child Actor"

Lenny Henry
294 Earl's Court Road
London SW5 9BB ENGLAND
"Actor"

Pamela Hensley
9526 Dalegrove Drive
Beverly Hills, CA 90210
"Actress"

Natasha Henstridge
12358 1/2 Ventura Blvd. #331
Studio City, CA 91604
"Actress"

Hans Werner Henze
La Leprara
via Del Fontonile
00047 Marino ITALY
"Composer, Conductor"

Richard Herd
P.O. Box 56297
Sherman Oaks, CA 91413
"Actor"

Jerry Herman
10847 Bellagio Road
Los Angeles, CA 90077
"Composer, Lyricist"

Herman's Hermits
11761 E. Speedway Blvd.
Tucson, AZ 85748
"Rock & Roll Group"

Pee Wee Herman
P.O. Box 29373
Los Angeles, CA 90029
"Actor"

Keith Hernandez
255 East 49th Street #28-D
New York, NY 10017
"Ex-Baseball Player"

Lynn Herring
21919 W. Canyon Drive
Topanga, CA 90291
"Actress"

Barbara Hershey
9830 Wilshire Blvd.
Beverly Hills, CA 90211
"Actress"

Oral Hershiser
1638 Via Tuscany
Winter Park, FL 32789
"Baseball Player"

Irene Hervey
c/o Jones
78-825 Osage Trail
Indian Wells, CA 92210
"Actress"

Jason Hervey
1755 Seaview Trail
Los Angeles, CA 90046
"Actor"

Eva Herzigova
107 Greene Street #200
New York, NY 10012
"Model"

Werner Herzog
Turkenstr. 91
D-80799 Munich 40 GERMANY
"Film Director"

Whitey Herzog
9426 Sappington Estates Dr.
St. Louis, MO 63127
"Baseball Manager"

Howard Hesseman
7146 La Presa
Los Angeles, CA 90068
"Actor, Director"

Charlton Heston
2859 Coldwater Canyon
Beverly Hills, CA 90210
"Actor, Director"

Christopher Hewett
1422 North Sweetzer #110
Los Angeles, CA 90069
"Actor, Director"

Don Hewitt
555 West 57th Street
New York, NY 10019
"Writer, Producer"

Jennifer Love Hewitt
4215 Glencoe Avenue #200
Marina del Rey, CA 90292
"Actress"

Martin Hewitt
2396 Fitzgerald Road
Simi Valley, CA 93065
"Actor"

Arthur Hewlett
10 Heath Drive
London NW3 ENGLAND
"Actor"

Donald Hewlett
Old King's Head
Whitstable, Kent ENGLAND
"Actor"

Thor Heyerdahl
E-38500 Guimar
(Tenerife) SPAIN
"Ethnologist, Explorer"

Anne Heywood
9966 Liebe Drive
Beverly Hills, CA 90210
"Actress"

Dwayne Hickman
P.O. Box 3352
Santa Monica, CA 90403
"Actor"

Catherine Hicks
15422 Brownwood Place
Los Angeles, CA 90077
"Actress"

Dan Hicks
P.O. Box 5481
Mill Valley, CA 94942
"Singer, Songwriter"

Jack Higgins
Septembertide
Mont De La Rocqque
Jersey Channel Islands
ENGLAND
"Writer"

Joel Higgins
24 Old Hill Road
Westport, CT 06880
"Actor"

Gerald Hiken
910 Moreno Avenue
Palo Alto, CA 94303
"Actor"

Hildegarde
230 East 48th Street
New York, NY 10017
"Singer"

Tommy Hilfiger
25 W. 39th St. #1300
New York, NY 10018
"Fashion Designer"

Anita Hill
300 Timberdell Road
Norman, OK 73019
"Professor of Law"

Arthur Hill
1515 Clubview Drive
Los Angeles, CA 90024
"Actor"

Faith Hill
480 Glen Arbor Circle
Cordova, TN 37018
"Singer"

Grant Hill
3777 Lapeer Road
Auburn Hills, MI 48057
"Basketball Player"

Steven Hill
18 Jill Lane
Monsey, NY 10952
"Actor"

Terrence Hill
P.O. Box 818
Stockbridge, MA 01262
"Actor"

Sir Edmund Hillary
278A Remuera Road
Auckland SE2 NEW ZEALAND
"Mountaineer"

Arthur Hiller
1218 Benedict Canyon
Beverly Hills, CA 90210
"Film Director"

Dame Wendy Hiller
Beaconsfield
Stratton Road
Buckinghamshire ENGLAND
"Actress"

John Hillerman
P.O. Box 218
Blue Jay, CA 92317
"Actor"

Carla Hills
3125 Chain Bridge Road NW
Washington, DC 20018
"Ex-Government Official"

Barron Hilton
28775 Sea Ranch Way
Malibu, CA 90265
"Hotel Executive"

John Hinckley, Jr.
St. Elizabeth's Hospital
2700 Martin Luther King Avenue
Washington, DC 20005
"Attempted to kill Ronald Reagan"

Gregory Hines
377 West 11th Street, PH. 4-A
New York, NY 10014
"Actor"

Mimi Hines
1605 South 11th Street
Las Vegas, NV 89109
"Actress"

Pat Hingle
P.O. Box 2228
Carolina Beach, NC 28428
"Actor"

Jurgen Hingsen
655 Circle Dr.
Santa Barbara, CA 93108
"Decathlon Athlete"

Martina Hingus
Seidenbbaum, Truebbach
CH-9477 SWITZERLAND
"Tennis Player"

Darby Hinton
4138 Troost Avenue
Studio City, CA 91604
"Actor"

James David Hinton
2808 Oak Point Drive
Los Angeles, CA 90068
"Actor"

S.E. Hinton
8955 Beverly Blvd.
Los Angeles, CA 90048
"Screenwriter"

Thora Hird
21 Leinster Mews
Lancaster Gate
London W2 3EX ENGLAND
"Actress"

Hiroshima
1460 4th Street #205
Santa Monica, CA 90401
"Jazz Group"

Elroy Hirsch
1440 Monroe Street
Madison, WI 53711
"Actor"

Judd Hirsch
888-7th Avenue #602
New York, NY 10017
"Actor"

Al Hirschfield
122 East 95th Street
New York, NY 10028
"Caricaturist"

Al Hirt
3530 Rue Delphine
New Orleans, LA 70131
"Trumpeter"

Shere Hite
PO Box 1037
New York, NY 10028
"Actress"

Don Ho
277 Lewers
Honolulu, HI 96814
"Singer, Songwriter"

Tony Hoare
430 Edgware Road
London W2 1EH ENGLAND
"Playwright"

Rose Hobart
23388 Mulholland Drive
Woodland Hills, CA 91364
"Actress"

Valerie Hobson
Old Barn Cottage
Upton Gey
Hampshire RG25 2RM
ENGLAND
"Actress"

David Hockney
2029 Century Park E. #300
Los Angeles, CA 90067
"Artist"

Patricia Hodge
76 Oxford Street
London W1N OAX ENGLAND
"Actress"

Stephanie Hodge
141 El Camino Drive #205
Beverly Hills, CA 90212
"Actress"

Joy Hodges
P.O. Box 1252
Cathedral City, CA 92235
"Actress"

Syd Hoff
P.O. Box 2463
Miami Beach, FL 33140
"Cartoonist"

James Hoffa, Jr.
2593 Hounds Chase Drive
Troy, MI 48096
"Union Leader"

Alice Hoffman
3 Hurlbut Street
Cambridge, MA 02138
"Screenwriter"

Basil Hoffman
4456 Cromwell
Los Angeles, CA 90027
"Actor"

Dustin Hoffman
1926 Broadway #305
New York, NY 10023
"Actor"

Isabella Hoffmann
121 N. San Vicente Blvd.
Beverly Hills, CA 90211
"Actress"

Susanna Hoffs
3575 Cahuenga Blvd. W. #450
Los Angeles, CA 90068
"Singer"

Hulk Hogan
130 Willadel Drive
Belleair, FL 34616
"Wrestler"

Paul Hogan
515 N. Robertson Blvd.
Los Angeles, CA 90048
"Actor"

Robert Hogan
344 West 89th Street #1B
New York, NY 10024
"Actor"

Drake Hogestyn
25370 1/2 Malibu Road
Malibu, CA 90265
"Actor"

Hal Holbrook
9100 Hazen Drive
Beverly Hills, CA 90210
"Actor"

Christopher Holder
733 N. Seward Street PH
Los Angeles, CA 90038
"Actor"

Sue Holderness
10 Rectory Close, Windsor
Berks. SL4 5ER ENGLAND
"Actress"

Hole
955 S. Carrillo Dr. #200
Los Angeles, CA 90048
"Grunge Band"

Hope Holiday
8538 Eastwood Road
Los Angeles, CA 90046
"Actress"

Xaviera Hollander
Stadionweg 17
1077 RU Amsterdam HOLLAND
"Author"

Lauren Holley
13601 Ventura Blvd. #99
Sherman Oaks, CA 91423
"Actress"

Polly Holliday
888-7th Avenue #2500
New York, NY 10106
"Actress"

Earl Holliman
4249 Bellingham Avenue
Studio City, CA 91604
"Actor"

Sen. Ernest F. Hollings (SC)
125 Russell Senator Office Bldg.
Washington, DC 20510
"Politician"

Celeste Holm
88 Central Park West
New York, NY 10023
"Actress"

Ian Holm
46 Albermarle Street
London W1X 4PP ENGLAND
"Actor"

Clint Holmes
697 Middle Neck Road
Great Neck, NY 11023
"Actor"

Jennifer Holmes
P.O. Box 6303
Carmel, CA 93921
"Actress"

Katie Holmes
217 E. Alameda Avenue #203
Burbank, CA 91502
"Actress"

Larry Holmes
101 Larry Holmes Drive #101
Easton, PA 18042
"Ex-Boxing Champion"

Jack Holt, Jr.
504 Temple Drive
Harrah, OK 73045
"Actor"

Lou Holtz
P.O. Box 518
Nortre Dame, IN 46556
"Football Coach"

Evander Holyfield
794 Highway 279
Fairburn, GA 30213
"Boxer"

Red Holzman
408 Oceanpoint Avenue
Cedarhurst, NY 11516
"Ex-Baseball Manager"

Honeymoon Suite
Box 70 - Station C
Queens St. West
Toronto, Ontario
M6J 3M7 CANADA
"Rock & Roll Group"

Dr. Hook
P.O. Box 121017
Nashville, TN 37212
"Rock & Roll Group"

John Lee Hooker
P.O. Box 170429
San Francisco, CA 94117
"Singer"

Benjamin Hooks
260 Fifth Avenue
New York, NY 10001
"Ex-N.A.A.C.P. President"

Jan Hooks
151 El Camino Drive
Beverly Hills, CA 90212
"Actress"

Kevin Hooks
P.O. Box 36D58
Los Angeles, CA 90036
"Actor, Director"

Robert Hooks
145 North Valley Street
Burbank, CA 91505
"Actor"

Burt Hooten
3619 Grandby Court
San Antonio, TX 78217
"Ex-Baseball Player"

Hootie & The Blowfish
917 Huger Street
Columbia, SC 29201
"Music Group"

William Hootkins
16 Berners Street
London W1 ENGLAND
"Actor"

Bob Hope
10346 Moopark
North Hollywood, CA 91602
"Actor, Comedian"

Dolores Hope
10346 Moopark
North Hollywood, CA 91602
"Mrs. Bob Hope"

Leslie Hope
151 El Camino Drive
Beverly Hills, CA 90212
"Actress"

Anthony Hopkins
7 High Park Road
Kew, Surrey TW9 3BL ENGLAND
"Actor"

Bo Hopkins
6620 Ethel Avenue
North Hollywood, CA 91606
"Actor"

Telma Hopkins
4122 Don Luis Drive
Los Angeles, CA 90008
"Actress, Singer"

Dennis Hopper
9830 Wilshire Blvd.
Beverly Hills, CA 90212
"Actor, Director"

Lena Horne
23 East 74th Street
New York, NY 10021
"Singer"

Marilyn Horne
165 West 57th Street
New York, NY 10019
"Mezzo-Soprano"

Harry Horner
728 Brooktree Road
Pacific Palisades, CA 90272
"Film Director"

Paul Hornung
5800 Creighton Hill Road
Louisville, KY 40207
"Ex-Football Player"

Bruce Hornsby
P.O. Box 3545
Williamburg, VA 23187
"Rock & Roll Group"

David Horowitz
P.O. Box 49915
Los Angeles, CA 90049
"TV Show Host"

Anna Maria Horsford
P.O. Box 48082
Los Angeles, CA 90048
"Actress"

Lee Horsley
15054 East Dartmouth
Aurora, CO 80014
"Actor"

Peter Horton
9560 Wilshire Blvd. #500
Beverly Hills, CA 90212
"Actor"

Robert Horton
5317 Anadsol Avenue
Encino, CA 91316
"Actor"

Willie Horton
15124 Warwick Street
Detroit, MI 48223
"Ex-Baseball Player"

Bob Hoskins
200 Fulham Road
London SW10 9PN ENGLAND
"Actor"

Robert Hossein
33 rue Galilee
75116 Paris, FRANCE
"Actor"

Richard C. Hottelet
120 Chestnut Hill Road
Wilton, CT 06897
"News Correspondent"

Dee Hoty
333 West 56th Street
New York, NY 10019
"Actress"

Charlie Hough
2266 Shade Tree Circle
Brea, CA 92621
"Ex-Baseball Manager"

John Hough
8 Queen Street
London W1X 7PH ENGLAND
"Film Director"

James Houghton
8585 Walnut Drive
Los Angeles, CA 90046
"Actor, Writer"

Katharine Houghton
165 W. 46th Street #1214
New York, NY 10036
"Actress"

Ralph Houk
3000 Plantation Road
Winter Haven, FL 33884
"Ex-Baseball Manger"

Jerry Houser
3236 Benda Street
Los Angeles, CA 90068
"Actor"

Cissy Houston
2160 North Central Road
Ft. Lee, NJ 07024
"Singer"

Thelma Houston
4296 Mount Vernon
Los Angeles, CA 90008
"Singer"

Whitney Houston
2160 North Central Road
Ft. Lee, NJ 07024
"Singer"

Arliss Howard
P.O. Box 9078
Van Nuys, CA 91409
"Actress"

Clint Howard
449 N. Florence Street
Burbank, CA 91505
"Actor"

Ken Howard
11718 Barrington Court #300
Los Angeles, CA 90049
"Actor"

Rance Howard
4286 Clybourne Avenue
Burbank, CA 91505
"Actor, Writer"

Ron Howard
9830 Wilshire Blvd.
Beverly Hills, CA 90210
"Actor, Director"

Susan Howard
P.O. Box 1456
Boerne, TX 78006
"Actress"

Traylor Howard
9560 Wilshire Blvd. #516
Beverly Hills, CA 90212
"Actor"

Gordie Howe
6645 Peninsula Drive
Traverse City, MI 49684
"Ex-Hockey Player"

Michael Howe
7 Floral Street
London WC2 ENGLAND
"Actor, Singer, Dancer"

Steve Howe
230 E. Union Street
Pasadena, CA 91101
"Guitarist"

C. Thomas Howell
151 El Camino Drive
Beverly Hills, CA 90212
"Actor"

Anne Howells
Milestone, Broomclose
Esher, Surrey, ENGLAND
"Opera Singer"

Sally Ann Howes
265 Liverpool Road
London N1 1LX ENGLAND
"Actress"

Freddie Hubbard
17609 Ventura Blvd. #212
Encino, CA 91316
"Musician"

Hubcaps
P.O. Box 1388
Dover, DE 19003
"Rock & Roll Group"

Season Hubley
46 Wavecrest Avenue
Venice, CA 90291
"Actress"

Whip Hubley
9000 Sunset Blvd #1200
Los Angeles, CA 90069
"Actor"

Cooper Huckabee
1800 East Cerrito Place #34
Los Angeles, CA 90068
"Actor"

David Huddleston
3518 Cahuenga Blvd. W. #216
Los Angeles, CA 90068
"Actor"

Bill Hudson
7023 Birdview
Malibu, CA 90265
"Singer, Actor"

Hudson Brothers
151 El Camino Drive
Beverly Hills, CA 90212
"Vocal Group"

Ernie Hudson
5711 Hoback Glen Road
Hidden Hills, CA 91302
"Actor"

Hues Corporation
1560 Broadway #1308
New York, NY 10036
"Vocal Trio"

Matthias Hues
3151 Cahuenga Blvd. W. #300
Los Angeles, CA 90068
"Actor"

Brent Huff
2203 Ridgemont Drive
Los Angeles, CA 90046
"Actor"

Billy Hufsey
14315 Crystal Creek Drive
Strongsville, OH 44136
"Actor"

Daniel Hugh-Kelly
130 West 42nd Street #2400
New York, NY 10036
"Actor"

Barnard Hughes
250 West 94th Street
New York, NY 10025
"Actor"

Finola Hughes
270 North Canon Drive #1064
Beverly Hills, CA 90210
"Actress"

Irene Hughes
500 N. Michigan Avenue #1039
Chicago, IL 60611
"Journalist"

Kathleen Hughes
8818 Rising Glen Place
Los Angeles, CA 90069
"Actress"

Miko Hughes
924 Westwood Blvd. #900
Los Angeles, CA 90024
"Actor"

Wayne H. Huizenga
One Blockbuster Plaza
Ft. Lauderdale, FL 33301
"Blockbuster Video Owner"

Thomas Hulce
175 - 5th Avenue #2409
New York, NY 10010
"Actor"

Bobby Hull
1439 S. Indiana Avenue
Chicago, IL 60605
"Hockey Player"

Britt Hume
3100 "N" St. NW #9
Washington, DC 20007
"News Correspondent"

Mary Margaret Humes
P.O. Box 1168-714
Studio City, CA 91604
"Actress, Model"

Englebert Humperdinck
10100 Sunset Blvd.
Los Angeles, CA 90077
"Singer"

Renee Humphrey
346 E. 63rd Street #4A
New York, NY 10021
"Actress"

Leann Hunley
1888 North Crescent Heights
Los Angeles, CA 90069
"Actress, Model"

Gayle Hunnicutt
174 Regents Park Road
London NW1 ENGLAND
"Actress"

Bonnie Hunt
9830 Wilshire Blvd.
Beverly Hills, CA 90212
"Actress"

Helen Hunt
9171 Wilshire Blvd. #406
Beverly Hills, CA 90210
"Actress"

Lamar Hunt
1601 Elm #2800
Dallas, TX 75021
"Football Team Owner"

Marsha Hunt
13131 Magnolia Blvd.
Sherman Oaks, CA 91423
"Actress"

Holly Hunter
19528 Ventura Blvd. #343
Tarzana, CA 91356
"Actress"

Jim "Catfish" Hunter
RR #1, Box 895
Hertford, NC 27944
"Ex-Baseball Player"

Kim Hunter
42 Commerce Street
New York, NY 10014
"Actress"

Rachel Hunter
23 Beverly Park
Beverly Hills, CA 90210
"Model"

Tab Hunter
223 North Guadalupe Street #292
Santa Fe, NM 87501
"Actor"

Isabelle Huppert
10 Avenue George V
75008 Paris, FRANCE
"Actress"

Douglas Hurd
5 Mitford Cottages, Westwell
Burford Oxon ENGLAND
"Government Official"

Gale Ann Hurd
270 North Canon Drive #1195
Beverly Hills, CA 90210
"Film Producer"

Elizabeth Hurley
3 Cromwell Place
London SW 2JE ENGLAND
"Model"

Rick Hurst
1230 North Horn #401
Los Angeles, CA 90069
"Actor"

John Hurt
46 Albermarle Street
London W1X 4PP ENGLAND
"Actor"

William Hurt
151 El Camino Drive
Beverly Hills, CA 90212
"Actor"

Ferlin Husky
1030 N. Woodland Drive
Kansas City, MO 64118
"Singer, Songwriter"

Rick Husky
13565 Lucca Dive
Pacific Palisades, CA 90272
"Actor, Writer, Producer"

King Hussein I
P.O. Box 1055
Amman, JORDAN
"Royalty"

Saddam Hussein
Al-Sijoud Palace
Baghdad, IRAQ
"Politician"

Olivia Hussey
4872 Topanga Canyon Blvd. #301
Woodland Hills, CA 91364
"Actress"

Ruth Hussey
3361 Don Pablo Drive
Carlsbad, CA 92008
"Actress"

Angelica Huston
57 Windward Avenue
Venice, CA 90291
"Actress"

Will Hutchins
P.O. Box 371
Glen Head, NY 11545
"Actor"

Sen. Kay Bailey Hutchinson(TX)
703 Hart Bldg.
Washington, DC 20510
"Politician"

Betty Hutton
Harrison Avenue
Newport, RI 02840
"Actress"

Danny Hutton
2437 Horseshoe Canyon Road
Los Angeles, CA 90046
"Singer, Songwriter"

Lauren Hutton
382 Lafayette Street #6
New York, NY10003
"Actress, Model"

Timothy Hutton
RR 2, Box 3318
Cushman Road
Patterson, NY 12563
"Actor"

Laura Huxley
6233 Mulholland Drive
Los Angeles, CA 90068
"Author"

Joe Hyams
10375 Wilshire Blvd. #4D
Los Angeles, CA 90024
"Author"

Peter Hyams
P.O. Box 10
Basking Ridge, NJ 07929
"Writer, Producer"

Alex Hyde-White
8271 Melrose Avenue #110
Los Angeles, CA 90046
"Actor"

Earle Hyman
484 West 43rd Street #33E
New York, NY 10036
"Actor"

Kenneth Hyman
Sherwood House
Tilehouse Lane
Denham, Bucks. ENGLAND
"Film Executive"

Joyce Hyser
10100 Santa Monica Blvd. #2500
Los Angeles, CA 90067
"Actress"

Lee Iacocca
30 Scenic Oaks
Bloomfield Hills, MI 48304
"Automobile Executive"

Ice Cube
(Oshea Jackson)
2155 Van Wick Street
Los Angeles, CA 90047
"Rap Singer, Actor"

Ice Tea
2287 Sunset Plaza Drive
Los Angeles, CA 90069
"Rap Singer, Actor"

Eric Idle
900 Allen, 7th Level
Glendale, CA 91201
"Actor, Director"

Billy Idol
7314 Woodrow Wilson Drive
Los Angeles, CA 90046
"Singer, Songwriter"

Julio Iglesias
5 Indian Creek Drive
Miami Beach, FL 33154
"Singer"

Rev. Ike
4140 Broadway
New York, NY 10004
"Evangelist"

Iman
111 East 22nd Street #200
New York, NY 10010
"Model"

Gary Imhoff
3500 West Olive Avenue #1400
Burbank, CA 91505
"Actor"

Don Imus
34-12 36th Street
Astoria, NY 11106
"Radio Talk Show Host"

Indigo Girls
315 Ponce DeLeon Avenue #755
Decatur, GA 30030
"Music Group"

Marty Ingels
701 North Oakhurst Drive
Beverly Hills, CA 90210
"Actor"

James Ingram
867 Muirfield Road
Los Angeles, CA 90005
"Singer"

John Inman
51A Oakwood Road
London NW11 6RJ ENGLAND
"Actor"

The Ink Spots
5100 DuPont Blvd. #10A
Ft. Lauderdale, FL 33308
"Vocal Group"

Roy Innis
800 Riverside Drive #6E
New York, NY 10032
"Activist"

Sen. Daniel Inouye (HI)
Senate Hart Bldg. #722
Washington, DC 20510
"Politician"

INXS
8 Hayes St.
#1 Neutray Bay
NSW 20891 AUSTRALIA
"Rock & Roll Group"

Kathy Ireland
P.O. Box 5353
Santa Barbara, CA 93150
"Model"

Donnie Iris
807 Darlington Road
Beaver Falls, PA 15010
"Singer"

Iron Butterfly
6400 Pleasant Park Drive
Chanhassen, MN 55317
"Rock & Roll Group"

Iron Maiden
1775 Broadway #433
New York, NY 10019
"Rock & Roll Group"

Jeremy Irons
200 Fulham Road
London SW10 9PN ENGLAND
"Actor"

Michael Ironside
2145 Sunset Crest Drive
Studio City, CA 91604
"Actor"

Monte Irvin
11 Douglas Court South
Homosassa, FL 32646
"Ex-Baseball Player"

Amy Irving
7920 Sunset Blvd. #400
Los Angeles, CA 90046
"Actress"

Michael Irving
1 Cowboy Parkway
Irving, TX 78063
"Football Player"

Hale Irwin
2801 Stonington Place
St. Louis, MO 63131
"Golfer"

Peter Isaacksen
4635 Placidia Avenue
North Hollywood, CA 91602
"Actor"

Chris Isaak
1655 38th Avenue
San Francisco, CA 94122
"Singer"

Isley Brothers
4229 Montieth Drive
Los Angeles, CA 90043
"R&B Group"

Ragib Ismail
332 Center Street
El Segundo, CA 90245
"Football Player"

Lance A. Ito
825 So. Madison Avenue
Pasadena, CA 91106
"Judge"

Zeljko Ivanek
145 West 45th Street #1204
New York, NY 10036
"Actor"

Dana Ivey
10100 Santa Monica Blvd. #2500
Los Angeles, CA 90067
"Actress"

Judith Ivey
15760 Ventura Blvd. #1730
Encino, CA 91436
"Actress"

James Ivory
250 W. 57th Street #1913-A
New York, NY 10019
"Actor"

Alan Jackson
1101 17th Avenue So.
Nashville, TN 37212
"Singer"

Anne Jackson
90 Riverside Drive
New York, NY 10024
"Actress"

Barry Jackson
29 Rathcoole Avenue
London N8 9LY ENGLAND
"Actor"

Bo Jackson
1765 Old Shell Road
Mobile, AL 36604
"Ex-Football & Baseball Player"

Donald Jackson
1080 Brocks
South Pickering
Ontario, CANADA

Freddie Jackson
231 West 58th Street
New York, NY 10019
"Singer"

Glenda Jackson
59 Fifth Street
London W1 ENGLAND
"Actress"

Janet Jackson
14755 Ventura Blvd. #1-170
Sherman Oaks, CA 91403
"Singer, Songwriter"

Jeremy Jackson
4444 Lankershim Blvd., #207
North Hollywood, CA 91602
"Singer"

Jermaine Jackson
4641 Hayvenhurst Avenue
Encino, CA 91316
"Singer, Songwriter"

Rev. Jesse Jackson
400 "T" Street N.W.
Washington, DC 20001
"Politician, Evangelist"

Rep. Jesse Jackson, Jr. (IL)
312 Cannon House Office Bldg.
Washington, DC 20515
"Son of Jesse Jackson"

Joe Jackson
6 Pembridge Road
Trinity House #200
London W11 ENGLAND
"Singer, Songwriter"

Jonathan Jackson
1825 North Pass Avenue
Burbank, CA 91505
"Actor"

Joshua Jackson
8211 Melrose Avenue #200
Los Angeles, CA 90046
"Actor"

Kate Jackson
P.O. Box 57593
Sherman Oaks, CA 91403
"Actress"

LaToya Jackson
30 Daniel Low Terrace #3-R
Staten Island, NY 10301
"Singer, TV Show Host"

Marlon Jackson
4641 Hayvenhurst Avenue
Encino, CA 91316
"Singer"

Mary Jackson
2055 Grace Avenue
Los Angeles, CA 90068
"Actress"

Mary Ann Jackson
1242 Alessandro Drive
Newbury Park, CA 91320
"Actress"

Maynard Jackson
68 Mitchell
Atlanta, GA 30303
"Ex-Mayor of Atlanta, GA"

Melody Jackson
6269 Selma Avenue #15
Los Angeles, CA 90028
"Actress"

Michael Jackson
Neverland Ranch
Los Olivos, CA 93441
"Singer, Songwriter"

Michael Jackson
1420 Moraga Drive
Los Angeles, CA 90049
"Talk Show Host"

Paul Jackson, Jr.
40 West 57th Street
New York, NY 10019
"Actor"

Phil Jackson
980 N. Michigan Avenue #1600
Chicago, IL 60611
"Basketball Coach"

Randy Jackson
4641 Hayvenhurst Drive
Encino, CA 91316
"Singer"

Rebbie Jackson
4641 Hayvenhurst Drive
Encino, CA 91316
"Singer"

Reggie Jackson
305 Amador Avenue
Seaside, CA 93955
"Ex-Baseball Player"

Samuel L. Jackson
5128 Encino Avenue
Encino, CA 91316
"Actor"

Sherry Jackson
4933 Encino Avenue
Encino, CA 91316
"Actress"

Stonewall Jackson
6007 Cloverland Drive
Brentwood, TN 37027
"Singer, Songwriter

Stoney Jackson
1602 North Fuller Avenue #102
Los Angeles, CA 90046
"Actor"

Tito Jackson
23726 Long Valley Road
Hidden Hills, CA 91302
"Singer"

Victoria Jackson
14631 Balgowan Road #2-5
Hialeah, FL 33016
"Actress"

Wanda Jackson
P.O. Box 891498
Oklahoma City, OK 73189
"Singer"

Sir Derek Jacobi
22 Chisham Road
London SW4 ENGLAND
"Actor"

Lou Jacobi
c/o William Morris
1325 Avenue of the Americas
New York, NY 10019
"Actor"

Lawrence-Hilton Jacobs
3804 Evans #2
Los Angeles, CA 90027
"Actor"

Billy Jacoby
P.O. Box 46324
Los Angeles, CA 90046
"Actor"

Laura Jacoby
P.O. Box 46324
Los Angeles, CA 90046
"Actress"

Scott Jacoby
P.O. Box 461100
Los Angeles, CA 90046
"Actor"

Henry Jaffe
7920 Sunset Blvd. #400
Los Angeles, CA 90046
"Film Producer"

Bianca Jagger
530 Park Avenue #18-D
New York, NY 10021
"Actress, Model"

Mick Jagger
304 West 81st Street
New York, NY 10024
"Singer"

Henry Jaglom
609 E. Channel Road
Santa Monica, CA 90402
"Actor"

John Jakes
19 West 44th Street #711
New York, NY 10036
"Author"

Ahmad Jamal
1995 Broadway #501
New York, NY 10023
"Musician"

Anthony James
1801 Avenue of the Stars #1250
Los Angeles, CA 90067
"Actor"

Clifton James
95 Buttonwood Drive
Dix Hills, NY 11746
"Actor"

Etta James
16409 Sally Lane
Riverside, CA 92504
"Singer"

Godfrey James
The Shack, Western Road
Pevensey Bay
East Sussex ENGLAND
"Actor"

John James
P.O. Box #9
Cambridge, NY 12816
"Actor"

Joni James
P.O. Box 7027
Westchester, IL 60154
"Singer"

Baroness P.D. James
37A Goldhawk Rd.
London W12 8QQ ENGLAND
"Writer"

Rick James
421 S. Beverly Dr. 8th Flr.
Beverly Hills, CA 90212
"Singer"

Sheila James-Kuehl
3201 Pearl Street
Santa Monica, CA 90405
"Actress"

Sonny James
818 - 18th Avenue
Nashville, TN 37203
"Singer, Songwriter"

Tommy James
Box 3074, Allwood Sta.
Clifton, NJ 07012
"Singer"

Paulene Jameson
7 Warrington Gardens
London W9 ENGLAND
"Actress"

Mae Jamison
P.O. Box 580317
Houston, TX 77258
"Astronaut"

Jan & Dean
1720 North Ross Street
Santa Ana, CA 92706
"Vocal Duo"

Jane's Addiction
8800 Sunset Blvd. #401
Los Angeles, CA 90069
"Rock & Roll Group"

Conrad Janis
1434 N. Genesee Avenue
Los Angeles, CA 90069
"Actor"

Dan Jansen
5040 S. 76th Street
Greenfield, WI 53220
"Ice Skater"

Famke Janssen
345 N. Maple Drive #397
Beverly Hills, CA 90210
"Actress"

Don January
14316 Hughes Lane
Dallas, TX 75240
"Golfer"

Lois January
225 North Crescent Drive #103
Beverly Hills, CA 90210
"Actress"

Lee Janzen
7512 Dr. Phillips Blvd. #50-906
Orlando, FL 32819
"Golfer"

Al Jardine
P.O. Box 36
Big Sur, CA 93920
"Singer, Musician"

Claude Jarman, Jr.
16 Tamai Vista Lane
Kentfield, CA 94904
"Actor"

Maurice Jarre
27011 Sea Vista Drive
Malibu, CA 90265
"Composer"

Al Jarreau
29171 Grayfox Street
Malibu, CA 90265
"Musician"

Tom Jarrell
77 West 66th Street
New York, NY 10023
"News Correspondent"

Gen.Wojciech Jaruzelski
ul Klonowa 1
009909 Warsaw, POLAND
"Military, Politician"

Graham Jarvis
15351 Via De Las Olas
Pacific Palisades, CA 90272
"Actor"

Lucy Jarvis
171 West 57th Street
New York, NY 10019
"TV Executive, Producer"

David Jason
25 Whitehall
London SWIA 2BS ENGLAND
"Actor"

Jason & The Scorchers
P.O. Box 1200235
Nashville, TN 37212
"Rock & Roll Group"

Harvey Jason
1280 Sunset Plaza Drive
Los Angeles, CA 90069
"Writer"

Sybil Jason
P.O. Box 40024
Studio City, CA 91604
"Actress"

Terry Jastrow
13201 Old Oak Lane
Los Angeles, CA 90049
"Director, Producer"

Michael Jayston
60 St. James's Street
London SW1 ENGLAND
"Actor"

**D.J. Jazzy Jeff &
The Fresh Prince**
298 Elizabeth Street #100
New York, NY 10012
"Rap Duo"

Gloria Jean
20309 Leadwell
Canoga Park, CA 91303
"Actress"

Marianne Jean-Baptiste
83-93 Shepparton Road
London MI 3DF ENGLAND
"Actress"

Anne Jeffreys
121 South Bentley Avenue
Los Angeles, CA 90049
"Actress"

Herb Jeffries
P.O. Box C
River Edge, NJ 07601
"Singer"

Lionel Jeffries
Guild House
Upper St. Martin's Lane
London WC2H 9EG ENGLAND
"Actor, Director"

Richard Jeni
9454 Wilshire Blvd. #405
Beverly Hills, CA 90212
"Comedian"

Carol Mayo Jenkins
606 North Larchmont Blvd. #309
Los Angeles, CA 90004
"Actress"

Hayes Alan Jenkins
809 Lafayette Drive
Akron, OH 44303
"Skater"

Jackie "Butch" Jenkins
Rt. #6, Box 541-G
Fairview, NC 28730
"Actor"

Bruce Jenner
P.O. Box 11137
Beverly Hills, CA 90213
"Athlete, Actor"

Peter Jennings
77 West 66th Street
New York, NY 10023
"News Anchor"

Waylon Jennings
824 Old Hickory Blvd.
Brentwood, TN 37027
"Singer, Songwriter"

Salome Jens
1716 Ridgedale Avenue
Los Angeles, CA 90026
"Actress"

Adele Jergens Langan
32108 Village 32
Camarillo, CA 93010
"Actress"

Michael Jeter
10100 Santa Monica Blvd. #2500
Los Angeles, CA 90067
"Actor"

Jethro Tull
2 Wansdown Place, Fulham
London SW6 ENGLAND
"Rock & Roll Goup"

Joan Jett
155 East 55th Street #6H
New York, NY 10022
"Rock & Roll Group"

Jewel
P.O. Box 33494
San Diego, CA 92163
"Singer"

Norman Jewison
3000 W. Olympic Blvd. #1314
Santa Monica, CA 90404
"Director, Producer"

Ann Jillian
151 El Camino Drive
Beverly Hills, CA 90212
"Actress, Singer"

Joyce Jilson
64 East Concord Street
Orlando, FL 32801
"Astrologer, Columnist"

Jim & Jesse
P.O. Box 27
Gallatin, TN 37066
"C&W Group"

Marlene Jobert
8-10 Blvd. de Courcelles
75008 Paris, FRANCE
"Actress"

Steve Jobs
900 Chesapeake Drive
Redwood City, CA 94063
"Computer Executive"

Billy Joel
280 Elm Street
Southampton, NY 11968
"Singer, Songwriter"

David Johanssen
200 West 58th Street
New York, NY 10019
"Actor"

Sir Elton John
Woodside
Crump Hill Road
Old Windsor, Berkshire ENGLAND
"Singer, Songwriter"

Pope John Paul II
Palazzo Apostolico Vaticano
Vatican City, ITALY
"Pope"

Tommy John
1585 Medina Rd.
Long Lake, MN 55356
"Ex-Baseball Player"

Gordon Johncock
1042 Becker Rd.
Hastings, MI 49058
"Race Car Driver"

Johnny Hates Jazz
321 Fulham Road
London ZW10 9QL ENGLAND
"Rock & Roll Group"

Glynis Johns
121 North San Vicente Blvd.
Beverly Hills, CA 90211
"Actress"

Anne-Marie Johnson
3500 W. Olive Avenue #1400
Burbank, CA 91505
"Actress"

Arte Johnson
2725 Bottlebrush Drive
Los Angeles, CA 90024
"Actor, Comedian"

Ben Johnson
926 Stonehaven Avenue
New Market, Ontario
L3X 1K7 CANADA
"Runner"

Brad Johnson
9830 Wilshire Blvd.
Beverly Hills, CA 90212
"Actor"

Don Johnson
P.O. Box 6909
Burbank, CA 91510
"Actor"

Earvin "Magic" Johnson
9100 Wilshire Blvd. #1060
Beverly Hills, CA 90212
"Ex-Basketball Player"

Georgann Johnson
218 North Glenroy Place
Los Angeles, CA 90049
"Actress"

Jill Johnson
43 Matheson Road
London W14 ENGLAND
"Actress"

Jimmy Johnson
2269 N.W. 199th Street
Miami, FL 33056
"Football Coach"

Kevin Johnson
201 East Jefferson Street
Phoenix, AZ 85004
"Basketball Player"

Kristin Johnson
8033 Sunset Blvd. #4020
Los Angeles, CA 90046
"Actress"

Lamont Johnson
900 Alameda Avenue
Monterey, CA 93940
"Director, Producer"

Laura Johnson
1917 Weepah Way
Los Angeles, CA 90046
"Actress"

Mrs. Lady Bird Johnson
LBJ Ranch Stonewall
Austin, TX 78701
"Ex-First Lady"

Lucie Baines Johnson
170 Crescent Road
Torontom Ont. M4W 1V2
CANADA
"Ex-President's Daughter"

Lynn-Holly Johnson
405 W. Riverside Drive #200
Burbank, CA 91506
"Actress"

Michael Johnson
3101 Iris Avenue #215
Boulder, CO 80301
"Track & Field"

Michelle Johnson
10100 Santa Monica Blvd. #2500
Los Angeles, CA 90067
"Actress"

Rafer Johnson
6071 Bristol Parkway #100
Culver City, CA 90230
"Actor"

Richard Johnson
18-21 Jermyn Street
London SW1Y 6NB ENGLAND
"Actor"

Russell Johnson
P.O. Box 11198
Bainbridge Island, WA 98110
"Actor"

Van Johnson
405 East 54th Street
New York, NY 10022
"Actor"

Lynn Johnston
3420 Main St. #700
Kansas City, MO 64111
"Cartoonist"

Tom Johnston Band
P.O. Box 878
Sonoma, CA 95476
"Rock & Roll Group"

Angelina Jolie
13340 Galewood Drive
Sherman Oaks, CA 91423
"Actress"

Chuck Jones
P.O. Box 2319
Costa Mesa, CA 92628
"Animated Cartoon Producer"

Davey Jones
P.O. Box 400
Beavertown, PA 17813
"Singer, Actor"

Dean Jones
500 N. Buena Vista
Burbank, CA 91521
"Actor"

Deacon Jones
1817 Crowchild Trail NW
Calgary, Alberta
T2M 4R6 CANADA
"Ex-Football Player"

Dub Jones
223 Glendale
Rusten, LA 71270
"Actor"

Gemma Jones
3 Goodwins Court
London WC2 ENGLAND
"Actor"

George Jones
Route #3, Box 150
Murphy, NC 28906
"Singer, Songwriter"

The Jones Girls
P.O. Box 6010, #761
Sherman Oaks, CA 91413
"Vocal Group"

Grace Jones
89 Fifth Avenue, 7th Floor
New York, NY 10003
"Model, Actress"

Dame Gwyneth Jones
P.O. Box 380
8040 Zurich SWITZERLAND
"Soprano"

Henry Jones
502 - 9th Street
Santa Monica, CA 90402
"Actor"

Howard Jones
Box 185, High Wycom.
Bucks. HP11 2E2 ENGLAND
"Singer, Songwriter"

Jack Jones
78-825 Osage Trail
Indian Wells, CA 92210
"Singer, Actor"

James Earl Jones
P.O. Box 610
Pawling, NY 12564
"Actor"

Janet Jones
9100 Wilshire Blvd. #1000W
Beverly Hills, CA 90212
"Actress"

Jeffrey Jones
3450 Wonder View Dr.
Los Angeles, CA 90068
"Actor"

Jenny Jones
454 North Columbus Drive
Chicago, IL 60611
"Talk Show Host"

L.Q. Jones
2144 1/2 N. Cahuenga Blvd.
Los Angeles, CA 90068
"Actor, Director"

Marcia Mae Jones
4541 Hazeltine Avenue #4
Sherman Oaks, CA 91423
"Actress"

Marilyn Jones
P.O. Box 69405
Los Angeles, CA 90069
"Actress"

Mick Jones
279 Central Park W. #19A
New York, NY 10024
"Actor"

Parnelli Jones
P.O. Box "W"
Torrance, CA 90507
"Race Car Driver"

Paula Jones
1 Third Place
Long Beach, CA 90802
"Sexual Harrassment Accuser"

Quincy Jones
3800 Barham Blvd. #503
Los Angeles, CA 90068
"Composer, Producer"

Rickie Lee Jones
476 Broome Street, #6A
New York, NY 10013
"Singer, Songwriter"

Sam J. Jones
10000 Santa Monica Blvd. #305
Los Angeles, CA 90067
"Actor"

Shirley Jones
701 North Oakhurst Drive
Beverly Hills, CA 90210
"Actress"

Star Jones
10877 Wilshire Blvd. #900
Los Angeles, CA 90024
"TV Reporter"

Terry Jones
68A Delancey Street
London NW1 7RY ENGLAND
"Actor, Writer, Director"

Tom Jones
4130 Stanbury Avenue
Sherman Oaks, CA 91403
"Singer"

Tommy Lee Jones
P.O. Box 966
San Saba, TX 76877
"Actor"

Trevor Jones
46 Avenue Road
Highgate,
London N6 5DR England
"Actor"

Erica Jong
121 Davis Hills Road
Weston, CT 06883
"Poet, Author"

The Jordanaires
1300 Divison Street #205
Nashville, TN 37203
"Music Group"

Hamilton Jordan
333 Main Avenue West
Nashville, TN 37902
"Former Government Offical"

James Carroll Jordan
8333 Lookout Mountain Avenue
Los Angeles, CA 90046
"Actor"

Lee Roy Jordan
2425 Burbank
Dallas, TX 75235
"Ex-Football Player"

Michael Jordan
676 N. Michigan Avenue #2940
Chicago, IL 60611
"Basketball Player"

Montel Jordan
250 West 57th Street #821
New York, NY 10107
"Singer"

Stanley Jordan
9000 Sunset Blvd. #1200
Los Angeles, CA 90069
"Guitarist"

Vernon E. Jordan, Jr.
1333 New Hampshire Ave. NW
#400
Washington, DC 20036
"Politician"

William Jordan
10806 Lindbrook Avenue #4
Los Angeles, CA 90024
"Actor"

Jackie Joseph
111 North Valley
Burbank, CA 91505
"Actress, Writer"

Jeffrey Joseph
121 North San Vicente Blvd.
Beverly Hills, CA 90211
"Actor"

Erland Josephson
Valhallavagen 10
11-422 Stockholm, SWEDEN
"Actor"

Louis Jourdan
1139 Maybrook
Beverly Hills, CA 90210
"Actor"

Journey
650 California Street #900
San Francisco, CA 94108
"Rock & Roll Group"

Milla Jovovich
23 Watts Street #600
New York, NY 10013
"Model, Actress"

Brenda Joyce
161040 S. Queens Drive #44
Bend, OR 90210
"Actress"

Elaine Joyce
724 North Roxbury Drive
Beverly Hills, CA 90210
"Actress"

Odette Joueux
1 rue Seguier
75006 Paris, FRANCE
"Writer"

Jackie Joyner-Kersee
P.O. Box 2220
Winnetka, CA 91396
"Track & Field Athlete"

Wally Joyner
P.O. Box 512
Rancho Santa Fe, CA 92067
"Ex-Baseball Player"

Judas Priest
3 East 54th, #1400
New York, NY 10022
"Music Group"

Ashley Judd
P.O. Box 680339
Franklin, TN 37068
"Actress"

Naomi Judd
P.O. Box 682068
Franklin, TN 37068
"Singer"

Gordon Jump
3285 Minnesota Avenue
Costa Mesa, CA 92625
"Actor, Director"

Katy Jurado
Apartado Postal 209
Cuernavaca, Moro. MEXICO
"Actress"

Peter Jurasik
969 1/2 Manzanita St.
Los Angeles, CA 90029
"Actor"

Sonny Jurgensen
P.O. Box 53
Mt. Vernon, VA 22121
"Ex-Football Player"

Charlie Justice
P.O. Box 819
Cherryville, NC 28021
"Violinist"

David Justice
40 Point Ridge
Atlanta, GA 30328
"Baseball Player"

K.C. & The Sunshine Band
4770 Biscayne Blvd., PH
Miami, FL 33137
"Rock & Roll Group"

Jim Kaat
2806 SE Dune Dr. #1208
Stuart, FL 34496
"Ex-Baseball Player"

Pauline Kael
2 Berkshire Heights Raod
Great Barrington, MA 02130
"Film Critic, Author"

Brian "Kato" Kaelin
8383 Wilshire Blvd. #954
Beverly Hills, CA 90211
"OJ's Ex-House Guest"

David Kagen
6457 Firmament Avenue
Van Nuys, CA 91406
"Actor"

Madeline Kahn
975 Park Avenue #9A
New York, NY 10028
"Actress, Singer"

Marvin Kalb
79 John F. Kennedy Street
Cambridge, MA 01238
"Journalist"

Patricia Kalember
1999 Avenue of the Stars #2850
Los Angeles, CA 90067
"Actress"

Al Kaline
945 Timberlake Drive
Bloomfield Hills, MI 48013
"Ex-Baseball Player"

Helena Kallianides
12830 Mulholland Drive
Beverly Hills, CA 90210
"Actress, Writer, Director"

Herbert Kalmbach
1056 Santiago Drive
Newport Beach, CA 92660
"Watergate Participant"

Stanley Kamel
9300 Wilshire Blvd. #410
Beverly Hills, CA 90210
"Actor"

Steve Kampmann
801 Alma Real
Pacific Palisades, CA 90272
"Actor, Writer"

Steven Kanaly
4663 Grand Avenue
Ojai, CA 93023
"Actor"

John Kander
12203 Octagon St.
Los Angeles, CA 90049
"Writer"

Bob Kane
8455 Fountain Avenue #725
Los Angeles, CA 90069
"Cartoonist"

Big Daddy Kane
151 El Camino Drive
Beverly Hills, CA 90212
"Rap Singer"

Carol Kane
8106 Santa Monica Blvd. #1426
Los Angeles, CA 90046
"Actress"

Fay Kanin
653 Ocean Front
Santa Monica, CA 90402
"Screenwriter"

Garson Kanin
210 Central Park South
New York, NY 10019
"Writer, Producer"

Stan Kann
570 North Rossmore Avenue
Los Angeles, CA 90004
"Actor"

Hal Kanter
15941 Woodvale Road
Encino, CA 91316
"Writer, Producer"

Mickey Kanter
5019 Klingle Street NW
Washington, DC 20016
"U.S. Trade Representative"

Gabriel Kaplan
9551 Hidden Valley Road
Beverly Hills, CA 90210
"Comedian, Actor"

Jonathan Kaplan
2413 Canyon Oak Dr.
Los Angeles, CA 90069
"Director"

Marvin Kaplan
7600 Claybeck Avenue
Burbank, CA 91505
"Actor"

Valerie Kapriski
10 Avenue George V
F-75008 Paris FRANCE
"Actress"

Mitzi Kapture
4705 Ruffin Road
San Diego, CA 92123
"Actress"

Donna Karan
550-7th Avenue #1500
New York, NY 10018
"Fashion Designer"

Kym Karath
2267 Roscomare Road
Los Angeles, CA 90077
"Actress"

Robert Kardashian
9722 Wendover Drive
Beverly Hills, CA 90212
"Attorney"

James Karen
4455 Los Feliz Blvd. #807
Los Angeles, CA 90027
"Actor"

John Karlen
911 - 2nd Street #16
Santa Monica, CA 90403
"Actor"

Fred Karlin
1187 Coast Village Road #1-339
Montecito, CA 93108
"Composer, Conductor"

Phil Karlson
3094 Patricia Avenue
Los Angeles, CA 90064
"Director"

Richard Karn
1317 Fifth Street #200
Santa Monica, CA 90401
"Actor"

Bela Karolyi
RR #1-Box 140
Huntsville, TX 77340
"Gymnastic Coach"

Anatoly Karpov
Luzhnetskaya 8
Moscow 119270 RUSSIA
"Chess Champion"

Alex Karras
7943 Woodrow Wilson Drive
Los Angeles, CA 90046
"Ex-Football Player, Actor"

Yousuf Karsh
1 Rideau Street
Ottawa Ontario
K1N 9S7 CANADA
"Photographer"

Lawrence Kasdan
10345 West Olympic Blvd.
Los Angeles, CA 90064
"Director, Producer"

Casey Kasem
138 North Mapleton Drive
Los Angeles, CA 90077
"Radio-TV Personality"

Jean Kasem
138 North Mapleton Drive
Los Angeles, CA 90077
"Radio-TV Personality"

John Kassir
P.O. Box 5617
Beverly Hills, CA 90210
"Comedian"

Dr. Irene Kassorla
10231 Charing Cross Road
Los Angeles, CA 90077
"Psychologist, Author"

William Katt
23508 Canzonet Street
Woodland Hills, CA 91367
"Actor"

Julie Kavner
25154 Malibu Road #2
Malibu, CA 90265
"Actress"

Charles Kay
18 Epple Road
London SW6 ENGLAND
"Actor"

Dianne Kay
1559 Palisades Drive
Pacific Palisades, CA 90272
"Actress"

Lila Kaye
47 Courtfield Road #9
London SW7 4DB ENGLAND
"Actress"

Melvina Kaye
P.O. Box 6085
Burbank, CA 90510
"Singer"

Lainie Kazan
9903 Santa Monica Blvd #283
Beverly Hills, CA 90212
"Singer, Actress"

James Keach
P.O. Box 548
Agoura, CA 91376
"Actor"

Stacy Keach, Jr.
27525 Winding Way
Malibu, CA 90265
"Actor"

Stacy Keach, Sr.
8749 Sunset Blvd.
Los Angeles, CA 90069
"Actor"

Jean Kean
28128 West Pacific Coast Hwy.
Malibu, CA 90265
"Actress"

Staci Keanan
8730 Sunset Blvd. #220W
Los Angeles, CA 90069
"Actress"

Bill Keane
5815 E. Joshua Tree Lane
Paradise Valley, AZ 85253
"Cartoonist"

Diane Keane
23 Primrose Hill
Charleton Mackrell
Summerset ENGLAND
"Actress"

James Keane
10206 Camarillo Place #6
North Hollywood, CA 91602
"Actor"

Michael Kearns
1616 Garden Street
Glendale, CA 91201
"Actor"

Diane Keaton
1015 N. Roxbury Drive
Beverly Hills, CA 90210
"Actress, Director"

Michael Keaton
11901 Santa Monica Blvd. #547
Los Angeles, CA 90025
"Actor"

Lila Kedrova
50 Forest Manor Road #3
Willowdale Ontario
M2J 1M1 CANADA
"Actress"

Don Keefer
4146 Allot Avenue
Sherman Oaks, CA 91423
"Actor"

Howard Keel
394 Red River Road
Palm Desert, CA 92211
"Actor, Singer"

William Keene
435 29th Street
Manhattan Beach, CA 90266
"Actor"

Catherine Keener
7920 Sunset Blvd. #400
Los Angeles, CA 90069
"Actress"

Bob Keeshan
(Capt. Kangaroo)
40 West 57th Street #1600
New York, NY 10019
"TV Show Host"

Garrison Keillor
45 E. 7th Street
St. Paul, MN 55101
"Author, Radio Personality"

Betty Lou Keim
10642 Arnel Place
Chatsworth, CA 91311
"Actress"

David Keith
9595 Wilshire Blvd. #801
Beverly Hills, CA 90212
"Actor"

Penelope Keith
66 Berkeley House
Hay Hill
London SW3 ENGLAND
"Actress"

Robert Kelker-Kelly
4544 Van Noord Avenue
Studio City, CA 91604
"Actor"

George Kell
P.O. Box 70
Swifton, AR 72471
"Ex-Baseball Player"

Marthe Keller
5 rue St. Dominique
75007 Paris, FRANCE
"Actress"

Mary Page Keller
151 El Camino Drive
Beverly Hills, CA 90212
"Actress"

Sally Kellerman
7944 Woodrow Wilson Drive
Los Angeles, CA 90046
"Actress"

DeForrest Kelley
415 N. Camden Drive #121
Beverly Hills, CA 90210
"Actor"

Kitty Kelley
3037 Dunbarton Avenue NW
Washington, DC 20007
"Author"

Sheila Kelley
10390 Santa Monica Blvd. #300
Los Angeles, CA 90025
"Actress"

Barbara Kelly
5 Kidderpore Avenue
London NW3 7SX ENGLAND
"Actress"

David Kelley
2210 Wilshire Blvd. #998
Santa Monica, CA 90403
"Actor"

Moira Kelly
P.O. Box 5617
Beverly Hills, CA 90210
"Actress"

Paula Kelly
7020 La Presa Drive
Los Angeles, CA 90068
"Actress, Dancer"

Roz Kelly
5614 Lemp Avenue
North Hollywood, CA 91601
"Actress"

Linda Kelsey
500 S. Sepulveda Blvd. #500
Los Angeles, CA 90049
"Actress"

Ed Kemmer
11 Riverside Drive #17PE
New York, NY 10022
"Actor"

Jack Kemp
1776 "I" Street NW #800
Washington, DC 20006
"Ex-Football Player, Politician"

Jeremy Kemp
Danbury Street #6A
London N18 JJ ENGLAND
"Actor"

Shawn Kemp
190 Queen Anne Avenue N.
Suite #200
Seattle, WA 98109
"Basketball Player"

Suzy Kendall
Dentham House #4
Hampstead
NW 3 ENGLAND
"Actress"

Justice Anthony Kennedy
1-1st Street N.E.
Washington, DC 20543
"Supreme Court Justice"

Burt Kennedy
13138 Magnolia Blvd.
Sherman Oaks, CA 91423
"Film Writer, Director"

Caroline Kennedy-Schlosseberg
641 6th Avenue
New York, NY 10011
"Ex-President's Daughter"

Sen. Edward Kennedy (MA)
315 Russell Office Bldg.
Washington, DC 20510
"Politician"

Ethel Kennedy
1147 Chain Bridge Road
McLean, VA 22101
"Mrs. Robert Kennedy"

George Kennedy
10100 Santa Monica Blvd. #2500
Los Angeles, CA 90067
"Actor"

Jayne Kennedy-Overton
224 Barbour Street
Playa del Rey, CA 90293
"Actress, Model"

John F. Kennedy, Jr.
20 North Moore Street
New York, NY 10013
"Ex-President's Son"

Rep. Joseph Kennedy II (MA)
122 Longworth House Bldg.
Washington, DC 20510
"Politician"

Leon Isaac Kennedy
9427 Via Monique
Burbank, CA 91504
"Actor, Producer"

Mimi Kennedy
9000 Sunset Blvd. #1200
Los Angeles, CA 90069
"Actress"

Nigel Kennedy
9A Penzance Place
London W11 4PE ENGLAND
"Violinist"

Robert F. Kennedy, Jr.
78 North Broadway
White Plains, NY 10603
"Robert Kennedy's Son"

Ted Kennedy, Jr.
636 Chain Bridge Road
McLean, VA 22101
"Sen. Ted Kennedy's Son"

Mr. Kenneth
19 East 54th Street
New York, NY 10022
"Hairstylist"

Patsy Kensit
132 Loundoun Road
St. John's Woods
London NW8 OND ENGLAND
"Actress"

Jean Kent
2-4 Noel Street
London W1V 3RB ENGLAND
"Actress"

Lord Philip Kentner
1 Mallord Street
London SW3 ENGLAND
"Musician"

Kentucky Headhunters
212 Third Avenue North #301
Nashville, TN 37201
"Music Group"

Shell Kepler
3123 Belden Drive
Los Angeles, CA 90068
"Actress"

Ken Kercheval
P.O. Box 325
Goshen, KY 40026
"Actor"

Kirk Kerkorian
4835 Koval Lane
Las Vegas, NV 89109
"Business Executive"

Joanna Kerns
P.O. Box 49216
Los Angeles, CA 90049
"Actress"

Sandra Kerns
620 Resolano Drive
Pacific Palisades, CA 90272
"Actress"

Deborah Kerr
Los Monteras
E-29600 Marbella
Malaga, SPAIN
"Actress"

Jean Kerr
1 Beach Avenue
Larchmont, NY 10538
"Dramatist"

John Kerr
2975 Monterey Road
San Marino, CA 91108
"Actor"

Sen. Robert Kerrey (NE)
Senate Hart Bldg. #303
Washington, DC 20510
"Politician"

Nancy Kerrigan
7 Cedar Avenue
Stoneham, MA 02180
"Ice Skater"

Sen. John Kerry (MA)
Senate Russell Bldg. #421
Washington, DC 20510
"Politician"

Sammy Kershaw
817 18th Avenue South
Nashville, TN 37203
"Singer"

Irwin Kershner
424 Sycamore Road
Santa Monica, CA 90402
"Director"

Brian Kerwin
304 W. 81st Street #2
New York, NY 10024
"Actor"

Hank Ketcham
P.O. Box 1997
Monterey, CA 93942
"Cartoonist"

Dave Ketchum
2318 Waterby Street
Westlake Village, CA 91361
"Writer, Producer"

Dr. Jack Kevorkian
4870 Lockhart Street
West Bloomfield, MI 48323
"Assists with Suicide "

Ted Key
1694 Glenhardie Road
Wayne, PA 19087
"Cartoonist"

Dr. Alan Keyes
1030 - 15th Street NW #700
Washington, DC 20005
"Talk Show Host"

Evelyn Keyes
999 North Doheny Drive #509
Los Angeles, CA 90069
"Actress"

Mark Keyloun
1320 N. Laurel #18
West Hollywood, CA 90048
"Actor"

Chaka Khan
P.O. Box 16680
Beverly Hills, CA 90209
"Singer"

Princess Yasmin Khan
146 Central Park West
New York, NY 10023
"Royalty"

Adnan Khashoggi
P.O. Box 6
Riyadh SAUDIA-ARABIA
"Arms Dealer"

Victor Kiam II
60 Main Street
Bridgeport, CT 06602
"Business Executive"

Sidney Kibrick
711 North Oakhurst Drive
Beverly Hills, CA 90210
"Actor"

Jason Kidd
777 Sports Street
Dallas, TX 75207
"Basketball Player"

Michael Kidd
1614 Old Oak Road
Los Angeles, CA 90049
"Actor, Dancer"

Margot Kidder
220 Pine Creek Road
Livingston, MT 59047
"Actress"

Nicole Kidman
333 North Maple Drive #135
Beverly Hills, CA 90210
"Actress"

Richard Kiel
40356-T Oak Park Way
Oakhurst, CA 93644
"Actor"

Richard Kiley
Ryerson Road
Warwick, NY 10990
"Actor"

Merle Kilgore
P.O. Box 850
Paris, TN 38242
"Singer, Songwriter"

Harmon Killebrew
P.O. Box 14550
Scottsdale, AZ 85267
"Ex-Baseball Player"

Jean-Claude Killey
13 Chemin Bellefontaine
1223 Cologny GE SWITZERLAND
"Skier"

Val Kilmer
P.O. Box 362
Tesuque, NM 87574
"Actor"

Eric Kilpatrick
6330 Simpson Avenue #3
North Hollywood, CA 91606
"Actor"

James L. Kilpatrick
White Walnut Hill
Woodville, VA 22749
"Columnist, Journalist"

Lincoln Kilpatrick
1710 Garth Avenue
Los Angeles, CA 90035
"Actor"

Ward Kimball
8910 Ardendale Avenue
San Gabriel, CA 91775
"Animation Director"

Bruce Kimmel
12230 Otsego Street
North Hollywood, CA 91607
"Writer, Director"

Richard Kind
1345 N. Hayworth Avenue #112
Los Angeles, CA 90046
"Actor"

Roslyn Kind
8871 Burton Way, #303
Los Angeles, CA 90048
"Actress"

Alan King
888-7th Avenue, 38th Floor
New York, NY 10106
"Comedian, Actor"

Andrea King
1225 Sunset Plaza Drive #3
Los Angeles, CA 90069
"Actress"

B.B. King
1414 Sixth Avenue
New York, NY 10019
"Singer, Guitarist"

Ben E. King
P.O. Box 1094
Teaneck, NJ 07666
"Singer, Songwriter"

Billie Jean King
445 N. Wells #404
Chicago, IL 60610
"Tennis Player"

Cammie Conlon King
511 Cypress Street, #2
Ft. Bragg, CA 95437
"Actress"

Carole King
509 Hartnell Street
Monterey, CA 93940
"Singer, Songwriter"

Coretta Scott King
234 Sunset Avenue N.W.
Atlanta, GA 30314
"Mrs. Martin Luther King, Jr."

Don King
871 W. Oakland Blvd.
Ft. Lauderdale, FL 33311
"Fight Promoter"

Evelyn "Champagne" King
2746 N. Green Valley Pkwy., #499
Las Vegas, NV 89014
"Singer"

Larry King
10801 Lockwood Drive #230
Silver Springs, MD 20901
"TV Talk Show Host"

Mabel King
23388 Mulholland Drive
Woodland Hills, CA 91364
"Actress"

Morgana King
504 W. 168th Street
New York, NY 10032
"Singer"

Perry King
3647 Wrightwood Drive
Studio City, CA 91604
"Actor"

Regina King
9229 Sunset Blvd. #315
Los Angeles, CA 90069
"Actress"

Rodney King
9100 Wilshire Blvd. #250-W
Beverly Hills, CA 90212
"Beaten Motorist"

Stephen King
47 West Broadway
Bangor, ME 04401
"Novelist"

Zalman King
1393 Rose Avenue
Venice, CA 90291
"Writer"

Roger Kingdom
322 Mall Blvd. #303
Monroeville, PA 15146
"Track & Field Athlete"

Ben Kingsley
Stratford Upon Avon
New Penworth House
Warwickshire 0V3 7QX
ENGLAND
"Actor"

The Kingsmen
1720 North Ross Avenue
Santa Ana, CA 92706
"Rock & Roll Group"

Alex Kingston
9255 Sunset Blvd. #710
Los Angeles, CA 90069
"Actress"

The Kingston Trio
P.O. Box 34397
San Diego, CA 92103
"Vocal Trio"

The Kinks
29 Rushton Mews
London W11 1RB ENGLAND
"Rock & Roll Group"

Kathleen Kinmont
6651 Vineland Avenue,
No. Hollywood, CA 91606
"Actress"

Greg Kinnear
3000 W. Alameda Ave., #2908
Burbank CA 91523
"Actor"

Michael Kinsley
5602 Lakeview Drive #J
Kirkland, WA 98033
"Political Commentator"

Nastassja Kinski
1000 Bel Air Place
Los Angeles, CA 90077
"Actress, Model"

Bruce Kirby
629 N. Orlando Avenue #3
Los Angeles, CA 90048
"Actor"

Durward Kirby
29 Pheasant Ridge Road
Ossinging, NY 10562
"Screenwriter"

Phyllis Kirk
321-M South Beverly Drive
Beverly Hills, CA 90212
"Actress"

Clare Kirkconnell
515 South Irving Blvd.
Los Angeles, CA 90020
"Actress"

Gelsey Kirkland
191 Silver Moss Drive
Vero Beach, FL 32963
"Dancer"

Lane Kirkland
815-16th Street N.W.
Washington, DC 20006
"Union Executive"

Sally Kirkland
151 El Camino Drive
Beverly Hills, CA 90212
"Actress"

Terry Kiser
9911 West Pico Blvd. #1060
Los Angeles, CA 90035
"Actor, Comedian"

KISS
8730 Sunset Blvd. #175
Los Angeles, CA 90069
"Rock & Roll Group"

Dr. Henry Kissinger
435 East 52nd Street
New York, NY 10022
"Politician"

Tawny Kitaen
650 Town Center Drive #1000
Costa Mesa, CA 92626
"Actress"

Michael Kitchen
4 Windmill Street
London W1P 1HF ENGLAND
"Actor"

Tom Kite
5999 Long Champ Court
Austin, TX 78746
"Golfer"

Eartha Kitt
125 Boulder Ridge Road
Scarsdale, NY 10583
"Singer, Actress"

Franz Klammer
Mooswald 22
A-9712 Friesach, AUSTRIA
"Skier"

Calvin Klein
205 West 39th Street
New York, NY 10018
"Fashion Designer"

Robert Klein
67 Ridge Crest Road
Briarcliff, NY 10510
"Comedian, Actor"

Werner Klemperer
44 West 62nd Street, 10th Floor.
New York, NY 10023
"Actor"

Kevin Kline
1636 3rd Avenue #309
New York, NY 10128
"Actor"

Richard Kline
14322 Mulholland Drive
Los Angeles, CA 9007
"Actor"

Don Klosterman
2220 Avenue of the Stars #2502
Los Angeles, CA 90067
"Ex-Football Player"

Patricia Klous
18095 Karen Drive
Encino, CA 91316
"Actress"

Jack Klugman
22548 Pacific Coast Highway
Malibu, CA 90265
"Actor, Writer"

Evel Knievel
160 East Flamingo Road
Las Vegas, NV 89109
"Daredevil"

Bobby Knight
Indiana University Basketball
Bloomington, IN 47405
"Basketball Coach"

Gladys Knight
2801 Yorkshire Avenue
Henderson, NV 89014
"Singer"

Michael E. Knight
10100 Santa Monica Blvd.
Suite #2500
Los Angeles, CA 90067
"Actor"

Shirley Knight
19528 Ventura Blvd. #559
Tarzana, CA 91356
"Actress"

Wayne Knight
3242 Oakshire Drive
Los Angeles, CA 90068
"Actor"

Mark Knopfler
16 Lamberton Place
London W11 2SH ENGLAND
"Rock Musician"

Don Knotts
1854 South Beverly Glen #402
Los Angeles, CA 90025
"Actor"

Buddy Knox
940 Brunette Avenue
Coquitiam BC V3K 1C9 CANADA
"Singer, Songwriter"

Chuck Knox
11220 N.E. 53rd Street
Kirkland, WA 98033
"Football Coach"

Elyse Knox-Harmon
2236A Encinitas Blvd.
Encinitas, CA 92024
"Actress"

Terence Knox
8942 Wilshire Blvd.
Beverly Hills, CA 90211
"Actor"

Jeff Kober
P.O. Box 16758
Beverly Hills, CA 90209
"Actor"

Mayor Edward I. Koch
1290 Avenue of the Stars
30th Floor
New York, NY 10104
"Ex-Mayor"

Howard W. Koch
704 North Crescent Drive
Beverly Hills, CA 90210
"Director, Producer"

Walter Koenig
P.O. Box 4395
North Hollywood, CA 91607
"Actor, Writer"

Helmut Kohl
Marbacher Str. 11
D-6700 Ludwigshafen/Rhein
GERMANY
"Politician"

Sen. Herbert Kohl (WI)
Senate Hart Bldg. #330
Washington, DC 20510
"Politician"

Mayor Teddy Kollek
22 Jaffa Road
Jerusalem, ISRAEL
"Politician"

Dorothy Konrad
10650 Missouri Avenue #2
Los Angeles, CA 90025
"Actress"

Kool & The Gang
89 Fifth Avenue #700
New York, NY 10003
"R&B Group""

Kool Moe Dee
151 El Camino Drive
Beverly Hills, CA 90212
"Rap Singer"

Dean R. Koontz
P.O. Box 9529
Newport Beach, CA 92658
"Writer"

Dr. C. Everett Koop
5924 Maplewood Park Place
Bethesda, MD 20814
"Ex-Surgeon General"

Bernie Kopel
19413 Olivos
Tarzana, CA 91356
"Actor, Writer"

Arnold Kopelson
901 N. Roxbury Drive
Beverly Hills, CA 90210
"Film Producer"

Karen Kopins
145 S. Fairfax Avenue #310
Los Angeles, CA 90036
"Actress"

Ted Koppel
11810 Glenn Mill Road
Potomac, MD 20854
"TV Show Host"

Olga Korbut
4705 Masters Court
Duluth, MN 30136
"Gymnast"

Marla Korda
304 N. Screenland Drive
Burbank, CA 91505
"Actress"

Michael Korda
1230 Avenue of the Americas
New York, NY 10019
"Writer"

Harvey Korman
1136 Stradella
Los Angeles, CA 90077
"Actor, Director"

Bernie Kosar
6969 Ron Park Place
Youngstown, OH 44512
"Football Player"

Lauren Koslow
17520 Mayall Street
Northridge, CA 91325
"Actress"

David Kossoff
45 Roe Green Close
College Lane
Hatfield, Herts. ENGLAND
"Actor, Writer"

Irwin Kostal
3149 Dona Susana Drive
Studio City, CA 91604
"Conductor"

Yaphet Kotto
10100 Santa Monica Blvd. #2490
Los Angeles, CA 90067
"Actor"

Sandy Koufax
100 N. Broadway #2100
St. Louis, MO 63102
"Ex-Baseball Player"

Nancy Kovack
27 Oakmont Drive
Los Angeles, CA 90049
"Actress"

Martin Kove
19155 Rosita Street
Tarzana, CA 91356
"Actor"

Harley Jane Kozak
2329 Stanley Hills Drive
Los Angeles, CA 90046
"Actor"

Linda Kozlowski
9150 Wilshire Blvd. #205
Beverly Hills, CA 90212
"Actress"

Jeroen Krabbe
107 Van Eeghenstraat
1071 EZ Amsterdam, HOLLAND
"Actor"

Ken Kragen
240 Baroda
Los Angeles, CA 90077
"Talent Agent"

Jane Krakoroski
P.O. Box 5617
Beverly Hills, CA 90210
"Actress"

Jack Kramer
231 North Glenroy Place
Los Angeles, CA 90049
"Tennis Player"

Stanley Kramer
2530 Shira Drive
Valley Village, CA 91607
"Film Director"

Stephanie Kramer
9300 Wilshire Blvd. #555
Beverly Hills, CA 90212
"Actress, Director"

Judith Krantz
166 Groverton Place
Los Angeles, CA 90077
"Author"

Peter Kraus
Kaiserplatz 7
8000 Munich 40 GERMANY
"Actor"

Brian Krause
10683 Santa Monica Blvd.
Los Angeles, CA 90025
"Actor"

Alison Krauss
1017 16th Avenue So.
Nashville, TN 37212
"Singer"

Lenny Kravitz
14681 Harrison Street
Miami, FL 33176
"Singer"

Paul Kreppel
14300 Killion Street
Van Nuys, CA 91401
"Actor"

Kreskin
P.O. Box 1383
West Caldwell, NJ 07006
"Psychic"

Robbie Krieger
8033 Sunset Blvd. #76
Los Angeles, CA 90046
"Actress'

Alice Krige
132 S. Rodeo Drive #300
Beverly Hills, CA 90212
"Actress'

Wortham Krimmer
1642 Redesdale Avenue
Los Angeles, CA 90026
"Actor"

Kris Kross
9380 SW 72nd Street #B-220
Miami, FL 33173
"R&B Duo"

Sylvia Kristal
8955 Norma Place
Los Angeles, CA 90069
"Actress"

Marta Kristen
3575 Cahuenga Blvd. W. #500
Los Angeles, CA 90068
"Actress"

Kris Kristofferson
P.O. Box 2147
Malibu, CA 90265
"Singer, Actor, Writer"

William Kristol
6625 Jill Court
McLean, VA 22101
"Political Conservative"

Joan Kroc
8939 Villa La Jolla Drive #201
La Jolla, CA 92037
"Ray Kroc's Widow"

Marty Krofft
7710 Woodrow Wilson Drive
Los Angeles, CA 90046
"Puppeteer, Producer"

Sid Krofft
7710 Woodrow Wilson Drive
Los Angeles, CA 90046
"Puppeteer, Producer"

Hardy Kruger
P.O. Box 726
Crestline, CA 92325
"Actor"

Jack Kruschen
P.O. Box 10143
Canoga Park, CA 91309
"Actor"

Mike Krzyzewski
Duke University Basketball
Durham, NC 27706
"Basketball Coach"

Stanley Kubrick
P.O. Box 123
Borehamwood, Herts.
ENGLAND
"Film Director"

Lisa Kudrow
1122 S. Robertson Blvd. #15
Los Angeles, CA 90035
"Actress"

Toni Kukoc
1901 West Madison Street
Chicago, IL 60612
"Basketball Player"

Buzz Kulik
10425 Charing Cross Road
Los Angeles, CA 90024
"Writer, Producer"

Mitch Kupchak
156 N. Gunston Drive
Los Angeles, CA 90049
"Ex-Basketball Player"

Akira Kurosawa
Seijo 2-21-6
Setagaya-Ku
Tokyo, JAPAN
"Film Director"

Swoosie Kurtz
320 Central Park West
New York, NY 10025
"Actress"

Kay Kuter
6207 Satsuma Avenue
North Hollywood, CA 91606
"Actress"

Michelle Kwan
44450 Pinetree Drive #103
Plymouth, MI 48071
"Ice Skater"

Nancy Kwan
1317 Fifth Street #200
Santa Monica, CA 90401
"Actress"

Burt Kwouk
2-4 Noel Street
London W1V 3RB ENGLAND
"Actor"

L

Patti LaBelle
1212 Grennox Road
Wynnewood, PA 19096
"Singer, Actress"

Matthew Laborteaux
4555 Mariota Avenue
Toluca Lake, CA 91602
"Actor"

Patrick Laborteaux
1450 Belfast Drive
Los Angeles, CA 90069
"Actor"

Jerry Lacy
10100 Santa Monica Blvd. #2500
Los Angeles, CA 90067
"Actor, Writer, Director"

Alan Ladd, Jr.
312 N. Faring Road
Los Angeles, CA 90077
"Film Executive"

Alana Ladd
1420 Moraga Drive
Los Angeles, CA 90049
"Actress"

Cheryl Ladd
P.O. Box 1329
Santa Ynez, CA 93460
"Actress, Singer"

David Ladd
9212 Hazen Drive
Beverly Hills, CA 90210
"Actor"

Diane Ladd
P.O. Box 17111
Beverly Hills, CA 90209
"Actress"

Margaret Ladd
444-21st Street
Santa Monica, CA 90402
"Actress"

Dr. Arthur Laffer
5375 Executive Square #330
La Jolla, CA 92037
"Economist"

Perry Lafferty
335 South Bristol Avenue
Los Angeles, CA 90049
"TV Executive"

Guy LaFleur
9050 Blvd. del Acadie
Montreal PQ H4N 2S5 CANADA
"Hockey Player"

Christine Lahti
1122 S. Robertson Blvd. #15
Los Angeles, CA 90035
"Actress"

Francis Lai
4146 Lankershim Blvd. #401
North Hollywood, CA 91602
"Composer"

Cleo Laine
Wavendon (Old Rectory)
Milton Keynes
MK17 8LT ENGLAND
"Singer"

Frankie Laine
P.O. Box 6910
San Diego, CA 92166
"Singer, Actor"

Melvin Laird
1730 Rhode Island Avenue
Washington, DC 20036
"Ex-Government Official"

Ricki Lake
401 Fifth Avenue
New York, NY 10016
"TV Show Host"

Sir Freddie Laker
138 Cheapside
London EC2V 6BL ENGLAND
"Business Executive"

Jack LaLanne
P.O. Box 1023
San Luis Obispo, CA 93406
"Exercise Instructor"

Donny Lalonde
2554 Lincoln Blvd. #729
Venice, CA 90291
"Boxer"

Hedy Lamarr
568 Orange Drive #47
Altamonte Springs, FL 32701
"Actress"

Lorenzo Lamas
3727 W. Magnolia Blvd. #807
Burbank, CA 91505
"Actor"

Gil Lamb
755 Madrid Circle
Palm Springs, CA 92262
"Actor"

Jack Lambert
222 Highland Drive
Carmel, CA 93921
"Ex-Football Player"

Jerry Lambert
P.O. Box 25371
Charlotte, NC 28212
"Singer"

L.W. Lambert
Route #1
Olin, NC 28860
"C&W Singer"

Robert Lamm
1113 Sutton Way
Beverly Hills, CA 90210
"Musician, Songwriter"

Darryl Lamonica
8796 North 6th Street
Fresno, CA 93720
"Ex-Football Player"

Jake Lamotta
235 Beacon Drive
Phoenixville, PA 19460
"Boxer"

Zohra Lampert
100 West 57th Street
New York, NY 10019
"Actress"

Jim Lampley
3347 Tareco Drive
Los Angeles, CA 90068
"Sportscaster"

Mark LaMura
10100 Santa Monica Blvd. #2500
Los Angeles, CA 90067
"Actor"

Bert Lance
P.O. Box 637
Calhoun, GA 30701
"Politician"

Martin Landau
7455 Palo Vista Drive
Los Angeles, CA 90046
"Actor"

David L. Lander
5819 Saint Laurent Drive
Agoura Hills, CA 91301
"Actor, Writer"

Ann Landers
435 North Michigan Avenue
Chicago, IL 60611
"Columnist"

Audrey Landers
3112 Nicka Drive
Los Angeles, CA 90077
"Actress, Singer"

Judy Landers
9849 Denbigh
Beverly Hills, CA 90210
"Actress, Model"

Steve Landesburg
355 North Genesee Avenue
Los Angeles, CA 90036
"Actor"

John Landis
9402 Beverly Crest Drive
Beverly Hills, CA 90210
"Film Writer, Director"

Joe Lando
151 El Camino Drive
Beverly Hills, CA 90212
"Actor"

Michael Landon, Jr
3736 Calle Jazmin
Calabasas, CA 91302
"Actor"

Paul Landres
5343 Amestoy Avenue
Encino, CA 91316
"TV Director"

Sen. Mary Landrieu (LA)
4301 S. Prier
New Orleans, LA 70125
"Politician"

Moon Landrieu
4301 South Prieur
New Orleans, LA 70125
"Ex-Mayor"

Tom Landry
5336 Rock Cliff Place
Dallas, TX 75209
"Ex-Football Coach"

Vytatis Landsbergis
Parliment House
Vilnius, LITHUANIA
"Politician"

Valerie Landsburg
22745 Chamera Lane
Topanga, CA 90290
"Actress"

Andre Landzaat
7500 Devista Drive
Los Angeles, CA 90046
"Actor"

Abby Lane
444 North Faring Road
Los Angeles, CA 90077
"Actress, Singer"

Charles Lane
321 Gretna Green Way
Los Angeles, CA 90049
"Actor"

Christy Lane
1225 Apache Lane
Madison, TN 37115
"Singer"

Diane Lane
25 Sea Colony Drive
Santa Monica, CA 90405
"Actress"

Dick "Night Train" Lane
18100 Meyer
Detroit, MI 48235
"Ex-Football Player"

Nathan Lane
P.O. Box 1249
White River Junction, VT 05001
"Actor"

Eric Laneuville
5138 W. Slauson Avenue
Los Angeles, CA 90056
"Actor"

June Lang-Morgan
12756 Kahlenberg Lane
North Hollywood , CA 91607
"Actress"

Katherine Kelly Lang
7800 Beverly Blvd. #3371
Los Angeles, CA 90036
"Actress"

K.D. Lang
P.O. Box 33800, Station D
Vancouver B.C.
V6J 5C7 CANADA
"Singer"

Robert Lang
68 St. James's Street
London SW1A 1PH ENGLAND
"Actor"

Harry Langdon
181 N. McCadden Place
Los Angeles, CA 90004
"Photographer"

Hope Lange
803 Bramble
Los Angeles, CA 90049
"Actress"

Ted Lange
18653 Venura Blvd. #131-B
Tarzana, CA 91356
"Actor, Writer, Director"

Heather Langenkamp
9229 Sunset Blvd. #311
Los Angeles, CA 90069
"Actress"

Bernhard Langer
1120 S.W. 21st Lane
Boca Raton, FL 33486
"Golfer"

Frances Langford
P.O. Box 96
Jensen Beach, FL 33457
"Singer"

Murray Langston
RR #3, Box 4630-31
Tehachapi, CA 93561
"Comedian, Actor"

Lester Lanin
157 West 57th Street
New York, NY 10019
"Band Leader"

Kim Lankford
9911 W. Pico Blvd. #1060
Los Angeles, CA 90035
"Actress"

Angela Lansbury
635 Bonhill Road
Los Angeles, CA 90049
"Actress"

Sherry Lansing
10451 Bellagio Road
Los Angeles, CA 90077
"Film Executive"

Anthony LaPaglia
955 S. Carrillo Drive #300
Los Angeles, CA 90048
"Actor"

Alison La Placa
4526 Wilshire Blvd.
Los Angeles, CA 90010
"Actress"

Guy LaPointe
4568 E. des Bousquets
Augustin PQ 6A3 1C4 CANADA
"Hockey Player"

Joe Lara
8383 Wilshire Blvd. #954
Beverly Hills, CA 90211
"Actor"

John Larch
4506 Varna Avenue
Sherman Oaks, CA 91403
"Actor"

Ring Lardner, Jr.
55 Central Park West
New York, NY 10023
"Writer"

Rep. Steve Largent (OK)
Cannon House Office Bldg. #410
Washington, DC 20515
"Politician"

Sheila Larkin
9229 Sunset Blvd. #311
Los Angeles, CA 90069
"Actress"

Julius LaRosa
67 Sycamore Lane
Irvington, NY 10533
"Actor, Singer"

John Larroquette
P.O. Box 6910
Malibu, CA 90264
"Actor"

Don Larsen
P.O. Box 2863
Hayden Lake, ID 83835
"Ex-Baseball Player"

Darrell Larson
8380 Melrose Avenue #207
Los Angeles, CA 90069
"Actor"

Gary Larson
4900 Main Street #900
Kansas City, MO 62114
"Cartoonist"

Glen Larson
351 Delfern Drive
Los Angeles, CA 90077
"TV Writer, Producer"

Jack Larson
449 Skyewiay Road North
Los Angeles, CA 90049
"Actor"

Wolf Larson
10600 Holman Avenue, #1
Los Angeles, CA 90024
"Actor"

Danny LaRue
57 Gr. Cumberland Place
London W1M 7LJ ENGLAND
"Actor"

Eva La Rue-Callahan
11661 San Vicente Blvd. #307
Los Angeles, CA 90049
"Actress"

Florence La Rue
4300 Louis Avenue
Encino, CA 91316
"Singer"

Tony LaRussa
4549 Dunsmore Avenue #3
Tampa, FL 33611
"Baseball Manager"

Vincent LaRusso
419 Park Avenue So.#1009
New York, NY 10016
"Actor"

Eriq LaSalle
P.O. Box 2396
Beverly Hills, CA 90213
"Actor"

Tommy Lasorda
1473 West Maxzim Avenue
Fullerton, CA 92633
"Baseball Manager"

Louise Lasser
200 East 71st Street #20C
New York, NY 10021
"Actor, Writer"

Sydney Lassick
2734 Bellevue
Los Angeles, CA 90026
"Actor"

Fred Lasswell
1111 N. Westshore Blvd. #604
Tampa, FL 33607
"Cartoonist"

Louise Latham
9229 Sunset Blvd. #311
Los Angeles, CA 90069
"Actress"

Queen Latifah
151 El Camino Drive
Beverly Hills, CA 90212
"Rap Singer"

Matt Lattanzi
P.O. Box 2710
Malibu, CA 90265
"Actor"

Niki Lauda
San Costa de Baix
Santa Eucalia IBIZA
SPAIN
"Race Car Driver, Author"

Estee Lauder
767 Fifth Avenue
New York, NY 10153
"Fashion Designer"

Matt Lauer
30 Rockefeller Plaza #701
New York, NY 10112
"TV Show Host"

John Laughlin
11815 Magnolia Blvd., #2
North Hollywood, CA 91607
"Actor"

Tom Laughlin
P.O. Box 25355
Los Angeles, CA 90025
"Actor, Producer"

Cyndi Lauper
826 Broadway #400
New York, NY 10003
"Singer, Songwriter"

Matthew Laurance
1951 Hillcrest Road
Los Angeles, CA 90068
"Actor"

Ralph Lauren
1107-5th Avenue
New York, NY 10028
"Fashion Designer"

Tammy Lauren
8899 Beverly Blvd., #716
Los Angeles, CA 90048
"Actress"

Arthur Laurents
P.O. Box 582
Quoque, NY 11959
"Writer"

Dan Lauria
601 North Cherokee Avenue
Los Angeles, CA 90004
"Actor"

Piper Laurie
3130 Oakshire Drive
Los Angeles, CA 90068
"Actress"

Ed Lauter
1800 Avenue of the Stars #400
Los Angeles, CA 90067
"Actor"

Rod Laver
P.O. Box 4798
Hilton Head, SC 29928
"Tennis Player"

Linda Lavin
P.O. Box 2847
Wilmington, NC 28402
"Actress, Director"

John Phillip Law
1339 Miller Drive
Los Angeles, CA 90069
"Actor"

Patricia Kennedy Lawford
1 Sutton Place South
New York, NY 10021
"Widow of Peter Lawford"

Lucy Lawless
100 Universal City Plaza #415A
Universal City, CA 91608
"Actress"

Carol Lawrence
12337 Ridge Circle
Los Angeles, CA 90049
"Actress, Singer"

Joey Lawrence
16130 Ventura Blvd. #550
Encino, CA 91436
"Actor"

Linda Lawrence
4926 Commonwealth
La Canada, CA 91011
"Actress"

Marc Lawrence
2200 N. Vista Grande Avenue
Palm Springs, CA 92262
"Actor, Director"

Martin Lawrence
9560 Wilshire Blvd. #516
Beverly Hills, CA 90212
"Actor"

Patricia Lawrence
33 St. Luke's Street
London SW3 ENGLAND
"Actress"

Sharon Lawrence
P.O. Box 462048
Los Angeles, CA 90046
"Actress"

Tracy Lawrence
2100 West End Avenue #1000
Nashville, TN 37203
"Singer"

Vicki Lawrence-Schultz
6000 Lido Avenue
Long Beach, CA 90803
"Actress, Singer"

Hubert Laws
1078 South Ogden Drive
Los Angeles, CA 90019
"Flutist"

Leigh Lawson
162-170 Wardour Street
London W1V 3AT ENGLAND
"Actress"

Paul Laxalt
1455 Pennsylvania Avenue NW
Washington, DC 20004
"Ex-Senator"

George Lazenby
P.O. Box 55306
Sherman Oaks, CA 91413
"Actor"

Buddy Lazier
8135 West Crawfordsville
Indianapolis, IN 46224
"Race Car Driver"

Nicholas Lea
110-55 Brooks Bank Blvd. #10, No.
Vancouver BC V7J 3S5 CANADA
"Actor"

Rep. Jim Leach (IA)
Rayburn House Office Bldg. #2186
Washington, DC 20515
"Politician"

Robin Leach
1 Dag Hammarskjold Plaza
21st Floor
New York, NY 10017
"TV Personality"

Cloris Leachman
2041 Mandeville Canyon
Los Angeles, CA 90049
"Actress"

Sen. Patrick J. Leahy (VT)
Senate Russell Bldg. #433
Washington, DC 20510
"Politician"

Amanda Lear
Immanuelkirschtr. 33
D-10405 Berlin GERMANY
"Singer, Actress"

Norman Lear
1999 Avenue of the Stars #500
Los Angeles, CA 90067
"TV Writer, Producer"

Michael Learned
1600 N. Beverly Drive
Beverly Hills, CA 90210
"Actress"

Denis Leary
9560 Wilshire Blvd. #516
Beverly Hills, CA 90212
"Commedian"

Sabrina Le Beauf
354 Indiana Avenue
Venice, CA 90291
"Actress"

Matt LeBlanc
11766 Wilshire Blvd. #1470
Los Angeles, CA 90025
"Actor"

Kelly LeBrock
P.O. Box 57593
Sherman Oaks, CA 91403
"Actress, Model"

John Le Carre
9 Gainsborough Gardens
London NW3 1BJ ENGLAND
"Writer"

Jean LeClerc
RD #2 Freborn Street
St. Albans, VT 05478
"Actor"

Francis Lederer
1385 E. El Alameda
Palm Springs, CA 92252
"Actor, Director"

Chris Ledoux
4205 Hillsboro Road #208
Nashville, TN 37215
"Singer, Songwriter"

Anna Lee
1240 N. Doheny Drive
Los Angeles, CA 90069
"Actress"

Brenda Lee
26 Fall Creek Drive #6
Branson, MO 65516
"Singer"

Christopher Lee
21 Golden Square #200
London W1R 3PA ENGLAND
"Actor"

Dickey Lee
168 Orchid Drive
Pearl River, NY 10965
"Singer"

Dorothy Lee
2664 Narcissus Street
San Diego, CA 92106
"Actress"

Hyapatia Lee
15127 Califa Street
Van Nuys, CA 91411
"Actress, Model"

Jason Scott Lee
P.O. Box 1083
Pearl City, HI 96782
"Actor"

Kathy Lee
204 River Edge Lane
Seiverville, TN 37862
"Singer"

Michelle Lee
830 Birchwood
Los Angeles, CA 90024
"Actress, Singer"

Peggy Lee
11404 Bellagio Road
Los Angeles, CA 90024
"Singer, Actress"

Ruta Lee
2623 Laurel Canyon Road
Los Angeles, CA 90046
"Actress"

Dr. Sammy Lee
16537 Harbour Lane
Huntington Beach, CA 92649
"Physician, Athlete"

Sheryl Lee
151 El Camino Drive
Beverly Hills, CA 90212
"Actress"

Spike Lee
40 Acres & A Mule Film Works
124 De Kalb Avenue #2
Brooklyn, NY 11217
"Actor, Film Director"

Stan Lee
387 Park Avenue South
New York, NY 10016
"Cartoonist"

Beverly Leech
9150 Wilshire Blvd. #175
Beverly Hills, CA 90212
"Actress"

Richard Leech
27 Clayland's Road
London SW8 1NX ENGLAND
"Actor"

Phil Leeds
8831 Sunset Blvd. #304
Los Angeles, CA 90069
"Actor"

Jane Leeves
9560 Wilshire Blvd. #516
Beverly Hills, CA 90212
"Actress"

Michel Legrand
157 W. 57th Street
New York, NY 10019
"Pianist, Composer"

John Leguizamo
151 El Camino Dr.
Beverly Hills, CA 90212
"Actor"

Jim Lehrer
3556 Macomb Street NW
Washington, DC 20016
"Broadcast Journalist"

Ron Leibman
10530 Strathmore Drive
Los Angeles, CA 90024
"Actor, Writer"

Annie Leibovitz
55 Vandam Street
New York, NY 10013
"Photographer"

Janet Leigh
1625 Summitridge Drive
Beverly Hills, CA 90210
"Actress"

Jennifer Jason Leigh
2400 Whitman Place
Los Angeles, CA 90068
"Actress"

Mike Leigh
8 Earlham Grove
London N22 ENGLAND
"Film Writer, Director"

Laura Leighton
9560 Wilshire Blvd. #516
Beverly Hills, CA 90210
"Actress"

David Leisure
8428-C Melrose Place
Los Angeles, CA 90069
"Actor"

Donovan Leitch
8794 Lookout Mountain Avenue
Los Angeles, CA 90046
"Actor"

Claude LeLouch
15 Avenue Foch
F-75016 Paris, FRANCE
"Director, Producer"

Paul Le Mat
1100 North Alta Loma #805
Los Angeles, CA 90069
"Actor"

Michael Lembeck
13530 Erwin Street
Van Nuys, CA 91401
"Actor"

Mario Lemieux
630 Academy Street
Sewickley, PA 15143
"Hockey Player"

Christopher Lemmon
80 Murray Drive
South Glastonbury, CT 06073
"Actor"

Jack Lemmon
141 South El Camino Drive #201
Beverly Hills, CA 90212
"Actor, Director"

Bob Lemon
95 Fairway Lakes
Myrtle Beach, SC 29577
"Baseball Manager"

Meadowlark Lemon
13610 N. Scottsdale Road #1026
Scottsdale, AZ 85254
"Ex-Basketball Player"

Greg Lemond
5250 Nell Road #101
Reno, NV 89502
"Bicyclist"

Ivan Lendl
400 5 1/2 Mile Road
Goshen, CT 05756
"Tennis Player"

Julian Lennon
30 Ives Street
London SW3 2ND ENGLAND
"Singer, Composer"

Sean Lennon
1 West 72nd Street
New York, NY 10023
"Singer, Composer"

Lennon Sisters
1984 State Highway 165
Branson, MO 65616
"Vocal Group"

Annie Lennox
35 - 37 Park Gate Road
Unit #2 Ransome's Dock
London SW1 4NP ENGLAND
"Singer"

Jay Leno
P.O. Box 7885
Burbank, CA 91510
"TV Show Host, Comedian"

Rula Lenska
306-16 Euston Road
London NW13 ENGLAND
"Actress"

Kay Lenz
5719 Allot Avenue
Van Nuys, CA 91401
"Actress"

Rick Lenz
12955 Calvert Street
Van Nuys, CA 91401
"Actor"

Melissa Leo
853-7th Avenue #9A
New York, NY 10019
"Actress"

Valerie Leon
2-3 Golden Square #42-43
London WIR 3AD ENGLAND
"Actress"

Tea Leoni
2300 W. Victory Blvd.
Burbank, CA 91506
"Actress"

Buck Leonard
605 Atlantic Ave.
Rocky Mount, NC 27807
"Ex-Baseball Player"

Elmore Leonard
2192 Yarmouth Road
Bloomfield Village, MI 48301
"Author, Screenwriter"

Lu Leonard
8525 S.W. Pfaffle Street #5
Tigard, OR 97223
"Actress"

Robert Sean Leonard
P.O. Box 454
Sea Isle City, NJ 08243
"Actor"

Sugar Ray Leonard
4401 East West Highway #303
Bethesda, MD 20914
"Boxer"

Tea Leoni
10683 Santa Monica Blvd.
Los Angeles, CA 90025
"Actress"

Michael Lerner
8347 Sunset View
Los Angeles, CA 90069
"Actress"

Gloria LeRoy
3500 West Olive Avenue #1400
Burbank, CA 91505
"Actress"

Aleen Leslie
1700 Lexington Road
Beverly Hills, CA 90210
"Writer"

Bethel Leslie
393 West End Avenue #11C
New York, NY 10024
"Actress, Writer"

Joan Leslie
2228 North Catilina Avenue
Los Angeles, CA 90027
"Actress"

Lenn Lesser
934 N. Evergreen St.
Burbank, CA 91505
"Actor"

Ketty Lester
5931 Comey Avenue
Los Angeles, CA 90034
"Actress"

Mark Lester
25437 Cumberland Lane
Calabasas, CA 91302
"Singer, Actor"

Richard Lester
River Land
Petersham Surrey, ENGLAND
"Film Director, Composer"

Terry Lester
145 S. Fairfax Avenue #310
Los Angeles, CA 90036
"Actor"

Tom Lester
794 Foley Street
Jackson, MS 39202
"Actor"

Jared Leto
405 S. Beverly Drive #500
Beverly Hills, CA 90212
"Actor"

David Letterman
1697 Broadway
New York, NY 10019
"TV Show Host"

Shelby Leverington
1801 Avenue of the Stars #1250
Los Angeles, CA 90067
"Actress"

Le Vert
110-112 Lantoga Road #D
Wayne, PA 19087
"Singer, Songwriter"

Sen. Carl Levin (MI)
Senate Russell Bldg. #459
Washington, DC 20510
"Politician"

Ira Levin
425 Madison Avenue
New York, NY 10017
"Author"

Rep. Sander Levin (MI)
House Rayburn Bldg. #2909
Washington, DC 20515
"Politician"

Ted Levine
1999 Ave. of the Stars #2850
Los Angeles, CA 90067
"Actor"

Barry Levinson
8942 Wilshire Blvd.
Beverly Hills, CA 90211
"Film Writer, Director"

Gene Levitt
9200 Sunset Blvd., PH. 25
Los Angeles, CA 90069
"TV Writer, Director"

Monica Lewinsky
c/o Marcia Lewis
700 New Hampshire Avenue NW
Washington, DC 20037
"Ex-White House Intern"

Al Lewis
P.O. Box 277
New York, NY 10044
"Actor"

Carl Lewis
P.O. Box 571990
Houston, TX 77082
"Track & Field Athlete"

Clea Lewis
1999 Avenue of the Stars, #2850
Los Angeles, CA 90067
"Actress"

Dawnn Lewis
P.O. Box 56718
Sherman Oaks, CA 91413
"Actress"

Geoffrey Lewis
19756 Collier
Woodland Hills, CA 91364
"Actor"

Huey Lewis
P.O. Box 779
Mill Valley, CA 94942
"Singer"

Jennifer Lewis
P.O. Box 5617
Beverly Hills, CA 90210
"Actress"

Jerry Lewis
3160 W. Sahara Avenue #816
Las Vegas, NV 89102
"Comedian, Actor"

Jerry Lee Lewis
P.O. Box 23162
Nashville, TN 37202
"Singer, Composer"

Rep. John Lewis (GA)
Cannon House Office Bldg. #229
Washington, DC 20515
"Politician"

Juliette Lewis
151 El Camino Drive
Beverly Hills, CA 90212
"Actress"

Lennox Lewis
811 Totowa Road #100
Totowa, NJ 07512
"Boxer"

Ramsey Lewis
180 N. LaSalle Street #220C
Chicago, IL 60601
"Pianist, Composer"

Richard Lewis
345 N. Maple Drive #300
Beverly Hills, CA 90210
"Actor"

Shari Lewis
603 North Alta Drive
Beverly Hills, CA 90210
"Ventriloquist"

John Leyton
53 Keyes House, Dophin Sq.
London SW1V 3NA ENGLAND
"Actor"

Richard Libertini
2313 McKinley Avenue
Venice, CA 90291
"Actor"

Jeremy Licht
4355 Clybourn Avenue
Toluca Lake, CA 91602
"Actor"

G. Gordon Liddy
9112 Riverside Drive
Ft. Washington, MD 20744
"Talk Show Host"

Sen. Joseph I Lieberman (CT)
Senate Hart Bldg. #316
Washington, DC 20510
"Politician"

Judith Light
1475 Sierra Vista Drive
Aspen, CO 81611
"Actress"

Gordon Lightfoot
1365 Yonge Street #207
Toronto, Ontario
M4T 2P7 CANADA
"Singer, Songwriter"

Leonard Lightfoot
446 South Orchard Drive
Burbank, CA 91506
"Actor"

Tom Ligon
227 Waverly Place
New York, NY 10014
"Actor"

Rush Limbaugh
366 Madison Avenue #700
New York, NY 10117
"Radio & TV Talk Show Host"

Scott Lincoln
1305 N. Laurel #111
Los Angeles, CA 90046
"Actor"

DeDe Lind
P.O. Box 1712
Boca Raton, FL 33429
"Model"

Ann Morrow Lindbergh
P.O. Box 157
Peacham, VT 05682
"Aviatrix, Author"

Hal Linden
100 Universal City Plaza #507-3D
Universal City, CA 91608
"Actor, Director"

Kate Linden
9111 Wonderland Avenue
Los Angeles, CA 90046
"Actress"

Astrid Lindgren
Dalagatan 46
11314 Stockholm, SWEDEN
"Author"

Delroy Lindo
151 El Camino Drive
Beverly Hills, CA 90212
"Actor"

Eric Lindros
1 Pattison Place
Philadelphia, PA 19148
"Hockey Player"

Mark Lindsay
P.O. Box 210
Elk City, ID 83525
"Singer, Composer"

Mort Lindsey
6970 Fernhill Drive
Malibu, CA 90265
"Composer, Conductor"

Robert Lindsay
1 Robert Street
London WC2N 6BH ENGLAND
"Actor"

Jon Lindstrom
10100 Santa Monica Blvd. #2490
Los Angeles, CA 90067
"Actor"

Pia Lindstrom
30 Rockefeller Plaza
Suite #700
New York, NY 10020
"Film Critic"

Art Linkletter
1100 Bel Air Road
Los Angeles, CA 90077
"TV Personality"

Jack Linkletter
765 Baker Street
Costa Mesa, CA 92626
"TV Personality"

Mark Linn-Baker
27702 Fairweather Street
Canyon Country, CA 91351
"Actor"

Teri Ann Linn
4267 Marina City Drive #312
Marina del Rey, CA 90292
"Actress"

Laura Linney
8942 Wilshire Blvd.
Beverly Hills, CA 90211
"Actress"

Joanne Linville
3148 Fryman Road
Studio City, CA 91604
"Actress"

Ray Liotta
16829 Monte Hermosa Drive
Pacific Palisades, CA 90272
"Actor"

Tara Lipinski
888 Dennison Court
Bloomfield Hills, MI 48302
"Ice Skater"

Dennis Lipscomb
9200 Sunset Blvd. #1130
Los Angeles, CA 90069
"Actor"

Peggy Lipton
7920 Sunset Blvd. #400
Los Angeles, CA 90046
"Actress"

Robert Lipton
9300 Wilshire Blvd. #410
Beverly Hills, CA 90212
"Actor"

Lisa Lisa
747-10th Avenue
New York, NY 10019
"R&B Group"

Verna Lisi
Via di Filomarino 4
Rome, ITALY
"Actress"

Stephen Liska
15050 Sherman Way #167
Van Nuys, CA 91405
"Actor"

John Lithgow
1319 Warnall Avenue
Los Angeles, CA 90024
"Actor"

Little River Band
9850 Sandalfoot Blvd. #458
Boca Raton, FL 33428
"Rock & Roll Group"

Rich Little
5485 W. Flamingo Road #105
Las Vegas, NV 89103
"Actor, Comedian"

Little Richard
Hyatt Sunset Hotel
8401 Sunset Blvd.
Los Angeles, CA 90069
"Singer, Songwriter"

Tawny Little
5515 Melrose Avenue
Los Angeles, CA 90038
"TV Show Host"

Big Tiny Little
West 3985 Taft Drive
Spokane, WA 98208
"Singer, Songwriter"

Gene Littler
P.O. Box 1919
Rancho Santa Fe, CA 92067
"Golfer"

Robyn Lively
P.O. Box 8212
Universal City, CA 91608
"Actress"

Barry Livingston
8271 Melrose Avenue #202
Los Angeles, CA 90046
"Actor"

Stanley Livingston
P.O. Box 1782
Studio City, CA 91604
"Actor"

Keri Lizer
13410 Killion Street
Sherman Oaks, CA 91401
"Actress"

LL Cool J
160 Varick Street
New York, NY 10013
"Rap Singer"

Doug Llewelyn
8075 West Third Street #303
Los Angeles, CA 90048
"Actor"

Christopher Lloyd
P.O. Box 491264
Los Angeles, CA 90049
"Actor"

Emily Lloyd
9560 Wilshire Blvd. #516
Beverly Hills, CA 90212
"Actress"

Kathleen Lloyd
116 Rosehedge Lane
Agoura, CA 91301
"Actress"

Norman Lloyd
1813 Old Ranch Road
Los Angeles, CA 90049
"Actor, Director"

Tony Lo Bianco
15301 Ventura Blvd. #345
Sherman Oaks, CA 91403
"Actor, Writer, Director"

Amy Locane
8942 Wilshire Blvd.
Beverly Hills, CA 90211
"Actress"

Dick Locher
435 N. Michigan Avenue
Chicago, IL 60611
"Cartoonist"

Brad Lockerman
1800 Avenue of the Stars #400
Los Angeles, CA 90067
"Actor"

Anne Lockhart
191 Upper Lake Road
Thousand Oaks, CA 91361
"Actress"

June Lockhart
P.O. Box 3207
Santa Monica, CA 90403
"Actress"

Heather Locklear
1836 Courtney Terrace
Los Angeles, CA 90046
"Actress, Model"

Gary Lockwood
3083 1/2 Rambla Pacifica
Malibu, CA 90265
"Actor"

David Lodge
8 Sydney Road
Richmond, Surrey, ENGLAND
"Actor"

Phyllis Logan
47 Courtfield Road #9
London SW7 4DB ENGLAND
"Actress"

Robert Logan
11532 Chiquita Street
Stuido City, CA 91604
"Actor"

Robert Loggia
544 Bellagio Terrace
Los Angeles, CA 90049
"Actor, Director"

Kenny Loggins
670 Oak Springs Lane
Santa Barbara, CA 93108
"Singer, Songwriter"

Gina Lollobrigida
Via Appino Antica 223
I-00178 Rome, ITALY
"Actress"

Herbert Lom
76 Oxford Street
London W1N 0AX ENGLAND
"Actor"

Jeremy London
P.O. Box 5617
Beverly Hills, CA 90210
"Actor"

Julie London
16074 Royal Oaks
Encino, CA 91436
"Actress, Singer"

John Lone
1740 Broadway, 22nd Floor
New York, NY 10019
"Actor"

Howie Long
514 S. Juanita Avenue
Redondo Beach, CA 902774
"Ex-Football Player"

Shelley Long
15237 Sunset Blvd.
Pacific Palisades, CA 90272
"Actress"

Johnny Longdon
5401 Palmer Drive
Banning, CA 92220
"Actor"

Tony Longo
24 Westwind Street
Marina del Rey, CA 90292
"Actor"

Mike Lookinland
2036 Highland View Circle
Salt Lake City, UT 84109
"Actor"

Rod Loomis
12600 Miranda Street
No. Hollywood, CA 91607
"Actor"

Al Lopez
3601 Beach Street
Tampa, FL 33609
"Ex-Baseball Player"

Jennifer Lopez
P.O. Box 57593
Sherman Oaks, CA 91403
"Actress"

Mario Lopez
P.O. Box 4736
Chatsworth, CA 91311
"Actor"

Nancy Lopez
2308 Tara Drive
Albany, GA 31707
"Golfer"

Trini Lopez
1139 Abrigo Road
Palm Springs, CA 92762
"Singer, Actress"

Stefan Lorant
215 West Mountain Road
Lenox, MA 01240
"Photojournalist, Author"

Marjorie Lord
1110 Maytor Place
Beverly Hills, CA 90210
"Actress"

Traci Lords
P.O. Box 16758
Beverly Hills, CA 90209
"Actress"

Sophia Loren
1151 Hidden Valley Road
Thousand Oaks, CA 91360
"Actress"

Gloria Loring
4125 Parva Avenue
Los Angeles, CA 90027
"Singer, Actress"

Lisa Loring
11130 Huston Street #6
No. Hollywood, CA 91601
"Actress"

Joan Lorring
345 East 68th Street
New York, NY 10021
"Actress"

Ronnie Lott
11342 Canyon View Circle
Cupertino, CA 95014
"Ex-Football Player"

Sen. Trent Lott (MS)
Senate Russell Bldg. #487
Washington, DC 20510
"Politician"

Dorothy Loudon
101 Central Park West
New York, NY 10023
"Actress"

Greg Louganis
P.O. Box 4130
Malibu, CA 90264
"Diver"

Lori Loughlin
1122 S. Robertson Blvd. #15
Los Angeles, CA 90036
"Actress"

Julia Louis-Dreyfus
9150 Wilshire Blvd. #205
Beverly Hills, CA 90212
"Actress"

Tina Louise
310 East 46th Street #18T
New York, NY 10017
"Actress"

Col. Jack R. Lousma
2722 Roseland Street
Ann Arbor, MI 48103
"Astronaut"

Charlie Louvin
3160 Highway 64 E.
Wartrace, TN 37183
"Singer"

Courtney Love
9072 Wonderland Park Avenue
Los Angeles, CA 90046
"Singer"

Mike Love
24563 Ebelden Avenue
Santa Clarita, CA 91321
"Singer, Songwriter"

Peter Love
P.O. Box 4826
Valley Village, CA 91617
"Actor"

Love & Rockets
4, The Lakes
Bushey, Hertsfordshire
WD2 1HS ENGLAND
"Rock & Roll Group"

Linda Lovelace
120 Enterprise
Secaucus, NJ 07094
"Actress"

Patty Loveless
P.O. Box 1407
White House, TN 37188
"Singer"

James Lovell
5725 East River Road
Chicago, IL 60611
"Astronaut"

Loverboy
406-68 Water Street
Gastown, Vancouver B.C.
VGB 1AY CANADA
"Rock & Roll Group"

Lyle Lovett
c/o General Delivery
Klein, TX 77391
"Singer"

Candy Loving
2112 Broadway
Santa Monica, CA 90404
"Model"

Jon Lovitz
4735 Vivinana Drive
Tarzana, CA 91356
"Actor"

Dale Lowdermilk
P.O. Box 5743
Montecito, CA 93150
"Actor"

Barry Lowe
31 South Audley Street
London W1 ENGLAND
"Actor"

Chad Lowe
7920 Sunset Blvd. 4th Flr.
Los Angeles, CA 90046
"Actor"

Rob Lowe
646 Romero Canyon Road
Santa Barbara, CA 93108
"Actor"

Carey Lowell
8942 Wilshire Blvd.
Beverly Hills, CA 90211
"Model, Actress"

George Lucas
P.O. Box 2459
San Rafael, CA 94912
"Writer, Producer, Director"

Jerry Lucas
P.O. Box 728
Templeton, CA 93465
"Ex-Basketball Player"

Susan Lucci
P.O. Box 621
Quogue, NY 11959
"Actress"

Gloria Luchenbill
415 South Shirley Place
Beverly Hills, CA 90212
"Actress"

Laurance Luckenbill
P.O. Box 636
Cross River, NY 10518
"Actor"

William Lucking
10100 Santa Monica Blvd. #700
Los Angeles, CA 90067
"Actor"

Sid Luckman
5303 St. Charles Road
Bellwood, IL 60104
"Ex-Football Player"

Robert Ludlum
P.O. Box 235
Bedford Hills, NY 10507
"Author"

Lorna Luft
108 East Matilija Street
Ojai, CA 93023
"Actress"

Sen. Richard Lugar (IN)
306 Hart Office Bldg.
Washington, DC 20510
"Politician"

Bela Lugosi, Jr.
520 N. Central Avenue #800
Glendale, CA 91203
"Actor"

James Luisi
14315 Riverside Drive #1
Sherman Oaks, CA 91423
"Actor"

Johnny Lujack
6321 Crow Valley Drive
Bettendorf, IA 52722
"Ex-Football Player"

Lulu
2 King Street
London SW1Y 6QL ENGLAND
"Singer, Actress"

Lulabel & Scottie
P.O. Box 171132
Nashville, TN 37217
"Vocal Group"

Carl Lumbly
1999 Avenue of the Stars #2850
Los Angeles, CA 90067
"Actor"

Sidney Lumet
1 West 81st Street
New York, NY 10024
"Film Writer, Director"

Joanna Lumley
P.O. Box 1AS
London W1A 1AS ENGLAND
"Actress"

Robert Ludlum
P.O. Box 235
Bedford Hills, NY 10507
"Novelist"

Barbara Luna
18026 Rodarte Way
Encino, CA 91316
"Actress"

Deanna Lund
545 Howard Street
Salem, VA 24153
"Actress"

Lucille Lund
3424 Shore Heights Drive
Malibu, CA 90265
"Actress"

Dan Lundberg
3347 Bonnie Hill Drive
Los Angeles, CA 90068
"Writer"

Joan Lunden
1965 Broadway #400
New York, NY 10023
"TV Show Host"

Dolph Lundgren
151 El Camino Drive
Beverly Hills, CA 90212
"Bodybuilder, Actor"

Jessica Lundy
151 El Camindo Drive
Beverly Hills, CA 90212
"Actress"

Patti LuPone
40 West 57th Street
New York, NY 10019
"Singer"

Peter Lupus
2401 S. 24th Street #110
Phoenix, AZ 85034
"Actor"

Nellie Lutcher
1524 La Baig Avenue
Los Angeles, CA 90028
"Pianist, Vocalist"

Frank Luz
606 North Larchmont Blvd. #309
Los Angeles, CA 90004
"Actor"

Greg Luzinski
620 Jackson Road
Medford, NJ 08055
"Ex-Baseball Player"

Jimmy Lydon
1317 Los Arboles Avenue N.W.
Albuquerque, NM 87107
"Actor"

A.C. Lyles
2115 Linda Flora
Los Angeles, CA 90024
"Writer, Producer"

David Lynch
P.O. Box 93624
Los Angeles, CA 90093
"TV Writer

Kelly Lynch
1970 Mandeville Canyon Road
Los Angeles, CA 90049
"Actress"

Richard Lynch
8271 Melrose Avenue #202
Los Angeles, CA 90046
"Actor"

Adrian Lyne
9876 Beverly Grove Drive
Beverly Hills, CA 90210
"Film Director"

Carol Lynley
3349 Cahuenga Blvd. W. #2
Los Angeles, CA 90068
"Actress"

Betty Lynn
10424 Tennessee Avenue
Los Angeles, CA 90064
"Actress"

Loretta Lynn
P.O. Box 120369
Nashville, TN 37212
"Singer"

Dame Vera Lynn
Ditchling
Sussex ENGLAND
"Singer, Actress"

Lynyrd Skynyrd
3423 Piedmont Road NE #220
Atlanta, GA 30305
"Music Group"

Sue Lyon
2019 N. Bronson Avenue
Los Angeles, CA 90068
"Actress"

Jeffrey Lyons
205 W. 57th Street
New York, NY 10019
"Film Critic"

Phyllis Lyons
9171 Wilshire Blvd. #441
Beverly Hills, CA 90210
"Actress"

Robert F. Lyons
1801 Avenue of the Stars #1250
Los Angeles, CA 90067
"Actor"

M

Andrea McArdle
713 Disaton Street
Philadelphia, PA 19111
"Actress"

Alex McArthur
10435 Wheatland Avenue
Sunland, CA 91040
"Actor"

Martina McBride
406-68 Water Street
Vancouver BC V6B 1A4
CANADA
"Singer"

Amanda McBroom
9107 Wilshire Blvd. #300
Beverly Hills, CA 90212
"Singer, Songwriter"

Sen. John McCain (AZ)
Senate Russell Bldg. #241
Washington, DC 20510
"Politician"

Mitzi McCall
3635 Wrightwood Drive
Studio City, CA 91604
"Actress"

Irish McCalla
920 Oak Terrace
Prescott, AZ 86301
"Actress"

Lon McCallister
P.O. Box 6030
Stateline, NV 89449
"Actor"

David McCallum
68 Old Brompton Road
London SW7 3LQ ENGLAND
"Actor"

Napoleon McCallum
1320 Harbor Bay Parkway
Alameda, CA 94502
"Football Player"

Mercedes McCambridge
2500 Torrey Pines Road #1203
La Jolla, CA 92037
"Actress"

Chuck McCann
2941 Briar Knoll Drive
Los Angeles, CA 90046
"Actor, Comedian"

Les McCann
4031 Panama Court
Piedmont, CA 94611
"Musician, Composer"

Fred McCarren
9200 Sunset Blvd. #710
Los Angeles, CA 90069
"Actor"

Chris McCarron
218 Wildwood Lane
Sierra Madre, CA 91024
"Jockey"

Andrew McCarthy
8942 Wilshire Blvd.
Beverly Hills, CA 90211
"Actor"

Eugene McCarthy
271 Hawlin Road
Woodville, VA 22749
"Ex-Senator"

Jenny McCarthy
345 N. Maple Drive #185
Beverly Hills, CA 90210
"MTV Host/Model"

Kevin McCarthy
14854 Sutton Street
Sherman Oaks, CA 91403
"Actor"

Lin McCarthy
233 North Swall Drive
Beverly Hills, CA 90210
"Actor"

Nobu McCarthy
9229 Sunset Blvd., #311
Los Angeles, CA 90069
"Actor"

Sir Paul McCartney
1 Soho Square
London W1 ENGLAND
"Singer, Composer"

Tim McCarver
1518 Youngford Road
Gladwynne, PA 19035
"Ex-Baseball Player"

Chris McCarty
9105 Carmelita Avenue #101
Beverly Hills, CA 90210
"Singer, Songwriter"

Constance McCashin
2037 Desford Drive
Beverly Hills, CA 90210
"Actress"

McCaughey Septuplets
615 N. First
Carlisle, IA 50047
"Muti-Birth Babies"

Peggy McCay
8811 Wonderland Avenue
Los Angeles, CA 90046
"Actress"

Rue McClanahan
9454 Wilshire Blvd. #405
Beverly Hills, CA 90212
"Actress"

Sarah McClendon
3133 Connecticut Avenue NW #215
Washington, DC 20008
"News Correspondent"

Sean McClory
6612 Whitley Terrace
Los Angeles, CA 90069
"Actor, Director"

Leigh McCloskey
6032 Philip Avenue
Malibu, CA 90265
"Actor"

Paul McCloskey
580 Mountain Home Road
Woodside, CA 94062
"Ex-Congressman"

Marc McClure
1420 Beaudry Blvd.
Glendale, CA 91208
"Actor"

Edie McClurg
145 S. Fairfax Avenue #310
Los Angeles, CA 90036
"Actress"

Bill McCollum
799 United Nation Plaza
New York, NY 10017
"U.S. Ambassador to the U.N."

Matt McColm
9000 Sunset Blvd. #1200
Los Angeles, CA 90069
"Stuntman"

Matthew McConaughey
P.O. Box 1145
Malibu, CA 90265
"Actor"

Judith McConnell
3300 Bennett Drive
Los Angeles, CA 90068
"Actress"

Sen. Mitch McConnell (KY)
Senate Russell Bldg. #361A
Washington, DC 20510
"Politician"

Marilyn McCoo-Davis
2639 Lavery Court #5
Newbury Park, CA 91320
"Singer"

John McCook
7800 Beverly Blvd. #3371
Los Angeles, CA 90036
"Actor, Writer, Director"

Carolyn McCormick
2372 Veteran Avenue #102
Los Angeles, CA 90064
"Actress"

Kent McCord
6767 Forest Lawn Dr. #115
Los Angeles, CA 90068
"Actor"

Mary McCormack
P.O. Box 67335
Los Angeles, CA 90067
"Actress"

Patty McCormack
14723 Magnolia Blvd.
Sherman Oaks, CA 91403
"Actress"

Maureen McCormick
1925 Century Park E. #2320
Los Angeles, CA 90067
"Actress"

Pat McCormick
7709 Rhodes Avenue
North Hollywood, CA 91605
"Comedian"

Pat McCormick
P.O. Box 250
Seal Beach, CA 90740
"Swimmer"

Alec McCowen
3 Goodwins Court
St. Martin's Lane
London WG2 ENGLAND
"Actor"

Charlie McCoy
P.O. Box 158558
Nashville, TN 37215
"Singer, Guitarist"

Mark McCoy
7120 Hawthorne #18
Los Angeles, CA 90046
"Actor"

Matt McCoy
4526 Wilshire Blvd.
Los Angeles, CA 90010
"Actor"

George McCrae
495 S.E. 10th Court
Hialeah, FL 33010
"Singer, Songwriter"

Gwen McCrae
495 S.E. 10th Court
Hialeah, FL 33010
"Singer, Songwriter"

Jody McCrea
Country Road 395
P.O. Box 195
Hondo, NM 89336
"Actor"

Julie McCullough
8033 Sunset Blvd. #353
Los Angeles, CA 90046
"Model"

Kimberly McCullough
9200 Sunset Blvd. #1130
Los Angeles, CA 90069
"Actress"

Shanna McCullough
7920 Alabama Avenue
Canoga Park, CA 91304
"Actress"

James McDaniel
8730 Sunset Blvd., #480
Los Angeles, CA 90069
"Actor"

Mel McDaniel
P.O. Box 150845
Nashville, TN 37215
"Singer"

Brian McDermott
27 Upper Berkeley Street
London W1 ENGLAND
"Actor"

Dylan McDermott
P.O. Box 25516
Los Angeles, CA 90025
"Actor"

James McDivitt
9146 Cherry Avenue
Rapid City, MI 49676
"Astrouaut"

Christopher McDonald
8033 Sunset Blvd. #4011
Los Angeles, CA 90046
"Actor"

"Country" Joe McDonald
P.O. Box 7064
Berkeley, CA 94707
"Singer"

Grace McDonald
6115 Lincoln Drive
Minneapolis, MN 55436
"Singer, Dancer"

Mary McDonnell
P.O. Box 6010-540
Sherman Oaks, CA 91413
"Actress"

Mary McDonough
6858 Cantelope Avenue
Van Nuys, CA 91405
"Actress"

Frances McDormand
333 West End Avenue #12C
New York, NY 10023
"Actress"

Malcolm McDowall
76 Oxford Street
London W1N OAX ENGLAND
"Actor"

Roddy McDowall
3110 Brookdale Road
Studio City, CA 91604
"Actor"

Ronnie McDowell
P.O. Box 268
Russellville, AL 35653
"Singer"

Peter McEnery
9 Cork Street
London W1 ENGLAND
"Actor"

John McEnroe
23712 Malibu Colony Road
Malibu, CA 90265
"Tennis Player"

Reba McEntire
40 Music Spuare W.
Nashville, TN 37203
"Singer"

Geraldine McEwan
308 Regent Street
London W1 ENGLAND
"Actress"

Gates McFadden
1999 Avenue of the Stars
Suite #2850
Los Angeles, CA 90067
"Actor"

Robert C. McFarlane
3414 Prospect Street N.W.
Washington, DC 20007
"Ex-Government Official"

Bobby McFerrin
826 Broadway #400
New York, NY 10003
"Singer"

Paul McGann
6A Danbury Street
London N1 8JU ENGLAND
"Actor"

Darren McGavin
P.O. Box 2939
Beverly Hills, CA 90213
"Actor"

Henry McGee
47 Courtfield Road #20
London SW7 4DB ENGLAND
"Actor"

Kirk McGee
P.O Box 626
Franklin, TN 37064
"Singer"

Vonetta McGee
1801 Avenue of the Stars #902
Los Angeles, CA 90067
"Actress"

Howard McGinnin
151 El Camino Drive
Beverly Hills, CA 90212
"Actor, Singer"

Kelly McGillis
303 Whitehead Street
Key West, FL 33040
"Actress"

Ted McGinley
1925 Century Park East #2320
Los Angeles, CA 90067
"Actor"

Mike McGlone
8942 Wilshire Blvd.
Beverly Hills, CA 90211
"Actor"

Patrick McGoohan
16808 Bollinger Drive
Pacific Palisades, CA 90272
"Actor, Writer, Producer"

Elizabeth McGovern
17319 Magnolia Blvd.
Encino, CA 91316
"Actress"

George McGovern
4012 Linnean Avenue NW
Washington, DC 20008
"Ex-Senator"

Maureen McGovern
163 Amsterdam Avenue #174
New York, NY 10023
"Singer"

Tim McGraw
3310 West End Avenue #500
Nashville, TN 37203
"Singer"

Tug McGraw
2595 Wallingford Road
San Marino, CA 91108
"Ex-Baseball Player"

Ewan McGregor
503/504 Lotts Road
The Chambers, Chelsea Harbour
SW10 OXF ENGLAND
"Actor"

Dorothy McGuire
10351 Santa Monica Blvd. #300
Los Angeles, CA 90025
"Actress"

McGuire Sisters
100 Rancho Circle
Las Vegas, NV 89119
"Vocal Group"

Mark McGwire
1704 Alamo Plaza #322
Alamo, CA 94507
"Baseball Player"

Stephen McHattie
9229 Sunset Blvd. #710
Los Angeles, CA 90069
"Actor"

Gardner McKay
252 Lumahai Place
Honolulu, HI 96825
"Actor"

Jim McKay
2805 Sheppard Road
Monkton, MD 21111
"Sportscaster"

John McKay
1 Buccaneer Road
Tampa, FL 33607
"Ex-Football Coach"

Peggy McKay
8811 Wonderland Avenue
Los Angeles, CA 90046
"Actress"

Michael McKean
833 Thornhill Road
Calabasas, CA 91302
"Actor"

Donna McKechnie
127 Broadway #220
Santa Monica, CA 90401
"Actress"

Todd McKee
32362 Lake Pleasant Drive
Westlake Village, CA 91361
"Actor"

Danica McKellar
9200 Sunset Blvd. #900
Los Angeles, CA 90069
"Actress"

Sir Ian McKellen
25 Earl's Terrace
London W8 ENGLAND
"Actor"

Virginia McKenna
67 Glebe Place
London SW3 5JB ENGLAND
"Actress"

Julia McKenzie
Richmond Park
Kingston Surrey, ENGLAND
"Actress"

Doug McKeon
818-6th Street #202
Santa Monica, CA 90403
"Actor"

Nancy McKeon
P.O. Box 6778
Burbank, CA 91510
"Actress"

Philip McKeon
11409 Dona Dorotea Drive
Studio City, CA 91604
"Actor"

Leo McKern
29 Roehampton Gate
London SW15 5JR ENGLAND
"Actor"

Tamara McKinney
4935 Parkers Mill Road
Lexington, KY 40502
"Skier"

Rod McKuen
1155 Angelo Drive
Beverly Hills, CA 90210
"Singer, Poet"

Andrew McLaglen
P.O. Box 1056
Friday Harbor, WA 98250
"Film Director"

Denny McLain
11994 Hyne Road
Brighton, MI 48116
"Ex-Baseball Player"

John McLaughlin
1211 Connecticut Avenue N.W.
Washington, DC 20036
"News Correspondent"

Don McLean
119 West 57th Street
New York, NY 10019
"Singer, Songwriter"

Allyn Ann McLerie
3344 Campanil Drive
Santa Barbara, CA 93109
"Actress"

Rachel McLish
120 S. El Camino Drive #116
Beverly Hills, CA 90212
"Actress"

Ed McMahon
12000 Crest Court
Beverly Hills, CA 90210
"TV Show Host"

Jenna McMahon
435 Palisades Ave.
Santa Monica, CA 90402
"Writer, Producer"

Jim McMahon
9520 Viking Drive
Eden Prarie, MN 55344
"Football Player"

John McMartin
250 W. 57th St. #703
New York, NY 10107
"Actor"

Susan Carpenter McMillan
1744 Oak Lane
San Marino, CA 91108
"Paula Jones' Promoter"

Jim McMullen
515 Mt. Holyoke Avenue
Pacific Palisades, CA 90272
"Actor"

Sam McMurray
4728 1/2 Forman Lane
North Hollywood, CA 91602
"Actor"

Larry McMurtry
P.O. Box 552
Archer City, TX 76351
"Screenwriter"

Steve McNair
335 South Hollywood
Memphis, TN 38104
"Football Player"

Terrence McNally
218 West 10th Street
New York, NY 10014
"Dramatist"

Brian McNamara
11730 National Blvd. #19
Los Angeles, CA 90064
"Actor"

Robert McNamara
2412 Tracy Place N.W.
Washington, DC 20008
"Banker, Government"

William McNamara
21154 Entrada Road
Topanga, CA 90290
"Actor"

Kate McNeil
9229 Sunset Blvd. #710
Los Angeles, CA 90069
"Actress"

Robert Duncan McNeill
861 Burrell Street
Marina del Rey, CA 90292
"Actor"

Kristy McNichol
151 El Camino Drive
Beverly Hills, CA 90212
"Actress"

Chad McQueen
8306 Wilshire Blvd. #438
Beverly Hills, CA 90211
"Actor"

Neile McQueen
2323 Bowmont Drive
Beverly Hills, CA 90210
"Actress"

Gerald McRaney
1012 Royal Street
New Orleans, LA 70116
"Actor, Director"

Jim McReynolds
P.O. Box 304
Gallatin, TN 37066
"Singer, Guitarist"

Jesse McReynolds
P.O. Box 304
Gallatin, TN 37066
"Singer, Guitarist"

Ian McShane
11620 Wilshire Blvd. #700
Los Angeles, CA 90025
"Actor"

**Timothy Mcveigh-
#12076-06**4
9595 West Quincy Avenue
Littleton, CO 80123
"Bombing Convict"

Tyler McVey
14130 Weddington Street
Van Nuys, CA 91401
"Actor"

Christie McVie
9477 Lloydcrest Drive
Beverly Hills, CA 90210
"Singer, Songwriter"

Caroline McWilliams
10390 Santa MOnica Blvd. #300
Los Angeles, CA 90025
"Actress"

James MacArthur
74092 Covered Wagon Trail
Palm Desert, CA 92260
"Actor"

Mrs. Jean MacArthur
Waldorf Towers
100 East 50th Street
New York, NY 10022
"Widower of Douglas MacArthur"

Ralph Macchio
451 Deerpark Avenue
Dix Hills, NY 11746
"Actor"

Simon MacCorkindale
520 Washington Blvd. #187
Marina del Rey, CA 90292
"Actor"

Dr. Jeffrey MacDonald
#00131-177
Federal Correctional Institute
27072 Ballston
Sheridan, OR 97378
"Accused of Killing His Family"

Andie MacDowell
939 8th Avenue #400
New York, NY 10019
"Actress"

Ali MacGraw
10345 West Olympic Blvd. #200
Los Angeles, CA 90064
"Actress, Model"

Jeff MacGregor
151 El Camino Drive
Beverly Hills, CA 90212
"TV Personality"

Mario Machado
5750 Briarcliff Road
Los Angeles, CA 90068
"Actor"

Stephen Macht
248 South Rodeo Drive
Beverly Hills, CA 90212
"Actor"

Sen. Connie Mack (FL)
Senate Hart Bldg. #517
Washington, DC 20510
"Politician"

Warner Mack
1136 Sunnymeade Drive
Nashville, TN 37216
"Singer, Guitarist"

Bob Mackie
225 W. 39th Street
New York, NY 10018
"Custome Designer"

Gisele MacKenzie
10643 Riverside Drive
Toluca Lake, CA 91602
"Actress"

Patch MacKenzie
3500 West Olive Avenue #1400
Burbank, CA 91505
"Actress"

David Macklin
5410 Wilshire Blvd. #227
Los Angeles, CA 90036
"Actor"

Janet MacLachlan
1919 North Taft Avenue
Los Angeles, CA 90068
"Actress"

Kyle MacLachlan
132 S. Rodeo Drive #300
Beverly Hills, CA 90212
"Actor"

Shirley MacLaine
25200 Old Malibu Road
Malibu, CA 90265
"Actress"

Gavin MacLeod
1025 Fifth Avenue
New York, NY 10028
"Actor"

Patrick Macnee
P.O. Box 1685
Palm Springs, CA 92263
"Actor"

Robert Macneil
356 West 58th Street
New York, NY 10019
"News Correspondent"

Jeff MacNelly
64 E. Concord St.
Orlando, FL 32801
"Cartoonist"

Elle MacPherson
414 East 52nd Street PH-B
New York, NY 10022
"Model"

Meredith MacRae
11759 Iowa Avenue
Los Angeles, CA 90025
"Actress"

Bill Macy
10130 Angelo Circle
Beverly Hills, CA 90210
"Actor"

William H. Macy
405 S. Beverly Drive #500
Beverly Hills, CA 90212
"Actor"

Dave Madden
13034 Delano
Van Nuys, CA 91406
"Actor"

John Madden
5955 Coronado Blvd.
Pleasanton, CA 94588
"Sportscaster"

Lester Maddox
3155 Johnson Ferry Road N.E.
Marietta, GA 30062
"Ex-Governor"

Greg Maddux
8124 Desert Jewel Circle
Las Vegas, NV 89128
"Ex-Baseball Player"

Amy Madigan
151 El Camino Drive
Beverly Hills, CA 90212
"Actress"

Bill Madlock
18 Meeting House Lane
Shelton, CT 06484
"Ex-Baseball Player"

Madonna
4519 Cockerham Drive
Los Angeles, CA 90027
"Singer, Actress"

Michael Madsen
9830 Wilshire Blvd.
Beverly Hills, CA 90212
"Actor"

Virginia Madsen
9830 Wilshire Blvd.
Beverly Hills, CA 90212
"Actress"

Debra Sue Maffett
1525 McGavock Street
Nashville, TN 37203
"Actress, Model"

Brandon Maggart
9200 Sunset Blvd. #710
Los Angeles, CA 90069
"Actor"

Ann Magnuson
1317 Maltman Avenue
Los Angeles, CA 90026
"Proformance Artist"

Tobey Maguire
7920 Sunset Blvd. #400
Los Angeles, CA 90046
"Actress"

Kathy Maisnik
1800 N. Vine Street #120
Los Angeles, CA 90028
"Actress"

Valerie Mahaffey
121 North San Vicente Blvd.
Beverly Hills, CA 90211
"Actress"

George Maharis
13150 Mulholland Drive
Beverly Hills, CA 90210
"Actor"

Bill Maher
7800 Beverly Blvd. #D
Los Angeles, CA 90036
"Actor"

Robert Maheu
3523 Cochise Lane
Las Vegas, NV 89109
"Actor"

Cardinal Roger Mahony
1531 West 9th Street
Los Angeles, CA 90012
"Clergy"

Phil Mahre
White Pass Drive
Naches, WA 98937
"Skier"

Steve Mahre
2408 North 52nd Avenue
Yakima, WA 98908
"Skier"

Norman Mailer
142 Columbia Heights
Brooklyn, NY 11201
"Author"

Beth Maitland
8485-E Melrose Place
Los Angeles, CA 90069
"Actress"

John Major
8 Stuckley Road
Huntingdon
Cambs, ENGLAND
"Ex-Prime Minister"

Lee Majors
3000 Holiday Drive, PH #1
Ft. Lauderdale, FL 33316
"Actor"

Tommy Makem
2 Longmeadow Road
Dover, NH 03820
"Singer"

Chris Makepeace
Box 1095, Station "Q"
Toronto, Ontario
M4T 2P2 CANADA
"Actor"

Mako
6477 Pepper Tree Lane
Somis, CA 93066
"Actor"

Kristina Malandro
P.O. Box 491035
Los Angeles, CA 90049
"Actress"

Karl Malden
1845 Mandeville Canyon
Los Angeles, CA 90049
"Actor"

Wendy Malick
1999 Avenue of the Stars #2850
Los Angeles, CA 90067
"Actress"

Art Malik
47 Courtfield Rd. #20
London SW7 4DB ENGLAND
"Actor"

Ross Malinger
6212 Banner Aveune
Los Angeles, CA 90038
"Actor"

John Malkovich
P.O. Box 1171
Weston, CT 06883
"Actor"

Carole Mallory
2300-5th Avenue
New York, NY 10037
"Model, Actress, Author"

Bruce Malmuty
9981 Robin Drive
Beverly Hills, CA 90210
"Screenwriter, Director"

Dorothy Malone
P.O. Box 7287
Dallas, TX 75209
"Actress"

Karl Malone
301 W. South Temple
Salt Lake City, UT 84101
"Basketball Player"

Moses Malone
1001 N. 4th Street
Milwaukee, WI 53203
"Ex-Basketball Player"

Nancy Malone
11624 Sunshine Terrace
Studio City, CA 91604
"Actress, Director"

Patty Maloney
6767 Forest Lawn Dr. #101
Los Angeles, CA 90068
"Actress"

Leonard Maltin
10424 Whipple Street
Toluca Lake, CA 91602
"Film Critic, Author"

The Mamas & The Papas
108 E. Matilija Street
Ojai, CA 93023
"Rock & Roll Group"

David Mamet
P.O. Box 381589
Cambridge, MA 02238
"Writer"

Charles T. Manatt
4814 Woodway Lane N.W.
Washington, DC 20016
"Politician"

Melissa Manchester
15822 High Knoll Road
Encino, CA 91436
"Singer, Songwriter"

William Manchester
P.O. Box 329 Wesleyan Station
Middletown, CT 06457
"Author"

Ray "Boom Boom" Mancini
12524 Indianapolis Street
Los Angeles, CA 90066
"Boxer"

Nick Mancuso
10100 Santa Monica Blvd. #2490
Los Angeles, CA 90067
"Actor"

Robert Mandan
247 S. Beverly Drive #102
Beverly Hills, CA 90212
"Actor"

Howie Mandel
8942 Wilshire Blvd.
Beverly Hills, CA 90211
"Actor, Comedian"

Johnny Mandel
28946 Cliffside Drive
Malibu, CA 90265
"Composer, Conductor"

Loring Mandel
555 West 57th Street #1230
New York, NY 10019
"Screenwriter"

Nelson Mandela
51 Plain Street
Johannesburg 2001
SOUTH AFRICA
"Social Activist, Politician"

Winnie Mandela
Orlando West, Soweto
Johannesburg SOUTH AFRICA
"Social Activist"

Barbara Mandrell
605-C N. Main Street
Ashland City, TN 37015
"Singer, Singwriter"

Erline Mandrell
605-C N. Main Street
Ashland City, TN 37015
"Actress, Drummer"

Louise Mandrell
2046 Parkway
Pigeon Forge, TN 37863
"Singer, Musician"

Costas Mandylor
151 El Camino Drive
Beverly Hills, CA 90212
"Actor"

Larry Maneti
4615 Winnetka
Woodland Hills, CA 91364
"Actor"

Barry Manilow
5443 Beethoven Street
Los Angeles, CA 90066
"Singer, Composer"

Tom Mankiewicz
1609 Magnetic Terrace
Los Angeles, CA 90069
"Writer, Producer"

Wolf Mankowitz
Bridge House
Ahakista, County Cork
Kilcrohane 11 IRELAND
"Author, Producer, Dramatist"

Abby Mann
1240 La Collina Drive
Beverly Hills, CA 90210
"Writer, Producer"

Delbert Mann
401 South Burnside Avenue
Suite #11D
Los Angeles, CA 90036
"Director, Producer"

Johnny Mann
78516 Gorham Lane
Indio, CA 92203
"Composer, Conductor"

Michael Mann
13746 Sunset Blvd.
Pacific Palisades, CA 90272
"Writer, Producer"

David Manners
717 Santeclto Street
Santa Barbara, CA 93105
"Actor"

Dorothy Manners
744 North Dohney Drive
Los Angeles, CA 90069
"Actress"

Miss Manners
1651 Harvard Street N.W.
Washington, DC 20009
"Etiquette Expert"

Irene Manning
3165 La Mesa Drive
Santa Carlos, CA 94070
"Actress, Singer, Author"

Dinah Manoff
21244 Ventura Blvd. #101
Woodland Hills, CA 91364
"Actress"

Nigel Mansell
Station Road, Box 1
Ballasalle
Isle of Man ENGLAND
"Race Car Driver"

Charles Manson #B33920
Pelican Bay State Prison
5905 Lake Earl Drive
Crescent City, CA 95531
"Convicted Serial Killer"

Marilyn Manson
83 Riverside Drive
New York, NY 10024
"Singer"

Paul Mantee
9057A Nemo Street
West Hollywood, CA 90069
"Actor"

Joe Mantegna
10415 Sarah Street
Toluca Lake, CA 91602
"Actor"

John Mantley
4121 Longridge Avenue
Sherman Oaks, CA 91423
"Screenwriter"

Randolph Mantooth
2735 Hollyridge Drive
Los Angeles, CA 90068
"Actor"

Martin Manulis
242 Copa de Oro Road
Los Angeles, CA 90077
"TV Producer"

Ralph Manza
550 Hygeia Avenue
Leucadia, CA 92024
"Actor"

Ray Manzarek
232 South Rodeo Drive
Beverly Hills, CA 90212
"Keyboardist"

Marla Maples
725 Fifth Avenue
New York, NY 10022
"Actress"

Adela Mara
1928 Mandeville Canyon
Los Angeles, CA 90049
"Dancer, Actress"

Diego Maradona
Brandsen 805
1161 Capital Federal ARGENTINA
"Soccer Player"

Sophie Marceau
10 Avenue George V
F-75008 Paris FRANCE
"Actress"

Marcel Marceau
P.O. Box 411197
San Francisco, CA 94141
"Mime"

Mario Marcelino
1418 North Highland Avenue #102
Los Angeles, CA 90028
"Actress, Writer"

Jane March
5 Jubilee Place #100
London SW3 3TD ENGLAND
"Actress"

Guy Marchand
40 rue Francois Ier
F-75008 Paris, FRANCE
"Actor"

Nancy Marchand
250 West 89th Street
New York, NY 10024
"Actress"

Vanessa Marcil
P.O. Box 691736
W. Hollywood, CA 90069
"Actress"

Imelda Marcos
Leyte Providencia Dept.
Tolosa, Leyte PHILIPPINES
"Politician"

Adrea Marcovicci
3761 Reklaw Drive
Studio City, CA 91604
"Actress, Singer"

HRH The Princess Margaret
Kensington Palace
London W8 5AF ENGLAND
"Royalty"

Stuart Margolin
4727 Wilshire Blvd. #600
Beverly Hills, CA 90210
"Actor, Director"

Miriam Margolyes
121 North San Vicente Blvd.
Beverly Hills, CA 90211
"Actress"

Julianna Margulies
405 S. Beverly Drive #500
Beverly Hills, CA 90212
"Actress"

Juan Marichal
9458 NW 54 Doral Circle Lane
Miami, FL 33128
"Ex-Baseball Player"

Anne Marie
120 Hickory Street
Madison, TN 37115
"Actress, Model"

Lisa Marie
1041 N. Formosa Avenue W10
W. Hollywood, CA 90046
"Actress"

Teena Marie
1000 Laguna Road
Pasadena, CA 91105
"Actress"

Marilyn
33-34 Cleveland Street
London W1 ENGLAND
"Singer"

Richard Marin
(Cheech & Chong)
3880 Clay Street
San Francisco, CA 94118
"Actor, Comedian"

Ed Marinaro
1466 North Doheny Drive
Los Angeles, CA 90069
"Ex-Football Player, Actor"

Dan Marino
3415 Stallion Lane
Ft. Lauderdale, FL 33331
"Football Player"

Monte Markhan
P.O. Box 607
Malibu, CA 90265
"Actor"

Marky Mark
63 Pilgrim Road
Braintree, MA 02184
"Rap Singer"

Ziggy Marley
Jack's Hill
Kingston, JAMAICA
"Raggae Singer"

Jean Marlow
32 Exeter Road
London NW2 ENGLAND
"Actress"

Christian Marquand
45 rue de Belle Chasse
75007 Paris FRANCE
"Actor"

Gabriel Garcia Marques
Fuego 144
Pedregal de San Angel
Mexico DF MEXICO
"Author"

Forrest Mars
6885 Elm Street
McLean, VA 22101
"Candy Executive"

Kenneth Mars
9911 West Pico Blvd. #1060
Los Angeles, CA 90035
"Actor"

Branford Marsalis
3 Hastings Square
Cambridge, MA 02139
"Saxophonist"

Wynton Marsalis
3 Lincoln Center #2911
New York, NY 10023
"Trumpeter"

Marian Marsh
P.O. Box 1
Palm Desert, CA 92260
"Actress"

Marshall Tucker Band
100 West Putnam
Greenwich, CT 06830
"Music Group"

E.G. Marshall
RFD #2, Oregon Road
Mt. Kisco, NY 10549
"Actor"

Garry Marshall
10459 Sarah Street
Toluca Lake, CA 91602
"Writer, Producer"

James Marshall
30710 Monte Lado Drive
Malibu, CA 90265
"Author"

Ken Marshall
8721 Melrose Avenue #110
Los Angeles, CA 90046
"Actor"

Penny Marshall
8942 Wilshire Blvd.
Beverly Hills, CA 90212
"Actress"

Peter Marshall
16714 Oakview Drive
Encino, CA 91316
"Actor, TV Show Host"

Trudy Marshall
1852 Marcheeta Place
Los Angeles, CA 90069
"Actress"

William Marshall
P.O. Box 331212
Pacoima, CA 91331
"Actor"

Donna Martell
17833 Chatsworth
Granada Hills, CA 91344
"Actress"

Frank Marth
8538 Eastwood Road
Los Angeles, CA 90046
"Actor, Singer"

Martika
8995 Elevado Avenue
Los Angeles, CA 90069
"Actress"

Dewey Martin
1371 E. Avenue De Los Arboles
Thousand Oaks, CA 91360
"Actor"

Andrea Martin
14619 Bestor Blvd.
Pacific Palisades, CA 90272
"Actress"

Barney Martin
12838 Milbank Street
Studio City, CA 91604
"Actor"

Dick Martin
11030 Chalon Road
Los Angeles, CA 90077
"Actor, Writer, Comedian"

Eric Martin Band
P.O. Box 5952
San Francisco, CA 94101
"Rock & Roll Group"

Helen Martin
1440 North Fairfax #109
Los Angeles, CA 90046
"Actress"

Jared Martin
9300 Wilshire Blvd. #500
Beverly Hills, CA 90212
"Actor"

Kellie Martin
5918 Van Nuys Blvd.
Van Nuys, CA 91401
"Actress"

Millicent Martin
P.O. Box 101
Redding, CT 06875
"Singer, Actresss"

Nan Martin
33604 Pacific Coast Hwy.
Malibu, CA 90265
"Actress"

Pamela Sue Martin
1199 Forest Avenue #275
Pacific Grove, CA 93951
"Actress, Producer"

Steve Martin
P.O. Box 929
Beverly Hills, CA 90213
"Actor"

Todd Martin
1751 Pinnacle Dr. #1500
McLean, VA 22102
"Actor"

Tony Martin
10724 Wilshire Blvd. #1406
Los Angeles, CA 90024
"Actor, Singer"

Wink Martindale
5744 Newcastle
Calabasas, CA 91302
"Game Show Host"

A. Martinez
6835 Wild Life Road
Malibu, CA 90265
"Actor"

Al Martino
927 North Rexford Drive
Beverly Hills, CA 90210
"Singer'

Leslie Martinson
2288 Coldwater Canyon
Beverly Hills, CA 90210
"TV Director"

The Marvelettes
9936 Majorca Place
Boca Raton, FL 33434
"R & B Group"

Greg Marx
14755 Ventura Blvd. #343
Sherman Oaks, CA 91403
"Actor"

Mrs. Harpo Marx
37631 Palm View Road
Rancho Mirage, CA 92270
"Harpo Marx's Widower"

Richard Marx
15250 Ventura Blvd. #900
Sherman Oaks, CA 91403
"Conductor"

Ron Masak
5440 Shirley Avenue
Tarzana, CA 91356
"Actor"

Joseph Mascolo
3818 Blue Canyon Drive
Studio City, CA 91604
"Actor"

Hugh Masekela
230 Park Avenue #1512
New York, NY 10169
"Trumpeter"

Jackie Mason
145 W. 57th Street
New York, NY 10019
"Comedian"

Marlyn Mason
8242 Hillside Avenue
Los Angeles, CA 90069
"Actress, Singer"

Marsha Mason
320 Galisted Street #305
Santa Fe, NM 87401
"Actress"

Tom Mason
853-7th Avenue #9A
New York, NY 10019
"Actor"

Osa Massen
10501 Wilshire Blvd. #704
Los Angeles, CA 90024
"Actress"

Andrew Masset
11635 Huston
No. Hollywood, CA 91607
"Actor"

Anna Massey
76 Oxford Street
London W1N 0AX ENGLAND
"Actress"

Ben Masters
9255 Sunset Blvd. #710
Los Angeles, CA 90069
"Actor"

Chase Masterson
P.O. Box 611
Waterbury, CT 06720
"Actress"

Mary Stuart Masterson
P.O. Box 1249
White River Junction, VT 05001
"Actress"

Mary Elizabeth Mastrantonio
9465 Wilshire Blvd.
Beverly Hills, CA 90210
"Actress"

Richard Masur
121 North San Vicente Blvd.
Beverly Hills, CA 90211
"Actor, Writer"

Mary Matalin
P.O. Box 18686
Washington, DC 20036
"Political Consultant"

Jerry Mathers
31103 Rancho Viejo Road #2143
San Juan Capistrano, CA 92675
"Actor"

Don Matheson
10275 1/2 Missouri Ave.
Los Angeles, CA 90025
"Actor"

Richard Matheson
P.O. Box 81
Woodland Hills, CA 91364
"Writer"

Tim Matheson
9171 Wilshire Blvd. #406
Beverly Hills, CA 90210
"Actor"

Kerwin Mathews
67-A Buena Vista Terrace
San Francisco, CA 94117
"Actor"

Bob Mathias
7469 East Pine Avenue
Fresno, CA 93727
"Athlete, Actor"

Mirielle Mathieu
12 rue du Boise de Blulogne
F-92200 Neuilly FRANCE
"Singer"

Johnny Mathis
3500 West Olive Avenue
Suite #750
Burbank, CA 91505
"Singer"

Samantha Mathis
P.O. Box 480137
Los Angeles, CA 90048
"Orchestra Leader"

Melissa Mathison
655 MacCulloch Drive
Los Angeles, CA 90049
"Screenwriter"

Marlee Matlin
7920 Sunset Blvd. #400
Los Angeles, CA 90046
"Actress"

Walter Matthau
278 Toyopa Drive
Pacific Palisades, CA 90272
"Actor"

Kathy Mattea
900 Division Street
Nashville, TN 37203
"Singer"

Roland Matthes
Storkower Street 118
D-10407 Berlin GERMANY
"Swimmer"

Eddie Matthews
13744 Recuerdo Dr.
Del Mar, CA 92014
"Ex-Baseball Player"

Don Mattingly
RR #5, Box 74
Evansville, IN 47711
"Baseball Player"

Robin Mattson
77 West 66th Street
New York, NY 10023
"Actress"

Victor Mature
P.O. Box 706
Rancho Santa Fe, CA 92067
"Actor"

Billy Mauch
538-C W. Northwest Highway
Palatine, IL 60067
"Actor"

Bobby Mauch
538-C W. Northwest Highway
Palatine, IL 60067
"Actor"

Gene Mauch
71 Princeton
Rancho Mirage, CA 92270
"Baseball Manager"

Bill Mauldin
112 8th Street
Seal Beach, CA 90740
"Cartoonist

Brad Maule
4136 Dixie Canyon
Sherman Oaks, CA 91423
"Actor"

Nicole Maurey
21 Chemin Vauillons
78160 Marly-le-roi FRANCE
"Actress"

Claire Maurier
11 rue de la Montague-le-Breuil
91360 Epinay sur Orge, FRANCE
"Actress"

Max Maven
7095 Hollywood Blvd. #382
Hollywood, CA 90028
"Mind Reader"

The Mavericks
P.O. Box 23329
Nashville, TN 37202
"Music Group"

Peter Max
118 Riverside Drive
New York, NY 10024
"Artist, Designer"

Frank Maxwell
447 San Vicente Blvd. #301
Santa Monica, CA 90401
"Actor"

Lois Maxwell
150 Carlton Street #200
Toronto, Ontario CANADA
"Actress"

Billy May
4 San Remo
San Clemente, CA 92672
"Composer"

Brian May
The Old Bakehouse
16A Barnes High Street
London SW13 9LW ENGLAND
"Composer"

Donald May
4616 Los Feliz Blvd. #2
Los Angeles, CA 90027
"Actor"

Elaine May
145 Central Park West
New York, NY 10023
"Actress, Writer, Director"

Wendell Mayes
1504 Bel Air Road
Los Angeles, CA 90077
"Screen writer"

Curtis Mayfield
P.O. Box 724677
Atlanta, GA 31139
"Singer"

Don Maynard
6545 Butterfield Drive
El Paso, TX 79932
"Ex-Football Player"

Asa Maynor
P.O. Box 1641
Beverly Hills, CA 90213
"Actress, Producer"

Virginia Mayo
109 East Avenue De Los Arboles
Thousand Oaks, CA 91360
"Actress"

Whitman Mayo
10100 Santa Monica Blvd. #2500
Los Angeles, CA 90067
"Actor"

Melanie Mayron
7510 Sunset Blvd.
Los Angeles, CA 90046
"Actress, Writer"

Willie Mays
P.O. Box 2410
Menlo Park, CA 94026
"Ex-Baseball Player"

Debi Mazar
9560 Wilshire Blvd. #516
Beverly Hills, CA 90212
"Actress"

Bill Mazeroski
RR 6, Box 130
Greensburg, PA 15601
"Ex-Baseball Player"

Julia Meade
1010 Fifth Avenue
New York, NY 10021
"Actress"

Jayne Meadows-Allen
15201 Burbank Blvd.
Van Nuys, CA 91411
"Actress"

Kristen Meadows
8383 Wilshire Blvd. #954
Beverly Hills, CA 90211
"Actress"

Colm Meaney
9560 Wilshire Blvd. #516
Beverly Hills, CA 90212
"Actor"

Anne Meara
1999 Avenue of the Stars #2850
Los Angeles, CA 90067
"Actress, Comedienne"

Rick Mears
204 Spyglass Lane
Jupiter, FL 33477
"Race Car Driver"

Meatloaf
Box 65, Stockport
Cheshire SK3 0JY ENGLAND
"Singer, Composer"

Peter Medak
1712 Stanley Avenue
Los Angeles, CA 90046
"Film Director"

Mike Medavoy
9110 Hazen Drive
Beverly Hills, CA 90210
"Film Executive"

Patricia Medina
10590 Wilshire Blvd. #1202
Los Angeles, CA 90024
"Actress"

Michael Medved
1224 Ashland Avenue
Santa Monica, CA 90405
"Writer, Film Critic"

Thomas Meehan
Brook House
Obtuse Road
Newtown, CT 06470
"Screenwriter"

Edwin Meese
1075 Springhill Road
McLean, VA 22102
"Ex-Government Official"

Zubin Mehta
27 Oakmont Drive
Los Angeles, CA 90049
"Violinist"

Randy Meisner
3706 Eureka Drive
Studio City, CA 91604
"Singer, Songwriter"

Eddie Mekka
3518 Cahuenga Blvd. W. #216
Los Angeles, CA 90068
"Actor"

Melanie
11806 N. 56th Street #B
Tampa, FL 33617
"Singer"

Ib Melchoir
8228 Marmont Lane
Los Angeles, CA 90069
"Writer, Producer"

John Mellencamp
Rt. 1, Box 361
Nashville, IN 47448
"Singer, Songwriter"

Daniel Melnick
1123 Sunset Hills Drive
Los Angeles, CA 90069
"Film Producer"

Sid Melton
5347 Cedros Avenue
Van Nuys, CA 91410
"Actor"

Allen Melvin
271 North Bowling Green Way
Los Angeles, CA 90049
"Actor"

Murray Melvin
535 Kings Road
19 Plaza #2
London SW10 OSZ ENGLAND
"Actor"

Men At Work
15 Blue Street
North Sydney NSW 2060 AUS-
TRALIA
"Rock & Roll Group"

Erik Menedez #1878449
CSP-Sac
P.O. Box 290066
Represa, CA 95671
"Charged for Killing Parents"

Lyle Menedez #1887106
California Correctional Institution
P.O. Box 1031
Tehachapi, CA 93581
"Charged for Killing Parents"

Sergio Mendez
4849 Encino Avenue
Encino, CA 91316
"Pianist, Songwriter"

John Mengatti
8322 Beverly Blvd. #200
Los Angeles, CA 90048
"Actor"

Gian Carlo Menotti
Gilford Haddington
East Lothian
EH41 4JF SCOTLAND
"Composer"

Menudo
2895 Biscayne Blvd. #455
Miami, FL 33137
"Rock & Roll Group"

Sir Yehudi Menuhin
Buhlstr
CH-3780 Gstaad-Neuret
SWITZERLAND
"Violinist"

Heather Menzies
P.O. Box 5973-1006
Sherman Oaks, CA 91403
"Actress"

Marian Mercer
25901 Piuma
Calabasas, CA 91302
"Actress"

Natalie Merchant
9830 Wilshire Blvd.
Beverly Hills, CA 90212
"Singer"

Paul Mercurio
53-55 Brisbane Street
Surryhills, Sydney
NSW 2010 AUSTRALIA
"Actor"

Don Meredith
P.O. Box 597
Santa Fe, NM 87504
"Ex-Football Player"

James Meredith
427 Eastview Street
Jackson, MS 39206
"First Black Attend U of MS"

Lee Ann Meriwether
P.O. Box 260402
Encino, CA 91326
"Actress"

Jan Merlin
9016 Wonderland Avenue
Los Angeles, CA 90046
"Actor, Director"

Dawn Merrick
8281 Melrose Avenue #200
Los Angeles, CA 90046
"Actress"

Dina Merrill
405 East 54th Street #12A
New York, NY 10022
"Actress"

Robert Merrill
79 Oxford Drive
New Rochelle, NY 10801
"Baritone"

Teresa Merritt
192-06 110th Road
St. Albans, NY 11412
"Actress"

Dale Messick
435 N. Michigan Avenue #1417
Chicago, IL 60611
"Cartoonist"

Jim Messina
P.O. Box 770850
Orlando, FL 32877
"Singer, Songwriter"

Reinhold Messner
St. Magdalena 52
I-39040 Villnoss ITALY
"Mountaineer, Author"

Metallica
729 7th Avenue #1400
New York, NY 10019
"Rock & Roll Group"

Laurie Metcalf
11845 Kling Street
North Hollywood, CA 91607
"Actress"

Burt Metcalfe
11800 Brookdale Lane
Studio City, CA 91604
"TV Writer, Producer"

Art Metrano
9300 Wilshire Blvd. #410
Beverly Hills, CA 90212
"Actor"

Howard Metzenbaum
4512 Foxhill Crescent NW
Washington, DC 20007
"Ex-Senator"

Jim Metzler
10100 Santa Monica Blvd. #2500
Los Angeles, CA 90067
"Actor"

Nicholas Meyer
9830 Wilshire Blvd.
Beverly Hills, CA 90212
"Writer, Producer"

Russ Meyer
3121 Arrowhead Drive
Los Angeles, CA 90068
"Film Writer, Producer"

Ari Meyers
875 Comstock #11C
Los Angeles, CA 90024
"Actress"

Kweisi Mfume
3000 Druld Park Drive
Baltimore, MD 21215
"N.A.A.C.P. Director"

Miami Sound Machine
6205 Bird Road
Miami, FL 33155
"Rock & Roll Group"

Bob Michael
1029 N. Glenwood Street
Peoria, IL 61606
"Former Congressman"

George Michael
338 N. Foothill Road
Beverly Hills, CA 90210
"Singer, Composer"

Prince Michael of Kent
Kensington Palace
London N5 ENGLAND
"Royalty"

Princess Michael of Kent
Kensington Palace
London N5 ENGLAND
"Royalty"

Al Michaels
c/o ABC Sports
47 West 66th Street
New York, NY 10023
"Sports Announcer"

Lorne Michaels
88 Central Park West
New York, NY 10023
"TV Writer, Producer"

Marilyn Michaels
185 West End Avenue
New York, NY 10023
"Comedienne"

Keith Michell
130 West 57th Street #10-A
New York, NY 10019
"Actor"

Guy Michelmore
72 Goldsmith Avenue
London, W3 6HN England
"Actor"

Bette Midler
135 Watts Street #400
New York, NY 10013
"Singer, Actress, Comedienne"

Mighty Morphin Power Rangers
26020-A Avenue Hall
Valencia, CA 91355
"Martial Arts Fighting Characters"

Mike & The Mechanics
9000 Sunset Blvd. #1200
Los Angeles, CA 90069
"Rock & Roll Group

George Mikell
23 Shuttleworth Road
London SW11 ENGLAND
"Actor"

Sen. Barbara A. Mikulski (MD)
Senate Hart Bldg. #709
Washington, DC 20510
"Politician"

Alyssa Milano
25 Sea Colony Drive
Santa Monica, CA 90405
"Actress"

Joanna Miles
2062 North Vine Street
Los Angeles, CA 90068
"Actress"

Sarah Miles
Chithurst Manor
Trotton, nr. Petersfield
Hampshire GU31 5EU ENGLAND
"Actor, Singer"

Sylvia Miles
240 Central Park South #191
New York, NY 10019
"Actress"

Vera Miles
P.O. Box 1704
Big Bear Lake, CA 92315
"Actress"

John Milford
334 South Bentley Avenue
Los Angeles, CA 90049
"Actor"

Tomas Milian
Via Giosue Carducci 10
1-00187 Rome ITALY
"Actor"

Michael Milken
4543 Tara Drive
Encino, CA 91436
"Stock Broker"

Ann Miller
618 North Alta Drive
Beverly Hills, CA 90210
"Actress, Dancer"

Arthur Miller
Box 320 RR #1 Tophet Road
Roxbury, CT 06783
"Author, Dramatist"

Cheryl Miller
6767 Forest Lawn Drive #115
Los Angeles, CA 90068
"Sports Analyst"

Denise Miller
814 N. Mansfield Avenue
Los Angeles, CA 90038
"Actress"

Dennis Miller
40 W. 57th Street
New York, NY 10019
"TV Show Host"

Denny Miller
733 N. Seward Street, PH
Los Angeles, CA 90038
"Actor"

Jason Miller
436 Spruce Street #600
Scranton, PA 18503
"Actor, Writer, Director"

Jeremy Miller
5255 Vesper Avenure
Van Nuys, CA 91411
"Actor"

Jody Miller
Rt. #3
Blanchard, OK 73010
"Singer"

Johnny Miller
P.O. Box 2260
Napa, CA 94558
"Golfer"

Johnny Lee Miller
8730 Sunset Blvd. #490
Los Angeles, CA 90069
"Actor"

Jonathan Miller
63 Gloucester Crescent
London NW1 ENGLAND
"Film Director"

Linda G. Miller
242 Conway Avenue
Los Angeles, CA 90024
"Actress"

Mitch Miller
345 West 58th Street
New York, NY 10019
"Musician, Composer"

Penelope Ann Miller
P.O. Box 7369
Santa Monica, CA 90406
"Actress"

Reggie Miller
11116 Catamaran Court
Indianapolis, IN 46236
"Basketball Player"

Shannon Miller
P.O. Box 5103
Edmond, OK 73083
"Gymnast"

Sidney Miller
2724 Bottlebrush Drive
Los Angeles, CA 90077
"Actor, Director"

Spike Milligan
9 Orme Court
London W2 ENGLAND
"Actor, Director"

Alley Mills
444 Carol Canal
Venice, CA 90291
"Actress"

Donna Mills
2660 Benedict Canyon
Beverly Hills, CA 90210
"Actress, Model"

Hayley Mills
81 High Street
Hampton, Middlesex, ENGLAND
"Actress"

Sir John Mills
Hill House
Denham Village
Buckinghamshire ENGLAND
"Actor"

Juliet Mills
340 East 64th Street #25
New York, NY 10021
"Actress"

Stephanie Mills
1995 Broadway #501
New York, NY 10023
"Singer"

Martin Milner
10100 Santa Monica Blvd. #2490
Los Angeles, CA 90067
"Actor, Radio Personality"

Ronnie Milsap
3015 Theater Drive
Myrtle Beach, SC 29577
"Singer, Songwriter"

Yvette Mimieux
500 Perugia Way
Los Angeles, CA 90077
"Actress, Writer"

Jan Miner
P.O. Box 293
Southbury, CT 06488
"Actress"

Anthony Minghella
31/32 Soho Square
London W1V 5DG ENGLAND
"Actor"

Charles Mingus
484 W. 43rd Street #43-S
New York, NY 10036
"Bassist"

Liza Minnelli
160 Central Park South
New York, NY 10019
"Actress, Singer"

Kylie Minogue
10 Bovington Road
London SW6 2AP, ENGLAND
"Singer"

Michael Minor
280 S. Beverly Drive #400
Beverly Hills, CA 90212
"Actor"

Minnie Minoso
805 Main Road
Independence, MO 64056
"Ex-Baseball Player"

Miou-Miou
10 Avenue George V
75008 Paris, FRANCE
"Actress"

Walter Mirisch
647 Warner Avenue
Los Angeles, CA 90024
"Film Executive, Producer"

Helen Mirren
55 Park Lane
London W1Y 3DD ENGLAND
"Actress"

Missing Persons
11935 Laurel Hills Road
Studio City, CA 91604
"Rock & Roll Group"

Mr. Mister
P.O. Box 69343
Los Angeles, CA 90069
"Rock & Roll Group"

Don Mitchell
1930 South Marvin
Los Angeles, CA 90016
"Actor"

Capt. Edgar Mitchell
5968 Western Way
Lake Worth, FL 33463
"Astronuat"

Ex-Sen. George Mitchell
8280 Greensboro Drive
McLean, VA 22102
"Politician"

James Mitchell
330 West 72nd Street #12C
New York, NY 10023
"Actor"

Joni Mitchell
1505 W. 2nd Avenue #200
Vancouver BC V6H 3Y4
CANADA
"Singer, Songwriter"

Kim Mitchell
41 Britain Street #305
Toronto, Ont. M5A 1R7 CANADA
"Singer, Guitarist"

Sasha Mitchell
9057 A Nemo Street
W. Hollywood, CA 90069
"Actress"

Shirley Mitchell
8730 Sunset Blvd. #200W
Los Angeles, CA 90069
"Actress"

Warren Mitchell
28 Sheldon Avenue
London N6 ENGLAND
"Actor"

Marvin Mitchelson
2500 Apollo Drive
Los Angeles, CA 90046
"Talent Agent"

Carrie Mitchum
3500 W. Olive Avenue #1400
Burbank, CA 91505
"Actress"

John Mitchum
15612 Liberty Circle
Nevada City, CA 95959
"Actor"

Rosi Mittermaier
Winkelmoosalm
D-83242 Reit im Winkel
GERMANY
"Skier"

Kim Miyori
121 North San Vicente Blvd.
Beverly Hills, CA 90211
"Actress"

Larry Mize
106 Greystone Court
Columbus, GA 31904
"Golfer"

Mary Ann Mobley
2751 Hutton Drive
Beverly Hills, CA 90210
"Actress"

Jayne Modean
10000 Santa Monica Blvd.
Suite #305
Los Angeles, CA 90025
"Actress"

The Modernaires
RD #1, Box 91
Tannersville, PA 18372
"Vocal Group"

Matthew Modine
9696 Culver Blvd. #203
Culver City, CA 90232
"Actor"

John Moffatt
59A Warrington Street
London W9 ENGLAND
"Actor"

Katy Moffatt
PO Box 334
O'Fallon, IL 62269
"Singer, Songwriter"

D.W. Moffett
450 N. Rossmore Avenue #401
Los Angeles, CA 90004
"Actor"

Jay Mohr
9200 Sunset Blvd. #1130
Los Angeles, CA 90069
"Actor"

Al Molinaro
P.O. Box 9218
Glendale, CA 91226
"Actor"

Richard Moll
1119 N. Amalfi Drive
Pacific Palisades, CA 90272
"Actor"

Thomas L. Monaghan
3001 Earhart
Ann Arbor, MI 48106
"Domino Pizza Owner"

Paul Monash
912 Alto Cedro Drive
Beverly Hills, CA 90210
"Writer, Producer"

Walter Mondale
2116 Irving Avenue S.
Minneapolis, MN 55405
"Ambassador"

Rick Monday
149 42nd Avenue
San Mateo, CA 94403
"EX-Baseball Player"

Eddie Money
P.O. Box 429094
San Francisco, CA 94142
"Singer"

Corbett Monica
PO Box 801406
Miami, FL 33280
"Comedian, Actor"

The Monkees
8369A Sausalito Avenue
West Hills, CA 91304
"Rock & Roll Group"

Bob Monkhouse
118 Beaufort Street
London SW3 6BU ENGLAND
"Actor, Writer"

Earl Monroe
535 Boulevard
Kenilworth, NJ 07033
"Ex-Basketball Player"

Joe Montagna
10415 Sarah Street
Toluca Lake, CA 91602
"Actor"

Ashley Montague
321 Cherry Hill Road
Princeton, NJ 08540
"Model"

Lee Montague
5 Keats Close
London NW3 ENGLAND
"Actor"

Ricardo Montalban
1423 Oriole Drive
Los Angeles, CA 90069
"Actor, Director"

Joe Montana
21515 Hawthorne Blvd. #1250
Torrance, CA 90503
"Football Player"

Monte Montana
10326 Montana Lane
Agua Dulce, CA 91350
"Actor"

Kelly Monteith
P.O. Box 11669
Knoxville, TN 37939
"Comedian, Writer"

Liliane Montevecchi
24 W. 40th St. #1700
New York, NY 10011
"Singer"

George Montgomery
P.O. Box 2187
Rancho Mirage, CA 92270
"Actor"

John Michael Montgomery
P.O. Box 639
Danville, KY 40423
"Singer"

Ron Moody
Ingleside
41 The Green, Southgate
London N14 ENGLAND
"Actor"

Rev. Donn Moomaw
3124 Corda Drive
Los Angeles, CA 90049
"Clergy"

Rev. Sun Myung Moon
4 West 43rd Street
New York, NY 10010
"Cult Leader"

Warren Moon
1 Lakeside Estate Drive
Missouri City, TX 77459
"Football Player"

Archie Moore
145 Hugenot Street
New Rochelle, NY 10301
"Boxer"

Clayton Moore
4720 Parkolivo
Calabasas, CA 91302
"Actor"

Constance Moore
10450 Wilshire Blvd. #1-B
Los Angeles, CA 90024
"Actress"

Demi Moore
955 S. Carrillio Drive #200
Los Angeles, CA 90048
"Actress"

Dickie Moore
150 West End Avenue #26C
New York, NY 10023
"Actor"

Dudley Moore
73 Market Street
Venice, CA 90291
"Actor, Writer, Pianist"

Julianne Moore
8912 Burton Way
Beverly Hills, CA 90211
"Actress"

Mary Tyler Moore
510 East 86th Street #21A
New York, NY 10028
"Actress"

Melba Moore
c/o HUSH
231 West 58th Street
New York, NY 10019
"Singer"

Roger Moore
2-4 Noel Street
London W1V 3RB ENGLAND
"Actor"

Terry Moore
10366 Wilshire Blvd. #5
Los Angeles, CA 90024
"Actress"

Jim Mora
6928 Saints Drive
Metairie, LA 70003
"Football Coach"

Esai Morales
1147 South Wooster Street
Los Angeles, CA 90035
"Actor"

Erin Moran
1800 Avenue of the Stars, #400
Los Angeles, CA 90067
"Actress"

Peggy Moran
3101 Village #3
Camarillo, CA 93010
"Actress"

Tony Mordente
4541 Comber
Encino, CA 91316
"Film Director"

Jeanne Moreau
5 rue Clemont Marot
F-75008 Paris, FRANCE
"Actress"

Rita Moreno
1620 Amalfi Drive
Pacific Palisades, CA 90272
"Actress"

Cindy Morgan
280 South Beverly Drive #400
Beverly Hills, CA 90212
"Actress"

Debbie Morgan
8091 Selma Avenue
Los Angeles, CA 90046
"Actress"

Elaine Morgan
24 Aberfford Road
Mountain Ash
Glamorgan ENGLAND
"Playwright"

Harry Morgan
13172 Boca De Canon Lane
Los Angeles, CA 90049
"Actor, Director"

Jane Morgan
27740 Pacific Coast Highway
Malibu, CA 90265
"Actress"

Jaye P. Morgan
1185 La Grange Avenue
Newbury Park, CA 91320
"Actress"

Joe Morgan
3239 Danvill Blvd. #A
Alamo, CA 94507
"Ex-Baseball Player"

Lorrie Morgan
P.O. Box 78
Spencer, TN 37212
"Singer"

Michelle Morgan
5 rue Jacques Dulud
92200 Neuily, FRANCE
"Actress"

Robert M. Morganthau
1085 Park Avenue
New York, NY 10028
"Attorney"

Cathy Moriarity
1100 Alta Loma Road #801
West Hollywood, CA 90069
"Actress"

Michael Moriarty
200 West 58th Street #3B
New York, NY 10019
"Actor"

Patricia Morison
400 South Hauser Blvd.
Los Angeles, CA 90036
"Actress, Singer"

Alanis Morissette
75 Rockefeller Plaza #2100
New York, NY 10019
"Singer"

Noriyuki "Pat" Morita
P.O. Box 491278
Los Angeles, CA 90049
"Actor, Comedian"

Louisa Moritz
405 Cliffwood Avenue
Los Angeles, CA 90049
"Actress, Model"

Karen Morley
5320 Ben Avenue #3
North Hollywood, CA 91607
"Actress"

Alonzo Morning
701 Areana Blvd.
Miami, FL 33136
"Basketball Player"

Giorgio Moroder
9438 Civic Center Drive #101
Beverly Hills, CA 90210
"Composer, Conductor"

David Morphet
101 Honor Oak Road
London SE23 3LB ENGLAND
"Writer, Producer"

Dr. Desmond Morris
78 Danbury Road
Oxford, ENGLAND
"Zoologist, Author"

Dick Morris
20 Beeholm Road
West Redding, CT 06896
"Political Consultant"

Garret Morris
3740 Barham Blvd. #E116
Los Angeles, CA 90068
"Actor"

Gary Morris
2829 Dogwood Place
Nashville, TN 37204
"Actor, Singer"

Greg Morris
2829 Dogwood Place
Nashville, TN 37204
"Actor"

Howard Morris
2723 Carmar Drive
Los Angeles, CA 90046
"Actor, Director"

Phil Morris
704 Strand
Manhattan Beach, CA 90266
"Actor"

Mark Morrison
28 Kensington Church St.
London W8 4EP ENGLAND
"Singer"

Toni Morrison
185 Nassau Street
Princeton, NJ 08544
"Writer"

Van Morrison
12304 Santa Monica Blvd. #300
Los Angeles, CA 90025
"Singer, Songwriter"

Karen Morrow
9400 Readcrest Drive
Beverly Hills, CA 90210
"Actress"

Rob Morrow
151 El Camino Drive
Beverly Hills, CA 90212
"Actor"

David Morse
8721 Santa Monica Blvd. #21
W. Hollywood, CA 90069
"Actor"

Barry Morse
Box 7064, Edison
Alberta T7E 1V4 CANADA
"Actor"

Robert Morse
13830 Davana Terrace
Sherman Oaks, CA 91403
"Actor"

Craig Morton
19021 - 35th Place
Lake Oswego, OR 97034
"Ex-Football Player"

Gary Morton
40241 Clubview Drive
Rancho Mirage, CA 92270
"Comedian"

Joe Morton
606 North Larchmont Blvd.
Suite #309
Los Angeles, CA 90004
"Actor"

John Moschitta, Jr.
11601 Dunston Way #206
Los Angeles, CA 90049
"Actor"

Tad Mosel
149 Eastside Dr., Box 24-B
Concord, NH 03301
"Playwright"

Sen. Carol Moseley-Braun
Senate Hart Building #320
Washington, DC 20510
"Politician"

Mark Mosley
P.O. Box 17247
Washington, DC 20041
"Ex-Football Player"

Albert Moses
15 Overstone Road
Harpenden, Herts.
AL5 5PN ENGLAND
"Actor"

Billy Moses
405 Sycamore Road
Santa Monica, CA 90402
"Actor"

Edwin Moses
P.O. Box 120
Indianapolis, IN 46206
"Track & Field Athlete"

Roger E. Moseley
4470 Sunset Blvd. #107-342
Los Angeles, CA 90027
"Actor"

Kate Moss
5 Jubilee Place #100
London SW3 3TD ENGLAND
"Model"

Ronn Moss
7800 Beverly Blvd. #3371
Los Angeles, CA 90036
"Actor"

Sterling Moss
46 Shepherd Street, Mayfair
London W1Y 8JN ENGLAND
"Actor"

Donny Most
280 South Beverly Drive #400
Beverly Hills, CA 90212
"Actor"

Manny Mota
3926 Los Olivos Lane
La Crescenta, CA 91214
"Ex-Baseball Player"

Mark Mothersbaugh
2164 Sunset Plaza Drive
Los Angeles, CA 90046
"Writer"

Motley Crue
6255 Sunset Blvd. #1111
Hollywood, CA 90028
"Rock & Roll Group"

Stewart Mott
515 Madison Avenue
New York, NY 10022
"Philanthropist"

Mickey Mouse Club
P.O. Box 10200
Lake Buena Vista, FL 32830
"Fan Club"

Movita
2766 Motor Avenue
Los Angeles, CA 90064
"Actress"

Tia & Tamera Mowry
7813 Sunset Blvd.
Los Angeles, CA 90046
"Actress"

Bill Moyers
524 West 57th Street
New York, NY 10019
"News Correspondent"

Sen. Daniel Moynihan (NY)
Senate Russell Bldg. #464
Washington, DC 20510
"Politician"

Pres. Hosni Mubarak
Royal Palace
Cairo, EGYPT
"President of Egypt"

Roger Mudd
7167 Old Dominion Drive
McLean, VA 22101
"News Correspondent"

Armin Mueller-Stahl
c/o ZBF
Ordensmeisterstr. 15-1
D12099 Berlin GERMANY
"Actor"

Diana Muldaur
10100 Santa Monica Blvd. #2490
Los Angeles, CA 90067
"Actress"

Maria Muldaur
311 Oakdale Road
Charlotte, NC 28216
"Singer, Songwriter"

Patrick Muldoon
9300 Wilshire Blvd., #400
Beverly Hills, CA 90212
"Actor"

Shirley Muldowney
79559 North Avenue
Armada, MI 48005
"Race Car Driver"

Kate Mulgrew
11938 Foxboro Drive
Los Angeles, CA 90049
"Actress"

Chris Mulkey
918 Zenizia Avenue
Venice, CA 90291
"Actor"

Martin Mull
338 Chadbourne Avenue
Los Angeles, CA 90049
"Actor, Comedian, Writer"

Greg Mullavey
P.O. Box 46067
W. Hollywood, CA 90046
"Actor"

Lillian Muller
3435 Ocean Park Blvd. #206
Santa Monica, CA 90405
"Actress, Model"

Richard Mulligan
145 South Beachwood Drive
Los Angeles, CA 90004
"Actor"

Gardner Mulloy
800 NW 9th Avenue
Miami, FL 33136
"Tennis Player"

Dermot Mulroney
1180 S. Beverly Drive #618
Los Angeles, CA 90035
"Actor"

Billy Mumy
8271 Melrose Avenue #202
Los Angeles, CA 90046
"Actor"

The Muppets
P.O. Box 20726
New York, NY 10023
"Puppets"

Bobby Murcer
P.O. Box 75089
Oklahoma City, OK 73147
"Ex-Baseball Player"

George Murdock
5733 Sunfield Avenue
Lakewood, CA 90712
"Actor"

Rupert Murdoch
210 South Street
New York, NY 10002
"Publisher"

Sen. Frank Murkowski (AK)
Senate Hart Bldg. #706
Washington, DC 20510
"Politician"

Ben Murphy
3601 Vista Pacifica #17
Malibu, CA 90265
"Actor"

Dale Murphy
P.O. Box 4064
Atlanta, GA 30302
"Ex-Baseball Player"

Eddie Murphy
152 W. 57th Street #4700
New York, NY 10019
"Actor, Comedian"

John Cullen Murphy
14 Mead Avenue
Cos Cob, CT 06805
"Illustrator"

Michael Martin Murphy
207K Paseo Del Pueble Sur
Taos, NM 87571
"Singer, Guitarist"

Rosemary Murphy
220 East 73rd Street
New York, NY 10021
"Actress"

Anne Murray
406-68 Water Street
Vancouver B.C. V6B 14A
CANADA
"Singer"

Bill Murray
P.O. Box 2267
Redondo Beach, CA 90278
"Actor"

Don Murray
1215-F De La Vina Street
Santa Barbara, CA 93101
"Actor, Writer, Director"

Jan Murray
1157 Calle Vista
Beverly Hills, CA 90210
"Actor, Comedian"

Katherine Murray
2877 Kalakaua Avenue
Honolulu, HI 96815
"Dance Instructor"

Ruby Murray
10A Victoria Parade, Torquay
Devon ENGLAND
"Singer"

Kate Murtagh
15146 Moorpark Street
Sherman Oaks, CA 91403
"Actress"

Tony Musante
38 Bedford Street
New York, NY 10014
"Actor, Writer"

Brent Musburger
47 West 66th Street
New York, NY 10023
"Sportscaster"

Stan Musial
1655 Des Peres Rd. #125
St. Louis, MO 63131
"Ex-Baseball Player, Manager"

Marjorie Ann Mutchie
1169 Mary Circle
La Verne, CA 91750
"Actress"

Ornella Muti
Via Giovanni Bettolo 3
I-00195 Rome ITALY
"Actress"

Dikembe Mutombo
One CNN Center
South Tower, Suite 405
Atlanta, GA 30303
"Basketball Player"

Dee Dee Myers
30 Rockefeller Plaza
New York, NY 10112
"Ex-Press Secretary"

Mike Myers
9150 Wilshire Blvd. #350
Beverly Hills, CA 90212
"Actor"

Bess Myerson
3 East 71st Street
New York, NY 10021
"Columnist"

The Mystics
88 Anador Street
Staten Island, NY 10303
"Vocal Group"

John Naber
P.O. Box 50107
Pasadena, CA 91105
"Swimmer"

Jim Nabors
P.O. Box 10364
Honolulu, HI 96816
"Actor, Singer"

George Nader
893 Camino del Sur
Palm Springs, CA 92662
"Actor"

Michael Nader
200 West 57th Street #900
New York, NY 10019
"Actor"

Ralph Nader
1600-20th Street, NW
Washington, DC 20009
"Consumer Advocate"

Kathy Najimy
8383 Wilshire Blvd. #444
Beverly Hills, CA 90211
"Actress"

Joe Namath
7 Bay Harbor Road
Tequesta, FL 33469
"Ex-Football Player"

Nantucket
250 N. Kepler Road
Deland, FL 33724
"Rock & Roll Group"

Charles Napier
Star Rt. Box 60-H
Caliente, CA 93518
"Actor"

Hugo Napier
2207 N. Beachwood Drive
Los Angeles, CA 90068
"Actor"

Jack Narz
1906 Beverly Place
Beverly Hills, CA 90210
"TV Show Host"

Graham Nash
14930 Ventura Blvd. #205
Sherman Oaks, CA 91403
"Singer, Songwriter"

Richard Nash
19323 Oxnard Street
Tarzana, CA 91356
"Composer"

Ille Nastase
Calea Plevnei 14
Bucharest HUNGARY
"Tennis Player"

Marie-Jose Nat
10 rue Royale
75008 Paris, FRANCE
"Actress"

Kitten Natividad
5917 Oak Avenue, #148
Temple, City, CA 91780
"Actress, Model"

David Naughton
11774-B Moorpark Street
Studio City, CA 91604
"Actor, Singer"

James Naughton
8942 Wilshire Blvd.
Beverly Hills, CA 90211
"Actor"

Naughty by Nature
155 Morgan Street
Jersey City, NJ 07302
"Music Group"

Martina Navratilova
1266 E. Main Street #44
Stamford, CT 06902
"Tennis Player"

Patricia Neal
45 East End Avenue #4C
New York, NY 10028
"Actress"

Kevin Nealon
9363 Wilshire Blvd. #212
Beverly Hills, CA 90210
"Comedian"

Ronald Neame
2317 Kimridge Drive
Beverly Hills, CA 90210
"Film Director"

Holly Near
733-735 N. Main Street
Ann Arbor, MI 48104
"Singer"

Connie Needham
19721 Castlebar Drive
Rowland Heights, CA 91748
"Actress"

Hal Needham
2220 Avenue of the Stars #302
Los Angeles, CA 90067
"Writer, Producer"

Tracey Needham
9229 Sunset Blvd. #311
Los Angeles, CA 90069
"Actress"

Liam Neeson
200 Fulham Road
London SWI0 9PN ENGLAND
"Actress"

Taylor Negron
9000 Sunset Blvd. #1200
Los Angeles, CA 90069
"Actor"

Noel Neill
331 Sage Lane
Santa Monica, CA 90402
"Actress"

Sam Neill
P.O. Box 153, Noble Park
Victoria 3174 AUSTRALIA
"Actor"

LeRoy Neiman
1 West 67th Street
New York, NY 10023
"Artist"

Stacey Nelkin
2770 Hutton Drive
Beverly Hills, CA 90210
"Actress"

Kate Nelligan
40 W. 57th Street
New York, NY 10019
"Actress"

Barry Nelson
134 West 58th Street
New York, NY 10019
"Actor"

Byron Nelson
Rt. 3, Box 5
Litsey Road
Roanoke, TX 76262
"Golfer"

Craig Richard Nelson
8271 Melrose Avenue, #110
Los Angeles, CA 90046
"Actor"

Craig T. Nelson
28872 Boniface Drive
Malibu, CA 90265
"Actor, Writer"

David Nelson
4179 Valley Meadow Road
Encino, CA 91316
"Actor, Director"

Ed Nelson
1038 Marina Drive
Slidell, LA 70458
"Actor"

Frank Nelson
8906 Evanview Drive
Los Angeles, CA 90069
"Actor"

John Allen Nelson
10100 Santa Monica Blvd.
25th Floor
Los Angeles, CA 90067
"Actor"

Judd Nelson
409 N. Camden Drive #202
Beverly Hills, CA 90210
"Actor"

Tracy Nelson
13263 Ventura Blvd. #10
Studio City, CA 91604
"Actress"

Willie Nelson
Rt. #1
Briarcliff TT
Spicewood, TX 78669
"Singer, Songwriter"

Corin "Corkey" Nemec
701 N. Valley Street
Burbank, CA 91505
"Actor"

Franco Nero
Via di Monte del Gallo 26
I-00165 Rome, ITALY
"Actor"

Peter Nero
11806 N. 56th Street #B
Tampa, FL 33617
"Pianist"

Michael Nesmith
2828 Donald Douglas Loop N. #15
Santa Monica, CA 90405
"Singer, Producer"

Benjamin Netanyahue
38 Rehou King George
Tel Aviv 61231 ISRAEL
"Prime Minister"

Graig Nettles
963 Urania Avenue
Encinitas, CA 92024
"Ex-Baseball Player"

Lois Nettleton
11762-G Moorpark Street
Studio City, CA 91604
"Actress"

Bebe Neuwirth
144 Prospect Avenue
Princeton, NJ 08540
"Actress"

Aaron Neville
P.O. Box 750187
New Orleans, LA 70130
"Singer"

Claudette Nevins
3500 W. Olive Avenue #1400
Burbank, CA 91505
"Actress"

Nancy Nevinson
23 Mill Close, Fishbourne
Chichester ENGLAND
"Actress"

George Newbern
9150 Wilshire Blvd. #205
Beverly Hills, CA 90212
"Actor"

New Christy Minstrels
2112 Casitas Way
Palm Springs, CA 92264
"Vocal Group"

New Editon
151 El Camino Drive
Beverly Hills, CA 90212
"R&B Group"

New Grass Revival
P.O. Box 128037
Nashville, TN 37212
"C&W Group"

Bob Newhart
420 Amapola Lane
Los Angeles, CA 90077
"Actor, Comedian"

Samuel I. Newhouse, Jr.
950 Fingerboard Road
Staten Island, NY 10305
"Publishing Executive"

Anthony Newley
60 Old Brompton Road
London SW7 3LQ ENGLAND
"Singer, Actor, Writer"

Barry Newman
425 North Oakhurst Drive
Beverly Hills, CA 90210
"Actor"

Laraine Newman
10480 Ashton Avenue
Los Angeles, CA 90024
"Actress"

Nanette Newman
Seven Pines, Wentworth
Surrey GU25 4QP ENGLAND
"Actress"

Paul Newman
1120 - 5th Aveune #C
New York, NY 10128
"Actor"

Phyllis Newman
1501 Broadway #703
New York, NY 10036
"Actress"

Randy Newman
644 S. N. Doheny Drive
Los Angeles, CA 90069
"Singer, Songwriter"

Julie Newmar
204 South Carmelina Avenue
Los Angeles, CA 90049
"Actress, Model"

New Order
72 Chancellor's Road
London W6 9SG ENGLAND
"Rock & Roll Group"

New Riders of the Purple Sage
P.O. Box 3773
San Rafael, CA 94912
"Rock & Roll Group"

David Newsom
9229 Sunset Blvd. #710
Los Angeles, CA 90069
"Actor"

Tommy Newson
19315 Wells Drive
Tarzana, CA 91356
"Conductor"

Juice Newton
P.O. Box 3035
Rancho Santa Fe, CA 92067
"Singer"

Wayne Newton
3422 Happy Lane
Las Vegas, NV 89120
"Singer, Actor"

Olivia Newton-John
P.O. Box 2710
Malibu, CA 90265
"Singer, Actress"

Richard Ney
800 South San Rafael Avenue
Pasadena, CA 91105
"Actor"

Dustin Nguyen
465 No. Sierra Bonita Avenue #8
Los Angeles, CA 90036
"Actor"

Michelle Nicastro
1800 Avenue of the Stars, #400
Los Angeles, CA 90067
"Actress"

Denise Nicholas
932 Longwood Avenue
Los Angeles, CA 90019
"Actress, Singer"

Fayard Nicholas
23388 Mulholland Drive #5
Woodland Hills, CA 91364
"Dancer"

Harold Nicholas
789 West End Avenue
New York, NY 10025
"Dancer"

Bobby Nichols
8681 Glenlyon Coourt
Fort Meyers, FL 33912
"Golfer"

Mike Nichols
15 East 69th Street
New York, NY 10021
"Film Writer, Director"

Nichelle Nichols
22647 Ventura Blvd.
Woodland Hills, CA 91364
"Actress"

Stephen Nichols
11664 National Blvd. #116
Los Angeles, CA 90064
"Actor"

Terry Nichols
#08157-031
9595 West Quincy Avenue
Littleton, CO 80123
"Convict"

Jack Nicholson
15760 Ventura Blvd. #1730
Encino, CA 91436
"Actor"

Jack Nicklaus
11760 U.S. Highway 1 #6
North Palm Beach, FL 33408
"Golfer"

Sen. Don Nickles (OK)
Senate Hart Bldg. #133
Washington, DC 20510
"Politician"

Stevie Nicks
P.O. Box 7855
Alhambra, CA 91802
"Singer, Songwriter"

Julia Nickson
1206 S. Hudson Avenue
Los Angeles, CA 90019
"Actress"

Alex Nicol
1496 San Leandro Park
Santa Barbara, CA 93108
"Actor"

Joe Niekro
2707 Fairway Drive S.
Plant City, FL 33567
"Ex-Baseball Player"

Phil Niekro
6382 Nichols Road
Flowery Branch, GA 30542
"Ex-Basetball Player"

Brigitte Nielsen
P.O. Box 57593
Sherman Oaks, CA 91403
"Actress"

Leslie Nielsen
1622 Viewmont Drive
Los Angeles, CA 90069
"Actor"

Birgit Nilsson
P.O. Box 527
Stockholm, SWEDEN
"Soprano"

Leonard Nimoy
2300 W. Victory Blvd., #C-384
Burbank, CA 91506
"Actor, Writer, Director"

Yvette Nipar
121 N. San Vicente Blvd.
Beverly Hills, CA 90211
"Actress"

Paul Nitze
1619 Massachusetts Ave. N.W.
Suite #811
Washington, DC 20036
"Statesman"

Barbara Niven
145 S. Fairfax Avenue #310
Los Angeles, CA 90036
"Actress"

Mrs. Hjordis Niven
CH-1837 Chateau D'Oex
SWITZERLAND
"David Niven's Widower"

David Niven, Jr.
1457 Blue Jay Way
Los Angeles, CA 90069
"Son of David Niven"

Agnes Nixon
774 Conestoga Road
Rosemont, PA 19010
"TV Writer, Producer"

Julia Nixon-Eisenhower
Foxall Lane
Berwyn, PA 19312
"Ex-President's Daughter"

Norm Nixon
607 Marguerita Avenue
Santa Monica, CA 90402
"Ex-Basketball Player"

Yannick Noah
20 rue Billancourt
F-92100 Boulogne FRANCE
"Tennis Player"

Chelsea Noble
P.O. Box 8665
Calabasas, CA 91372
"Actress"

James Noble
80 Baavater Lane
Black Rock, CT 06605
"Actor"

Lyn Nofziger
2000 Pennsylvania Ave. NW #365
Washington, DC 20037
"Political Advisor"

Dr. Thomas Noguchi
1110 Avoca Avenue
Pasadena, CA 91105
"Coroner"

Natalija Nogulich
11841 Kiowa Avenue #7
Los Angeles, CA 90049
"Actress"

Philippe Noiret
104 rue des Sablons
F-78750 Mareil-Marly FRANCE
"Actor"

Christopher Nolan
158 Vernon Avenue
Dublin, IRELAND
"Poet, Author"

Kathleen Nolan
360 East 55th Street
New York, NY 10022
"Actress"

Tom Nolan
1335 North Ontario Street
Burbank, CA 91505
"Writer"

Gena Lee Nolin
2135 Groveland Drive
Los Angeles, CA 90046
"Actress"

Chuck Noll
201 Grant Street
Sewickley, PA 15143
"Ex-Football Coach"

Nick Nolte
6174 Bonsall Drive
Malibu, CA 90265
"Actor"

Hideo Nomo
1000 Elysian Park Avenue
Los Angeles, CA 90012
"Baseball Player"

Kathleen Noone
12747 Riverside Drive #208
Valley Village, CA 91607
"Actress"

Peter Noone
875 Avenue of the Americas #1908
New York, NY 10001
"Singer"

Clayton Norcross
951 Galloway Street
Pacific Palisades, CA 90272
"Actor"

Gen. Manuel Noriega
#38699-079
P.O. Box 979132
Miami, FL 33197
"Prisoner of War"

Greg Norman
501 N. AIA Suite
Jupiter, FL 33477
"Golfer"

Maide Norman
455 E. Charleston Road #132-B
Palo Alto, CA 94306
"Actress"

Christopher Norris
19528 Ventura Blvd. #323
Tarzana, CA 91356
"Actress"

Chuck Norris
P.O. Box 872
Navosota, TX 77868
"Actor"

Jay North
290 NE First Avenue
Lake Butler, FL 32054
"Actor"

Oliver North
P.O. Box 9771
McLean, VA 22102
"Former Military Lt. Col."

Wayne Northrup
21919 West Canon Drive
Topanga, CA 90290
"Actor"

Edward Norton
8000 Sunset Blvd. #300
Los Angeles, CA 90046
"Actor"

Ken Norton
20451 Puerto Vallerta Drive
Laguna Niguel, CA 92677
"Boxer, Actor"

Deborah Norville
P.O. Box 426
Mill Neck, NY 11765
"TV Show Host"

Jack Noseworthy
606 N. Larchmont Blvd. #309
Los Angeles, CA 90004
"Actor"

Chris Noth
9560 Wilshire Blvd. #516
Beverly Hills, CA 90212
"Actor"

Michael Nouri
14 West 68th Street #12
New York, NY 10023
"Actor"

William Novack
3 Ashton
Newton, MA 02159
"Author"

Robert Novak
1750 Pennsylvania Avenue N.W.
Suite #1312
Washington, DC 20006
"News Journalist, Columnist"

Don Novello
P.O. Box 245
Fairfax, CA 94930
"Actor, Writer, Comedian"

Danny Nucci
3500 W. Olive Avenue #1400
Burbank, CA 91505
"Actor"

Eddie Nugent
P.O. Box 1266
New York, NY 10150
"Actor"

Ted Nugent
8000 Eckert
Concord, MI 49237
"Singer, Guitarist"

Sam Nunn
915 Main Street
Perry, GA 31060
"Politician"

France Nuyen
9255 Sunset Blvd., #515
Los Angeles, CA 90069
"Actress"

Carrie Nye
200 West 57th Street #900
New York, NY 10019
"Actress"

Louis Nye
1241 Corsica Drive
Pacific Palisdaes, CA 90272
"Actor, Comedian"

Oak Ridge Boys
2102 West Linden Avenue
Nashville, TN 37212
"C&W Group"

Oasis
8A Wyndham Place
London W1X 1PP ENGLAND
"Gospel Group"

John Oates
130 West 57th Street #12B
New York, NY 10019
"Singer, Songwriter"

Hugh O'Brian
10880 Wilshire Blvd. #1500
Los Angeles, CA 90024
"Actor"

Conan O'Brien
30 Rockefeller Plaza
New York, NY 10019
"Talk Show Host"

Cubby O'Brien
2839 N. Surrey Drive
Carrollton, TX 75004
"Actor"

Dan O'Brien
P.O. Box 9344
Moscow, ID 83843
"Decathlete"

Margaret O'Brien
1250 La Peresa Drive
Thousand Oaks, CA 91362
"Actress"

Billy Ocean
Ascot
Berkshire ENGLAND
"Singer"

Jerry O'Connell
151 El Camino Drive
Beverly Hills, CA 90212
"Actor"

Mark O'Conner
7957 Nita Avenue
Canoga Park, CA 91304
"Violinist"

Carroll O'Connor
30826 Broad Beach Road
Malibu, CA 90265
"Actor, Writer, Director"

Des O'Connor
23 Eyot Gardens
London W6 9TR ENGLAND
"Singer"

Donald O'Connor
P.O. Box 20204
Sedona, AZ 86341
"Actor, Director"

Glynnis O'Connor
2400 Whitman Avenue
Los Angeles, CA 90068
"Actress"

Sandra Day O'Connor
1-1st Street, Northeast
Washington, DC 20543
"Supreme Court Justice"

Tim O'Connor
P.O. Box 458
Nevada City, CA 95959
"Actor"

Anita O'Day
1862 Vista del Mar
Hollywood, CA 90028
"Entertainer, Singer"

Tony O'Dell
417 Griffith Park Drive
Burbank, CA 91506
"Actor"

Chris O'Donnell
P.O. Box 220250
St. Louis, MO 63112
"Actor"

Rosie O'Donnell
235 No. Broadway
Nyack, NY 10960
"Actress"

Martha O'Driscoll
22 Indian Creek Village
Miami Beach, FL 33154
"Actress"

Al Oerter
5485 Avenieda Pescadera
Ft. Meyers, FL 33931
"Executive, Discus Thrower"

Ian Ogilvy
68 St. James's Street
London SW1A 1LE ENGLAND
"Actor"

Lani O'Grady
4181 W. Kling Street #54
Burbank, CA 91505
"Actress"

Soon-Teck Oh
128 N. Kenwood Street
Burbank, CA 91505
"Actor"

Jenny O'Hara
1801 Avenue of the Stars #902
Los Angeles, CA 90067
"Actress"

Maureen O'Hara
P.O. Box 1400
Christiansted 00820
St. Croix, VIRGIN ISLANDS
"Actress"

Michael O'Hare
280 S. Beverly Drive #400
Beverly Hills, CA 90212
"Actor"

Dan O'Herlihy
24 W. 40th Street #1700
New York, NY 10018
"Actor"

Michael O'Keeffe
1344 North Spaulding
Los Angeles, CA 90046
"Actor"

Paul O'Keefe
225 W. 83rd Street #9-5
New York, NY 10027
"Actor"

Miles O'Keeffe
1725-B Madison Avenue #625
Memphis, TN 38104
"Actor"

Ken Olandt
3500 West Olive #1400
Burbank, CA 91505
"Actor"

Mike Oldfield
115-A Glenthorne Road
London W6 OLJ ENGLAND
"Musician, Composer"

Sally Oldfield
100 Chalk Farm Road
London NW1 ENGLAND
"Singer"

Gary Oldman
76 Oxford Street
London W1N OAX ENGLAND
"Actor"

Michael O'Leary
8075 West 3rd Street #303
Los Angeles, CA 90048
"Actress"

Ken Olefson
6720 Hillpark Drive #301
Los Angeles, CA 90068
"Actor"

Ken Olin
5855 Topanga Canyon #410
Woodland Hills, CA 91367
"Actor"

Lena Olin
40 West 57th Street
New York, NY 10019
"Actress"

Jane Oliver
23-50 Waters Edge Dr.
Bayside, NY 11360
"Singer"

Edward James Olmos
18034 Ventura Blvd. #228
Encino, CA 91316
"Actor"

Gerald O'Loughlin
P.O. Box 340832
Arleta, CA 91334
"Actor, Director"

Ashley Olsen
8916 Ashcroft Avenue
Los Angeles, CA 90048
"Actress"

Mary Kate Olsen
8916 Ashcroft Avenue
Los Angeles, CA 90048
"Actress"

Merlin Olsen
P.O. Box 3148
Park City, UT 84060
"Ex-Football Player"

Nancy Olsen
945 North Alpine Drive
Beverly Hills, CA 90210
"Actress"

James Olson
250 West 57th Street #2223
New York, NY 10019
"Actor"

Saltan of Oman
The Palace
Muslat OMAN
"Royalty"

Kate O'Mara
11 Southwick Mews
London W2 1JG ENGLAND
"Actress"

Sydney Omarr
201 Ocean Avenue #1706-B
Santa Monica, CA 90402
"Astrologer, Writer"

Athina Onassis
88 Avenue Foch
75016 Paris FRANCE
"Richest Girl in the World"

Griffin O'Neal
21368 Pacific Coast Highway
Malibu, CA 90265
"Screenwriter"

Ryan O'Neal
21368 Pacific Coast Highway
Malibu, CA 90265
"Actor"

Shaquille O'Neal
3110 Main Street #225
Santa Monica, CA 90405
"Basketball Player"

Tatum O'Neal
300 Central Park West #16-G
New York, NY 10024
"Actress"

Dick O'Neil
443 S. Oakhurst Dr., PH 401
Beverly Hills, CA 90212
"Actor"

Jennifer O'Neil
1191 Cross Creek Road
Franklin, TN 37067
"Actress, Model"

Ron O'Neil
10100 Santa Monica Blvd., #2500
Los Angeles, CA 90067
"Actor"

Ed O'Neill
9150 Wilshire Blvd. #350
Beverly Hills, CA 90212
"Actor"

Yoko Ono Lennon
1 West 72nd Street
New York, NY 10023
"Singer, Songwriter"

Michael Ontkean
P.O. Box 1212
Malibu, CA 90265
"Actor"

Marcel Ophuls
10 rue Ernst-Deloison
92200 Neuilly, FRANCE
"Director, Producer"

Jerry Orbach
10100 Santa Monica Blvd., #2490
Los Angeles, CA 90067
"Actor"

Cyril O'Reilly
8091 Selma Avenue
Los Angeles, CA 90046
"Actor"

Tony Orlando
3220 Falls Parkway
Branson, MO 65616
"Singer"

Yuri Orlov
Cornell University
Newman Laboratory
Ithica, NJ 14853
"Scientist"

Julia Ormond
308 Regent St.
London W1R 5AL ENGLAND
"Actress"

Bobby Orr
300 Boylston Street #605
Boston, MA 02116
"Ex-Hockey Player"

Brian Orser
1600 James Naismith Dr.
Gloucester Ontario
K1B 5N4 CANADA
"Skater"

Joan Osbourne
83 Riverside Drive
New York, NY 10024
"Singer"

Jeffrey Osbourne
P.O. Box 3718
Los Angeles, CA 90078
"Singer, Songwriter"

Ozzy Osbourne
P.O. Box 3718
Los Angeles, CA 90078
"Singer, Songwriter"

Tom Osburne
University of Nebraska Football
Lincoln, NE 68588
"Football Coach"

Milo O' Shea
40 West 72nd Street #17-A
New York, NY 10023
"Actor"

Nagisa Osima
4-11-5, Kugenuma-Matsugaoka
Fujisawa-Shi 251 JAPAN
"Director"

K.T. Oslin
1103-16th Avenue
Nashville, TN 37212
"Singer"

Haley Joel Osment
3000 W. Alameda Avenue
Burbank, CA 91523
"Actor"

Cliff Osmond
630 Bienvenida
Pacific Palisades, CA 90272
"Screenwriter"

Donny Osmond
36 Avignon
Newport Beach, CA 92657
"Singer"

Ken Osmond
9863 Wornom Avenue
Sunland, CA 91040
"Actor"

Marie Osmond
3325 N. University Avenue
Provo, UT 84604
"Singer, Actress"

The Osmonds
P.O. Box 7122
Branson, MO 65616
"Vocal Group"

Jeff Osterhage
210-D North Cordova
Burbank, CA 91505
"Actor"

Bibi Osterwald
341 Carrol Park West
Long Beach, CA 90815
"Actress"

Gilbert O'Sullivan
6 Deep Meadow Road
Barrington, RI 02806
"Singer"

Johnny Otis
2608 Ninth Street
Berkeley, CA 94710
"Singer, Guitarist"

Annette O'Toole
360 Morton Street
Ashland, OR 97520
"Actress"

Peter O'Toole
31/32 Soho Square
London W1V 5DG ENGLAND
"Actor"

Merlene Ottey
P.O. Box 120
Indianapolis, IN 46206
"Track & Field"

Park Overall
4843 Arcola Avenue
North Hollywood, CA 91601
"Actress"

Paul Overstreet
909 Meadowlark Lane
Goodletteville, TN 37072
"Singer"

Michael Ovitz
9465 Wilshire Blvd. #750
Beverly Hills, CA 90212
"Talent Agent"

Randy Owen
Rt. #4
Ft. Payne, AL 35967
"Guitarist, Singer"

Buck Owens
3223 Sillect Avenue
Bakersfield, CA 93308
"Singer, Songwriter"

Gary Owens
17856 Via Vallarta
Encino, CA 91316
"Radio/TV Performer"

Catherine Oxenberg
505 S. Beverly Hills, CA 90212
Beverly Hills, CA 90212
"Actress, Model"

Frank Oz
P.O. Box 20750
New York, NY 10023
"Puppeteer"

Jack Paar
9 Chateau Ridge Drive
Greenwich, CT 06830
"Ex-TV Show Host

Pablo Cruise
P.O. Box 779
Mill Valley, CA 94941
"Rock & Roll Group"

Judy Pace
4139 Cloverdale
Los Angeles, CA 90008
"Actress"

Al Pacino
301 W. 57th Street #16
New York, NY 10019
"Actor"

Kelly Packard
5433 Beethoven Street
Los Angeles, CA 90066
"Actress"

Joanna Pacula
1465 Lindacrest Drive
Beverly Hills, CA 90210
"Actress"

Anita Page
929 Rutland Avenue
Los Angeles, CA 90042
"Actress"

Bettie Page
P.O. Box 2594
Woodinville, WA 98072
"50's Pin-up Girl"

Genevieve Page
52 rue de Vaugirard
75006 Paris FRANCE
"Actress"

Jimmy Page
29/33 Berner's Street
London W1P 4AA ENGLAND
"Guitarist"

LaWanda Page
1056 West 84th Street
Los Angeles, CA 90044
"Actress"

Patti Page
71537 Highway #K
Rancho Mirage, CA 92270
"Singer"

Debra Paget
737 Kuhlman Road
Houston, TX 77024
"Actress"

Ashraf Pahlavi
12 Avenue Montaigne
75016 Paris FRANCE
"Royalty"

David Paich
5323 Bellaire Avenue
No. Hollywood, CA 91607
"Composer, Conductor"

Elaine Paige
Arlon, Pinewood Road
Iver. Buckinghamshire
SL0 0NH ENGLAND
"Actress"

Janis Paige
1700 Rising Glen Road
Los Angeles, CA 90069
"Actress"

Rev. Ian Paisley
The Parsonage
17 Cyprus Avenue
Belfast BT5 5NT IRELAND
"Clergyman"

Alan Pakula
330 West 58th Street #5-H
New York, NY 10019
"Writer, Producer"

Holly Palance
2753 Roscomare
Los Angeles, CA 90077
"Actress"

Jack Palance
785 Tucker Road #G-206
Tehachapi, CA 93561
"Actor, Director"

Ron Palillo
448 W. 44th Street
New York, NY 10036
"Actor"

Michael Palin
68A Delancey Street
London W1 ENGLAND
"Actor, Writer"

Arnold Palmer
100 Avenue of Champions
Palm Beach Gardens, FL 33418
"Golfer"

Betsy Palmer
40 Jordan Drive
River Edge, NJ 07661
"Actress"

Gregg Palmer
5726 Graves Avenue
Encino, CA 91316
"Actor"

Gretchen Palmer
15301 Ventura Blvd. #345
Sherman Oaks, CA 91403
"Actress"

Jim Palmer
P.O. Box 590
Cooperstown, NY 13325
"Ex-Baseball Player, Model"

Peter Palmer
478 Severn
Tampa, FL 33606
"Actor"

Robert Palmer
584 Broadway #1201
New York, NY 10012
"Singer, Songwriter"

Chazz Palminteri
375 Greenwich St.
New York, NY, 10013
"Actor"

Bruce Paltrow
304-21st Street
Santa Monica, CA 90402
"Actor"

Gwyneth Paltrow
9830 Wilshire Blvd.
Beverly Hils, CA 90212
"Actress"

May Pang
1619 Third Avenue #9D
New York, NY 10128
"John Lennon's Mistress"

Stuart Pankin
9150 Wilshire Blvd. #350
Beverly Hills, CA 90212
"Actor"

Joe Pantaliano
2313 - 30th Street
Santa Monica, CA 90405
"Actor"

Irene Papas
Xenokratous 39
Athens-Kolanaki, GREECE
"Actress"

Milt Pappas
205 Thompson Drive
Wheaton, IL 60187
"Ex-Baseball Player"

Anna Paquin
P.O. Box 9585
Wellington, New Zealand
"Actress"

Ara Paraseghian
51767 Oakbrook Court
Granger, IN 46539
"Former College Coach"

Jack Pardee
P.O. Box 272
Grause, TX 77857
"Ex-Football Coach"

Michael Pare
2804 Pacific Avenue
Venice, CA 90291
"Actor"

Gail Parent
2001 Mandeville Canyon
Los Angeles, CA 90024
"Screenwriter"

Judy Parfitt
924 Westwood Blvd. #900
Los Angeles, CA 90024
"Actress"

Corey Parker
10431 Scenario Lane
Los Angeles, CA 90077
"Actor"

Dave Parker
7864 Ridge Road
Cincinnati, OH 45237
"Ex-Baseball Player"

Eleanor Parker
2195 La Paz Way
Palm Springs, CA 92262
"Actress"

Fess Parker
P.O. Box 908
Los Olivos, CA 93441
"Actor"

Jameson Parker
1604 North Vista Avenue
Los Angeles, CA 90046
"Actor"

Mary Louise Parker
151 El Camino Drive
Beverly Hills, CA 90212
"Actress"

Robert B. Parker
555 W. 57th Street #1230
New York, NY 10019
"Author"

Sarah Jessica Parker
P.O. Box 69646
Los Angeles, CA 90069
"Actress"

Suzy Parker
770 Hot Springs Road
Santa Barbara, CA 93103
"Actress"

Willard Parker
74580 Fairway Drive
Indian Wells, CA 92260
"Actor"

Camilla Parker-Bowles
Ray Mill House
Reybridge. nr. Chippenham
Wiltshire ENGLAND
"Prince Charles' Friend"

Heather Parkhurst
8383 Wilshire Blvd. #954
Beverly Hills, CA 90211
"Actress"

Barbara Parkins
1317 - 5th Street #200
Santa Monica, CA 90401
"Actress"

Michael Parkinson
58 Queen Anne Street
London W1M 0DX ENGLAND
"Writer"

Andrew Parks
1830 Grace Avenue
Los Angeles, CA 90028
"Actor"

Rosa Parks
9336 Wildemere Street
Detroit, MI 48206
"Mother of Civil Rights"

Lee Roy Parnell
P.O. Box 120073
Nashville, TN 37212
"Singer"

Van Dyke Parks
1801 Century Park E. #2400
Los Angeles, CA 90067
"Actress"

Julie Parrish
P.O. Box 247
Santa Monica, CA 90406
"Actress"

Peter Parros
15 Carter Road
West Orange, NJ 07052
"Actor"

Estelle Parsons
505 West End Avenue
New York, NY 10024
"Actress"

Karyn Parsons
8428-C Melrose Place
Los Angeles, CA 90069
"Actress"

Nancy Parsons
121 North San Vicente Blvd.
Beverly Hills, CA 90211
"Actress"

Dolly Parton
P.O. Box 150307
Nashville, TN 37215
"Singer, Actress"

Stella Parton
P.O. Box 120295
Nashville, TN 37212
"Singer"

Derek Partridge
96 Broadway
Bexley Heath
Kent DA6 7DE ENGLAND
"Actor"

Francoise Pascal
89 Riverview Gardens
London SW12 ENGLAND
"Actress"

Adrian Pasdar
4250 Wilshire Blvd.
Los Angeles, CA 90010
"Actor"

Robert Pastorelli
2751 Holly Ridge Drive
Los Angeles, CA 90068
"Actor"

Michael Pate
21 Bukdarra Road
Bellevue Hill 2023
AUSTRALIA
"Actor"

Joe Paterno
830 McKee Street
State College, PA 16803
"College Football Coach"

Mandy Patinkin
200 West 90th Street
New York, NY 10024
"Actress"

Tatjana Patitz
111 E. 22nd Street #200
New York, NY 10010
"Model"

Jason Patric
10683 Santa Monica Blvd.
Los Angeles, CA 90025
"Actor"

Butch Patrick
P.O. Box 587
Farmingville, NY 11738
"Actor"

Robert Patrick
2700 La Cuesta Drive
Los Angeles, CA 90046
"Playwright"

Floyd Patterson
Springtown Road
P.O. Box 336
New Paltz, NY 12561
"Boxer"

Lorna Patterson
13530 Erwin Street
Van Nuys, CA 91401
"Actress"

Neva Patterson
2498 Maneville Canyon Road
Los Angeles, CA 90049
"Actress"

Sandi Patti
P.O. Box 2940
Anderson, IN 46018
"Singer"

Adrian Paul
1154 South Point View Street
Los Angeles, CA 90035
"Actor"

Alexandra Paul
5433 Beethoven Street
Los Angeles, CA 90066
"Actress"

Don Michael Paul
3104 Walnut Avenue
Manhattan Beach, CA 90266
"Actor"

Les Paul
78 Deerhaven Road
Mahwah, NJ 07430
"Guitarist"

Richard Paul
3614 Willowcrest Avenue
Studio City, CA 91604
"Actor"

Jane Pauley
271 Central Park West #10-E
New York, NY 10024
"TV Show Host"

Albert Paulsen
733 N. Seward Street PH
Los Angeles, CA 90038
"Actor"

Marisa Pavan
4 Allee des Borouillards
F-75018 Paris, FRANCE
"Actress"

Corey Paven
2515 McKinney #930, Box 10
Dallas, TX 75201
"Golfer"

Luciano Pavarotti
Via Giardini
I-41040 Saliceta
Panaro ITALY
"Tenor"

Ria Pavia
3500 West Olive Avenue, #1400
Burbank, CA 91505
"Actress"

Bill Paxton
151 El Camino Drive
Beverly Hills, CA 90212
"Actor"

Johnny Paycheck
P.O. Box 916
Hendersonville, TN 37077
"Singer"

David Paymer
1506 Pacific Street
Santa Monica, CA 90405
"Actor"

Freda Payne
245 S. Spalding Drive #302
Beverly Hills, CA 90212
"Singer"

Amanda Pays
3541 North Knoll Drive
Los Angeles, CA 90068
"Actress, Model"

Walter Payton
13400 S. Budler Road
Plainfield, IL 60544
"Ex-Football Player"

Vinnie Pazienda
64 Waterman Avenue
Cranston, RI 02910
"Boxer"

E. J. Peaker
4935 Densmore Avenue
Encino, CA 91436
"Actress"

Guy Pearce
Box 478
Kings Cross NSW 2011 AUSTRA-
LIA
"Actor"

Pearl Jam
417 Denny Way, #200
Seattle, WA 98109
"Rock & Roll Group"

Drew Pearson
1701 Eden Valley Lane
Plano, TX 75075
"Ex-Football Player"

Durk Pearson
P.O. Box 1067
Hollywood, FL 33022
"Scientist, Author"

Pebbles
530 Howard Street #200
San Francisco, CA 94105
"Singer"

Gregory Peck
P.O. Box 837
Beverly Hills, CA 90213
"Actor"

Nia Peeples
P.O. Box 5617
Beverly Hills, CA 90210
"Actress"

Rodney Peete
10683 Santa Monica Blvd.
Los Angeles, CA 90025
"Football Player"

I. M. Pei
600 Madison Avenue
New York, NY 10022
"Architect"

Ashley & Courtney Peldon
P.O. Box 57593
Sherman Oaks, CA 91403
"Actress"

Amanda Peet
10100 Santa Monica Blvd. #2500
Los Angeles, CA 90067
"Actress"

Courtney Peldon
P.O. Box 57593
Sherman Oaks, CA 91403
"Actress"

Pele
Praca dos Tres Poderes
Palacio de Planalto BR
70150900 Brasilia DF BRAZIL
"Soccer Player"

Lisa Pelikan
P.O. Box 57593
Sherman Oaks, CA 91403
"Actress"

Meeno Peluce
2713 North Keystone
Burbank, CA 91504
"Actor"

Elizabeth Pena
274 Muerdago Road
Topanga, CA 90290
"Actress"

Teddy Pendergrass
1505 Flat Rock Road
Narberth, PA 19072
"Singer, Songwriter"

Austin Pendleton
155 East 76th Street
New York, NY 10021
"Comedian"

Thao Penghlis
7187 Macapa Drive
Los Angeles, CA 90068
"Actor"

The Penguins
708 West 137th Street
Gardena, CA 90247
"Vocal Group"

Susan Penhaligon
109 Jermyn Street
London SW1 ENGLAND
"Actress"

Ce Ce Peniston
250 West 57th Street #821
New York, NY 10107
"Singer"

Chris Penn
9560 Wilshire Blvd. #516
Beverly Hills, CA 90212
"Actor"

Leo Penn
6728 Zumirez Drive
Malibu, CA 90265
"Filmwriter, Director"

Sean Penn
2049 Century Park East #2500
Los Angeles, CA 90067
"Actor"

Jonathan Penner
924 Westwood Blvd. #900
Los Angeles, CA 90024
"Actor"

Ann Pennington
701 N. Oakhurst Drive
Beverly Hills, CA 90210
"Actress, Model"

Janice Pennington
433 N. Camden Drive #600
Beverly Hills, CA 90210
"Model, Actress"

Michael Pennington
41 Marlborough Hill
London NW8 ENGLAND
"Actor"

Chris Pennock
25150 1/2 Malibu Road
Malibu, CA 90265
"Actor"

Joe Penny
10453 Sarah
North Hollywood, CA 91602
"Actor"

Sidney Penny
6894 Parson Trail
Tujunga, CA 91042
"Actress"

Roger Penske
13400 Outer Drive West
Detroit, MI 48239
"Auto Racing Executive"

Willie Pep
130 Hartford Avenue
Wethersfield, CT 06109
"Boxer"

Joe Pepitone
32 Lois Lane
Farmingdale, NY 11735
"Ex-Baseball Player"

Barry Pepper
3817 Puget Dr., Vancouver
BC V6L 2T8 CANADA
"Actor"

Charles Percy
1691-34th Street NW
Washington, DC 20007
"Ex-Senator"

Shimon Peres
10 Hayarkon Street
Box 3263
Tel Aviv 3263 ISRAEL
"Politician"

Rosie Perez
10683 Santa Monica Blvd.
Los Angeles, CA 90025
"Actress"

Vincent Perez
10 avenue George V
F-75008 Paris, France
"Actor"

Elizabeth Perkins
9830 Wilshire Blvd.
Beverly Hills, CA 90212
"Actress"

Jack Perkins
235 E. 45th Street
New York, NY 10017
"Actor"

Millie Perkins
2511 Canyon Drive
Los Angeles, CA 90068
"Actress"

Sam Perkins
131 Privateer Mall
Marina del Rey, CA 90292
"Basketball Player"

Rhea Perlman
P.O. Box 491246
Los Angeles, CA 90049
"Actress"

Ron Perlman
P.O. Box 5617
Beverly Hills, CA 90210
"Actress"

Mme. Isabel Peron
Moreto 3
Los Jeronimos, E-28014
Madrid SPAIN
"Politician"

H. Ross Perot
1700 Lakeside Square
Dallas, TX 75251
"Data Executive"

Gigi Perreau
268 North Bowling Green Way
Los Angeles, CA 90049
"Actress"

Valerie Perrine
Via Toscana 1
I-00187 Rome ITALY
"Actress, Model"

Barbara Perry
6926 La Presa Drive
Los Angeles, CA 90068
"Actress"

Felton Perry
540 South St. Andrews Place
Suite #5
Los Angeles, CA 90020
"Actor"

Gaylord Perry
P.O. Box 1958
Kill Devil Hills, NC 27948
"Ex-Baseball Player"

Jeff Perry
8458 Ridpath Avenue
Los Angeles, CA 90046
"Actor"

John Bennett Perry
606 N. Larchmont Blvd. #309
Los Angeles, CA 90004
"Actor"

Luke Perry
8484 Wilshire Blvd. #745
Beverly Hills, CA 90211
"Actor"

Matthew Perry
7204 Chelan Way #505
Los Angeles, CA 90068
"Actor"

Steve Perry
959 Cinnamon Drive
Leemore, CA 93245
"Singer, Composer"

William Perry
8017 Rising Ridge Road
Bethesda, MD 20817
"Ex-Secretary of Defense"

Bill Pertwee
25 Whitehall
London SW1A 2BS ENGLAND
"Actor"

Nehemia Persoff
5847 Tampa Avenue
Tarzana, CA 91356
"Actor"

Joe Pesci
P.O. Box 6
Lavallette, NJ 08735
"Actor"

Donna Pescow
9300 Wilshire Blvd. #555
Beverly Hills, CA 90212
"Actress"

Pet Shop Boys
27A Pembridge Way #8
London WII 3EP ENGLAND
"Rock & Roll Group"

Peter, Paul & Mary
121 Mt. Herman Way
Ocean Grove, NJ 07756
"Vocal Trio"

Bernadette Peters
323 West 80th Street
New York, NY 10024
"Actress"

Brock Peters
1420 Rising Glen Road
Los Angeles, CA 90069
"Actor, Writer, Director"

Jean Peters
507 North Palm Drive
Beverly Hills, CA 90210
"Actress"

Jon Peters
630 Siena Way
Los Angeles, CA 90077
"Film Producer"

Mike Peters
1269 - 1st Street #8
Sarasota, FL 34236
"Cartoonist"

Roberta Peters
64 Garden Road
Scarsdale, NY 10583
"Singer"

Pat Petersen
1634 Veteran Avenue
Los Angeles, CA 90025
"Actor"

Paul Petersen
14530 Denker Avenue
Gardena, CA 90247
"Actor"

William L. Petersen
8942 Wilshire Blvd.
Beverly Hills, CA 90211
"Actor"

Wolfgang Petersen
10202 W. Washington Blvd.
Lean Building
Culver City, CA 90232
"Film Director"

Oscar Peterson
2421 Hammond Road
Mississagua, Ontario
L5K 1T3 CANADA
"Musician"

Dan Petry
1808 Cartlen Drive
Placentia, CA 92670
"Ex-Baseball Player"

Daniel Petrie
13201 Haney Place
Los Angeles, CA 90049
"TV Director"

Kyle Petty
135 Longfield Drive
Mooresville, NC 28115
"Race Car Driver"

Lori Petty
12301 Wilshire Blvd. #200
Los Angeles, CA 90025
"Actress"

Richard Petty
Rt. #4, Box 86
Randleman, NC 27317
"Race Car Driver"

Tom Petty
4626 Encino Avenue
Encino, CA 91316
"Rock & Roll Singer"

Penny Peyser
22039 Alizondo Drive
Woodland Hills, CA 91367
"Actress"

Dedee Pfeiffer
8271 Melrose Avenue #110
Los Angeles, CA 90046
"Actress"

Michelle Pfeiffer
721 Fairview Street
Burbank, CA 91505
"Actress"

Jo Ann Pflug
1270 Peachtree Battle Avenue NW
Atlanta, GA 30327
"Actress"

Joaquin (Leaf) Phoenix
1450 Belfast Drive
Los Angeles, CA 90069
"Actor"

Regis Philbin
101 W. 67th Street #51A
New York, NY 10023
"TV Show Host"

HRH Prince Philip
Duke of Edinburgh
Buckingham Palace
London SW1 ENGLAND
"Royalty"

Ryan Phillippe
10100 Santa Monica Blvd. #2500
Los Angeles, CA 90067
"Actor"

John Phillips
108 E. Matilija Street
Ojai, CA 93023
"Actor"

Joseph C. Phillips
8730 Sunset Blvd. #480
Los Angeles, CA 90069
"Actor"

Julia Phillips
2534 Benedict Canyon
Beverly Hills, CA 90210
"Film Producer"

Julianne Phillips
1999 Avenue of the Stars #2850
Los Angeles, CA 90067
"Actress, Model"

Lou Diamond Phillips
1122 S. Robertson Blvd. #15
Los Angeles, CA 90035
"Actor"

Mackenzie Phillips
10110 Empyrean Way #304
Los Angeles, CA 90067
"Actress, Singer"

Michelle Phillips
P.O. Box 67758
Beverly Hills, CA 90209
"Actress, Singer"

Sam Phillips
729 7th Avenue #1600
New York, NY 10019
"Singer"

Sian Phillips
14 Petherton Road
London N5 ENGLAND
"Actress"

Robert Picardo
P.O. Box 5617
Beverly Hills, CA 90210
"Actor"

Mike Piazza
Box 864, Oakwood Lane
Valley Forge, PA 19481
"Baseball Player"

Paloma Picasso
37 West 57th Street
New York, NY 10019
"Designer"

Michel Piccoli
11 rue de Lions St. Paul
4e Paris, FRANCE
"Actor"

Paul Picerni
19119 Wells Drive
Tarzana, CA 91356
"Actor"

Donald Pickering
Back Court
Manor House
Eastleach, Glos. ENGLAND
"Actor"

Cindy Pickett
151 El Camino Drive
Beverly Hills, CA 90212
"Actress"

Wilson Pickett
102 Ryders Lane
East Brunswick, NJ 08816
"Singer"

Christina Pickles
137 South Westgate Avenue
Los Angeles, CA 90049
"Actress"

Vivian Pickles
91 Regent Street
London W1R 8RU ENGLAND
"Actress"

Ronald Pickup
54 Crouch Hall Road
London N8 ENGLAND
"Actor"

Charles Pierce
4445 Cartwright Avenue #309
North Hollywood, CA 91602
"Impersonator"

David Hyde Pierce
8730 Sunset Blvd. #480
Los Angeles, CA 90069
"Actor"

Mary Pierce
5500 - 34th Street West
Bradenton, FL 34210
"Tennis Player"

Eric Pierpoint
10929 Morrison Street #14
North Hollywood, CA 91601
"Actor"

Jimmy Piersall
1105 Oakview Drive
Wheaton, IL 60187
"Ex-Baseball Player"

Geoff Pierson
9150 Wilshire Blvd. #175
Beverly Hills, CA 90212
"Actor"

Amy Pietz
P.O. Box 157
Oak Creek, WI 53154
"Actress"

Tim Pigott-Smith
125 Gloucester Road
London SW7 4TE ENGLAND
"Actor"

Mitch Pileggi
9229 Sunset Blvd. #315
Los Angeles, CA 90069
"Actor"

Ray Pillow
2802 Columbine Place
Nashville, TN 37204
"Singer"

Bronson Pinchot
9150 Wilshire Blvd. #350
Beverly Hills, CA 90212
"Actor"

Philip Pine
7034 Costello Avenue
Van Nuys, CA 91405
"Actor"

Robert Pine
4212 Ben Avenue
Studio City, CA 91604
"Actor, Director"

Lou Piniella
1005 Taray De Avila
Tampa, FL 33613
"Baseball Manager"

Jada Pinkett-Smith
9560 Wilshire Blvd. #516
Beverly Hills, CA 90212
"Actress"

Pink Floyd
43 Portland Road
London W11 ENGLAND
"Rock & Roll Group"

Gordon Pinsent
180 Bloor Street West
Toronto, Ontario
M5S 2V6 CANADA
"Actor, Writer"

Vada Pinson
710 31st Street
Oakland, CA 94609
"Baseball Player"

Sir Harold Pinter
83 Eastbourne Mews
London W2 6LQ ENGLAND
"Screenwriter"

Scottie Pippen
2320 Shady Lane
Highland Park, IL 60035
"Basketball Player"

Joe Piscopo
P.O. Box 258
Bernardsville, NJ 07924
"Actor"

Marie-France Pisier
3, Quai Malaquais
75006 Paris, FRANCE
"Actress"

Dean Pitchford
1701 Queens Road
Los Angeles, CA 90069
"Lyricist, Producer"

Maria Pitillo
8912 Burton Way
Beverly Hills, CA 90211
"Actress"

Gene Pitney
8901 - 6 Mile Road
Caledonia, WI 53108
"Singer"

Brad Pitt
2705 Glendower
Los Angeles, CA 90027
"Actor"

Ingrid Pitt
2-4 Noel Street
London W1V 3RB ENGLAND
"Actress"

Mary Kay Place
2739 Motor Avenue
Los Angeles, CA 90064
"Actress, Writer"

Robert Plant
8942 Wilshire Blvd.
Beverly Hills, CA 90211
"Singer, Songwriter"

Scott Plant
151 El Camino Drive
Beverly Hills, CA 90212
"Actor"

Platinum Blonde
P.O. Box 1223, Station F.
Toronto, Ontario
M4Y 2T8 CANADA
"Rock & Roll Group"

Howard Platt
9200 Sunset Blvd. #1130
Los Angeles, CA 90069
"Actor"

Oliver Platt
29 East 9th Street
New York, NY 10003
"Actor"

The Platters
2756 N. Green Valley Parkway #449
Las Vegas, NV 89014
"Vocal Group"

Gary Player
3930 RCA Blvd. #3001
Palm Beach Gardens, FL 33410
"Golfer"

John Pleshette
2643 Creston Drive
Los Angeles, CA 90068
"Actor, Writer"

Suzanne Pleshette
P.O. Box 1492
Beverly Hills, CA 90213
"Actress"

George Plimpton
541 East 72nd Street
New York, NY 10021
"Author"

Martha Plimpton
40 West 57th Street
New York, NY 10019
"Model, Actress"

Joan Plowright
76 Oxford Street
London W1R 1RB ENGLAND
"Actress"

Eve Plumb
3518 Cahuenga Blvd. W. #216
Los Angeles, CA 90068
"Actress"

Amanda Plummer
1925 Century Park E. #2320
Los Angeles, CA 90067
"Actress"

Christopher Plummer
49 Wampum Hill Road
Weston, CT 06883
"Actor"

Glenn Plummer
1999 Avenue of the Stars #2850
Los Angeles, CA 90067
"Actor"

Scotty Plummer
909 Parkview Avenue
Lodi, CA 95240
"Singer"

Jim Plunkett
51 Kilroy Way
Atherton, CA 94025
"Ex-Football Player"

Steve Plytas
70 Lansbury Avenue, Feltham
Middlesex TW14 OJR ENGLAND
"Actor"

Rosanna Podesta
Via Bartolemeo Ammanatti 8
00187 Rome, ITALY
"Actress"

Sylvia Poggioli
c/o National Public Radio
2025 "M" Street NW
Washington, DC 20036
"News Correspondent"

Buster Poindexter
200 West 58th Street
New York, NY 10019
"Singer"

Anita Pointer
12060 Crest Court
Beverly Hills, CA 90210
"Singer"

Priscilla Pointer
151 El Camino Drive
Beverly Hills, CA 90211
"Actress"

Ruth Pointer
1900 Avenue of the Stars #1640
Los Angeles, CA 90067
"Singer"

Pointer Sisters
1900 Avenue of the Stars, #1640
Los Angeles, CA 90067
"Vocal Trio"

Poison
1750 N. Vine Street
Hollywood, CA 90028
"Rock & Roll Group"

Sydney Poitier
9255 Doheny Road
Los Angeles, CA 90069
"Actor, Writer, Producer"

Roman Polanski
43 Avenue Montaigne
75008 Paris, FRANCE
"Actor, Writer, Director"

The Police
194 Kensington Park Road
London W11 2ES ENGLAND
"Rock & Roll Group"

Sydney Pollack
13525 Lucca Drive
Pacific Palisades, CA 90272
"Writer, Producer"

Tracy Pollan
7 Peabody Court
Teaneck, NJ 07666
"Actress"

Jonathan Pollard
Federal Reformatory
Marion, IL 62959
"Israeli Spy, Traitor"

Michael J. Pollard
520 S. Burnside Avenue #12-A
Los Angeles, CA 90036
"Actor"

Abraham Polonsky
135 S. McCarty Drive #4
Beverly Hills, CA 90212
"Filmwriter"

Danny Ponce
14539 Teton Drive
Hacienda Heights, CA 91745
"Actor"

LuAnne Ponce
3500 West Olive Avenue, #1400
Burbank, CA 91505
"Actress"

Carlo Ponti
6 rue Charles Bonnet
CH-1206 Geneve SWITZERLAND
"Film Producer"

Iggy Pop
P.O. Box 561
Pine Bush, NY 12565
"Singer"

Albert Popwell
1427 - 3rd Street #205
Santa Monica, CA 90401
"Actor"

Paulina Porizkova
130 West 57th Street #5E
New York, NY 10019
"Model"

Jean Porter
3945 Westfall Drive
Encino, CA 91436
"Actress"

Nyree Dawn Porter
28 Berkeley Square
London W1X 6HD ENGLAND
"Actress"

Vladimir Posner
1125-16th Street N.W.
Washington, DC 20036
"Russian Spokesman"

Markie Post
10153 1/2 Riverside Drive
Suite #333
Toluca Lake, CA 91602
"Actress"

Tom Poston
2930 Deep Canyon Drive
Beverly Hills, CA 90210
"Actor"

Carol Potter
151 El Camino Drive
Beverly Hills, CA 90210
"Actress"

Annie Potts
P.O. Box 29400
Los Angeles, CA 90029
"Actress"

Cliff Potts
8383 Wilshire Blvd. #954
Beverly Hills, CA 90211
"Actor"

Ely Pouget
2190 Beach Knoll Road
Los Angeles, CA 90049
"Actor"

CCH Pounder
121 North San Vicente Blvd.
Beverly Hills, CA 90211
"Actor"

Paula Poundstone
1223 Broadway #162
Santa Monica, CA 90404
"Comedienne, TV Show Host"

Maury Povich
250 West 57th Street #26-W
New York, NY 10019
"TV Show Host"

Gen Colin L. Powell
909 No. Washington Street #767
Alexandria, VA 22314
"Ex-Military Leader"

Jane Powell
150 West End Avenue #26C
New York, NY 10023
"Actress"

Randolph Powell
2644 Highland Avenue
London W1 ENGLAND
"Actor"

Robert Powell
10 Pond Place
London SW3 ENGLAND
"Actor"

Susan Powell
6333 Bryn Mawr Drive
Los Angeles, CA 90068
"Actress"

Romina Power
I-72020 Cellino San Marco
(Brindise) ITALY
"Actress"

Taryn Power
843 N. Sycamore Avenue
Los Angeles, CA 90038
"Actress"

Tyrone Power, Jr.
12190 1/2 Ventura Blvd. #324
Studio City, CA 91604
"Son of Tyrone Power"

Udana Power
1962 Beachwood Drive #202
Los Angeles, CA 90068
"Actress"

Mala Powers
10543 Valley Spring Lane
North Hollywood, CA 91602
"Actress"

Stefanie Powers
P.O. Box 5087
Sherman Oaks, CA 91403
"Actress"

Susan Powter
256 S. Spalding Drive
Beverly Hills, CA 90212
"Actress"

Laurie Prange
1519 Sargent Place
Los Angeles, CA 90026
"Actress"

Joan Prather
31647 Sea Level Drive
Malibu, CA 90265
"Actress"

Judson Pratt
8745 Oak Park Avenue
Northridge, CA 91325
"Actor"

Josephine Premice
755 West End Avenue
New York, NY 10023
"Actress, Singer, Dancer"

Paula Prentiss
719 North Foothill Road
Beverly Hills, CA 90120
"Actress"

Micheline Presle
6 rue Antoine Dubois
F 75006 Paris, FRANCE
"Actress"

Lisa-Marie Presley
1167 Summit Drive
Beverly Hills, CA 90210
"Elvis' Daughter"

Priscilla Presley
1167 Summit Drive
Beverly Hills, CA 90210
"Actress, Model"

Sen. Larry Pressler (SD)
P.O. Box 1372
Sioux Falls, SD 57102
"Politician"

Lawrence Pressman
15033 Encanto Drive
Sherman Oaks, CA 91403
"Actor"

Billy Preston
4271 Garthwaite Avenue
Los Angeles, CA 90008
"Singer"

Kelly Preston
15020 Ventura Blvd. #710
Sherman Oaks, CA 91403
"Actress"

The Pretenders
28 Kensington Church Street
London W8 4EP ENGLAND
"Vocal Group"

Andre Previn
8 Sherwood Lane
Bedford Hills, NY 10507
"Composer, Conductor"

Francoise Previne
5 rue Brenzin
75015 Paris, FRANCE
"Actor"

Hermann Prey
Fichtenstr. 12
D-82152 Krailling
GERMANY
"Baritone"

Leontyne Price
9 Van Dam Street
New York, NY 10003
"Soprano"

Lloyd Price
22236-C Boca Rancho Dr.
Boca Raton, FL 33428
"Actor"

Marc Price
8444 Magnolia Drive
Los Angeles, CA 90046
"Actor"

Mark Price
2923 Streetsboro Road
Richfield, OH 44286
"Basketball Player"

Nick Price
300 S. Beach Road
Hobe Sound, FL 33455
"Golfer"

Ray Price
P.O. Box 1986
Mt. Pleasant, TX 75230
"Singer"

Nancy Priddy
329 N. Wetherly Drive #101
Beverly Hills, CA 90211
"Actress"

Charlie Pride
P.O. Box 670507
Dallas, TX 75367
"Singer"

Maxi Priest
1350 Avenue of the Americas
New York, NY 10019
"Singer"

Pat Priest
1199 Forest Avenue #275
Pacific Grove, CA 93951
"Actor"

Jason Priestley
11766 Wilshire Blvd. #1610
Los Angeles, CA 90025
"Actor"

Barry Primus
2735 Creston Drive
Los Angeles, CA 90068
"Actor, Director"

Prince (formely known as)
9401 Kiowa Trail
Chanhassen, MN 55317
"Singer, Songwriter, Actor"

Clayton Prince
3500 West Olive Avenue, #1400
Burbank, CA 91505
"Actor"

Jonathan Prince
10340 Calvin Avenue
Los Angeles, CA 90025
"Actor"

Victoria Principal
120 S. Spalding Drive #205
Beverly Hills, CA 90212
"Actress"

Andrew Prine
3364 Longridge Avenue
Sherman Oaks, CA 91403
"Actor"

Joan Pringle
3500 West Olive #1400
Burbank, CA 91505
"Actress"

Freddie Prinz Jr.
P9830 Wilshire Blvd.
Beverly Hills, CA 90212
"Actor"

Sir Victor S. Pritchett
12 Regent's Park Terrace
London NW1 ENGLAND
"Author"

Jurgen Prochnow
8942 Wilshire Blvd.
Beverly Hills, CA 90211
"Actor"

The Proclaimers
P.O. Box 309
Edinburgh EH9 1JE SCOTLAND
"Rock & Roll Group"

Ronnie Prophet
1227 Saxon Drive
Nashville, TN 37215
"Singer, Songwriter"

Robert Prosky
306 - 9th Street
Washington, DC 20003
"Actor"

Paul Provenza
P.O. Box 5617
Beverly Hills, CA 90210
"Actor"

Dorothy Provine
8832 Ferncliff N.E.
Bainbridge Island, WA 98110
"Actress"

Dave Prowse
12 Marshalsea Road
London SE1 1HL ENGLAND
"Actor"

Jeanne Pruett
1300 Division Street #103
Nashville, TN 37203
"Singer"

Jonathan Pryce
233 Park Avenue South
10th Floor
New York, NY 10003
"Actor"

Nicholas Pryor
8787 Shoreham Drive #302
Los Angeles, CA 90069
"Actor"

Rain Pryor
846 N. Clybourn Avenue
Burbank, CA 91505
"Actress, Musician"

Richard Pryor
16847 Bosque Drive
Encino, CA 91436
"Actor, Comedian"

Public Enemy
298 Elizabeth Street
New York, NY 10012
"Rap Group"

Wolfgang Puck
805 North Sierra Drive
Beverly Hills, CA 91765
"Chef, Restaurateur"

Gary Puckett
11088 Indian Lore Ct.
San Diego, CA 92127
"Singer, Songwriter"

Tito Pueett
15 Gregg Court
Tappan, NY 10983
"Jazz Musician"

Tommy Puett
16621 Cerulean Court
Chino Hills, CA 91709
"Actor"

Keshia Knight Pulliam
P.O. Box 866
Teaneck, NJ 07666
"Actress"

Bill Pullman
8750 Hollway Drive
Los Angeles, CA 90069
"Actor"

Liselotte Pulver
Villa Bip, Perroy
Kanton Vandois SWITZERLAND
"Actress"

Dr. Bernard Punsley
1415 Granvia Altemeia
Rancho Palos Verdes, CA 90274
"Actor"

Lee Purcell
3300 Foothill Blvd
P.O. Box 1258
La Crescenta, CA 91224
"Actress"

Sarah Purcell
6525 Esplanada Street
Playa del Rey, CA 90293
"Actress"

Edmund Purdom
via Giosue Carducci
I0-00187 Rome ITALY
"Actor"

Linda Purl
10417 Ravenwood Court
Los Angeles, CA 90077
"Actress"

John Putch
3972 Sunswept Drive
Studio City, CA 91604
"Actor"

Mario Puzo
866 Manor Lane
Bay Shore, NY 11706
"Author, Screenwriter"

Thomas Pynchon
34 Beacon Street
Boston, MA 02108
"Author"

Natasha Pyne
43A Princess Road
Regent's Park
London NW1 8JS ENGLAND
"Actress"

Monty Python
68a Delancy Street
London NW1 70W ENGLAND
"Comedy Group"

Dennis Quaid
9665 Wilshire Blvd. #200
Beverly Hills, CA 90212
"Actor"

Randy Quaid
P.O. Box 17372
Beverly Hills, CA 90209
"Actor"

Robert Quarry
11032 Moorpark St. #A-3
No. Hollywood, CA 91602
"Actor"

Suzi Quatro
Hellkamp 17
D-20255 Hamburg GERMANY
"Singer"

Anna Quayle
4 Guilford Road, Brighton
Essex ENGLAND
"Actress"

Dan Quayle
6263 N. Scottsdale Road #292
Scottsdale, AZ 85250
"Ex-Vice President U.S.A."

Marilyn Tucker-Quayle
6263 N. Scottsdale Road #292
Scottsdale, AZ 85250
"Wife of Dan Quayle"

Queen
16A High St. Barnes
London SW13 9LW ENGLAND
"Rock & Roll Group"

Diana Quick
162 Wardour Street
London W1V 3AT ENGLAND
"Actress"

Quiet Riot
P.O. Box 24455
New Orleans, LA 70184
"Rock & Roll Group"

Joan Quigley
1055 California Street #14
San Francisco, CA 94108
"Astrologer"

Linnea Quigley
P.O. Box 43
Newbury Park, CA 91320
"Actress, Model"

Denis Quilley
22 Willow Road
London NW3 ENGLAND
"Actor, Singer"

Kathleen Quinlan
P.O. Box 861
Rockaway, OR 97136
"Actress"

Aileen Quinn
170 West End Avenue #3K
New York, NY 10023
"Actress"

Anthony Quinn
P.O. Box 479
Bristol, RI 02809
"Actor, Director"

Anthony Tyler Quinn
8949 Sunset Blvd. #201
Los Angeles, CA 90069
"Actor"

Danny Quinn
8271 Melrose Avenue #202
Los Angeles, CA 90046
"Actor"

Francesco Quinn
1230 North Horn Avenue #730
Los Angeles, CA 90069
"Actor"

Glenn Quinn
10458 IIona
Los Angeles, CA 90064
"Actor"

Martha Quinn
7920 Sunset Blvd., #400
Los Angeles, CA 90046
"TV Personality"

Sally Quinn
3014 "N" Street NW
Washington, DC 20007
"Journalist"

Robin Quivers
350 E. 79th Street #16H
New York, NY 10021
"Talk Show Personality"

Mrs. Jutchak (Lea) Rabin
Rehov Abba Hillel 14, 15th Flr.
Ramat-Gun ISRAEL
"Widow of Yitzhak Rabin"

Alan Rachins
1274 Capri
Pacific Palisades, CA 90272
"Actor, Writer, Director"

Cassidy Rae
1801 Ave. of the Stars #902
Los Angeles, CA 90067
"Actress"

Charlotte Rae
10790 Wilshire Blvd. #903
Los Angeles, CA 90024
"Actress"

Deborah Raffin
301 N. Canon Drive #207
Beverly Hills, CA 90210
"Actress"

Kaye Lani Rae Rafko
4932 Frary Lane
Monroe, MI 48161
"Former Miss America"

Hashemi Rafsanjani
The Majlis
Tehran, IRAN
"President of Iran"

Gerald Rafshoon
3028 "Q" Street N.W.
Washington, DC 20006
"Former Presidential Aide"

John S. Ragin
5706 Briarcliff Road
Los Angeles, CA 90068
"Actor"

William Ragsdale
8899 Beverly Blvd. #410
Los Angeles, CA 90048
"Actor"

Bobby Rahal
P.O. Box 39
Hilliard, OH 43026
"Race Car Driver"

Steve Railsback
11684 Ventura Blvd. #581
Studio City, CA 91604
"Actor"

Gillian Raine
13 Billing Road
London SW10 ENGLAND
"Actress"

Luise Rainer
54 Eaton Square
London SW1 ENGLAND
"Actress"

Ford Rainey
3821 Carbon Canyon
Malibu, CA 90265
"Actor"

Bonnie Raitt
1344 Spaulding
Los Angeles, CA 90046
"Singer"

John Raitt
1164 Napoli Drive
Pacific Palisades, CA 90272
"Actor"

Sheryl Lee Ralph
938 South Longwood
Los Angeles, CA 90019
"Actress"

Vera Hruba Ralston
4121 Crecienta Drive
Santa Barbara, CA 93110
"Actress"

Raul Ramirez
Avenida Ruiz
65 Sur Ensenda
Baja California, MEXICO
"Tennis Player"

Harold Ramis
160 Euclid Avenue
Glencoe, IL 60022
"Actor, Writer, Director"

Pres. Fidel Ramos
Malacanang Palace
Manila PHILIPPINES
"Politician"

Charlotte Rampling
1 Ave. Emile Augier
F-78290 Croissy-Sur Seine
FRANCE
"Actress"

Logan Ramsey
12932 Killion Street
Van Nuys, CA 91401
"Actor"

Tony Randall
1 West 81st Street #6-D
New York, NY 10024
"Actor, Director"

Teddy Randazzo
5254 Oak Island Road
Orlando, FL 32809
"Singer"

Theresa Randle
1018 Meadowbrook Avenue
Los Angeles, CA 90019
"Actress"

Boots Randolph
2416 Music Valley Dr. #139-140
Nashville, TN 37214
"Saxophonist"

John Randolph
1850 North Whitley Place
Los Angeles, CA 90028
"Actor"

Joyce Randolph
295 Central Park West #18-A
New York, NY 10024
"Actress"

Willie Randolph
648 Juniper Place
Franklin Lakes, NJ 07417
"Ex-Baseball Player"

Rep. Charles B. Rangel (NY)
House Rayburn Bldg. #2354
Washington, DC 20515
"Politician"

Crown Price Ranier III
Grimaldi Palace
Monte Carlo, MONACO
"Royalty"

Prunella Ransome
59 Frith Street
London W1 ENGLAND
"Actress"

Sally Jessy Raphael
510 West 57th Street #200
New York, NY 10019
"TV Show Host"

David Rasche
1040 S. Sepulveda Blvd. #218
Los Angeles, CA 90025
"Actor"

Ahmad Rashad
30 Rockefeller Plaza #1411
New York, NY 10020
"Ex-Football Player, Sportcaster"

Phylicia Rashad
888 7th Avenue #602
New York, NY 10106
"Actress"

Dan Rather
524 West 57th Street
New York, NY 10019
"Newscaster"

RATT
1818 Illion Street
San Diego, CA 92110
Rock & Roll Group"

John Ratzenberger
7080 Hollywood Blvd., #1118
Los Angeles, CA 90028
"Actor"

Eddy Raven
1071 Bradley Road
Gallatin, TN 37066
"Singer, Songwriter"

Lou Rawls
109 Fremont Place
Los Angeles, CA 90005
"Singer"

Gene Rayburn
245 Fifth Avenue
New York, NY 10016
"TV Show Host"

Collin Raye
612 Humboldt Street
Reno, NV 89509
"Singer"

Marguerite Raye
1329 North Vista #106
Los Angeles, CA 90046
"Actress"

Gene Raymond
250 Trino Way
Pacific Palisades, CA 90272
"Actor"

Paula Raymond
P.O. Box 86
Beverly Hills, CA 90213
"Actress"

Peggy Rea
10231 Riverside Drive #203
Toluca Lake, CA 91602
"Actress"

Stephen Rea
861 Sutherland Avenue
London W9 ENGLAND
"Actor"

James Read
9229 Sunset Blvd. #315
Los Angeles, CA 90069
"Actor"

Ralph Read
P.O. Box 1990
Chesapeake, VA 23327
"Christian Spokesman"

Maureen Reagan
1121 "L" Street #806
Sacramento, CA 95814
"Ex-President's Daughter"

Michael Reagan
4740 Allott Avenue
Sherman Oaks, CA 91403
"Ex-President's Son"

Nancy Reagan
668 St. Cloud Road
Los Angeles, CA 90077
"Ex-First Lady, Actress"

Ronald Reagan
668 St. Cloud Road
Los Angeles, CA 90077
"Actor, Ex-President"

Ron Reagan, Jr.
2612 28th Avenue W.
Seattle, WA 98199
"TV Show Host, Dancer"

Jeff Reardon
4 Martwood Lane
Palm Beach Gardens, FL 33410
"Ex-Baseball Player"

Rex Reason
20105 Rhapsody Road
Walnut, CA 91789
"Actor"

Rhodes Reason
P.O. Box 503
Gladstone, OR 97027
"Actor"

Charles "Bebe" Rebozo
524 Fernwood Drive
Key Biscayne, FL 33149
"Financier"

Peter Reckell
8033 Sunset Blvd. #4016
Los Angeles, CA 90046
"Actor"

Leon Redbone
179 Aquestong Road
New Hope, PA 18938
"Singer, Guitarist"

Juli Redding
P.O. Box 1806
Beverly Hills, CA 90212
"Actress"

Helen Reddy
820 Stanford
Santa Monica, CA 90403
"Singer"

Quinn Redeker
15315 Magnolia Blvd. #429
Sherman Oaks, CA 91403
"Actor, Writer"

Robert Redford
1101-E Montana Avenue
Santa Monica, CA 90403
"Actor, Director"

Lynn Redgrave
21342 Colina Drive
Topanga, CA 90290
"Actress"

Vanessa Redgrave
21 Golden Square
London W1R 3PA ENGLAND
"Actress"

Red Hot Chili Peppers
11116 Aqua Vista #39
North Hollywood, CA 91602
"Music Group"

Marge Redmond
420 Madison Avenue #1400
New York, NY 10017
"Actress"

Sumner Redstone
200 Elm Street
Dedham, MA 02026
"Media Executive"

Gabrielle Reece
5111 Ocean Front Walk #4
Marina del Rey, CA 90291
"Model"

Alaina Reed-Hall
10636 Rathburn
Northridge, CA 91326
"Actress"

Jerry Reed
153 Rue De Grande
Brentwood, TN 37027
"Singer, Actor"

Margaret Reed
524 West 57th Street #5330
New York, NY 10019
"Actress"

Oliver Reed
76 Oxford Street
London WIN OAX ENGLAND
"Actor"

Pamela Reed
10390 Snata Monica Blvd. #300
Los Angeles, CA 90025
"Actress"

Rex Reed
1 West 72nd Street #86
New York, NY 10023
"Film Critic"

Walter Reed
3400 Paul Sweet Road #B-209
Santa Cruz, CA 95065
"Actor"

Della Reese
P.O. Box 2812
Beverly Hills, CA 90210
"Singer, Actress"

Pee Wee Reese
1400 Willow Avenue
Louisville, KY 40204
"Ex-Baseball Player"

Christopher Reeve
RR #2
Bedford, NY 10506
"Actor"

Del Reeves
1300 Division Street #102
Nashville, TN 37203
"Singer"

Keanu Reeves
9460 Wilshire Blvd., #700
Beverly Hills, CA 90212
"Actor"

Martha Reeves
P.O. Box 1987
Paramount, CA 90723
"Singer"

Steve Reeves
P.O. Box 807
Valley Center, CA 92082
"Actor, Bodybuilder"

Joe Regalbuto
724-24th Street
Santa Monica, CA 90402
"Actor"

Donald T. Regan
240 McLaws Circle #142
Williamsburg, VA 23185
"Former Secretary of Treasury"

Duncan Regehr
2501 Main Street
Santa Monica, CA 90405
"Actor"

Paul Regina
2911 Canna Street
Thousand Oaks, CA 91360
"Actor"

Regine
502 Park Avenue
New York, NY 10022
"Singer"

William Rehnquist
111 2nd Street NE
Washington, DC 20002
"Supreme Court Chief Justice"

Daphne Maxwell Reid
11342 Dona Lisa Drive
Studio City, CA 91604
"Actress"

Elliott Reid
1850 N. Whitley Avenue
Los Angeles, CA 90028
"Actor, Writer"

Frances Reid
235 Oceano Drive
Los Angeles, CA 90049
"Actress"

Tim Reid
11342 Dona Lisa Drive
Studio City, CA 91604
"Actor"

Charles Nelson Reilly
2341 Gloaming Way
Beverly Hills, CA 90210
"Actor"

John Reilly
602 North Las Palmas Avenue
Los Angeles, CA 90004
"Actor"

Tom Reilly
8200 Wilshire Blvd. #218
Beverly Hills, CA 90211
"Actor"

Carl Reiner
714 North Rodeo Drive
Beverly Hills, CA 90210
"Actor, Director"

Rob Reiner
335 N. Maple Drive #135
Beverly Hills, CA 90210
"Actor, Director"

Judge Reinhold
626 Santa Monica Blvd. #113
Santa Monica, CA 90405
"Actor"

Ann Reinking
40 West 57th Street
New York, NY 10019
"Actor"

Paul Reiser
11845 West Olympic Blvd. #1125
Los Angeles, CA 90064
"Actor"

R.E.M.
P.O. Box 128288
Nashville, TN 37212
"Rock & Roll Group"

Bert Remsen
5722 Mammoth Avenue
Van Nuys, CA 91401
"Actor"

Line Renaud
5 rue de Bois de Boulogne
F-75016 Paris FRANCE
"Actress"

Liz Renay
3708 San Angelo Avenue
Las Vegas, NV 89102
"Burlesque"

Brad Renfro
P.O. Box 53454
Knoxville, TN 37950
"Actor"

Janet Reno
Department of Justice
10th & Constitution
Washington, DC 20530
"U.S. Attorney General"

Faye Resnick
301 N. Canon Drive #203
Beverly Hills, CA 90210
"Nicole Brown-Simpson's Friend"

Alain Resnis
70 rue des Plantes
75014 Paris, FRANCE
"Film Director"

Mary Lou Retton
44450 Pinetree Drive #103
Plymouth, MI 48170
"Gymnast, Actress"

Paul Reubens
P.O. Box 29373
Los Angeles, CA 90029
"Actor"

Gloria Reuben
P.O. Box 5617
Beverly Hills, CA 90210
"Actress"

Paul Revere & The Raiders
P.O. Box 544
Graingeville, ID 83530
"Rock & Roll Group"

Clive Revill
15029 Encanto Drive
Sherman Oaks, CA 91403
"Actor"

Ernie Reyes, Jr.
12561 Willard Street
No. Hollywood, CA 91605
"Actor"

Burt Reynolds
16133 Jupiter Farms Road
Jupiter, FL 33478
"Actor, Director"

Debbie Reynolds
305 Convention Center Drive
Las Vegas, NV 89109
"Actress"

Gene Reynolds
2034 Castillian Drive
Los Angeles, CA 90068
"Actor, Director"

James Reynolds
1925 Hanscom Drive
South Pasadena, CA 91030
"Actor"

Kevin Reynolds
151 El Camino Drive
Beverly Hills, CA 90212
"Film Director"

Ving Rhames
751-24th Street
Santa Monica, CA 90402
"Actor"

Alicia Rhett
50 Tradd Street
Charleston, SC 29401
"Actress"

Barbara Rhoades
90 Old Redding Road
Weston, CT 06883
"Actress"

Cynthia Rhodes
15250 Ventura Blvd. #900
Sherman Oaks, CA 91403
"Actress, Dancer"

Donnelly Rhodes
1148 - 4th Street #206
Santa Monica, CA 90403
"Actor"

Dusty Rhodes
8577A Boca Glades Blvd. W.
Boca Raton, FL 33434
"Wrestler"

Madlyn Rhue
148 South Maple Drive, Apt. #D
Beverly Hills, CA 90212
"Actress"

John Rhys-Davies
1933 Cold Canyon Road
Calabasas, CA 91302
"Actor"

Alfonso Ribeiro
3353 Blair Drive
Los Angeles, CA 90068
"Actor"

Abraham Ribicoff
425 Park Avenue
New York, NY 10022
"Ex-Senator"

Giovanni Ribisi
5750 Wilshire Blvd. #580
Los Angeles, CA 90036
"Actor"

Christina Ricci
8942 Wilshire Blvd.
Beverly Hills, CA 90211
"Actress"

Anne Rice
1239 First Street
New Orleans, LA 70130
"Writer"

Bobby G. Rice
505 Canton Pass
Madison, TN 37115
"Singer"

Jerry Rice
2 Brittany Meadows
Atherton, CA 94025
"Football Player"

Jim Rice
RR #8
Anderson, SC 29621
"Ex-Baseball Player"

Adam Rich
21848 Vantage Avenue
Chatsworth, CA 91311
"Actor"

Christopher Rich
15760 Ventura Blvd. #1730
Encino, CA 91436
"Actor"

Elaine Rich
500 South Sepulveda Blvd.
Los Angeles, CA 90049
"Producer"

John Rich
2501 Colorado Ave. #350
Santa Monica, CA 90404
"Writer, Producer"

Matty Rich
9560 Wilshire Blvd. #500
Beverly Hills, CA 90210
"Director"

Cliff Richard
Portsmouth Road
Box 46A, Esher
Surrey KT10 9AA ENGLAND
"Singer, Actor"

Maurice Richard
10950 Peloquin
Montreal PQ H2C 2KB CANADA
"Hockey Player"

Ann Richard
P.O. Box 684746
Austin, TX 78768
"Ex-Governor"

Ariana Richards
256 S. Robertson Blvd. #8200
Beverly Hills, CA 90211
"Actress"

Beah Richards
1842 South Sycamore Avenue
Los Angeles, CA 90019
"Actress"

Denise Richards
P.O. Box 5617
Beverly Hills, CA 90210
"Actress"

Evan Richards
1800 Avenue of the Starts, #400
Los Angeles, CA 90067
"Actor"

Kieth Richards
"Redlands" West Whittering
Near Chichester Sussex
ENGLAND
"Actor"

Michael Richards
12730 Halkirk Street
Studio City, CA 91604
"Actor"

Elliot Richardson
1100 Crest Lane
McLean, VA 22101
"Diplomat"

Ian Richardson
131 Lavender Sweep
London SW11 ENGLAND
"Actor"

Miranda Richardson
Forest Hill
195 Devonshire Road
London SE 23 ENGLAND
"Actress"

Natasha Richardson
200 Fulham Road
London SWIO 9PN ENGLAND
"Actress, V. Redgrave's Daughter"

Patricia Richardson
196 Granville Avenue
Los Angeles, CA 90049
"Actress"

Salli Richardson
1999 Avenue of the Stars #2850
Los Angeles, CA 90067
"Actress"

Lionel Richie
P.O. Box 9055
Calabasas, CA 91372
"Singer, Songwriter"

Peter Mark Richman
5114 Del Moreno Drive
Woodland Hills, CA 91364
"Actor"

Branscombe Richmond
5706 Calvin Avenue
Tarzana, CA 91356
"Actor/Stuntman"

Jason James Richter
10683 Santa Monica Blvd.
Los Angeles, CA 90025
"Actor"

Don Rickles
23750 Malibu Road
Malibu, CA 90265
"Comeidan, Actor"

Alan Rickman
76 Oxford Street
London W1N 0AX ENGLAND
"Actor"

Dr. Sally Ride
9500 Gillman Drive
MS 0221
La Jolla, CA 92093
"Astronaut"

Andrew Ridgeley
8800 Sunset Blvd. #401
Los Angeles, CA 90069
"Singer, Composer"

Leni Riefenstahl
Tengstrasse 20
D-80798 Munich
GERMANY
"Film Director"

Peter Riegert
25 Sea Colony Drive
Santa Monica, CA 90405
"Actor"

Joshua Rifkind
4526 Wilshire Blvd. #200
Los Angeles, CA 90010
"Conductor"

Cathy Rigby
110 East Wilshire #200
Fullerton, CA 92632
"Gymnast"

Diana Rigg
2-4 Noel Street
London W1V 3RB ENGLAND
"Actress"

Righteous Brothers
9841 Hot Springs Drive
Huntington Beach, CA 92646
"Vocal Group"

Robin Riker-Halsey
1089 North Oxford Avenue
Los Angeles, CA 90029
"Actress"

Meshulam Riklis
23720 Malibu Colony Road
Malibu, CA 90265
"Film Producer"

Jeaniie C. Riley
105 Ewingville Drive
Franklin, TN 37064
"Singer"

Pat Riley
180 Arvida Parkway
Miami, FL 33156
"Basketball Coach"

LeAnn Rimes
1801 Whitehall Lane
Garland, TX 75043
"Singer"

Molly Ringwald
9454 Wilshire Blvd. #405
Beverly Hills, CA 90212
"Actress"

Lisa Rinna
3500 W. Olive #1400
Burbank, CA 91505
"Actress"

Mayor Richard Riordan
200 North Spring Street
Los Angeles, CA 90012
"Mayor of Los Angeles"

Cal Ripken, Jr.
2330 W. Juppa Road #333
Lutherville, MD 21093
"Baseball Player"

Cal Ripken Sr.
410 Clover Street
Aberdeen, MD 21001
"Baseball Coach"

Rodney Allen Rippey
3939 Veselich Avenue #351
Los Angeles, CA 90039
"Actor"

Robby Rist
P.O. Box 867
Woodland Hills, CA 91365
"Actor"

Clint Ritchie
10000 Riverside Drive #6
Toluca Lake, CA 91602
"Actor"

Michael Ritchie
12305 Fifth Helena Drive
Los Angeles, CA 90049
"Director, Producer"

The Ritchie Family
4100 West Flagler #B-2
Miami, FL 33134
"Vocal Group"

Lee Ritenour
11808 Dorothy Street #108
Los Angeles, CA 90049
"Guitarist"

John Ritter
15030 Ventura Blvd. #806
Sherman Oaks, CA 91403
"Actor"

Mrs. Tex Ritter
14151 Valley Vista
Sherman Oaks, CA 91423
"Tex Ritter's Widow"

Chita Rivera
1325 Avenue of the Americas
New York, NY 10019
"Actress, Singer, Dancer"

Geraldo Rivera
524 West 57th Street #1100
New York, NY 10019
"TV Show Host, Author"

Jorge Rivero
Salvador Novo 71
Cuyoacan 21 D.F. MEXICO
"Actor"

Joan Rivers
1 East 62nd Street
New York, NY 10021
"Comedienne, TV Show Host"

Johnny Rivers
3141 Coldwater Canyon Lane
Beverly Hills, CA 90210
"Singer, Songwriter"

Jacques Rivette
20 Blvd. de la Bastille
75012 Paris, FRANCE
"Film Director"

Phil Rizzuto
912 Westminister Avenue
Hillside, NJ 07205
"Ex-Baseball Player"

Jason Robards
200 West 57th Street #900
New York, NY 10019
"Actor"

Sam Robards
2530 Riverbend Drive
Crested Butte, CO 81224
"Actor"

Sen. Charles Robb (VA)
Senate Russell Bldg. #154
Washington, DC 20510
"Politician"

Lynda Bird Johnson-Robb
612 Chain Bridge Raod
Mc Lean, VA 22101
"Ex-President's Daughter"

Seymour Robbie
9980 Liebe Drive
Beverly Hills, CA 90210
"TV Director"

Brian Robbins
752 North Orange Drive
Los Angeles, CA 90038
"Actor"

Mrs. Marty Robbins
713-18th Avenue South
Nashville, TN 37203
"Marty Robbins's Widow"

Tim Robbins
40 West 57th Street
New York, NY 10019
"Actor"

Jane Robelot
524 West 57th Street
New York, NY 10019
"TV Show Host"

Beverly Roberts
30912 Ariana Lane
Laguna Niguel, CA 92677
"Actress"

Cokie Roberts
5315 Bradley Blvd.
Bethesda, MD 20814
"News Correspondent"

Doris Roberts
6225 Quebec Drive
Los Angeles, CA 90068
"Actress, Director"

Eric Roberts
132 S. Rodeo Drive #300
Beverly Hills, CA 90212
"Actor"

Jake "The Snake" Roberts
P.O. Box 3859
Stamford, CT 06905
"Wrestler"

Julia Roberts
6220 Del Valle Drive
Los Angeles, CA 90048
"Actress"

Louie Roberts
2401-12th Avenue South
Nashville, TN 37203
"Singer, Guitarist"

Oral Roberts
7777 Lewis Street
Tulsa, OK 74130
"Evangelist"

Pernell Roberts
20395 Seaboard Road
Malibu, CA 90265
"Actor"

Robin Roberts
504 Terrace Hill Road
Temple Terrace, FL 33617
"Ex-Baseball Player"

Tanya Roberts
2126 Ridgemont Drive
Los Angeles, CA 90046
"Actress"

Tony Roberts
970 Park Avenue #8-N
New York, NY 10028
"Actor"

Cliff Robertson
325 Dunmere Drive
La Jolla , CA 92037
"Actor, Writer, Director"

Dale Robertson
P.O. Box 850707
Yukon, OK 73085
"Actor"

Oscar Robertson
621 Tusculum Avenue
Cincinatti, OH 45226
"Ex-Basketball Player"

Pat Robertson
1000 Centerville Turnpike
Virginia Beach, VA 23463
"Evangelist"

Andrew Robinson
2671 Byron Place
Los Angeles, CA 90046
"Actor"

Brooks Robinson
36 S. Charles Street #2000
Baltimore, MD 21201
"Ex-Baseball Player"

Chris Robinson
9300 Wilshire Blvd. #410
Beverly Hills, CA 90212
"Actor, Director"

David Robinson
P.O. Box 530
San Antonio, TX 78292
"Basketball Player"

Frank Robinson
15557 Aqua Verde Drive
Los Angeles, CA 90024
"Ex-Baseball Player & Manager"

Glen Robinson
1001 North Fourth Street
Milwaukee, WI 53203
"Basketball Player"

Holly Robinson
10683 Santa Monica Blvd.
Los Angeles, CA 90025
"Actress"

Jay Robinson
13757 Milbank Avenue
Sherman Oaks, CA 91403
"Actor"

Mary Robinson
799 United Nations Plaza
New York, NY 10017
"Politician"

Randall Robinson
1744 "R" Street NW
Washington, DC 20009
"Social Activist"

Smokey Robinson
17085 Rancho Street
Encino, CA 91316
"Singer, Songwriter"

Andy Robustelli
30 Spring Street
Stamford, CT 06901
"Ex-Football Player"

Alex Rocco
1755 Ocean Oaks Road
Carpinteria, CA 93013
"Actor"

Eugene Roche
9911 West Pico Blvd., #PH-A
Los Angeles, CA 90035
"Actor"

Debbie Rochon
P.O. Box 1299
New York, NY 10009
"Actress"

Lela Rochon
250 W. 57th Street #1610
New York, NY 10107
"Actress"

Chris Rock
527 N. Azusa Avenue #231
Covina, CA 91722
"Comedian"

David Rockefeller, Jr.
30 Rockefeller Plaza #506
New York, NY 10112
"Businessman"

Sen. John D. Rockefeller IV (WV)
Senate Hart Bldg. #109
Washington, DC 20510
"Politician"

Mrs. Nelson Rockefeller
812 Fifth Avenue
New York, NY 10024
"Wife of Nelson Rockefeller"

Sharon Rockefeller
1940 Shepherd Street NW
Washington, DC 20011
"Wife of John D. Rockefeller"

Robert Rockwell
650 Toyopa Drive
Pacific Palisades, CA 90272
"Actor"

Marcia Rodd
11738 Moorpark Street #C
Studio City, CA 91604
"Actress"

Anton Rodgers
The White House
Lower Basildon
Berkshire ENGLAND
"Actor"

Jimmie Rodgers
P.O. Box 685
Forsyth, MO 65653
"Singer, Songwriter"

Dennis Rodman
4809 Seashore Drive
Newport Beach, CA 92663
"Basketball Player"

Chi Chi Rodriguez
1720 Merriman Road
P.O. Box 5118
Akron, OH 44334
"Golfer"

Johnny Rodriguez
P.O. Box 23162
Nashville, TN 37202
"Singer, Songwriter"

Paul Rodriguez
435 N. Camden Drive #400
Beverly Hills, CA 90210
"Comedian"

Tommy Roe
P.O. Box 26037
Minneapolis, MN 55426
"Singer, Songwriter"

Daniel Roebuck
P.O. Box 950597
Mission Hills, CA 91395
"Actor"

Nicholas Roeg
14 Courtnell Street
London W2 5BX ENGLAND
"Film Director"

Maurice Roeves
1800 Avenue of the Stars, #400
Los Angeles, CA 90067
"Actor"

Bill Rogers
353 The Marketplace
Fanuil Hall
Boston, MA 02109
"Runner"

Charles "Buddy" Rogers
1147 Pickfair Way
Beverly Hills, CA 90210
"Actor"

Mr. Rogers (Fred)
4802 - 5th Avenue
Pittsburgh, PA 15213
"TV Show Host"

Joy Rogers
4141 West Kling Street #3
Burbank, CA 91505
"Actress"

Kenny Rogers
P.O. Box 24240
Nashville, TN 37202
"Singer, Songwriter"

Melody Rogers
2051 Nicols Canyon
Los Angeles, CA 90046
"Actress, TV Show Host"

Mimi Rogers
11693 San Vicente Blvd. #241
Los Angeles, CA 90049
"Actress"

Paul Rogers
9 Hillside Gardens
London N6 5SU ENGLAND
"Actor"

Roy Rogers, Jr.
P.O. Box 1507
Apple Valley, CA 92307
"Actor, Singer, Guitarist"

Suzanne Rogers
11266 Canton Drive
Studio City, CA 91604
"Actress"

Tristan Rogers
8550 Hollyway Drive #301
Los Angeles, CA 90069
"Actor"

Wayne Rogers
11828 La Grange Avenue
Los Angeles, CA 90025
"Actor, Writer, Director"

Fred Roggin
3000 West Alameda Avenue
Burbank, CA 91523
"TV Show Host"

Eric Rohmer
26 Ave. Pierre-Ler-De-Serbie
F-75016 Paris, FRANCE
"Film Director"

Al Roker
2200 Fletcher Drive
FT. Lee, NJ 07024
"TV Weatherman"

Ether Rolle
P.O. Box 8986
Los Angeles, CA 90008
"Actress"

Rolling Stones
P.O. Box 6152
New York, NY 10028
"Rock & Roll Group"

Ed Rollins
510 King Street, #302
Alexandria, VA 22314
"Political Consultant"

Sonny Rollins
193 Brighton Avenue
Boston, MA 02134
"Saxophonist"

Freddie Roman
101 West 57th Street
New York, NY 10019
"Comedian"

Roman Holiday
P.O. Box 475
London W1 ENGLAND
"Rock & Roll Group"

Ruth Roman
1225 Cliff Drive
Laguna Beach, CA 92651
"Actress"

Richard Romanus
1840 Camino Palmero
Los Angeles, CA 90046
"Actor"

George Romero
3364 Lake Road North
Sanibel, FL 33957
"Filmmaker, Screenwriter"

Ned Romero
9255 Sunset Blvd. #515
Los Angeles, CA 90069
"Actor"

Linda Ronstadt
644 North Doheny
Los Angeles, CA 90069
"Singer"

Michael Rooker
P.O. Box 5617
Beverly Hills, CA 90210
"Actor"

Andy Rooney
254 Rowayton Avenue
Rowayton, CT 06853
"Writer, Actor, Director"

Mickey Rooney
P.O. Box 5028
Westlake Village, CA 91362
"Actor"

Axl Rose
9229 Sunset Blvd., #607
Los Angeles, CA 90069
"Singer"

Charlie Rose
356 W. 58th St., 10th Floor
New York, NY 10019
"Talk Show Host"

Jamie Rose
3500 W. Olive Avenue #1400
Burbank, CA 91505
"Actress"

Rose Marie
6916 Chisholm Avenue
Van Nuys, CA 91406
"Singer"

Murray Rose
3305 Carse Drive
Los Angeles, CA 90028
"Swimmer"

Pete Rose
8144 Glades Road
Boca Raton, FL 33434
"Ex-Baseball Player"

Sherrie Rose
1758 Laurel Canyon Blvd.
Los Angeles, CA 90046
"Actress"

Roseanne
5664 Cahuenga Blvd. #433
No. Hollywood, CA 91601
"Actress"

Alan Rosenberg
10468 Ilona Ave.
Los Angeles, CA 90064
"Actor"

Barney Rosenzweig
308 North Sycamore #502
Los Angeles, CA 90036
"TV Writer, Producer"

Ken Rosewall
111 Pentacost Avenue
Turramurra NSW 2074
AUSTRALIA
"Tennis Player"

Francesco Rosi
Via Gregoriana 36
I-00187 Rome, ITALY
"Film Director"

Charlotte Ross
9200 Sunset Blvd. #1130
Los Angeles, CA 90069
"Actress"

Diana Ross
P.O. Box 11059
Glenville Station
Greenwich, CT 06831
"Singer, Actress"

Jonathan Ross
34/42 Cleveland Street
London W1P 5SB ENGLAND
"Actor"

Katherine Ross
33050 Pacific Coast Hwy.
Malibu, CA 90265
"Actress"

Marion Ross
20929 Ventura Blvd. #47
Woodland Hills, CA 91364
"Actress"

Stan Ross
1410 North Gardner
Los Angeles, CA 90046
"Actor"

Tracey Ross
12304 Santa Monica Blvd., #104
Los Angeles, CA 90025
"Actress"

Isabella Rossellini
745 Fifth Avenue #814
New York, NY 10151
"Actress"

Carol Rossen
1119-23rd Street #8
Santa Monica, CA 90403
"Actress"

Norman Rossington
27 Parliament Hill
London NW3 ENGLAND
"Actor"

Dan Rostenkowski
1372 West Evergreen Street
Chicago, IL 60027
"Ex-Congressman"

Walt Rostow
1 Wildwind Point
Austin, TX 78746
"Economist"

Miklos Rosza
2936 Montcalm Drive
Los Angeles, CA 90046
"Composer"

Kyle Rote
24700 Deepwater Pt. Drive #14
St. Michaels, MD 21663
"Ex-Football Player"

Andrea Roth
10100 Santa Monica Blvd. #2500
Los Angeles, CA 90067
"Actress"

David Lee Roth
455 Bradford Street
Pasadena, CA 91105
"Singer, Songwriter"

Matt Roth
P.O. Box 5617
Beverly Hills, CA 90210
"Actor"

Tim Roth
15250 Ventura Blvd. #900
Sherman Oaks, CA 91403
"Actor"

Sen. William Roth, Jr. (DE)
Senate Hart Bldg. #104
Washington, DC 20510
"Politician"

Richard Roundtree
8091 Selma Avenue
Los Angeles, CA 90046
"Actor"

Mickey Rourke
9150 Wilshire Blvd., #350
Beverly Hills, CA 90212
"Actor"

The Roustabouts
P.O. Box 25371
Charlotte, NC 28212
"Bluegrass Group"

Carl T. Rowan
3116 Fessenden Street NW
Washington, DC 20008
"Columnist"

Kelly Rowan
574 West End Avenue #4
New York, NY 10024
"Actor"

Alan Rowe
8 Sherwood Close
London SW13 ENGLAND
"Actor"

Debbie Rowe-Jackson
435 N. Roxbury Drive
Beverly Hills, CA 90210
"Michael Jackson's wife"

Misty Rowe
P.O. Box 11152
Greenwich, CT 06831
"Actress"

Nicholas Rowe
52 Shaftesbury Avenue
London WIV 7DE ENGLAND
"Poet, Dramatist"

Betty Rowland
125 N. Barrington Avenue #103
Los Angeles, CA 90049
"Burlesque"

Dave Rowland
P.O. Box 121089
Nashville, TN 37212
"Singer"

Gena Rowlands
7917 Woodrow Wilson Drive
Los Angeles, CA 90046
"Actress"

Patsy Rowlands
265 Liverpool Rd.
London N1 1LX ENGLAND
"Actress"

Steve Roxton
6 Thornton Road, Leytonstone
London E11 ENGLAND
"Actor"

Billy Joe Royal
P.O. Box 50572
Nashville, TN 37205
"Singer, Songwriter"

Darrell Royal
10507 La Costa Drive
Austin, TX 78747
"Ex-Football Coach"

Kenneth Royce
3 Abbott's Close, Andover
Hants. SP11 7NP ENGLAND
"Author"

Pamela Roylance
292 S. La Cienega Blvd. #217
Beverly Hills, CA 90211
"Actress"

Pete Rozelle
P.O. Box 9686
Rancho Santa Fe, CA 92067
"Former Football Commissioner"

Mike Rozier
I-85 & Suwanee Road
Suwanee, GA 30174
"Football Player"

Zelda Rubinstein
8730 Sunset Blvd. #270
Los Angeles, CA 90069
"Actress"

Paul Rudd
10228 Russett Avenue
Sunland, CA 91040
"Actor"

Al Ruddy
1601 Clearview Drive
Beverly Hills, CA 90210
"Film Writer, Producer"

Herbert Rudley
13056 Maxella Ave. #1
Marina del Rey, CA 90292
"Actor"

Rita Rudner
2934 Beverly Glen Circle #389
Los Angeles, CA 90077
"Comedienne"

Mercedes Ruehl
P.O. Box 178
Old Chelsea Station
New York, NY 10011
"Actress"

Rufus
7250 Beverly Blvd #200
Los Angeles, CA 90036
"R&B Group"

Tracy Ruiz-Conforto
14314-174th Avenue N.E.
Redmond, WA 98052
"Swimmer"

Janice Rule
105 West 72nd Street #12B
New York, NY 10023
"Actress"

Donald Rumsfeld
400 N. Michigan Avenue #405
Chicago, IL 60611
"Ex-Government Official"

Dr. Robert Runcie
Archbishop of Canterbury
Lambeth Palace
London SW1 7JU ENGLAND
"Archbishop"

Run D.M.C.
160 Varick Street
New York, NY 10013
"Rap Group"

Jennifer Runyon
5130 N. Lakemont Lane
Boise, ID 83703
"Actress"

RuPaul
6671 Sunset Blvd. #1590
Hollywood, CA 90028
"Singer"

Barbara Rush
1709 Tropical Avenue
Beverly Hills, CA 90120
"Actress"

Geoffrey Rush
9830 Wilshire Blvd.
Beverly Hills, CA 90212
"Actor"

Jennifer Rush
145 Central Park West
New York, NY 10023
"Singer"

Salman Rushdie
c/o Gillon Aitken
29 Fernshaw Road
London SW10 OTG ENGLAND
"Author"

Patrice Rushen
P.O. Box 6278
Altadena, CA 91003
"Singer"

Jared Rushton
10653 Riverside Drive
Toluca Lake, CA 91602
"Actor"

Robert Rusler
10683 Santa Monica Blvd.
Los Angeles, CA 90025
"Actor"

Betsy Russell
13926 Magnolia Blvd.
Sherman Oaks, CA 91423
"Actress"

Bing Russell
229 E. Gainsborough Road
Thousand Oaks, CA 91360
"Actor"

Brenda Russell
9000 Sunset Blvd. #1200
Los Angeles, CA 90069
"Singer"

Harold Russell
34 Old Town Road
Hyannis, MA 02601
"Government Official"

Jane Russell
2934 Torito Road
Santa Barbara, CA 93108
"Actress"

Johnny Russell
P.O. Box Drawer 37
Hendersonville, TN 37075
"Singer, Songwriter"

Ken Russell
7 Bellmount Wood Land
Watford, Hert. ENGLAND
"Film Director"

Kimberly Russell
11617 Laurelwood
Studio City, CA 91604
"Actress"

Kurt Russell
1900 Avenue of the Stars #1240
Los Angeles, CA 90067
"Actor"

Mark Russell
3201 33rd Place NW
Washington, DC 20008
"Satirist, Comedian"

Nipsey Russell
353 West 57th Street
New York, NY 10019
"Comedian, Writer, Director"

Theresa Russell
9454 Lloyd Crest Drive
Beverly Hills, CA 90210
"Actress"

Rene Russo
10435 Whipple Street
No. Hollywood, CA 91602
"Actress"

Ann Rutherford
826 Greenway Drive
Beverly Hills, CA 90210
"Actress"

Johnny Rutherford
4919 Black Oak Lane
Fort Worth, TX 76114
"Race Car Driver"

Kelly Rutherford
PO Box 492266
Los Angeles, CA 90049
"Actress"

Susan Ruttan
P.O. Box 862
Vashon, WA 98070
"Actress"

Frank Ryan
4204 Woodland
Burbank, CA 91505
"Actress"

Meg Ryan
11718 Barrington Court #508
Los Angeles, CA 90049
"Actress"

Mitchell Ryan
30355 Mulholland Drive
Cornell, CA 91301
"Actor"

Nolan Ryan
200 W. South Street #B
Alvin, TX 77511
"Ex-Baseball Player"

Peggy Ryan
1821 East Oakley Blvd.
Las Vegas, NV 89104
"Actress"

Bobby Rydell
917 Bryn Mawr Avenue
Narberth, PA 19072
"Singer"

Christopher Rydell
911 North Sweetzer #C
Los Angeles, CA 90069
"Actor"

Mark Rydell
1 Topsail
Marina del Rey, CA 90292
"Actor, Director"

Winona Ryder
350 Park Avenue #900
New York, NY 10022
"Actress"

Ann Ryerson
935 Gayley Avenue
Los Angeles, CA 90024
"Actress"

Leony Rysanek
D-88682
Attenbeuren GERMANY
"Soprano"

Jim Ryun
Rt. 3, Box 62-B
Lawrence, KS 66044
"Track Athlete"

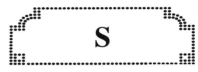

Gabriela Sabatini
Ap. Int. 14 Suc. 27
1427 Buenos Aires ARGENTINA
"Tennis Player"

Michael Sabatino
13538 Valleyheart Drive
Sherman Oaks, CA 91423
"Actor"

Brett Saberhagen
5535 Amber Circle
Calabasas, CA 91302
"Baseball Player"

Robert Sacchi
203 N. Gramercy Place
Los Angeles, CA 90004
"Actor"

Andrew Sachs
25 Whitehall
London SW1A 2BS ENGLAND
"Actor"

Madame Jehan El-Sadat
2310 Decatur Place N.W.
Washington, DC 20008
"Widower of Anwar"

Sade
10 Malborough Street
London W1V 2LP ENGLAND
"Singer, Songwriter"

William Sadler
9255 Sunset Blvd. #710
Los Angeles, CA 90069
"Actor"

Morley Safer
51 West 52nd Street
New York, NY 10019
"News Journalist"

William Safire
6200 Elmwood Road
Chevy Chase, MD 20815
"Columnist"

Katey Sagal
7095 Hollywood Blvd. #792
Los Angeles, CA 90028
"Actress"

Liz Sagal
4526 Wilshire Blvd.
Los Angeles, CA 90046
"Actress

Francoise Sagan
Equemauville F-14600
Honfleur FRANCE
"Author"

Jeff Sagansky
145 Ocean Avenue
Santa Monica, CA 90402
"TV Executive"

Carole Bayer Sager
10761 Bellagio Road
Los Angeles, CA 90077
"Singer, Songwriter"

Bob Saget
9150 Wilshire Blvd., #350
Beverly Hills, CA 90212
"Comedian"

Mort Sahl
2325 San Ysidro Drive
Beverly Hills, CA 90210
"Comedian, Writer"

Eva Marie Saint
10590 Wilshire Blvd. #408
Los Angeles, CA 90024
"Actress"

Lili St. Cyr
624 North Plymouth Blvd. #7
Los Angeles, CA 90004
"Entertainer"

Susan Saint James
854 North Genesee
Los Angeles, CA 90046
"Actress"

Jill St. John
1500 Old Oak Road
Los Angeles, CA 90077
"Actress"

Lyn St. James
2570 W. International Speedway #F
Daytona, FL 32114
"Race Car Driver"

Yves St. Laurent
5 Ave. du Marceau
75016 Paris FRANCE
"Fashion Designer"

Buffy Sainte-Marie
20 Duncan Street #200
Toronto, Ontario
M5H 3G8 CANADA
"Singer, Songwriter"

Pat Sajak
3400 Riverside Drive
Burbank, CA 91505
"TV Show Host"

Theresa Saldana
104-60 Queens Blvd. #1D
Forest Hills, NY 11375
"Actress"

Meredith Salenger
9255 Sunset Blvd. #1010
W. Hollywood, CA 90069
"Actress"

Soupy Sales
245 East 35th Street
New York, NY 10016
"Actor, Comedian"

J. D. Salinger
RR #3, Box 176
Cornish Flat, NH 03746
"Author"

Matt Salinger
21604 Paseo Serra
Malibu, CA 90265
"Actor"

Pierre Salinger
3114 "O" Street NW
Washington, DC 20007
"News Correspondent"

Jennifer Salt
9045 Elevado Street
West Hollywood, CA 90069
"Actress"

Salt-N-Pepa
1700 Broadway #500
New York, NY 10019
"Rap Group"

Emma Samms
2934 1/2 N. Beverly Glen Circle
Suite #417
Los Angeles, CA 90077
"Actress"

Pete Sampras
6352 Maclaurin Drive
Tampa, FL 33647
"Tennis Player"

Jeffrey D. Sams
9200 Sunset Blvd., #1130
Los Angeles, CA 90069
"Actor"

Ron Samuels
25 Judd Terrace
Rancho Mirage, CA 92270
"Talent Agent"

Aitana Sanchez-Gijon
8730 Sunset Blvd. #490
Los Angeles, CA 90069
"Actress"

Paul Sand
924 Westwood Blvd., #900
Los Angeles, CA 90024
"Actor"

Casey Sander
8271 Melrose Avenue #202
Los Angeles, CA 90046
"Actor"

Barry Sanders
1200 Featherstone Road
Pontiac, MI 48057
"Football Player"

Deion Sanders
10250 Meadow Crest Lane
Alpharetta, GA 30083
"Football & Baseball Player"

Doug Sanders
8828 Sandringham
Houston, TX 77024
"Golfer"

Jay O. Sanders
9229 Sunset Blvd. #710
Los Angeles, CA 90069
"Actor"

Richard Sanders
P.O. Box 1644
Woodinville, WA 98072
"Actor, Writer"

Summer Sanders
730 Sunrise Avenue
Roseville, CA 95661
"Swimmer"

William Sanderson
8271 Melrose Avenue #110
Los Angeles, CA 90046
"Actor"

Adam Sandler
5420 Worster Avenue
Van Nuys, CA 91401
"Actor"

Jay Sandrich
610 North Maple Drive
Beverly Hills, CA 90210
"Actor, Director"

Julian Sands
1287 Ozeta Terrace
Los Angeles, CA 90069
"Actor"

Tommy Sands
6671 Sunset Blvd. #1502
Hollywood, CA 90028
"Actor, Singer"

Baby Sandy
(Sandra Lee Henville Magee)
6846 Haywood
Tujunga, CA 91042
"Actress"

Gary Sandy
329 N. Wetherly Drive #101
Beverly Hills, CA 90211
"Actor"

Isabel Sanford
2501 Colorado Avenue #350
Santa Monica, CA 90404
"Actress"

Carlos Santana
P.O. Box 10348
San Rafael, CA 94912
"Singer"

Benito Santiago
2267 NW 199th Street
Miami, FL 33056
"Baseball Player"

Santo & Johnny
217 Edgewood Avenue
Clearwater, FL 34615
"Vocal Duo"

Ron Santo
1721 Meadow Lane
Bannockburn, IL 60015
"Ex-Baseball Player"

Penny Santon
1918 North Edgemont Street
Los Angeles, CA 90027
"Actress"

Reni Santoni
247 South Beverly Drive #102
Beverly Hills, CA 90212
"Actor"

Joe Santos
10100 Santa Monica Blvd. #700
Los Angeles, CA 90067
"Actor"

Mia Sara
P.O. Box 5617
Beverly Hills, CA 90210
"Actress"

HRH Sarah, Dutchess of York
Sunninghill Park
Windsor, Berks., ENGLAND
"Royalty"

Chris Sarandon
9540 Hidden Valley Road
Beverly Hills, CA 90210
"Actor"

Susan Sarandon
40 West 57th Street
New York, NY 10019
"Actress"

Gene Sarazen
Emerald Beach
P.O. Box 677
Marco, FL 33937
"Golfer"

Sen. Paul Sarbanes (MD)
Senate Hart Bldg. #309
Washington, DC 20510
"Politician"

Vincent Sardi, Jr.
234 West 44th Street
New York, NY 10036
"Restaurateur"

Michael Sarrazin
9920 Beverly Grove
Beverly Hills, CA 90210
"Actor"

Vidal Sassoon
1163 Calle Vista
Beverly Hills, CA 90210
"Hair Stylist"

Paul Satterfield
400 S. Beverly Drive #101
Beverly Hills, CA 90212
"Actor"

Ann Savage
1541 N. Hayworth Avenue #203
Los Angeles, CA 90046
"Actress"

Fred Savage
9830 Wilshire Blvd.
Beverly Hills, CA 90212
"Actor"

John Savage
11300 W. Olympic Blvd. #610
Los Angeles, CA 90064
"Actor"

Randy Savage
13300 Indian Rocks Road #304
Largo, FL 33774
"Wrestler"

Tracie Savage
6212 Banner Avenue
Los Angeles, CA 90038
"Actress"

Doug Savant
1015 East Angelo Avenue
Burbank, CA 91501
"Actor"

Jennifer Savidge
2705 Glendower Avenue
Los Angeles, CA 90027
"Actress"

David Saville
28 Colomb Street
London SW10 9EW ENGLAND
"Actor"

Richie Sambora
250 W. 57th Street #603
New York, NY 10107
"Guitarist"

Devon Sawa
1505 W. 2nd Ave. #200, Vancouver
BC V6H 3Y4 CANADA
"Actor"

Sawyer Brown
4219 Hillsboro Road #318
Nashville, TN 37215
"Rock & Roll Group"

Diane Sawyer
77 West 66th Street
New York, NY 10023
"Broadcast Journalist"

John Saxon
P.O. Box 492480
Los Angeles, CA 90049
"Actor, Writer"

Peggy Say
438 Lake Shore Drive
Cadiz, KY 42211
"Sister Of American Hostage"

Gale Sayers
624 Buck Road
Northbrook, IL 60062
"Ex-Football Player"

Raphael Sbarge
8281 Melrose Avenue #200
Los Angeles, CA 90046
"Actor"

Boz Scaggs
8900 Wilshire Blvd. #300
Beverly Hills, CA 90211
"Singer, Songwriter"

Prunella Scales
18-21 Jermyn Street
London SW1 ENGLAND
"Actress"

Antonin Scalia
6713 Wemberly Way
McLean, VA 22101
"Supreme Court Justice"

Jack Scalia
23049 Calvert Street
Woodland Hills, CA 91367
"Actor"

Michele Scarabelli
4720 Vineland Avenue #216
North Hollywood, CA 91602
"Actress"

Glenn Scarpelli
3480 Barham Blvd. #320
Los Angeles, CA 90068
"Actor"

Diana Scarwid
P.O. Box 3614
Savannah, GA 31404
"Actress"

Francesco Scavullo
216 East 63rd Street
New York, NY 10021
"Photographer"

Richard Schaal
303 S. Crescent Heights Blvd.
Los Angeles, CA 90048
"Actor, Writer, Director"

Johnathon Schaech
1122 S. Roxbury Drive
Los Angeles, CA 90035
"Actor"

George Schaeffer
1040 Woodland Drive
Beverly Hills, CA 90210
"TV Director, Producer"

William Schallert
14920 Ramos Place
Pacific Palisades, CA 90272
"Actor"

Anne Schedeen
816 Crestmore Place
Venice, CA 90291
"Actress"

Roy Scheider
P.O. Box 364
Sagaponack, NY 11962
"Actor"

Catherine Schell
Postfache 8000504 D-51005
Kain, GERMANY
"Actress"

Maria Schell
9400 Wolfsberg/Karnsten
AUSTRIA
"Actress"

Maximilian Schell
2869 Royston Place
Beverly Hills, CA 90210
"Actor"

Bo Schembechler
1904 Boulder Drive
Ann Arbor, MI 48104
"Ex-College Football Coach"

Paul Scherrer
9000 Sunset Blvd. #1200
Los Angeles, CA 90069
"Actor"

Vincent Schiavelli
450 N. Rossmore Avenue #206
Los Angeles, CA 90004
"Actor"

Bob Schieffer
2438 Belmont Road NW
Washington, DC 20008
"Broadcast Journalist"

Claudia Schiffer
5 Union Square West #500
New York, NY 10003
"Model"

Lalo Schifrin
710 North Hillcrest Road
Beverly Hills, CA 90210
"Composer, Conductor"

William Schilling
626 North Valley Street
Burbank, CA 91505
"Actor"

Walter M. Schirra, Jr.
16834 Via de Santa Fe
Rancho Santa Fe, CA 92067
"Astronaut"

Phyllis Schlafly
68 Fairmont
Alton, IL 62002
"Author, Politician"

Charlie Schlatter
13501 Contour Drive
Sherman Oaks, CA 91423
"Actor"

George Schlatter
400 Robert Lane
Beverly Hills, CA 90210
"Writer, Producer"

Arthur Schlesinger, Jr.
33 West 42nd Street
New York, NY 10036
"Historian, Author"

John Schlesinger
76 Oxford Street
London WIN OAX ENGLAND
"Film Director"

Dr. Laura Schlessinger
610 S. Ardmore Avenue
Los Angeles, CA 90005
"Radio Show Host"

Edwin Schlossberg
641 Avenue of the Americas
New York, NY 10011
"Artist"

Max Schmeling
Sonnenweg 1
D-21279 Hollenstedt
GERMANY
"Ex-Boxer"

Harold Schmi
Hohenzollernring 79
50672 Cologne Germany
"T.V. Show Host"

Helmut Schmidt
Neubergerweg 80/82
D-22419 Hamburg GERMANY
"Ex-Chancellor"

John Schneider
2644 E. Chevy Chase Drive
Glendale, CA 91401
"Actor, Writer, Singer"

Stephen Schnetzer
448 West 44th Street
New York, NY 10036
"Actor"

Gina Schock
P.O. Box 4398
North Hollywood, CA 91617
"Drummer, Singer"

Carolyn Hunt Schoellkopf
100 Crescent #1700
Dallas, TX 75201
"Businesswoman"

Daniel Schorr
3113 Woodley Road
Washington, DC 20008
"Broadcast Journalist"

Marge Schott
100 Riverfront Stadium
Cincinnati, OH 45202
"Baseball Team Owner"

David Schramm
3521 Berry Drive
Studio City, CA 91604
"Actor"

Tex Schramm
9355 Sunnybrook
Dallas, TX 75220
"Football Team Executive"

Avery Schreiber
6612 Ranchito
Van Nuys, CA 91405
"Actor, Comedian"

Barbet Schroeder
1478 North Kings Road
Los Angeles, CA 90069
"Film Director"

Patricia Schroeder
c/o Assoc. of Amer. Publishers
71 - 5th Avenue
New York, NY 10003
"Ex-Politician"

Rick Schroeder
9560 Wilshire Blvd. #500
Beverly Hills, CA 90212
"Actor"

Mark Schubb
9744 Wilshire Blvd. #308
Beverly Hills, CA 90212
"Actor"

John Schuck
702 California Court
Venice, CA 90291
"Actor"

Budd Schulberg
P.O. Box 707, Brookside
Westhampton Beach, NY 11978
"TV Writer"

Dr. Robert Schuller
464 South Esplanade
Orange, CA 92669
"Evangelist"

Dwight Schultz
7513 Fountain Avenue #204
Los Angeles, CA 90046
"Actor"

Charles Schulz
1 Snoopy Place
Santa Rosa, CA 95401
"Cartoonist"

Joel Schumacher
4000 Warner Blvd.
Bldg. 81 #117
burbank, CA 91522
"Writer, Producer"

Diane Schuur
33042 Ocean Ridge
Dana Point, CA 92629
"Singer"

Neil Schwartz
23427 Schoolcraft Avenue
Canoga Park, CA 91304
"Actor"

Sherwood Schwartz
1865 Carla Ridge Dr.
Beverly Hills, CA 90210
"TV Writer, Producer"

Arnold Schwarzenegger
3110 Main Street #300
Santa Monica, CA 90405
"Actor"

Elisabeth Schwarzkopf
Rebhusstr. 29
8126 Zunnikon
Zurich, SWITZERLAND
"Opera Singer"

Gen. Norman Schwarzkopf
400 North Ashley Drive #3050
Tampa, FL 33609
"Military Leader"

Eric Schweig
P.O. Box 5163
Vancouver BC V7B 1M4 CANADA
"Actor"

Til Schweiger
Im Klapperhof 33b.
D-50670 Koln GERMANY
"Actor"

David Schwimmer
10390 Santa Monica Blvd. #300
Los Angeles, CA 90025
"Actor"

Hanna Schygulla
17 rue Dumont-d'Urville
F-75016 Paris FRANCE
"Actress"

Patti Scialfa
11 Gimbel Place
Ocean, NJ 07712
"Singer"

Leonard Sciascia
Viale Scaduto 10/B
I-00144 Palermo, ITALY
"Author"

Annabella Sciorra
132 S. Rodeo Drive, #300
Beverly Hills, CA 90212
"Actress"

Mike Scioscia
444 Fargo Street
Thousand Oaks, CA 91360
"Baseball Player"

Dean Scofield
12304 Santa Monica Blvd. #104
Los Angeles, CA 90025
"Actor"

Paul Scofield
The Gables
Balcombe, Sussex ENGLAND
"Actor"

Tracy Scoggins
1131 Alta Loma Road #515
Los Angeles, CA 90069
"Actress, Model"

Peter Scolari
500 S. Sepulveda Blvd. #500
Los Angeles, CA 90049
"Actor"

The Scooters
15190 Encanto Drive
Sherman Oaks, CA 91403
"Rock & Roll Group"

Scorpions
P.O. Box 5220
D-30052 Hanover, GERMANY
"Rock & Roll Group"

Martine Scorsese
445 Park Avenue #700
New York, NY 10022
"Film Writer, Producer"

Campbell Scott
3211 Retreat Court
Malibu, CA 90265
"Actor"

Dr. Gene Scott
1615 Glendale Avenue
Glendale, CA 91205
"TV Show Host, Teacher"

George C. Scott
3211 Retreat Court
Malibu, CA 90265
"Actor, Director"

Jacqueline Scott
12456 Ventura Blvd. #1
Studio City, CA 91604
"Actress"

Judson Scott
10000 Santa Monica Blvd. #305
Los Angeles, CA 90067
"Actor"

Kathryn Leigh Scott
P.O. Box 17217
Beverly Hills, CA 90209
"Actress"

Lizabeth Scott
8277 Hollywood Blvd.
Los Angeles, CA 90069
"Actress"

Martha Scott
14054 Chandler Blvd.
Van Nuys, CA 91401
"Actress"

Pippa Scott
23431 Styles Street
Woodland Hills, CA 91367
"Actress"

Ridley Scott
9348 Civic Center Drive
Beverly Hills, CA 90210
"Film Director"

Williard Scott
30 Rockerfeller Plaza #304
New York, NY 10012
"TV Weatherman"

Renato Scotto
61 West 62nd Street #6F
New York, NY 10023
"Soprano"

Gen. Brent Scowcroft
6114 Wynnwood Road
Bethesda, MD 20816
"Ex-Military, Politician"

Earl Scruggs
P.O. Box 66
Madison, TN 37115
"Banjoist, Songwriter"

Vin Scully
1555 Capri Drive
Pacific Palisades, CA 90272
"Sportscaster"

Glenn T. Seaborg
1 Cyclotron Road
Berkeley, CA 94720
"Chemist"

Steven Seagal
4875 Louise
Encino, CA 91316
"Actor"

Bob Seagren
11801 Gwynne Lane
Los Angeles, CA 90077
"Actor"

Jenny Seagrove
302-308 Regent Street
London W1R 5AL ENGLAND
"Actress"

Seal
56 Beethoven Street
London W10 4LG ENGLAND
"Singer"

Bobby Seale
302 West Chelton Avenue
Philadelphia, PA 19144
"Activist, Author"

Dan Seals
153 Saunders Ferry Rd.
Hendersonville, TN 37075
"Singer, Songwriter"

Junior Seau
9449 Friars Road
San Diego, CA 92108
"Football Player"

Tom Seaver
Larkspur Lane
Greenwich, CT 06830
"Ex-Baseball Player"

John Sebastian
3520 Hayden Avenue
Culver City, CA 90232
"Singer, Songwriter"

Jon Secada
601 Brickell Key Dr. #200
Miami, FL 33131
"Singer"

Sir Harry Secombe
46 St. James's Place
London SW1 ENGLAND
"Actor, Singer"

Kyle Secor
538 North Mansfield Avenue
Los Angeles, CA 90036
"Actor"

Gen. Richard Secord
1 Pennsylvania Plaza #2400
New York, NY 10119
"Miltary Leader"

Neil Sedaka
888 - 7th Avenue #1600
New York, NY 10106
"Singer, Songwriter"

Frank Sedgman
28 Bolton Avenue
Hampton, Victoria 3188
AUSTRALIA
"Tennis Player"

Kyra Sedgwick
P.O. Box 668
Sharon, CT 06069
"Actress"

Pete Seeger
P.O. Box 431
Duchess Junction
Beacon, NY 12508
"Singer, Songwriter"

Erich Segal
53 The Pryors
East Heath Road
London NW3 1BP ENGLAND
"Author"

George Segal
515 N. Robertson Blvd.
Los Angeles, CA 90048
"Actor"

Jonathan Segal
P.O. Box 3059
Tel Aviv 61030 ISRAEL
"Actor"

Michael Segal
27 Cyprus Avenue, Finchley
London N3 1SS ENGLAND
"Actor"

Pamela Segall
9560 Wilshire Blvd. #500
Beverly Hills, CA 90212
"Actress"

Bob Seger
567 Purdy
Birmingham, MI 48009
"Singer"

Pancho Segura
La Costa Hotel & Spas
Costa Del Mar Road
Carlsbad, CA 92008
"Tennis Player"

Emmanuella Seigner
3 Quai Malaquais
F-75006 Paris FRANCE
"Actress"

Jerry Seinfeld
211 Central Park West
New York, NY 10024
"Comedian, Actor"

David Selby
15152 Encanto Drive
Sherman Oaks, CA 91403
"Actor"

Monica Seles
7751 Beeridge Road
Sarasota, FL 34241
"Tennis Player"

Bud Selig
c/o County Coliseum
Milwaukee, WI 53214
"Baseball Team Owner"

Connie Selleca
9255 Sunset Blvd. #1010
Los Angeles, CA 90069
"Actress"

Tom Selleck
331 Sage Lane
Santa Monica, CA 90402
"Actor"

Milton Selzer
575 San Juan Street
Santa Paul, CA 93060
"Actor"

The Serendipity Singers
P.O. Box 142
Wauconda, IL 60084
"Vocal Group"

Yahoo Serious
12/33 East Crescent Street
McMahons Point NSW 2060
AUSTRLIA
"Actor, Director"

Pepe Serna
2321 Hill Drive
Los Angeles, CA 90041
"Actor"

Sesame Street
One Lincoln Plaza
New York, NY 10022
"Children TV Show"

Brian Setzer
113 Wardour Street
London W1 ENGLAND
"Musician"

Johnny Seven
11213 McLennan Avenue
Granada Hills, CA 91344
"Actor, Director"

Joan Severance
9000 Sunset Boulevard, #1200
Los Angeles, CA 90069
"Actress, Model"

Doc Severinsen
4275 White Pine Lane
Santa Ynez, CA 93460
"Trumpeter"

The Sex Pistols
100 Wilshire Blvd. #1830
Santa Monica, CA 90401
"Music Group"

Jane Seymour
P.O. Box 548
Agoura, CA 91376
"Actress, Model"

Stephanie Seymour
5415 Oberlin Drive
San Diego, CA 92121
"Model"

Ted Shackelford
12305 Valleyheart Drive
Studio City, CA 91604
"Actor"

Paul Shaffer
1697 Broadway
New York, NY 10019
"Keyboardist"

Peter Shaffer
200 Fulham Road
London SW10 ENGLAND
"Screenwriter"

Steve Shagan
10390 Wilshire Blvd. #705
Los Angeles, CA 90024
"Writer, Producer"

Sec. Donna Shalala
200 Independence Avenue S.W.
Washington, DC 20201
"Sec. Health & Human Service"

Shalamar
707-18th Avenue So.
Nashville, TN 37203
"R&B Group"

Gen. John Shalikashvilli
The Pentagon, Room 2E872
Washington, DC 20301
"Joint Chief of Staff"

Gene Shalit
225 East 79th Street
New York, NY 10021
"Film Critic"

Gen. John Shalikashvili
The Pentagon, Room 2E872
Washington, DC 20301
"Military Leader"

Yitzhak Shamir
Kiriyat Ben Gurian
Jerusalem 91919 ISRAEL
"Politician"

Garry Shandling
9150 Wilshire Boulevard, #350
Beverly Hills, CA 90212
"Comedian, Actor, Director"

Shanice
8455 Fountain Avenue #530
Los Angeles, CA 90069
"Singer"

Ravi Shankar
17 Warden Court
Gowalia Tank Road
Bombay 36 INDIA
"Satarist"

Esther Shapiro
617 North Alta Drive
Beverly Hills, CA 90210
"TV Writer, Producer"

Richard Shapiro
617 North Alta Drive
Beverly Hills, CA 90210
"TV Writer, Producer"

Robert Shapiro
2590 Walingford Drive
Beverly Hills, CA 90210
"Attorney"

Omar Sharif
18 rue Troyan
F-75017 Paris FRANCE
"Actor"

Barbara Sharma
P.O. Box 29125
Los Angeles, CA 90029
"Actress"

Don Sharp
80 Castelnau
London SW13 9EX ENGLAND
"TV Writer, Executive"

Rev. Al Sharpton
1941 Madison Avenue #2
New York, NY 10035
"Social Activist"

William Shatner
P.O. Box 7401725
Studio City, CA 91604
"Actor"

Grant Shaud
8738 Applan Way
Los Angeles, CA 90046
"Actor"

Charles Shaughnessy
534 15th Street
Santa Monica, CA 90402
"Actor"

Mel Shavelson
11947 Sunshine Terrace
North Hollywood, CA 91604
"Writer, Producer"

Helen Shaver
9171 Wilshire Blvd. #436
Beverly Hills, CA 90210
"Actress"

Artie Shaw
2127 West Palos Court
Newbury Park, CA 91320
"Orchestra Leader"

Bernard Shaw
1050 Techwood Drive N.W.
Atlanta, GA 30318
"News Correspondent"

Martin Shaw
204 Belswins Lane
Hemel, Hempstead
Hertfordshire, ENGLAND
"Actor"

Stan Shaw
4526 Wilshire Blvd.
Los Angeles, CA 90010
"Actor"

Tommy Shaw
6025 The Comers Parkway #202
Norcross, GA 30092
"Singer, Songwriter"

David Shawyer
16 Rylett Road
London W12 ENGLAND
"Actor"

George Beverly Shea
1300 Harmon Place
Minneapolis, MN 55403
"Singer"

John Shea
955 South Carrillo Drive #300
Los Angeles, CA 90048
"Actor"

Rhonda Shear
317 North Palm Drive
Beverly Hills, CA 90210
"Actress, Model"

Harry Shearer
119 Ocean Park Blvd.
Santa Monica, CA 90405
"TV Writer, Director"

George Shearing
1220 General MacArthur Drive
Brentwood, TN 37027
"Actor"

Ally Sheedy
132 S. Rodeo Drive #300
Beverly Hills, CA 90212
"Actress"

Doug Sheehan
4019-137 Goldfinch Street
San Diego, CA 92103
"Actor"

Gail Sheehy
300 East 57th Street #18-D
New York, NY 10022
"Author, Journalist"

Charlie Sheen
10580 Wilshire Blvd.
Los Angeles, CA 90024
"Actor"

Martin Sheen
6916 Dune Drive
Malibu, CA 90265
"Actor, TV Director"

Craig Sheffer
5699 Kanan Road #275
Agoura, CA 91301
"Actor"

Johnny Sheffield
834 First Avenue
Chula Vista, CA 92011
"Actor"

David Sheiner
601 N. Orange Drive
Los Angeles, CA 90036
"Actor"

Sen. Richard C. Shelby (AL)
Senate Hart Bldg. #110
Washington, DC 20515
"Politician"

Deborah Sheldon
2265 Westwood Blvd. #251
Los Angeles, CA 90064
"Actress"

Sidney Sheldon
10250 Sunset Blvd.
Los Angeles, CA 90077
"Writer"

Art Shell
2318 Walker Drive
Lawrenceville, GA 30043
"Ex-Football Player"

Stephen Shellen
615 Yonge Street #401
Toronto, Ontario
M4Y IZ5 CANADA
"Actor"

Shenandoah
1028-B 18th Avenue So.
Nashville, TN 37212
"Music Group"

Cybill Shepherd
3930 Valley Meadow Road
Encino, CA 91436
"Actress, Model"

T.G. Sheppard
3341 Arlington Avenue #F-206
Toledo, OH 43614
"Singer"

Mark Shera
329 N. Wetherly Drive #101
Beverly Hills, CA 90211
"Actor"

Jamey Sheridan
8942 Wilshire Blvd.
Beverly Hills, CA 90211
"Actor"

Liz Sheridan
9255 Sunset Blvd. #515
Los Angeles, CA 90069
"Actress"

Nicollette Sheridan
8730 Shoreham Drive #A
Los Angeles, CA 90069
"Actress"

Bobby Sherman
1870 Sunset Plaza Drive
Los Angeles, CA 90069
"Singer, Actor"

Jenny Sherman
P.O. Box 73
Los Angeles, CA 90078
"Actress, Model"

Richard Sherman
9030 Harratt Street
Los Angeles, CA 90069
"Composer, Lyricist"

Robert Sherman
9030 Harratt Street
Los Angeles, CA 90069
"Composer, Lyricist"

Vincent Sherman
6355 Sycamore Meadows
Malibu, CA 90265
"Film Director"

Roberta Sherwood
14155 Magnolia Blvd. #126
Sherman Oaks, CA 91423
"Singer, Actress"

Pres. Edward Shevardnadze
c/o State Council
Tbilisi GEORGIA
"Politician"

Brooke Shields
2300 W. Sahara #630
Las Vegas, NV 89192
"Actress, Model"

James Shigeta
8271 Melrose Avenue #202
Los Angeles, CA 90046
"Actor"

Yoko Shimada
7245 Hillside Avenue #415
Los Angeles, CA 90046
"Actress"

Armin Shimerman
8730 Sunset Boulevard, #480
Los Angeles, CA 90069
"Actor"

Joanna Shimkus
9255 Doheny Road
Los Angeles, CA 90069
"Actress"

John Wesley Shipp
850 N. Kings Road #208
W. Hollywood, CA 90069
"Actor"

Talia Shire
16633 Ventura Blvd. #1450
Encino, CA 91436
"Actress"

The Shirelles
P.O. Box 100
Clifton, NJ 07011
"Singing Group"

William Shockley
6345 Balboa Blvd. #375
Encino, CA 91316
"Actor"

Bill Shoemaker
2553 Fairfield Place
San Marino, CA 91108
"Horse Racer"

Pauly Shore
8491 Sunset Blvd. #700
W. Hollywood, CA 90069
"Actor"

Roberta Shore
1620 E. 6480 South
Salt Lake City, UT 84121
"Actress"

Lonnie Shorr
141 S. El Camino Drive #205
Beverly Hills, CA 90212
"Comedian"

Bobby Short
444 East 57th Street #9E
New York, NY 10022
"Actor, Singer"

Martin Short
760 N. La Cienega Blvd. #200
Los Angeles, CA 90069
"Actor"

Frank Shorter
3800 Pleasant Ridge Road
Boulder, CO 80301
"Track Athlete"

Steve Shortridge
1707 Clearview Drive
Beverly Hills, CA 90210
"Actor"

Grant Show
937 South Tremaine
Los Angeles, CA 90019
"Actor"

Max Showalter
5 Gilbert Hill Road
Chester, CT 06412
"Actor"

Kathy Shower
8383 Wilshire Blvd. #954
Beverly Hills, CA 90210
"Actress"

Jean Shrimpton
Abbey Hotel
Penzance
Cornwall ENGLAND
"Actress"

Kin Shriner
3915 Benedict Canyon
Sherman Oaks, CA 91423
"Actor"

Wil Shriner
5313 Quakertown Avenue
Woodland Hills, CA 91364
"Actor, Writer, Comedian"

Eunice Kennedy Shriver
1325 "G" Street NW
Washington, DC 20005
"Ex-President's Sister"

Maria Shriver
3110 Main Street #300
Santa Monica, CA 90405
"Broadcast Journalist"

Pam Shriever
133 - 1st Street NE
St. Petersburg, FL 33701
"Tennis Player"

R. Sargent Shriver
1325 "G" Street NW
Washington, DC 20005
"Politician"

Sonny Shroyer
329 N. Wetherly Drive #101
Beverly Hills, CA 90211
"Actor"

Andrew Shue
2617 Outpost Drive
Los Angeles, CA 90068
"Actor"

Elisabeth Shue
P.O. Box 464
South Orange, NJ 07079
"Actress"

Don Shula
16 Indian Creek Island
Miami Lakes, FL 33154
"Football Coach"

Richard B. Shull
16 Gramercy Park
New York, NY 10003
"Actor"

George P. Shultz
776 Dolores Street
Stanford, CA 94305
"Ex-Government Official"

Jane Siberry
1505 W. 2nd Avenue #200
Vancouver, BC V6H 3Y4
CANADA
"Singer, Guitarist"

Hugh Sidey
1050 Connecticut Avenue
Washington, DC 20036
"Columnist"

Siegfried & Roy
1639 North Valley Drive
Las Vegas, NV 89109
"Circus Act"

Casey Siemaszko
P.O. Box 5617
Beverly Hills, CA 90210
"Actor"

Gregory Sierra
8050 Selma Avenue
Los Angeles, CA 90046
"Actor"

Sanford Sigoloff
320 Cliffwood Avenue
Los Angeles, CA 90049
"Business Executive"

Cynthia Sikes
250 Delfern Drive
Los Angeles, CA 90077
"Actress"

James B. Sikking
4526 Wilshire Blvd.
Beverly Hills, CA 90210
"Actor"

Karen Sillas
P.O. Box 725
Wading River, NY 11792
"Actress"

Beverly Sills
211 Central Park West #4F
New York, NY 10024
"Soprano"

Henry Silva
8747 Clifton Way #305
Beverly Hills, CA 90210
"Actor"

Ron Silver
955 S. Carrillo Drive #300
Los Angeles, CA 90048
"Actor"

Fred Silverman
12400 Wilshire Blvd. #920
Los Angeles, CA 90025
TV Executive, Producer"

Jonathan Silverman
4024 Radford Avenue #5
Studio City, CA 91604
"Actor"

Alicia Silverstone
60 McCreery Drive
Hillsborough, CA 94010
"Actress"

Dick Simmons
3215 Silver Cliff Drive
Prescott, AZ 86303
"Actor"

Gene Simmons
2650 Benedict Canyon
Beverly Hills, CA 90210
"Singer, Actor, Composer"

Jaason Simmons
5433 Beethoven Street
Los Angeles, CA 90066
"Actor"

Jean Simmons
636 Adelaide Way
Santa Monica, CA 90402
"Actress"

Richard Simmons
P.O. Box 5403
Beverly Hills, CA 90209
"Exercise Instructor"

Larry Simms
P.O. Box 55
Gray River, WA 98621
"Actor"

Phil Simms
252 West 71st Street
New York, NY 10023
"Ex-Football Player"

Neil Simon
10745 Chalon Road
Los Angeles, CA 90077
"Dramatist"

Paul Simon
Southern Illinois University
Carbondale, IL 62901
"Ex-Senator"

Paul Simon
110 W. 57th Street #300
New York, NY 10019
"Singer, Songwriter

Simone Simon
5 rue de Tilsitt
75008 Paris, FRANCE
"Actress"

William Simon
330 South Street
Morristown, NJ 07960
"Former Secretary of Treasury"

Nina Simone
7250 Franklin Avenue #115
Los Angeles, CA 90046
"Singer, Pianist"

Simple Minds
115A Glenthorne Road
London W6 OLJ ENGLAND
"Rock & Roll Group"

Simply Red
48 Princess Street
Manchester M1 6HR
ENGLAND
"Rock & Roll Group"

Arnelle Simpson
11661 San Vicente Blvd. #632
Los Angeles, CA 90049
"O.J.'s Daughter"

Jason Simpson
11661 San Vicente Blvd. #632
Los Angeles, CA 90049
"O.J.'s Son"

O.J. Simpson
11661 San Vicente Blvd. #632
Los Angeles, CA 90049
"Ex-Football Player"

Joan Sims
17 Esmond Court
Thackery Street
London W8 ENGLAND
"Actress"

Frank Sinatra
915 N. Foothill Road
Beverly HIls, CA 90210
"Singer, Actor"

Frank Sinatra, Jr.
2211 Florian Place
Beverly Hills, CA 90210
"Singer"

Nancy Sinatra, Jr.
P.O. Box 69453
Los Angeles, CA 90069
"Singer, Actress"

Ray Sinatra
1234 S. 8th Place
Las Vegas, NV 89104
"Composer, Conductor"

Tina Sinatra
30966 Broad Beach Road
Malibu, CA 90265
"Singer"

Sinbad
21704 Devonshire #13
Chatsworth, CA 91311
"Comedian, Actor"

Sinceros
25 Buliver Street
Shephard's Bush
London W12 8AR ENGLAND
"Rock & Roll Group"

Donald Sinden
60 Temple Fortune Lane
London NW11 ENGLAND
"Actor"

Lori Singer
9830 Wilshire Blvd.
Beverly Hills, CA 90212
"Actress"

Marc Singer
11218 Canton Drive
Studio City, CA 91604
"Actor"

John Singleton
P.O. Box 92547
Pasadena, CA 91107
"Director"

Margie Singleton
P.O. Box 567
Hendersonville, TN 37077
"Singer, Guitarist"

Penny Singleton
13419 Riverside Drive #C
Sherman Oaks, CA 91423
"Actress"

Gary Sinise
9830 Wilshire Blvd.
Beverly Hills, CA 90212
"Actor"

Curt Siomak
Old Southfork Ranch
43422 South Fork Drive
Three Rivers, CA 93271
"Writer, Producer"

Sirhan Sirhan #B21014
Corcoran State Prison
P.O. Box 8800
Corcoran, CA 93212
"Robert Kennendy's Killer"

Marina Sirtis
4526 Wilshire Blvd.
Los Angeles, CA 90010
"Actress"

Siskel & Ebert
108 W. Grand Avenue
Chicago, IL 60610
"Movie Critics"

Gene Siskel
1301 North Astor
Chicago, IL 60610
"Film Critic"

Jeremy Sisto
1724 North Vista Street
Los Angeles, CA 90046
"Actor"

Sister Sledge
151 El Camino Drive
Beverly Hills, CA 90212
"Vocal Group"

Tom Sizemore
1123 North Flores
W. Holloywood, CA 90069
"Actor"

Ricky Skaggs
380 Forest Retreat
Hendersonville, TN 37075
"Singer, Guitarist"

Tom Skerritt
9560 Wilshire Blvd. #516
Beverly Hills, CA 90212
"Actor"

Skid Row
240 Central Park South #2-C
New York, NY 10019
"Rock & Roll Group"

Moose Skowron
1118 Beachcomber Drive
Schaumburg, IL 60193
"Ex-Baseball Player"

Ione Skye
8794 Lookout Mountain Avenue
Los Angeles, CA 90046
"Actress"

Mark Slade
38 Joppa Road
Worcester, MA 01602
"Actor"

Jeremy Slate
1925 Century Park East #750
Los Angeles, CA 90067
"Actor"

Christian Slater
9150 Wilshire Blvd. #350
Beverly Hills, CA 90212
"Actor"

Helen Slater
1999 Avenue of the Stars, #2850
Los Angeles, CA 90067
"Actress"

Robert F. Slatzer
3033 Hollycrest Drive #2
Los Angeles, CA 90068
"Writer, Producer"

Enos Slaughter
959 Lawson Chapel Church Road
Roxboro, NC 27573
"Ex-Baseball Player"

Dr. Frank Slaughter
P.O. Box 14, Ortega Station
Jacksonville, FL 32210
"Author, Surgeon"

Percy Sledge
9850 Sandalfoot Blvd. #348
Boca Raton, FL 33428
"Singer"

Grace Slick
5996 Kanan Dume Road
Malibu, CA 90265
"Singer, Songwriter"

Curtis Sliwa
628 West 28th Street
New York, NY 10001
"Guardian Angles Founder"

James Sloyan
13740 Albers Street
Van Nuys, CA 91401
"Actor"

Mary Small
165 W. 66th Street
New York, NY 10023
"Actress"

Jean Smart
151 El Camino Drive
Beverly Hills, CA 90212
"Actress"

Smashing Pumpkins
8380 Melrose Avenue #210
Los Angeles, CA 90069
"Rock & Roll Group"

Eleanor Smeal
900 N. Stafford St. #1217
Arlington, VA 22003
"Social Activist"

Yakov Smirnoff
1990 South Bundy Drive #200
Los Angeles, CA 90025
"Comedian"

Allison Smith
1999 Avenue of the Stars#2850
Los Angeles, CA 90067
"Actress"

Anna Nicole Smith
200 Ashdale Avenue
Los Angeles, CA 90049
"Actress, Playmate"

Bubba Smith
5178 Sunlight Place
Los Angeles, CA 90016
"Actor, Football Player"

Buffalo Bob Smith
1005 Riverview Drive
Brielle, NJ 08730
"Actor"

Charlie Martin Smith
31515 Germaine Lane
Westlake Village, CA 91361
"Actor"

Connie Smith
2802 Columbine Place
Nashville, TN 37204
"Singer"

Cotter Smith
15332 Antioch Street #800
Pacific Palisades, CA 90272
"Actor"

Derek Smit
201 Bramblewood Lane
East Amherst, NY 14051
"Actor"

Emmitt Smith
1 Cowboy Parkway
Irving, TX 78063
"Football Player"

Harry Smith
524 West 57th Street
New York, NY 10019
"TV Show Host"

Ian Smith
Gwenoro Farm
Shurugwi ZIMBABWE
"Ex-Government Official"

Ilan Mitchell Smith
104-60 Queens Blvd. #10-C
Fox Hills, NY 11375
"Actor"

Jaclyn Smith
10398 Sunset Blvd.
Los Angeles, CA 90077
"Actress, Model"

Karin Smith
2300 Palisades Street
Los Osos, CA 93402
"Actress"

Kathy Smith
117 South Laxton Drive
Los Angeles, CA 90049
"Actress"

Keely Smith
28011 Paquet Place
Malibu, CA 90265
"Actress"

Kurtwood Smith
635 Frontenac Avenue
Los Angeles, CA 90065
"Actor"

Lane Smith
10000 Santa Monica Blvd. #305
Los Angeles, CA 90067
"Actor"

Lewis Smith
8271 Melrose Avenue #110
Los Angeles, CA 90046
"Actor"

Liz Smith
160 East 38th Street
New York, NY 10016
"Film Critic, Columnist"

Lois Smith
19 W. 44th Street #1000
New York, NY 10036
"Actress"

Madeline Smith
10 St. Martin's Court #100
London WC2N 4AJ ENGLAND
"Actress"

Dame Maggie Smith
76 Oxford Street
London W1N 0AX ENGLAND
"Actress"

Margo Smith
354 Cool Springs Blvd. #105
Franklin, TN 37067
"Singer"

Martha Smith
P.O. Box 2241
Beverly Hills, CA 90213
"Actress, Model"

O.C. Smith
1650 Broadway #508
New York, NY 10019
"Singer"

Ozzie Smith
P.O. Box 7117
Chesterfield, MO 63006
"Ex-Baseball Player"

Roger Smith
2707 Benedict Canyon
Beverly Hills, CA 90210
"Actor, Writer"

Sammi Smith
Route #4, Box 362
Bristow, OK 74010
"Singer"

Shawnee Smith
1999 Avenue of the Stars #2850
Los Angeles, CA 90067
"Actress"

Shelley Smith
182 South Mansfield Avenue
Los Angeles, CA 90036
"Actress"

Susan Smith
#4901-1104-94
Women's Correctional Facility
4450 Broad River Road
Columbia, SC 29210
"Convicted Child Killer"

Vince Smith
P.O. Box 1221
Pottsville, PA 17901
"Singer, Songwriter"

Wendy Smith
2925 Tuna Canyon Road
Topanga, CA 90290
"Actress"

Will Smith
8436 W. 3rd Street #650
Los Angeles, CA 90048
"Actor"

William Smith
3250 West Olympic Blvd. #67
Santa Monica, CA 90404
"Actor"

William Smithers
2202 Anacapa Street
Santa Barbara, CA 93105
"Actor"

Bill Smitrovich
5052 Rubio Avenue
Encino, CA 91436
"Actor"

Jimmy Smits
P.O. Box 49922
Barrington Station
Los Angeles, CA 90049
"Actor"

Dick Smothers
6442 Coldwater Canyon Ave. 107-B
N. Hollywood, CA 91606
"Comedian, Actor"

Tom Smothers
6442 Coldwater Canyon Ave. 107-B
N. Hollywood, CA 91606
"Comedian, Actor"

Marcus Smythe
12212 Califa Street
North Hollywood, CA 91607
"Actor"

Reggie Smythe
Whiteglass Caladonian Road
Hartlepool Cleveland, ENGLAND
"Cartoonist"

J.C. Snead
1751 Pinnacle Drive #1500
McLean, VA 22102
"Golfer"

Sam Snead
P.O. Box 839
Hot Springs, VA 24445
"Golfer"

Tom Sneva
3301 East Valley Vista Lane
Paradise Valley, AZ 85253
"Race Car Driver"

Mike Snider
P.O. Box 140710
Nashville, TN 37214
"Bluegrass Musician"

Wesley Snipes
1888 Century Park East #500
Los Angeles, CA 90067
"Actor"

Carrie Snodgress
16650 Schoenborn
Sepulveda, CA 91343
"Actress"

Snoop Doggy Dog
10900 Wilshire Blvd. #1230
Los Angeles, CA 90024
"Rap Singer"

Hank Snow
P.O. Box 1084
Nashville, TN 37202
"Singer, Songwriter"

Lord Snowdon
22 Lauceston Place
London, W1 England
"Photographer"

Tom Snyder
1225 Beverly Estates Drive
Beverly Hills, CA 90210
"Talk Show Host"

Barry Sobel
9000 Sunset Blvd. #1200
Los Angeles, CA 90069
"Comedian"

Steve Sohmer
2625 Larmar Road
Los Angeles, CA 90068
"TV Director"

Stephen Solarz
241 Dover Street
Brooklyn, NY 11235
"Ex-Congressman"

P.J. Soles
20940 Almazon
Woodland Hills, CA 91364
"Actress"

Alexander I. Solzhenitsyn
Plyushchikha Street
Moscow RUSSIA
"Author"

Suzanne Somers
8899 Beverly Blvd., #713
Los Angeles, CA 90048
"Actress, Singer"

Julie Sommars
9744 Wilshire Blvd. #308
Los Angeles, CA 90212
"Actress"

Elke Sommer
Atzelaberger Street 46
D-9I08O Marloffstein GERMANY
"Actress"

Stephen Sondheim
246 East 49th Street
New York, NY 10017
"Composer, Lyricist"

Kevin Sorbo
P.O. Box 410
Buffalo Center, IA 50424
"Actor"

Louise Sorel
10808 Lindbrook Drive
Los Angeles, CA 90024
"Actress"

Ted Sorenson
1285 Avenue of the Americas
New York, NY 10019
"Former Government Official"

Arleen Sorkin
1223 Wilshire Blvd. #815
Santa Monica, CA 90403
"Writer, Producer"

Mira Sorvino
41 W. 86th Street
New York, NY 10024
"Actress"

Paul Sorvino
110 East 87th Street
New York, NY 10128
"Actor"

Ann Sothern
P.O. Box 2285
Ketchum, ID 83340
"Actress"

Talisa Soto
9000 Sunset Blvd., #1200
Los Angeles, CA 90069
"Actress, Model"

David Soul
4201 Hunt Club Lane
Westlake Village, CA 91361
"Actor, Singer, Director"

David Souter
34 Cilley Hill Road
Weare, NH 03281
"Supreme Court Justice"

Joe South
3051 Claremont Road NE
Atlanta, GA 30329
"Singer, Songwriter"

J.D. Souther
P.O. Box 5617
Beverly Hills, CA 90210
"Singer, Songwriter"

Southern Belles
11150 West Olympic Blvd.
Suite #1100
Los Angeles, CA 90064
"Wrestling Tag Team"

Shawn Southwick
11445 Moorpark Avenue #17
Studio City, CA 91604
"Actress"

Catherine Spaak
Viale Parioli 59
00197 Rome, ITALY
"Actress"

Sissy Spacek
Rt. 22, #640
Cobham, VA 22929
"Actress"

Kevin Spacey
120 W. 45th Street #3600
New York, NY 10036
"Actor"

David Spade
9150 Wilshire Blvd. #350
Beverly Hills, CA 90212
"Actor"

James Spader
9530 Heather Road
Beverly Hills, CA 90210
"Actor"

Warren Spahn
RD #2
Hartshorne, OK 74547
"Ex-Baseball Player"

Joe Spano
73 Market Street
Venice, CA 90291
"Actor"

Vincent Spano
P.O. Box 4602
Valley Village, CA 91617
"Actor"

Camilla Spary
10140 Cielo Drive
Beverly Hills, CA 90210
"Actress"

Boris Spassky
Skatertny Pereulok 5
Moscow RUSSIA
"Chess Player"

Jeff Speakman
18935 Granada Circle
Northridge, CA 91326
"Actor"

Billy Joe Spears
2802 Columbine Place
Nashville, TN 37204
"Singer"

Sen. Arlen Specter (PA)
Senate Hart Bldg. #530
Washington, DC 20510
"Politician"

Phil Spector
1210 South Arroyo Blvd.
Pasadena, CA 91101
"Record Producer"

Ronnie Spector
39B Mill Plan Road #233
Danbury, CT 06811
"Singer"

Aaron Spelling
594 North Mapleton Drive
Los Angeles, CA 90077
"TV Producer"

Tori Spelling
5700 Wilshire Blvd. #575
Los Angeles, CA 90036
"Actress"

Gerry Spence
15 South Jackson
Jackson, WY 83001
"Attorney"

Bud Spencer
Via Cortina d'Ampezzo 156
00191 Rome, ITALY
"Actor"

Earl Charles Spencer
Althorpe House, Gr. Brington
Northamptonshire NN7 4HG
ENGLAND
"Princess Di's Brother"

Victor Spencer-Churchill
6 Cumberland Mansions
George Street
London W1 ENGLAND
"Viscount"

Wendy Jo Sperber
4110 Wetzel Drive
Sherman Oaks, CA 91423
"Actress"

Penelope Spheeris
8145 Laurelmont Drive
Los Angeles, CA 90046
"Director, Producer"

John Spencer
9200 Sunset Blvd. #1130
Los Angeles, CA 90069
"Actor"

Spice Girls
35-37 Parkgate Rd., Unit 32
Ransomes Dock
London SWII 4NP ENGLAND
"Female Music Group"

David Spielberg
3531 Bentley Avenue
Los Angeles, CA 90034
"Actor"

Steven Spielberg
P.O. Box 8520
Universal City, CA 91608
"Director, Producer"

Mickey Spillane
P.O. Box 265
Murrells Inlet, SC 29576
"Writer"

Sandy Spillman
1353 Alvarado Terrace
Los Angeles, CA 90017
"Actor"

Spinal Tap
15250 Ventura Blvd., #1215
Sherman Oaks, CA 91403
"Rock & Roll Group"

Brent Spiner
P.O. Box 5617
Beverly HIlls, CA 90210
"Actor"

Leon Spinks
P.O. Box 88771
Carol Stream, IL 60188
"Ex-Boxer"

Michael Spinks
250 West 57th Street
New York, NY 10107
"Boxer"

Spinners
65 West 55th Street #6C
New York, NY 10019
"Vocal Group"

Mark Spitz
383 Dalehurst
Los Angeles, CA 90077
"Swimmer"

Split Ends
136 New Kings Road
London SW6 ENGLAND
"Rock & Roll Group"

Michael Spound
3500 W. Olive Avenue #920
Burbank, CA 91505
"Actor"

Jerry Springer
454 N. Columbus Drive #200
Chicago, IL 60611
"Talk Show Host"

Dusty Springfield
7 Oak Thorpe Road
Palmer's Green
London N13 5HV ENGLAND
"Singer"

Rick Springfield
P.O. Box 261640
Encino, CA 91426
"Singer, Guitarist"

Bruce Springsteen
1224 Benedict Canyon
Beverly Hills, CA 90210
"Singer, Guitarist"

Steve Spurrier
12115 NW 1st Lane
Gainesville, FL 32907
"Football Coach"

Spyro Gyro
926 Horseshoe Road
Suffern, NY 10301
"Jazz Group"

Billy Squier
P.O. Box 1251
New York, NY 10023
"Singer, Guitarist"

Ken Stabler
Rt. Box, Gen. Del.
Orange Beach, AL 36561
"Ex-Football Player"

Robert Stack
321 St. Pierre Road
Los Angeles, CA 90077
"Actor"

Craig Stadler
1851 Alexander Bell Drive #410
Reston, VA 20191
"Golfer"

Jim Stafford
P.O. Box 6366
Branson, MO 65616
"Singer"

Jo Stafford
2339 Century Hill
Los Angeles, CA 90067
"Singer"

Nancy Stafford
13080 Mindanao Way #69
Marina del Rey, CA 90292
"Actress"

Thomas Strafford
3212 East Interstate #240
Oklahoma City, OK 73135
"Astronaut, Businessman"

Lesley Stahl
524 West 57th Street
New York, NY 10019
"Journalist"

Lisa Stahl
9229 Sunset Blvd., #710
Los Angeles, CA 90069
"Actress"

Joan Staley
24516-B Windsor Drive
Valencia, CA 91355
"Actress"

Lynn Stalmaster
12400 Wilshire Blvd. #920
Los Angeles, CA 90025
"Casting Director"

Frank Stallone
10668 Eastborne #206
Los Angeles, CA 90025
"Actor"

Sasha Stallone
9 Bevery Park
Beverly Hills, CA 90210
"Ex-Wife of Sylvester Stallone"

Sylvester Stallone
100 SE 32nd Road
Coconut Grove, FL 33129
"Actor"

John Stamos
9255 Sunset Blvd. #1010
Los Angeles, CA 90069
"Actor"

Terrence Stamp
4 Windmill Street
London W1P 1HF ENGLAND
"Actor"

John Standing
28 Broomhouse Road
London SW6 ENGLAND
"Actor"

Dennis Stanfill
908 Oak Grove Avenue
San Marino, CA 91108
"Business Executive"

Arnold Stang
P.O. Box 786
New Canaan, CT 06840
"Actor"

Eddie Stanky
2100 Spring Hill Road
Mobile, AL 36607
"Ex-Baseball Manager"

Bernadette Stanis
9300 Wilshire Blvd. #410
Beverly Hills, CA 90212
"Actress"

Florence Stanley
P.O. Box 48876
Los Angeles, CA 90048
"Actress"

Maurice Stans
211 South Orange Grove
Pasadena, CA 91105
"Government Official"

Lisa Stansfield
Box 59, Ashwall
Herfordshire SG 5NG ENGLAND
"Singer"

Harry Dean Stanton
14527 Mulholland Drive
Los Angeles, CA 90077
"Actor"

Jean Stapleton
5757 Wilshire Blvd. #PH-5
Los Angeles, CA 90036
"Actress"

Maureen Stapleton
1-14 Morgan Manor
Lenox, MA 01240
"Actress"

Willie Stargell
813 Tarpon Drive
Wilmington, NC 28409
Wilmington, NC 28409
"Ex-Baseball Player"

Koo Stark
52 Shaftesbury Avenue
London W1 ENGLAND
"Actress"

Ray Stark
232 South Mapleton Drive
Los Angeles, CA 90077
"TV Producer"

Bart Starr
2065 Royal Fern Lane
Birmingham, AL 35244
"Ex-Football Player"

Kay Starr
223 Ashdale Avenue
Los Angeles, CA 90077
"Singer"

Kenneth Starr
333 Constitution Avenue NW
Washington, DC 20001
"Attorney"

Ringo Starr
1541 Ocean Avenue, #200
Santa Monica, CA 90401
"Drummer, Actor"

Starship (Jefferson Airplane)
9850 Sandalfoot Blvd. #458
Boca Raton, FL 33428
"Rock & Roll Group"

Harold E. Stassen
310 Salem Church Road
Sunfish Lake, MN 55118
Ex-Governor"

Statler Brothers
P.O. Box 492
Hernando, MS 38632
"Vocal Group"

Roger Staubach
7912 Edelweiss Circle
Dallas, TX 75240
"Ex-Football Player"

Amy Steel
335 N. Maple Drive #360
Beverly Hills, CA 90210
"Actress"

Barbara Steele
2460 Benedict Canyon
Beverly Hills, CA 90210
"Actress"

Danielle Steele
P.O. Box 1637
Murray Hill Station
New York, NY 10156
"Novelist"

Tommy Steele
76 Oxford Street
London W1N 0AX ENGLAND
"Actor, Singer"

Mary Steenburgen
1201 Alta Loma
Los Angeles, CA 90069
"Actress"

Rod Steiger
6324 Zumirez Drive
Malibu, CA 90265
"Actor"

Ben Stein
4549 Via Vienta
Malibu, CA 90265
"Writer"

David Steinberg
4406 Haskell Avenue
Encino, CA 91436
"Comedian, Actor, Writer"

George Steinbrenner
P.O. Box 25077
Tampa, FL 33622
"Baseball Executive"

Gloria Steinem
118 East 73rd Street
New York, NY 10021
"Author, Feminist"

Jake Steinfeld
622 Toyopa Drive
Pacific Palisades, CA 90272
"Actor, Bodybuilder"

Ingemar Stenmark
Slalomvagen 9
92064 Tarnaby, SWEDEN
"Skier"

Princess Stephanie
Maison Clos St. Martin
F-St. Remy de Provence
FRANCE
"Royalty"

George Stephanopoulos
1717 De Sales Street NW
Washington, DC 20036
"White House Official"

Laraine Stephens
10800 Chalon Road
Los Angeles, CA 90077
"Actress"

Jan Stephenson
1231 Garden Street #204
Titusville, FL 32769
"Golfer"

Steppenwolf
108 E. Matilija
Ojai, CA 93023
"Rock & Roll Group"

Jan Sterling
3959 Hamilton Street #11
San Diego, CA 92104
"Actress"

Philip Sterling
4114 Benedict Canyon
Beverly Hills, CA 90210
"Actor"

Robert Sterling
121 South Bentley Avenue
Los Angeles, CA 90049
"Actor"

Howard Stern
40 West 57th Street #1400
New York, NY 10019
"Shock Radio Host"

Isaac Stern
211 Central Park West
New York, NY 10024
"Violinist"

Frances Sternahgen
152 Sutton Manor Road
New Rochelle, NY 10805
"Actress"

Andrew Stevens
9300 Wilshire Blvd. #400
Beverly Hills, CA 90212
"Actor"

Brinke Stevens
8033 Sunset Blvd. #556
Los Angeles, CA 90046
"Actress, Model"

Cat Stevens
(aka Yusef Islam)
Steinhauser Str. 3
81677 Munich GERMANY
"Singer, Songwriter"

Connie Stevens
426 S. Robertson Blvd.
Los Angeles, CA 90048
"Actress, Singer"

Craig Stevens
1308 N. Flores Street
Los Angeles, CA 90069
"Actor"

Fisher Stevens
5600 W. Taylor Street
Chicago, IL 60644
"Actor"

George Stevens, Jr.
John F. Kennedy Center
Washington, DC 20566
"Director, Producer"

Kay Stevens
478 Severn
Tampa, FL 33606
"Actress"

Morgan Stevens
14348 Roblar Place
Sherman Oaks, CA 91423
"Actor"

Ray Stevens
817 N. 2nd Street
San Jose, CA 95112
"Singer, Songwriter"

Rise Stevens
930 Fifth Avenue
New York, NY 10021
"Mezzo-Soprano"

Shadow Stevens
2570 Benedict Canyon
Beverly Hills, CA 90210
"Radio-TV personality"

Shawn Stevens
9555 Via Venezia
Burbank, CA 91504
"Actor"

Stella Stevens
2180 Coldwater Canyon
Beverly Hills, CA 90210
"Actress"

Sen. Ted Stevens (AK)
Senate Hart Bldg. #522
Washington, DC 20510
"Politician"

Warren Stevens
14155 Magnolia Blvd. #44
Sherman Oaks, CA 91403
"Actor"

Adlai Stevenson III
10 South La Salle Street #3610
Chicago, IL 60603
"Ex-Governor"

Parker Stevenson
4526 Wilshire Blvd.
Los Angeles, CA 90010
"Actor"

Teofilo Stevenson
Hotel Havana Libre
Havana, CUBA
"Boxer"

Catherine Mary Stewart
9220 Sunset Blvd. #230
Los Angeles, CA 90069
"Actress"

Freddie Stewart
4862 Excelente Drive
Woodland Hills, CA 91364
"Actor"

French Stewart
9825 Altman Avenue
Los Angeles, CA 90034
"Actor"

Jackie Stewart
24 Rte. de Divonne
1260 Nyon, SWITZERLAND
"Ex-Race Car Driver"

Martha Stewart
Lily Pond Lane
East Hampton, NY 11937
"Society Caterer, Author"

Patrick Stewart
P.O. Box 93999
Los Angeles, CA 90093
"Actor"

Payne Stewart
390 North Orange Avenue
Suite #2600
Orlando, FL 32801
"Golfer"

Peggy Stewart
11139 Hortense Street
North Hollywood, CA 91602
"Actress"

Rod Stewart
3500 W. Olive Avenue #920
Burbank, CA 91505
"Singer, Songwriter"

Michael Stich
Ernst-Barlach Street 44
D-25336 Elmshorn GERMANY
"Tennis Player"

Dorothy Stickney
13 East 94th Street
New York, NY 10023
"Actress"

David Ogden Stiers
121 North San Vicente Blvd.
Beverly Hills, CA 90211
"Actor, Director"

Robert Stigwood
122 E. 42nd Street
New York, NY 10017
"Film Producer"

Ben Stiller
9660 Wilshire Blvd. #516
Beverly Hills, CA 90212
"Actor"

Jerry Stiller
156-5th Avenue #820
New York, NY 10010
"Comedian, Actor, Writer"

Stephen Still
191 North Phelps Avenue
Winter Park, FL 32789
"Singer"

Sting
2 The Grove
Highgate Village
London N6 ENGLAND
"Singer, Actor, Composer"

Barbara Stock
12424 Wilshire Blvd., #840
Los Angeles, CA 90025
"Actress"

Adm. James B. Stockdale
Hoover Institution
Stanford, CA 94305
"Ross Perot's V.P. Select"

Karl-Heinz Stockhausen
Stockhausen-Verlag
D-51515 Kuerten, GERMANY
"Composer"

Dean Stockwell
P.O. Box 6248
Malibu, CA 90264
"Actor"

Guy Stockwell
6652 Coldwater Canyon Avenue
North Hollywood, CA 91606
"Actor"

John Stockwell
344 S. Rossmore Avenue
Los Angeles, CA 90029
"Actor"

Brandon Stoddard
241 North Glenroy Avenue
Los Angeles, CA 90049
"Film-TV Executive

Elvis Stojko
2 St. Clair Avenue E. #1500
Toronto, Ontario M4L 2R1
CANADA
"Ice Skater"

Rep. Louis Stokes (OH)
House Rayburn Bldg. #2365
Washington, DC 20515
"Politician"

David Stollery
3203 Bern Court
Laguna Beach, CA 92651
"Actor"

Eric Stoltz
9830 Wilshire Blvd.
Beverly Hills, CA 90212
"Actor"

Doug Stone
P.O. Box 943
Springfield, TN 37172
"Singer"

Marianne Stone
46 Abbey Road
London NW8 ENGLAND
"Actress"

Oliver Stone
520 Broadway #600
Santa Monica, CA 90401
"Film Writer, Director"

Rob Stone
8033 Sunset Blvd. #450
Los Angeles, CA 90046
"Actor"

Sharon Stone
P.O. Box 7304
North Hollywood, CA 91603
"Actress, Model"

Sly Stone
6467 Sunset Blvd. #1110
Hollywood, CA 90028
"Singer, Musician"

Tom Stoppard
Iver Grove, Iver
Bucks. ENGLAND
"Dramatist"

Larry Storch
330 West End Avenue #17-F
New York, NY 10023
"Actor"

Gale Storm
23831 Bluehill Bay
Dana Point, CA 92629
"Actress, Singer"

Tempest Storm
P.O. Box 15154
Newport Beach, CA 92659
"Burlesque"

John Stossel
211 Central Park West #15K
New York, NY 10024
"Broadcast Journalist"

Madeleine Stowe
10345 W. Olympic Blvd. #200
Los Angeles, CA 90064
"Actress"

Michael Stoyanov
8271 Melrose Avenue #110
Los Angeles, CA 90046
"Actor"

Beatrice Straight
150 E. 58th Street, 3rd Floor
New York, NY 10155
"Actress"

Julie Strain
602 De La Vista Avenue
Santa Barbara, CA 93103
"Actress"

George Strait
1000-18th Avenue South
Nashville, TN 37212
"Singer, Songwriter"

David Straithairn
9560 Wilshire Blvd. #516
Beverly Hills, CA 90212
"Actor"

Hank Stram
194 Belle Terre Blvd.
Covington, LA 70483
"Ex-Football Coach"

Robin Strand
4118 Elmer
North Hollywood, CA 91607
"Actor"

Susan Strasberg
P.O. Box 847
Pacific Palisades, CA 90272
"Actress"

Robin Strasser
3500 W. Olive Avenue #516
Burbank, CA 91505
"Actress"

Marcia Strassman
302 N. Almont Drive
Beverly Hills, CA 90211
"Actress"

Gil Stratton
4227-B Colfax Avenue #B
Studio City, CA 91604
"Sportscaster"

Peter Straub
53 West 85th Street
New York, NY 10026
"Novelist"

Peter Strauss
2176 Coldwater Canyon
Beverly Hills, CA 90210
"Actor"

Robert Strauss
1333 New Hampshire Ave. NW
Suite #400
Washington, DC 20005
"Politician"

Darryl Strawberry
P.O. Box 17868
Encino, CA 91416
"Baseball Player"

Stray Cats
113 Wardour Street
London W1 ENGLAND
"Rock & Roll Group"

Meryl Streep
9830 Wilshire Blvd.
Beverly Hills, CA 90212
"Actress"

Rebecca Street
247 S. Beverly Drive #102
Beverly Hills, CA 90212
"Actress"

Barbara Streisand
301 N. Carolwood
Los Angeles, CA 90077
"Singer, Actress, Director"

Amzie Strickland
1329 North Ogden Drive
Los Angeles, CA 90046
"Actress"

Gail Strickland
14732 Oracle Place
Pacific Palisades, CA 90272
"Actress"

Ray Stricklyn
852 North Genesee Avenue
Los Angeles, CA 90046
"Actor"

Sherry Stringfield
9560 Wilshire Blvd. #516
Beverly Hills, CA 90212
"Actress"

Elaine Stritch
125 Gloucester Road
London SW7 YTE ENGLAND
"Actress"

Don Stroud
17020 Sunset Blvd. #20
Pacific Palisades, CA 90272
"Actor"

Kerri Strug
2801 N. Camino Principal
Tucson, AZ 85715
"Gymnast"

Sally Struthers
9100 Wilshire Blvd., #1000
Beverly Hills, CA 90212
"Actress"

Gloria Stuart
884 South Bundy Drive
Los Angeles, CA 90049
"Actress"

Marty Stuart
119 17th Avenue South
Nashville, TN 37203
"Singer, Songwriter"

Maxine Stuart
1801 Avenue of the Stars #902
Los Angeles, CA 90067
"Actress"

Roy Stuart
4948 Radford Avenue
North Hollywood, CA 91602
"Actor"

Wes Studi
8380 Melrose Avenue #207
Los Angeles, CA 90069
"Actor"

Shannon Sturgess
15301 Ventura Blvd. #345
Sherman Oaks, CA 91403
"Actress"

William Styron
12 Rucum Road
Roxbury, CT 06783
"Author"

David Suchet
169 Queensgate #8A
London SW7 5EH ENGLAND
"Actor"

Alan Sues
9014 Dorrington Avenue
Los Angeles, CA 90048
"Actor"

Burt Sugarman
150 South El Camino Drive #303
Beverly Hills, CA 90212
"Rock & Roll Producer"

Helena Sukova
1 Avenue Grande Bretagne
Monte Carlo, Monaco
"Tennis Player"

Danny Sullivan
414 E. Cooper Street #201
Aspen, CO 81611
"Race Car Driver"

Susan Sullivan
8642 Allenwood Road
Los Angeles, CA 90046
"Actress"

Tom Sullivan
30 Glenmoor Drive
Englewood, CO 80110
"Singer, Songwriter"

Sultan of Brunei
Bandar Seri
Begawan BRUNEI
"Royalty"

Arthur Ochs Sulzberber
229 West 43rd Street
New York, NY 10036
"Newspaper Publisher"

Yma Sumac
P.O. Box 204
Beverly Hills, CA 90213
"Singer"

Cree Summer
131 South Orange Drive
Los Angeles, CA 90036
"Actress"

Donna Summer
18171 Eccles
Northridge, CA 91324
"Singer"

Eleanor Summerfield
10 Kildare Terrace
London W2 ENGLAND
"Actress"

Andy Summers
21A Noel Street
London W1V 3PD ENGLAND
"Singer, Songwriter"

Yale Summers
9490 Cherokee Lane
Beverly Hills, CA 90210
"Actor"

John Sununu
24 Samoset Drive
Salem, NH 03079
"Former Governor"

Nicolas Surovy
8787 Shoreham Drive
West Hollywood, CA 90069
"Actor"

Survivor
2114 West Pico Blvd.
Santa Monica, CA 90405
"Rock & Roll Group"

Todd Susman
10340 Keokuk Avenue
Chatsworth, CA 91311
"Actor"

Rick Sutcliff
25911 - 99th Street
Lee's Summit, MO 64053
"Baseball Player"

Donald Sutherland
760 North La Cienega Blvd. #300
Los Angeles, CA 90069
"Actor"

Joan Sutherland
111 West 57th Street
New York, NY 10019
"Soprano"

Kiefer Sutherland
132 So. Rodeo Drive, #300
Beverly Hills, CA 90212
"Actor"

James Sutorius
14014 Milbank Street #1
Sherman Oaks, CA 91423
"Actor"

Don Sutton
1145 Mountain Ivy Drive
Roswell, GA 30075
"Ex-Baseball Player"

Janet Suzman
11 Keats Grove, Hampsted
London NW3 ENGLAND
"Actress"

Bo Svenson
15332 Antioch Street #356
Pacific Palisades, CA 90272
"Actor"

Jimmy Swaggart
8912 World Ministry Avenue
Baton Rouge, LA 70810
"Evangelist"

Caskey Swaim
1605 North Cahuenga Blvd. #202
Los Angeles, CA 90028
"Actor"

Michael Swan
15315 Magnolia Blvd. #429
Sherman Oaks, CA 91403
"Actor"

Hilary Swank
3500 W. Olive Avenue #920
Burbank, CA 91505
"Actress"

Lynn Swann
600 Grant Street #4800
Pittsburgh, PA 15219
"Ex-Football Player"

Jackie Swanson
847 Iliff Street
Pacific Palisades, CA 90272
"Actress"

Kristy Swanson
2934 1/2 N. Beverly Glen Circle
#416
Los Angeles, CA 90077
"Actress"

Don Swayze
247 S. Beverly Drive #102
Beverly Hills, CA 90212
"Actor"

Patrick Swayze
132 S. Rodeo Drive, #300
Beverly HIlls, CA 90212
"Actor"

Keith Sweat
40 West 57th Street
New York, NY 10019
"Singer"

D.B. Sweeney
25144 Malibu Road
Malibu, CA 90265
"Actor"

Inga Swenson
10100 Santa Monica Blvd. #2500
Los Angeles, CA 90067
"Actress"

Jo Swerling, Jr.
25745 Vista Verde Drive
Calabasas, CA 91302
"Writer, Producer"

Nora Swinburne
52 Crammer Court
Whitehead's Grove
London SW3 3HW ENGLAND
"Actress"

Loretta Swit
10100 Santa Monica Blvd. #2490
Los Angeles, CA 90067
"Actress"

Ken Swofford
144 South Beverly Drive #405
Beverly Hills, CA 90212
"Actor"

Tracy Brooks Swope
8730 Sunset Blvd. #480
Los Angeles, CA 90069
"Actress"

Eric Sykes
9 Orme Court
London W2 ENGLAND
"Actor, Writer, Director"

The Sylvers
1900 Ave. of the Stars #1600
Los Angeles, CA 90067
"Vocal Group"

Sylvia Syms
47 West Square
London SE11 4SP ENGLAND
"Actress"

Mr. T
15208 La Maida Street
Sherman Oaks, CA 91403
"Actor"

Kristoffer Tabori
172 East 95th Street
New York, NY 10028
"Actor"

Cary-Hiroyuki Tagawa
8942 Wilshire Blvd.
Beverly Hills, CA 90211
"Actor"

Taj Mahal
1671 Appian Way
Santa Monica, CA 90401
"Musician"

Paul Tagliabueruss
410 Park Avenue
New York, NY 10022
"Football [NFL] Commissioner"

Miiko Taka
14560 Round Valley Drive
Sherman Oaks, CA 91403
"Actress"

Take Six
151 El Camino Drive
Beverly Hills, Ca 90212
"Vocal Group"

George Takei
419 N. Larchmont Blvd. #41
Los Angeles, CA 90004
"Actor"

Nita Talbot
3420 Merrimac Road
Los Angeles, CA 90049
"Actress"

Gloria Talbott
2066 Montecito Drive
Glendale, CA 91208
"Actress"

Gay Talese
154 East Atlantic Blvd.
Ocean City, NJ 08226
"Writer"

Maria Tallchief
2739 Elston Avenue
Chicago, IL 60747
"Ballerina"

Russ Tamblyn
2310 - 6th Street #2
Santa Monica, CA 90405
"Actor"

Jeffrey Tambor
5526 Calhoun Avenue
Van Nuys, CA 91401
"Actor"

Amy Tan
373 S. Robertson Blvd.
Beverly Hills, CA 90211
"Novelist"

Tangerine Dream
P.O. Box 29242
Oakland, CA 94604
"Rock & Roll Group"

Alain Tanner
Chemin Pt. du-jour 12
1202 Geneva, SWITZERLAND
"Film Director"

Roscoe Tanner
1109 Gnome Trail
Lookout Mountain, TN 37350
"Tennis Player"

Quentin Tarantino
7966 Beverly Blvd. #300
Los Angeles, CA 90048
"Actor, Director"

Jimmy Tarbuck
118 Beaufort Street
London SW3 6BU ENGLAND
"Comedian"

Fran Tarkington
1431 Garmon Ferry Road NW
Atlanta, GA 30327
"Ex-Football Player"

Bernie Taupin
450 N. Maple Drive #501
Beverly Hills, CA 90210
"Lyricist"

Benedict Taylor
4 Great Queen Street
London WC28 5DG ENGLAND
"Actor"

Buck Taylor
2899 Agoura Road #275
Westlake Village, CA 91361
"Actor"

Clarice Taylor
35 Hamilton Terrace
New York, NY 10031
"Actress"

Don Taylor
1111 San Vicente Blvd.
Santa Monica, CA 90402
"Film Director"

Elizabeth Taylor
P.O. Box 55995
Sherman Oaks, CA 91413
"Actress"

Holland Taylor
1355 North Laurel Avenue #7
Los Angeles, CA 90046
"Actress"

James Taylor
644 North Doheny Drive
Los Angeles, CA 90069
"Singer"

Josh Taylor
422 S. California Avenue
Burbank, CA 91505
"Actor"

Lawrence Taylor
122 Canterbury Lane
Williamsburg, VA 23188
"Ex-Football Player"

Leigh Taylor-Young
9229 Sunset Blvd. #710
Los Angeles, CA 90069
"Actress"

Lili Taylor
151 El Camino Drive
Beverly Hills, CA 90212
"Actress"

Meldrick Taylor
1158 N. York Road
Warminster, PA 18974
"Boxer"

Meshach Taylor
10100 Santa Monica Blvd
25th Floor
Los Angeles, CA 90067
"Actor"

Niki Taylor
8362 Pines Blvd., #334
Hollywood, FL 33024
"Model"

Noah Taylor
P.O. Box 5617
Beverly Hills, CA 90210
"Actor"

Regina Taylor
151 El Camino Drive
Beverly Hills, CA 90212
"Actress"

Renee Taylor
16830 Ventura Blvd. #326
Encino, CA 91436
"Actress, Writer"

Rip Taylor
1133 North Clark Street
Los Angeles, CA 90069
"Actor"

Rod Taylor
2375 Bowmont Drive
Beverly Hills, CA 90210
"Actor"

Roger Taylor
Salterwwell Farm
Moreton-In -The-Marsh
Gloucestershire ENGLAND
"Drummer"

Ludmilla Tcherina
42 cours Albert ler
75008 Paris, FRANCE
"Ballerina"

Lewis Teague
2190 N. Beverly Glen Blvd.
Los Angeles, CA 90077
"Film Director"

Tears For Fears
2100 Colorado Avenue
Santa Monica, CA 90404
"Rock & Roll Group"

Renata Tebaldi
1 Piazza Guastalla 20100
Milan ITALY
"Opera Singer"

Teenage Mutant Ninja Turtles
250 W. 57th Street #821
New York, NY 10107
"Fighting Team"

Dr. Edward U. Teller
Radiation Laboratory
P.O. Box 808
Livermore, CA 94550
"Physicist, Author"

Shirley Temple-Black
115 Lakeview Drive
Woodside, CA 94062
"Actress, Ex-Ambassador"

Christopher Templeton
11333 Moorpark Street
North Hollywood, CA 91602
"Actress"

The Temptations
1325 Avenue of the Americas
New York, NY 10019
"R&B Group"

Victoria Tennant
4526 Wilshire Blvd.
Los Angeles, CA 90010
"Actress"

Jon Tenney
9560 Wilshire Blvd. #516
Beverly Hills, CA 90212
"Actor"

Toni Tennille
P.O. Box 608
Zephyr Cove, NV 89448
"Singer"

Judy Tenuta
13504 Contour Drive
Sherman Oaks, CA 91423
"Comedienne"

Studs Terkel
850 West Castlewood
Chicago, IL 60640
"Novelist"

Malcolm Terris
14 England's Lane
London NW3 ENGLAND
"Actor"

Clark Terry
24 Westland Drive
Glen Cove, NY 11542
"Musician"

John Terry
P.O. Box 6010
Sherman Oaks, CA 91413
"Actor"

John Tesh
14755 Ventura Blvd. #1-916
Sherman Oaks, CA 91403
"TV Show Host"

Vinny Testaverde
936 Crenshaw Lake Road
Lutz, FL 33549
"Football Player"

Lauren Tewes
2739-31st Avenue, So.
Seattle, WA 98144
"Actress"

Baroness Margaret Thatcher
Chester Square Belgravia
London ENGLAND
"Former Prime Minister"

John Thaw
5 Denmark Street
London, WC2H 8LP England
"Actor"

Phyllis Thaxter
716 Riomar Drive
Vero Beach, FL 32963
"Actress"

Brynn Thayer
10100 Santa Monica Blvd. #2500
Los Angeles, CA 90067
"Actress"

Joe Theismann
5912 Leesburg Pike
Falls Church, VA 22041
"Ex-Football Player"

Brooke Theiss
9744 Wilshire Blvd. #308
Beverly Hills, CA 90212
"Actress"

Charlize Theron
1729 N. Sycamore Avenue
Hollywood, CA 90028
"Actress"

David Thewlis
76 Oxford Street
London W1N 0AX ENGLAND
"Actor"

Alan Thicke
10505 Sarah
Toluca Lake, CA 91602
"Actor, TV Show Host, Singer"

Ursula Thiess
1940 Bel Air Road
Los Angeles, CA 90077
"Actress"

Tiffani-Amber Thiessen
3500 W. Olive Avenue #1400
Burbank, CA 91505
"Actress"

Roy Thinnes
17258 Madison Avenue #634
Memphis, TN 38104
"Actor"

Third World
151 El Camino Drive
Beverly Hills, CA 90212
"Raggae Band"

Betty Thomas
3585 Woodhill Canyon
Studio City, CA 91604
"Actress"

B.J. Thomas
24 Music Square W. #208
Nashville, TN 37203
"Singer, Songwriter"

Clarence Thomas
1-1st Street N.E.
Washington, DC 20543
"Supreme Court Justice"

Damien Thomas
31 Kensington Church Street
London W8 4LL ENGLAND
"Actor"

Debi Thomas
22 East 71st Street
New York, NY 10021
"Ice Skater"

Ernest Thomas
3350 Barham Blvd.
Los Angeles, CA 90068
"Actor"

Frank Thomas
333 West 35th Street
Chicago, IL 60616
"Baseball Player"

Frankie Thomas
4045 Vineland Avenue #128
Studio City, CA 91604
"Actor"

Heather Thomas
1433 San Vicente Blvd.
Santa Monica, CA 90402
"Actress, Model"

Helen Thomas
2501 Calvert Street N.W.
Washington, DC 20008
"News Correspondent"

Isaiah Thomas
710 Lone Pine Road
Bloomfield, MI 48304
"Basketball Exec. &Ex-Player"

Jay Thomas
P.O. Box 5617
Beverly Hills, CA 90210
"Singer, Songwriter"

Jonathan Taylor Thomas
18711 Tiffeni Drive #17-203
Twain Harte, CA 95383
"Actor"

Kristin Scott Thomas
9830 Wilshire Blvd.
Beverly Hills, CA 90212
"Actress"

Marlo Thomas
420 East 54th Street #22-F
New York, NY 10022
"Actress, Writer"

Philip Michael Thomas
12615 West Dixie Hwy.
North Miami, FL 33161
"Actor"

R. David Thomas
4288 Dublin Erunville Road
Dublin, OH 43017
"Owner of Wendy's Restaurants"

Richard Thomas
4963 Los Feliz Blvd.
Los Angeles, CA 90027
"Actor, Director"

Harry Thomason
4000 Warner Blvd.
Bldg. 8, Room 147
Burbank, CA 91505
"Film Producer"

Tim Thomerson
2440 Long Jack Road
Encinitas, CA 92024
"Actor, Comedian"

Tony Thomopoulos
1280 Stone Canyon
Los Angeles, CA 90077
"Film Executive"

Andrea Thompson
14431 Ventura Blvd. #260
Sherman Oaks, CA 91423
"Actress"

Bobby Thompson
122 Sunlit Drive
Watchung, NJ 07060
"Banjoist"

Brian Thompson
3500 W. Olive Avenue #1400
Burbank, CA 91505
"Actor"

Daley Thompson
1 Church Row
Wandsworth Plain
London SW18 ENGLAND
"Track Athlete"

Emma Thompson
56 King's Road
Kingston-upon-Thames
KT2 5HF ENGLAND
"Actress"

Ernest Thompson
Rt. 1, Box 3248
Ashland, NH 03217
"Screenwriter"

Sen. Fred Thompson (IL)
701 Pennsylvania Avenue NW
Washington, DC 20004
"Politician"

Hank Thompson
5 Rushing Creek Court
Roanoke, TX 76262
"Singer, Songwriter"

Jack Thompson
12754 Sarah Street
Studio City, CA 91604
"Actor"

John Thompson
Georgetown University Basketball
Washington, DC 20057
"Basketball Coach"

Lea Thompson
P.O. Box 5617
Beverly Hills, CA 90210
"Actress"

Linda Thompson
3365 Cahuenga Blvd. W. #450
Los Angeles, CA 90068
"Actress"

Sada Thompson
P.O. Box 490
Southbury, CT 06488
"Actress"

Shawn Thompson
5319 Biloxi Avenue
North Hollywood, CA 91601
"Actor"

The Thompson Twins
9 Eccleston Street
London SW1 ENGLAND
"Rock & Roll Trio"

Gov. Tommy Thompson (WI)
115 East State Capitol
P.O. Box 7863
Madison, WI 53707
"Governor"

Gordon Thomson
3718 1/2 Multiview Drive
Los Angeles, CA 90068
"Actor"

Courtney Thorne-Smith
11693 San Vicente Blvd. #266
Los Angeles, CA 90049
"Actress"

Billy Bob Thornton
955 S. Carrillo Drive #200
Los Angeles, CA 90048
"Actor"

Jeremy Thorpe
2 Orme Square Bayswater
London W2 ENGLAND
"Political Leader"

Linda Thorson
145 West 45th Street #1204
New York, NY 10036
"Actress"

Three Degrees
19 The Willows
Maidenhead Road
Winsor, Berk. ENGLAND
"Rock & Roll Group"

Malachi Throne
11805 Mayfield Avenue #306
Los Angeles, CA 90049
"Actor"

Ingrid Thulin
Kevingerstrand 7b
Danderyd, SWEDEN
"Actress"

Uma Thurman
9830 Wilshire Blvd.
Beverly Hills, CA 90212
"Actress"

Sen. Strom Thurmond (SC)
217 Russell Senate Bldg.
Washington, DC 20510
"Politician"

Greta Thyssen
444 East 82nd Street
New York, NY 10228
"Actress"

Paul W. Tibbets
5574 Knollwood Drive
Columbus, OH 43227
"Singer"

Cheryl Tiegs
2 Greenwich Plaza #100
Greenwich, CT 06830
"Model"

Lawrence Tierney
2352 Penmar Avenue
Venice, CA 90291
"Actor"

Tiffany
13659 Victory Blvd. #550
Van Nuys, CA 91401
"Singer"

Pamela Tiffin
15 West 67th Street
New York, NY 10023
"Actress, Model"

Kevin Tighe
P.O. Box 453
Sedro Woolley, WA 98284
"Actor"

Nadja Tiller
Kathi-Kobus-Str.24
80797 Munich GERMANY
"Actress"

Mel Tillis
P.O. Box 1626
Branson, MO 65616
"Singer"

Pam Tillis
P.O. Box 1228575
Nashville, TN 37212
"Singer"

Floyd Tillman
4 Music Square East
Nashville, TN 37203
"Singer"

Johnny Tillotson
17530 Ventura Blvd. #108
Encino, CA 91316
"Singer"

Jennifer Tilly
270 N. Cannon Drive #1582
Beverly Hills, CA 90210
"Actress"

Meg Tilly
321 South Beverly Drive #M
Beverly Hills, CA 90212
"Actress"

Charlene Tilton
P.O. Box 1309
Studio City, CA 91614
"Actress"

Martha Tilton
760 Lausanne Road
Los Angeles, CA 90077
"Singer, Actress"

Grant Tinker
531 Barnaby Road
Los Angeles, CA 90077
"TV Executive"

Wayne Tipitt
8730 Sunset Blvd. #220W
Los Angeles, CA 90069
"Actor"

Sir Michael Tippett
48 Great Marlborough Street
London W1V 2BN ENGLAND
"Composer, Conductor"

Aaron Tippin
P.O. Box 41689
Nashville, TN 37204
"Singer"

Laurence Tisch
Island Drive North
Rye, NY 10580
"TV Executive"

Y.A. Tittle
PO Box 571
Lebanon, IN 46052
"Ex-Football Player"

Kenneth Tobey
10100 Santa Monica Blvd. #2500
Los Angeles, CA 90067
"Actor"

Oliver Tobias
Geranienstrasse 3
8022 Grunwald GERMANY
"Actor"

Beverly Todd
4888 Valley Ridge
Los Angeles, CA 90043
"Actress"

Hallie Todd
10100 Santa Monica Blvd.
Suite #700
Los Angeles, CA 90067
"Actress"

Richard Todd
Chinham Farm
Faringdon, Oxfordshire
ENGLAND
"Actor"

Alvin Toffel
2323 Bowmont Drive
Beverly Hills, CA 90210
"Author"

Tokyo Rose (Iva Toguri)
1443 Winnemac Street W.
Chicago, IL 60640
"Traitor"

Michael Tolan
9229 Sunset Blvd. #311
Los Angeles, CA 90069
"Actor"

John Toland
1 Long Ridge Road
Danbury, CT 06810
"Author"

Berlinda Tolbert
1800 Ave. of the Stars #400
Los Angeles, CA 90067
"Actress"

Susan Tolsky
10815 Acama Street
North Hollywood, CA 91602
"Actress"

David Toma
P.O. Box 854
Clark, NJ 07066
"Writer"

Alberto Tomba
I-40068 Castel de Britti
ITALY
"Skier"

Concetia Tomei
121 North San Vicente Blvd.
Beverly Hills, CA 90211
"Actress"

Marisa Tomei
120 W. 45th Street #3600
New York, NY 10036
"Actress"

Lily Tomlin
P.O. Box 27700
Los Angeles, CA 90027
"Comedian, Actress, Writer"

David Tomlinson
Brook Cottage
Mursley, Bucks. ENGLAND
"Actor"

Angel Tompkins
9812 Vidor Drive, #101
Los Angeles, CA 90035
"Actress"

James Toney
6305 Wellesley
West Bloomfield, MI 48322
"Boxer"

Tony! Toni! Tone!
484 Lake Park Avenue #21
Oakland, CA 94610
"Music Group"

Carrot Top
2438 N. Lincoln Avenue #300
Chicago, IL 60614
"Comedian"

Chaim Topol
22 Vale Court, Maidville
London W9 ENGLAND
"Actor, Director"

Peter Tork
1551 South Robertson Blvd.
Los Angeles, CA 90035
"Musician"

Mel Torme
1734 Coldwater Canyon
Beverly Hills, CA 90210
"Singer, Actor, Writer"

Rip Torn
130 West 42nd Street #2400
New York, NY 10036
"Actor, Director"

Dean Torrence
18932 Gregory Lane
Huntington Beach, CA 92646
"Singer, Songwriter"

Gwen Torrence
P.O. Box 361965
Decatur, GA 30036
"Track & Field"

Liz Torres
1206 Havenhurst Drive
Los Angeles, CA 90046
"Singer, Actress"

Robert Torti
13609 Chandler Blvd.
Van Nuys, CA 91401
"Actor"

Torvill & Dean
Box 16, Beeston
Nottingham NG9 ENGLAND
"Skating Duo"

Nina Totenberg
133 N. Carolina Avenue SE
Washington, DC 20003
"News Correspondent"

Toto
50 West Main Street
Ventura, CA 93001
"Rock & Roll Group"

Audrey Totter
1945 Glendon Avenue #301
Los Angeles, CA 90025
"Actress"

Constance Towers
2100 Century Park West #10263
Los Angeles, CA 90067
"Actress"

Robert Towne
1417 San Remo Drive
Pacific Palisades, CA 90272
"Film Writer, Director"

Harry Townes
201 Queensbury Drive SW #1
Huntsville, AL 35802
"Actor"

Barbara Townsend
1930 Century Park West #303
Los Angeles, CA 90067
"Actress"

Colleen Townsend
508 Seward Square S.E.
Washington, DC 20003
"Actress"

Pete Townshend
The Boathouse, Ranelagh Dr.
Twickenham TW1 1Q2 ENGLAND
"Singer"

Robert Townsend
2934 1/2 N. Beverly Glen Circle
Los Angeles, CA 90077
"Director, Actor, Comedian"

Tony Trabert
115 Knotty Pine Trail
Ponte Vedra, FL 32082
"Tennis Player"

The Tramps
P.O. Box 82
Great Neck, NY 10021
"R&B Group"

Fred Travalana
4515 White Oak Place
Encino, CA 91316
"Comedian, Actor, Writer"

Daniel J. Travanti
1077 Melody Road
Lake Forest, IL 60045
"Actor"

Kylie Travis
8732 St. Ives Drive
Los Angeles, CA 90069
"Actress"

Nancy Travis
231 S. Cliffwood Avenue
Los Angeles, CA 90049
"Actress"

Randy Travis
P.O. Box 121712
Nashville, TN 37212
"Singer, Songwriter"

Ellen Travolta
9255 Sunset Blvd. #515
Los Angeles, CA 90069
"Actress"

Joey Travolta
4975 Chimineas Avenue
Tarzana, CA 91356
"Actor"

John Travolta
15821 Ventura Blvd. #460
Studio City, CA 91436
"Actor, Singer"

Terri Treas
9000 Sunset Blvd. #1200
Los Angeles, CA 90069
"Actress"

Alex Trebek
10202 W. Washington Blvd.
Culver City, CA 90232
"Game Show Host"

Robert Trebor
3352 Broadway Blvd. #538
Garland, TX 75043
"Actor"

Les Tremayne
901 South Barrington Avenue
Los Angeles, CA 90049
"Actor"

Anne Tremko
10100 Santa Monica Blvd. #2500
Los Angeles, CA 90067
"Actress"

Charles Trenet
2 rue Anatole FRANCE
F-11100 Narbonne, FRANCE
"Singer, Songwriter"

Adam Trese
1724 N. Vista Street
Los Angeles, CA 90046
"Actor"

Lee Trevino
1901 W. 47th Place #200
Westwood, KS 66205
"Golfer"

Claire Trevor
22 Rue Villars
Newport Beach, CA 92660
"Actress"

Jean-Louis Trintignant
10 Ave. George V
75008 Paris FRANCE
"Actor"

Linda Tripp
27285 Boyce Mill Road
Greensboro, MD 21639
"Betrayed Monica Lewinsky"

Jean Tripplehorn
350 Fifth Avenue #3505
New York, NY 10118
"Actress"

Travis Tritt
1112 North Sherbourne Drive
Los Angeles, CA 90069
"Singer"

Bryan Trotter
165 Thousand Oaks Drive
Pittsburgh, PA 15241
"Hockey Player"

Bobby Troup
16074 Royal Oaks
Encino, CA 91436
"Actor, Comedian, Singer"

Tom Troup
8829 Ashcroft Avenue
Los Angeles, CA 90048
"Actor"

Garry Trudeau
459 Columbus Avenue #113
New York, NY 10024
"Cartoonist"

Mrs. Ernest Truex
3263 Via Altamura
Fallbrook, CA 92028
"Wife of Ernest Truex"

Donald Trump
721 Fifth Avenue
New York, NY 10022
"Real Estate Executive"

Ivana Trump
500 Park Avenue #500
New York, NY 10022
"Ex-Wife of Donald Trump"

Ivanka Trump
500 Park Avenue #500
New York, NY 10022
"Model"

Natalie Trundy
6140 Lindenhurst Avenue
Los Angeles, CA 90048
"Actress"

Irene Tsu
2760 Hutton Drive
Beverly Hills, CA 90210
"Actress"

Barry Tubb
121 North San Vicente Blvd.
Beverly Hills, CA 90211
"Actor"

Stanley Tucci
197 Oakdale Avenue
Mill Valley, CA 94941
"Actor"

Chris Tucker
9560 Wilshire Blvd. #516
Beverly Hills, CA 90210
"Composer, Actor"

Marshall Tucker Band
315 S. Beverly Drive, #206
Beverly Hills, CA 90212
"Rock & Roll Group"

Michael Tucker
197 Oakdale Avenue
Mill Valley, CA 94941
"Actor"

Tanya Tucker
901 - 6th Avenue South
Nashville, TN 37203
"Singer"

Tommy Tune
50 East 89th Street
New York, NY 10128
"Dancer, Director"

John Tunney
1819 Ocean Avenue
Santa Monica, CA 90401
"Ex-Senator"

Robin Tunney
c/o Myrna Jacoby
130 W 57th Street
New York, NY 10019
"Actress"

HRM King Tupou IV
Palace Officiale
Nuku'alofa TONGA
"Royalty"

Ann Turkel
9877 Beverly Grove
Beverly Hills, CA 90210
"Actress"

Christy Turlington
344 East 59th Street
New York, NY 10022
"Model"

Glynn Turman
10900 San Vicente Blvd. #340
Los Angeles, CA 90049
"Actor"

Dr. Debbye Turner
P.O. Box 12450
St. Louis, MO 63132
"Beauty Contest Winner"

Grant Turner
P.O. Box 414
Brentwood, TN 37027
"Singer"

Ike Turner
905 Viewpoint Drive
San Marcos, CA 92069
"Musician"

Janine Turner
9830 Wilshire Blvd.
Beverly Hills, CA 90212
"Actress"

Kathleen Turner
163 Amsterdam Avenue #210
New York, NY 10023
"Actress"

Ted Turner
1050 Techwood Drive NW
Atlanta, GA 30318
"Broadcast & Sports Executive"

Tina Turner
14755 Ventura Blvd. #772
Sherman Oaks, CA 91403
"Singer"

Scott Turow
Sears Tower #8000
Chicago, IL 60606
"Novelist"

Stanley Turrentine
P.O. Box 44555
Ft. Washington, MD 20749
"Musician"

John Turturro
16 North Street #2A
Ventura, CA 93001
"Actor"

Nicholas Turturro
5201 Calvin Avenue
Tarzana, CA 91356
"Actor"

Rita Tushingham
2-4 Noel Street
London W1V 3RB ENGLAND
"Actress"

Dorothy Tutin Browne
13 St. Martins Road
London SW9 ENGLAND
"Actress"

Desmond Tutu
7981 Orlando West, Box 1131
Johannesburg, SOUTH AFRICA
"Arch-Bishop"

Shania Twain
410 W. Elm Street
Greenwich, CT 06830
"Singer"

Shannon Tweed
9300 Wilshire Blvd. #410
Beverly Hills, CA 90212
"Actress, Model"

2 Live Crew
8400 N.E. 2nd Avenue
Miami, FL 33138
"Rap Group"

Twiggy
4 St. George's House
15 Hanover Square
London W1R 9AJ ENGLAND
"Actress, Singer"

Beverly Tyler
14585 Geronimo Trail
Reno, NV 89551
"Actress"

Bonnie Tyler
10 Great Marlborough Street
London W1V 2LP ENGLAND
"Singer, Songwriter"

Liv Tyler
305-2nd Avenue #903
New York, NY 10003
"Actress"

Willie Tyler
9955 Balboa Blvd.
Northridge, CA 91325
"Ventriloquist"

Hunter Tylo
11684 Ventura Blvd. #910
Studio City, CA 91604
"Model"

Michael Tylo
11684 Ventura Blvd. #910
Studio City, CA 91604
"Actor"

Susan Tyrell
1489 Scott Avenue
Los Angeles, CA 90026
"Actress"

Cicely Tyson
315 West 70th Street
New York, NY 10023
"Actress"

Mike Tyson
501 Fairway Drive
Deerfield Beach, FL 33441
"Boxer"

U2
119 Rockland Center #350
Nanvet, NY 10954
"Rock & Roll Group"

Peter Ueberroth
184 Emerald Bay
Laguna Beach, CA 92651
"Former Baseball Executive"

Bob Uecker
201 S. 46th Street
Milwaukee, WI 53214
"Actor, Baseball Announcer"

UFO
10 Sutherland
London W9 24Q ENGLAND
"Rock & Roll Group"

Leslie Uggams
3 Lincoln Center
New York, NY 10023
"Singer, Actress"

Anneliese Uhlig
1519 Escalona Drive
Santa Cruz, CA 95060
"Actress"

Dr. Art Ulene
10810 Via Verona
Los Angeles, CA 90024
"TV Medical Reporter"

Liv Ullman
Hafrsfjordgst. 7
0273 Oslo, NORWAY
"Actress"

Tracey Ullman
815 E. Colorado Street #210
Glendale, CA 91205
"Actress, Singer"

Skeet Ulrich
8942 Wilshire Blvd.
Beverly Hills, CA 90211
"Actor"

Blair Underwood
4116 N. Magnolia Blvd. #101
Burbank, CA 91505
"Actor"

Jay Underwood
9595 Wilshire Blvd. #505
Burbank, CA 90212
"Actor"

Johnny Unitas
5607 Patterson Road
Baldwin, MD 21013
"Ex-Football Player"

Al Unser
7625 Central N.W.
Albuquerque, NM 87105
"Race Car Driver"

Bobby Unser
7700 Central S.W.
Albuquerque, NM 87105
"Race Car Driver"

Bobby Unser Jr.
P.O. Box 25047
Albuquerque, NM 87125
"Race Car Driver"

John Updike
675 Hale Street
Beverly Farm, MA 01915
"Author"

Gene Upshaw
1102 Pepper Tree Drive
Great Falls, VA 22066
"Football Executive"

Robert Urich
10061 Riverside Drive #1026
Toluca Lake, CA 91602
"Actor, Writer"

Loen Uris
P.O. Box 1003
Shelter Island Hgts., NY 11965
Aspen, CO 81611
"Author"

Peter Ustinov
11 rue de Silly
92100 Boulogne, FRANCE
"Actor, Writer, Director"

Garrick Utely
8 Carburton Street
London W1P 7DT ENGLAND
"News Correspondent"

Brenda Vaccaro
17641 Tarzana Street
Encino, CA 91316
"Actress"

Jerry Vale
1100 N. Alta Loma Rd., #1404
Los Angeles, CA 90069
"Singer"

Nancy Valen
8306 Wilshire Blvd. #392
Beverly Hills, CA 90211
"Actress"

Jack Valenti
4635 Ashby Street NW
Washington, D C 20007
"Film Director"

Karen Valentine
P.O. Box 1410
Washington Depot, CT 06793
"Actress"

Scott Valentine
8091 Selma Avenue
West Hollywood, CA 90046
"Actor"

Valentino
2 E. 70th Street
New York, NY 10021
"Singer"

Fernando Valenzuela
3004 North Beachwod Drive
Los Angeles, CA 90027
"Baseball Player"

Alida Valli
Viale Liegi 42
00100 Rome, ITALY
"Actress"

Frankie Valli
6400 Pleasant Park Drive
Chanhassen, MN 55317
"Singer"

Raf Vallone
Viale R. Bacone #14
Rome, ITALY
"Actor"

Richard Van Allen
18 Octavia Street
London SW11 3DN ENGLAND
"Singer"

Joan Van Ark
10950 Alta View Drive
Studio City, CA 91604
"Actress"

Abigail Van Buren
P.O. Box 69440
Los Angeles, CA 90069
"Columnist"

Courtney B. Vance
9171 Wilshire Blvd. #406
Beverly Hills, CA 90210
"Actor"

Cyrus Vance
425 Lexington Avenue
New York, NY 10017
"Government Official"

Jean-Claude Van Damme
10926 Owensmouth Avenue
Chatsworth, CA 91316
"Actor"

Trish Van Devere
3211 Retreat Court
Malibu, CA 90265
"Actress"

Kiki Vandeweghe
4 Pennsylvania Plaza
New York, NY 10019
"Ex-Basketball Player"

Casper Van Dien
3500 W. Olive Avenue #1400
Burbank, CA 91505
"Actor"

Titos Vandis
1930 Century Park East #303
Los Angeles, CA 90067
"Actor"

Mamie Van Doren
428-31st Street
Newport Beach, CA 92663
"Actress, Singer"

Luther Vandross
3264 South Kihel Road
Kikel, HI 96753
"Singer"

Barry Van Dyke
27800 Blythdale Road
Agoura, CA 91301
"Actor"

Dick Van Dyke
23215 Mariposa De Oro
Malibu, CA 90265
"Actor"

Jerry Van Dyke
1705 Jameson Street
Benton, AR 72015
"Actor"

Amy Van Dyken
9638 Colinade Drive
Littleton, CO 80124
"Swimmer"

Charles Van Eman
12304 Santa Monica Blvd., #104
Los Angeles, CA 90025
"Actor"

Vangelis
195 Queens Gate
London W1 ENGLAND
"Composer"

Van Halen
10100 Santa Monica Blvd.
Suite #2460
Los Angeles, CA 90067
"Rock & Roll Group"

Alex Van Halen
12024 Summit Circle
Beverly Hills, CA 90210
"Musician"

Eddie Van Halen
3361 Coldwater Canyon
North Hollywood, CA 91604
"Guitarist, Songwriter"

Vanilla Ice
1290 Ave. of the Americas #4200
New York, NY 10104
"Rap Singer"

Vanity (Denise Mathews)
43521 Mission Blvd.
Fremont, CA 94539
"Singer, Actress"

Merete Van Kemp
10000 Santa Monica Blvd. #305
Los Angeles, CA 90067
"Actress"

Dick Van Patten
13920 Magnolia Blvd.
Sherman Oaks, CA 91423
"Actor"

James Van Patten
14411 Riverside Drive #15
Sherman Oaks, CA 91423
"Actor"

Joyce Van Patten
1321 North Hayworth
Los Angeles, CA 90046
"Actress"

Nels Van Patten
14411 Riverside Drive #18
Sherman Oaks, CA 91423
"Actor"

Tim Van Patten
13920 Magnolia Blvd.
Sherman Oaks, CA 91423
"Actor"

Vincent Van Patten
13926 Magnolia Blvd.
Sherman Oaks, CA 91423
"Actor"

Mario Van Peebles
9560 Wilshire Blvd. #516
Beverly Hills, CA 90212
"Actor, Writer, Director"

Ricky Van Shelton
P.O. Box 120548
Nashville, TN 37212
"Singer"

Deborah Van Valkenburgh
2025 Stanley Hills Drive
Los Angeles, CA 90046
"Actress"

Monique Van Vooren
165 East 66th Street
New York, NY 10021
"Actress, Singer"

Randy Vanwarmer
65 Music Square West
Nashville, TN 37203
"Singer, Songwriter"

Steve Van Zandt
322 West 57th Street
New York, NY 10019
"Singer, Guitarist"

The Vapors
44 Valmoral Drive
Woking, Surrey, ENGLAND
"Rock & Roll Group"

Jim Varney
1200 McGovock Street
Nashville, TN 37203
"Actor"

Victor Vasarely
83 re aux Reliaues
Annet-sur-Marne, FRANCE
"Artist"

Robert Vaughn
88 Salem View Drive
Ridgefield, CT 06877
"Actor, Director"

Vince Vaughn
532 N. Rossmore Avenue #103
Los Angeles, CA 90004
"Actor"

Bobby Vee (Velline)
P.O. Box 41
Saulk Rapids, MN 56379
"Singer, Songwriter"

Suzanne Vega
30 West 21st Street, #700
New York, NY 10010
"Singer"

Jorge Velasquez
770 Allerton Avenue
Bronx, NY 10467
"Horse Racer"

Eddie Velez
5439 Ellenvale Avenue
Woodland Hills, CA 91367
"Actor"

Reginald Vel Johnson
8637 Allenwood Drive
Los Angeles, CA 90046
"Actor"

Vendela
170 Fifth Avenue, 10th Floor
New York, NY 10010
"Model"

Ken Venturi
P.O. Box 5118
Akron, OH 44334
"Golf Instructor"

Gwen Verdon
26 Latimer Lane
Bronxville, NY 10708
"Actress, Dancer"

Elena Verdugo
P.O. Box 2048
Chula Vista, CA 92012
"Actress"

Ben Vereen
9255 Sunset Blvd. #804
Los Angeles, CA, 90069
"Dancer, Actor"

Dick Vermeil
51 W. 52nd Street
New York, NY 10019
"Sportcaster"

Henri Verneuil
21 rue du Bois-de-Boulogne
92200 Neuilly-sur-Seine
FRANCE
"Film Director"

John Vernon
15125 Mulholland Drive
Los Angeles, CA 90077
"Actor"

Kate Vernon
1999 Avenue of the Stars #2850
Los Angeles, CA 90067
"Actress"

Yvette Vickers
P.O. Box 292479
Phelan, CA 92329
"Actress"

James Victor
1944 N. Whitley Avenue #306
Los Angeles, CA 90036
"Actor"

Gore Vidal
1201 Alta Loma Road
Los Angeles, CA 90069
"Writer"

Peter Vidmar
6 Flores
Foothill Ranch, CA 92610
"Gymnast"

Abe Vigoda
8500 Melrose Avenue #208
West Hollywood, CA 90069
"Actor"

Richard Viguerie
7777 Leesburg Pike
Falls Church, VA 22043
"Professional Fund Raiser"

Bob Vila
10877 Wilshire Blvd. #900
Los Angeles, CA 90024
"Home Repair TV Host"

Guillermo Vilas
Avenue Foch 86
Paris, FRANCE
"Tennis Player"

The Village People
1560 Broadway, #1308
New York, NY 10036
"Music Group"

Jan-Michael Vincent
151 El Camino Drive
Beverly Hills, CA 90212
"Actor"

Virginia Vincent
1001 Hammond Street
Los Angeles, CA 90069
"Actress"

Melanie Vincz
2212 Earle Court
Redondo Beach, CA 90278
"Actress, Model"

Helen Vinson
2213 Carol Woods
Chapel Hill, NC 27514
"Actress"

Jesse Vint
10637 Burbank Blvd.
No. Hollywood, CA 91601
"Actress"

Bobby Vinton
P.O. Box 6010
Branson, MO 65616
"Singer"

Frank Viola
844 Sweetwater Island Circle
Longwood, FL 32779
"Baseball Player"

Lasse Viren
Suomen Urhellulirto Ry
Box 25002 00250
Helsinki 25 FINLAND
"Track Athlete"

Sal Visculo
6491 Ivarene Avenue
Los Angeles, CA 90068
"Actor"

Nana Visitor
9016 Wilshire Blvd. #363
Beverly Hills, CA 90211
"Actress"

Monica Vitti
Via F. 38, Siacci
00197 Rome, ITALY
"Actress"

Marina Vlady
10 Avenue de Marivauz
F-78600 Maisons Lafitte
FRANCE
"Actress"

Karl Micheal Vogler
Auweg 8, Seehof
D-82418 Seehausen
GERMANY
"Actor"

Jon Voight
9660 Oak Pass Road
Beverly Hills, CA 90210
"Actor"

Paul Volcker
International Economic Dept.
Princeton University
Princeton, NJ
"Former Monetary Treasurer"

Nedra Volz
5606 East Fairfield Street
Mesa, AZ 86205
"Actress"

Helene von Damm-Gurtler
Hotel Sacher bei der Oper
1010 Vienna, AUSTRIA
"Diplomat"

Lenny Von Dohlen
2271 Betty Lane
Beverly Hills, CA 90210
"Actor"

Betsy Von Fursterberg
230 Central Park West
New York, NY 10028
"Actress"

Diane von Furstenberg
389 West 12th Street
New York, NY 10014
"Fashion Designer"

Kurt Vonnegut, Jr.
P.O. Box 27
Sagaponack, NY 11962
"Author"

Max Von Sydow
avd C-G Rissberg
Box 5209
Stockholm 10245 SWEDEN
"Actor"

Richard von Weizsacker
Meisenstr. 6
D-14195 Berlin GERMANY
"Ex-President of Germany"

Lark Voorhies
10635 Santa Monica Blvd., #130
Los Angeles, CA 90025
"Actress"

Russell Wade
47-287 West Eldorado Drive
Indian Wells, CA 92260
"Actor"

Virginia Wade
Sharstead Court
Sittingbourne
Kent, ENGLAND
"Tennis Player"

Lanny Wadkins
6002 Kettering Court
Dallas, TX 75248
"Golfer"

Lyle Waggoner
4506 Pine Valley Place
Westlake Village, CA 91362
"Actor"

Chuck Wagner
1419 N. Hollywood Way
Burbank, CA 91505
"Actor"

Jack Wagner
1134 Alta Loma Road #115
West Hollywood, CA 90069
"Actor, Singer"

Jane Wagner
P.O. Box 27700
Los Angeles, CA 90027
"Writer, Producer"

Lindsay Wagner
P.O. Box 5002
Sherman Oaks, CA 91403
"Actress"

Natasha Gregson Wagner
1500 Old Oak Road
Los Angeles, CA 90049
"Actress"

Robert Wagner
P.O. Box 93339
Los Angeles, CA 90093
"Actor"

Porter Wagoner
P.O. Box 290785
Nashville, TN 37229
"Singer, Songwriter"

Ken Wahl
480 Westlake Blvd.
Malibu, CA 90265
"Actor"

Mark Wahlberg
63 Pilgrim Road
Braintree, MA 02184
"Actor, Talk Show Host"

Bea Wain
9955 Durant Drive, #305
Beverly Hills, CA 90212
"Singer"

Ralph Waite
73317 Ironwood Street
Palm Desert, CA 92260
"Actor, Director"

Terry Waite
Lambeth Palace
London SE1 7JU ENGLAND
"Clergy"

Tom Waits
P.O. Box 498
Valley Ford, CA 94972
"Singer, Songwriter"

Grete Waitz
Birgitte Hammers Vel 15-G
1169 Oslo NORWAY
"Track Athlete"

Andrzej Wajda
ul-Jezefa Hauke Bosaka 14
01-540 Warsaw POLAND
"Director"

Robert Walden
1450 Arroyo View Drive
Pasadena, CA 91103
"Actor"

Kurt Waldheim
1 Lobkowitz Platz
1010 Vienna, AUSTRIA
"Ex-President of Austria"

Janet Waldo
15725 Royal Oak Road
Encino, CA 91316
"Actress"

Lech Walesa
Polskistr. 53
Gdansk - (Danzig) POLAND
"Politician"

Alice Walker
327 - 25th Street #3
San Francisco, CA 94121
"Novelist"

Ally Walker
7920 Sunset Blvd. #400
Los Angeles, CA 90046
"Actress"

Arnetia Walker
20738 Deforest Street
Woodland Hills, CA 91364
"Actress"

Bree Walker
3347 Tareco Drive
Los Angeles, CA 90068
"Newscaster"

Clint Walker
10175 Joerschke Drive #1
Grass Valley, CA 95945
"Actor"

Doak Walker
P.O. Box 77329
Steamboat Springs, CO 80477
"Ex-Football Player"

Fiona Walker
13 Despard Road
London N19 ENGLAND
"Actress"

Hershell Walker
1 Cowboy Parkway
Irving, TX 75063
"Football Player"

Jimmy Walker
332 Southdown Road
Lloyd Harbor, NY 11754
"Actor, Comedian"

Junior Walker
141 Dunbar Avenue
Fords, NJ 08863
"Saxophonist"

Marcy Walker
9107 Wilshire Blvd. #700
Beverly Hills, CA 90210
"Actress"

Mort Walker
61 Studio Court
Stamford, CT 06903
"Cartoonist"

Nicholas Walker
6925 Tuna Canyon Road
Topanga, CA 90290
"Actor"

Polly Walker
4 Windmill Street
London WIP IHF ENGLAND
"Actress"

Chris Wallace
1717 DeSales Street
Washington, DC 20036
"Broadcast Journalist"

George Wallace
P.O. Box 667
Montgomery, AL 36101
"Former Governor"

George Wallace
8455 Fountain Avenue #401
W. Hollywood, CA 90069
"Comedian"

Marcia Wallace
1312 South Genesee Avenue
Los Angeles, CA 90019
"Actress"

Mike Wallace
555 West 57th Street
New York, NY 10019
"Broadcast Journalist"

Eli Wallach
200 West 57th Street #900
New York, NY 10019
"Actor"

The Great Wallendas
138 Frog Hollow Road
Churchville, PA 18966
"High Wire Act"

Deborah Walley
P.O. Box 1226
Sedona, AZ 86339
"Actress"

Jon Walmsley
13810 Magnolia Blvd.
Sherman Oaks, CA 91403
"Actor"

Martin Walser
Zum Hecht 36
D-88662 Uberlingen, GERMANY
"Author, Dramatist"

Bill Walsh
Stanford University Football
Stanford, CA 94305
"Ex-Football Coach"

Dylan Walsh
8942 Wilshire Blvd.
Beverly Hills, CA 90211
"Actor"

John Walsh
5151 Wisconsin Avenue
Washington , DC 20016
"Actor"

M. Emmet Walsh
4173 Motor Avenue
Culver City, CA 90232
"Actor"

Ray Walston
423 S. Rexford Drive #205
Beverly Hills, CA 90212
"Actor"

Jessica Walter
10530 Strathmore Drive
Los Angeles, CA 90024
"Actress"

Tracey Walter
257 North Rexford Drive
Beverly Hills, CA 90210
"Actor"

Barbara Walters
33 West 60th Street
New York, NY 10021
"News Journalist"

Hugh Walters
15 Christ Church Avenue
London NW6 7QP ENGLAND
"Actor"

Jaime Walters
4702 Ethel Avenue
Sherman Oaks, CA 91423
"Actor"

Julie Walters
76 Oxford Street
London W1N 0AX ENGLAND
"Actress"

Susan Walters
939-8th Avenue #400
New York, NY 10019
"Actress"

Bill Walton
1010 Myrtle Way
San Diego, CA 92103
"Ex-Basketball Player"

Jess Walton
4702 Ethel Avenue
Sherman Oaks, CA 91423
"Actress"

Darrell Waltrip
6780 Hudseth Road
Harrisburg, NC 28705
"Race Car Driver"

Joseph Wambaugh
3520 Kellogg Way
San Diego, CA 92106
"Novelist"

Joseph A. Wapner
16616 Park Lane Place
Los Angeles, CA 90049
"TV Show Judge"

Patrick Warburton
1800 Avenue of the Stars #400
Los Angeles, CA 90067
"Actor"

Fred Ward
1214 Cabrillo Avenue
Venice, CA 90291
"Actor"

Megan Ward
1999 Avenue of the Stars #2850
Los Angeles, CA 90067
"Actress"

Sela Ward
289 S. Robertson Blvd. #469
Beverly Hills, CA 90211
"Actress"

Skip Ward
P.O. Box 755
Beverly Hills, CA 90210
"Actor"

Jack Warden
23604 Malibu Colony Drive
Malibu, CA 90265
"Actor"

Clyde Ware
1252 North Laurel Avenue
Los Angeles, CA 90046
"Writer, Producer"

Herta Ware
P.O. Box 151
Topanga, CA 90290
"Actress"

Marsha Warfield
P.O. Box 691713
Los Angeles, CA 90069
"Actress, Comedienne"

Dr. William Warfield
P.O. Box 1573
Champaign, IL 61824
"Actor, Singer"

Steve Wariner
320 Main Street #240
Franklin, TN 37064
"Singer"

Richard Waring
1 Chester Close
Queens Ride
London SW13 OJE ENGLAND
"TV Writer"

Todd Waring
10 East 44th Street #500
New York, NY 10017
"Actor"

Billy Warlock
9229 Sunset Blvd. #315
Los Angeles, CA 90069
"Actor"

Cornelius Warmerdam
3976 North 1st Street
Fresno, CA 93726
"Track Athlete"

Sen. John Warner (VA)
Senate Russell Bldg. #225
Washington, DC 20510
"Politician"

Julie Warner
9830 Wilshire Blvd.
Beverly Hills, CA 90212
"Actress"

Malcolm-Jamal Warner
15303 Ventura Blvd. #1100
Sherman Oaks, CA 91403
"Actor"

Diane Warren
1896 Rising Glen Road
Los Angeles, CA 90069
"Singer"

Jennifer Warren
1675 Old Oak Road
Los Angeles, CA 90049
"Actress"

Lesley Ann Warren
2934 Beverly Glen Circle #372
Los Angeles, CA 90077
"Actress"

Michael Warren
189 Greenfield Avenue
Los Angeles, CA 90049
"Actor"

Ruth Warrick
903 Park Avenue
New York, NY 10021
"Actress"

Dionne Warwick
1583 Lindacrest Drive
Beverly Hills, CA 90210
"Singer"

Don Was
12831 Mulholland Drive
Beverly Hills, CA 90210
"Producer"

Denzel Washington
4701 Sancola
Toluca Lake, CA 91602
"Actor"

Dale Wasserman
1680 Valecroft Avenue
Westlake Village, CA 91361
"Playwright"

Lew Wasserman
911 North Foothill Road
Beverly Hills, CA 90210
"Film Executive"

Gedde Watanabe
1632 Westerly Terrace
Los Angeles, CA 90026
"Actor"

Waterboys
3 Monmouth Road
London W2 ENGLAND
"Rock & Roll Group"

John Waters
1018 N. Charles Street
Baltimore, MD 21201
"Director, Writer"

Sam Waterson
RR Box 232
West Cornwell, CT 06796
"Actor"

Carlene Watkins
15760 Ventura Blvd. #1730
Encino, CA 91436
"Actress"

Jody Watley
P.O. Box 6339
Beverly Hills, CA 90212
"Singer"

Angela Watson
16350 Ventura Blvd. #325
Encino, CA 91436
"Actress"

Tom Watson
1901 West 47th Place #200
Westwood, KS 66205
"Golfer"

James G. Watt
P.O. Box 3705
Jackson Hole, WY 83001
"Former Secretary of Interior"

Rep. J. C. Watts (OK)
1713 Longworth House Bldg.
Washington, DC 20510
"Politician"

Ruby Wax
503/4 The Chambers
Chelsea Harbour, Lots Rd.
London SWIO OXF ENGLAND
"Radio Show Hostess"

Rep. Henry A. Waxman (CA)
House Rayburn Bldg. #2204
Washington, DC 20515
"Politician"

Damon Wayans
7920 Sunset Blvd. #250
Los Angeles, CA 90046
"Actor"

Dwayne Wayans
16405 Mulholland
Los Angeles, CA 90049
"Actor"

Keenan Ivory Wayans
16405 Mulholland Drive
Los Angeles, CA 90049
"Actor"

Kim Wayans
1742 Granville Avenue #2
Los Angeles, CA 90025
"Actress"

Marlon Wayans
9200 Sunset Blvd. #106
Los Angeles, CA 90069
"Actor"

Shawn Wayans
7920 Sunset Blvd. #250
Los Angeles, CA 90046
"Comedian, Actor"

Fredd Wayne
117 Strand Street
Santa Monica, CA 90405
"Actor, Writer"

Michael Wayne
10425 Kling Street
North Hollywood, CA 91602
"Film Executive"

Patrick Wayne
10502 Whipple Street
North Hollywood, CA 91602
"Actor"

Shawn Weatherly
12203 Octagon Street
Los Angeles, CA 90049
"Actress, Model"

Carl Weathers
10960 Wilshire Blvd. #826
Los Angeles, CA 90024
"Actor"

Bob Weatherwax
16133 Soledad Canyon Road
Canyon Country, CA 91351
"Animal Trainer"

Dennis Weaver
P.O. Box 257
Ridgeway, CO 81432
"Actor"

Earl Weaver
501 Cypress Point Drive West
Pembroke Pines, FL 33027
"Ex-Baseball Manager"

Fritz Weaver
161 West 75th Street
New York, NY 10023
"Actor"

Sigourney Weaver
200 West 57th Street #1306
New York, NY 10019
"Actress"

Jimmy Webb
1560 North Laurel Avenue #109
Los Angeles, CA 90046
"Singer, Composer"

Lucy Webb
1360 N. Crescent Heights #3-B
Los Angeles, CA 90046
"Actress, Comedienne"

Andrew Lloyd Webber
Trump Tower
725 Fifth Avenue
New York, NY 10022
"Composer"

Chris Webber
31487 Northwestern Hwy.
Farmington Hills, MI 48334
"Basketball Player"

Steven Weber
8942 Wilshire Blvd.
Beverly Hills, CA 90211
"Actor"

Ann Wedgeworth
10100 Santa Monica Blvd. #2500
Los Angeles, CA 90067
"Actress"

Gene Weed
10405 Oklahoma Avenue
Chatsworth, CA 91311
"Writer, Producer"

Caspar Weinberger
700 New Hampshire Avenue NW
Washington, DC 20037
"Former Government Official"

Scott Weinger
9255 Sunset Blvd. #1010
West Hollywood, CA 90069
"Actor"

Carl Weintraub
10390 Santa Monica Blvd. #300
Los Angeles, CA 90025
"Actor"

Jerry Weintraub
27740 Pacific Coast Hwy.
Malibu, CA 90265
"Film Producer"

Peter Weir
Post Office
Palm Beach 2108 AUSTRALIA
"Film Director"

Tom Weiskepf
7580 East Gray Road
Scottsdale, AZ 85260
"Golfer"

Sam Weisman
4448 Tujunga Avenue
No. Hollywood, CA 91602
"Actor"

Michael T. Weiss
8635 Hayden Place
Culver City, CA 90232
"Actor"

Morgan Weisser
1030 Superba Avenue
Venice, CA 90291
"Actor"

Bruce Weitz
5030 Arundel Drive
Woodland Hills, CA 91364
"Actor"

Ezer Weizman
26 Hagiffen Street
Ramat, Haseram, ISRAEL
"Politician"

Raquel Welch
9903 Santa Monica Blvd. #514
Beverly Hills, CA 90212
"Actress, Singer, Writer"

Tahnee Welch
134 Duane Street #400
New York, NY 10013
"Actress"

Ann Weldon
11555 Dona Teresa Drive
Studio City, CA 91604
"Actress"

Mary Louise Weller
1416 North Havenhurst Drive #11
Los Angeles, CA 90046
"Actress"

Peter Weller
853 - 7th Avenue #9A
New York, NY 10019
"Actor"

Robb Weller
4249 Beck Avenue
Studio City, CA 91604
"TV Show Host"

William Wellman, Jr.
410 North Barrington Avenue
Los Angeles, CA 90049
"Actor"

Dawn Wells
4616 Ledge Avenue
North Hollywood, CA 91602
"Actress"

Kitty Wells
240 Old Hickory Blvd.
Madison, TN 35115
"Singer"

Sen. Paul Wellstone (MN)
717 Hart Office Bldg.
Washington, DC 20510
"Politician"

Eudora Welty
1119 Pinehurst Street
Jackson, MS 39202
"Author"

Señor Wences
204 West 55th Street #701A
New York, NY 10019
"Ventriliquist"

George Wendt
23458 W. Moon Shadows Dr.
Malibu, CA 90265
"Actor"

Lina Wertmuller
via Principessa Clotilde 5
00196 Rome, ITALY
"Film Director"

Adam West
P.O. Box 3477
Ketchum, ID 83340
"Actor"

Red West
12178 Ventura Blvd. #205
Studio City, CA 91604
"Actor, Author"

Shelly West
P.O. Box 158718
Nashville, TN 37215
"Singer"

Timothy West
46 North Side
Wandsworth Common
London SW18 ENGLAND
"Actor"

Dr. Ruth Westheimer
900 West 190th Street
New York, NY 10040
"Sex Theapist"

James Westmoreland
8019 1/2 West Norton Avenue
Los Angeles, CA 90046
"Actor"

Gen. William Westmoreland
107 1/2 Tradd Street
P.O. Box 1059
Charleston, SC 29401
"Military Leader"

David Weston
123A Grosvenor Road
London SW1 ENGLAND
"Actor"

Patricia Wetting
5855 Topanga Canyon #410
Woodland Hills, CA 91367
"Actress"

Frank Whaley
P.O. Box 5617
Beverly Hills, CA 90210
"Actor

Joanne Whaley
9207 Flicker Way
West Hollywood, CA 90069
"Actress"

Justin Whalin
3604 Holboro Drive
Los Angeles, CA 90027
"Actor"

Wil Wheaton
2820 Honolulu #255
Verdugo City, CA 91043
"Actor"

Lisa Whelchel
30408 Olympic Street
Castaic, CA 91384
"Actress"

Shannon Whirry
8091 Selma Drive
Los Angeles, CA 90046
"Actress"

Forest Whitaker
1990 South Bundy Drive #200
Los Angeles, CA 90025
"Actor"

Ian Whitcomb
P.O. Box 451
Altadena, CA 91001
"Singer, Actor, Producer"

Barry White
3395 S. Jones Blvd. #176
Las Vegas, NV 89102
"Singer, Songwriter"

Betty White
P.O. Box 491965
Los Angeles, CA 90049
"Actress"

Bradley White
8730 Sunset Blvd. #480
Los Angeles, CA 90069
"Actor"

Bryan White
1114 - 17th Avenue #102
Nashville, TN 37212
"Singer"

Byron "Whizzer" White
6801 Hampshire Road
McLean, VA 22101
"Ex-Supreme Court Justice"

Jaleel White
151 El Camino Drive
Beverly Hills, CA 90212
"Actor"

Jesse White
818 N. Doheny Drive #305
West Hollywood, CA 90069
"Actor"

Karyn White
3300 Warner Blvd.
Burbank, CA 91505
"Singer"

Michael Jai White
P.O. Box 5617
Beverly Hills, CA 90210
"Actor"

Reggie White
P.O. Box 10628
Green Bay, WI 54307
"Football Player"

Sharon White
380 Forest Retreat
Hendersonville, TN 37075
"Singer, Guitarist"

Thelma White
8431 Lennox Avenue
Panorama City, CA 91402
"Singer"

Vanna White
3400 Riverside Drive
Burbank, CA 91505
"TV Personality, Model"

Geoffrey Whitehead
81 Shaftesbury Avenue
London W1 ENGLAND
"Actor"

Billie Whitelaw
535 King's Road
19 The Plaza #2
London SW10 0SZ ENGLAND
"Actress"

The White's
P.O. Box 2158
Hendersonville, TN 37075
"C&W Group"

Heather Whitestone
P.O. Box 672801
Marietta, GA 30006
"Former Miss America"

Lynn Whitfield
8942 Wilshire Blvd.
Beverly Hills, CA 90211
"Actress"

Bradley Whitford
1999 Avenue of the Stars #2850
Los Angeles, CA 90067
"Actor"

Barbara Whiting
1085 Waddington Street
Birmingham, MI 48009
"Actress"

Margaret Whiting
41 West 58th Street #5A
New York, NY 10019
"Singer"

Slim Whitman
1300 Divison Street #103
Nashville, TN 37203
"Singer"

Stuart Whitman
749 San Ysidro Road
Santa Barbara, CA 93108
"Actor"

James Whitmore
4990 Puesta Del Sol
Malibu, CA 90265
"Actor"

James Whitmore, Jr.
1284 La Brea Drive
Thousand Oaks, CA 91362
"Actor"

Jane Whitney
5 TV Place
Needham, MA 02192
"TV Talk Show Host"

Phyllis Whitney
310 Madison Avenue #607
New York, NY 10017
"Actress"

Roger Whittaker
69-79 Fulham High Street
London SW6 3JW ENGLAND
"Singer, Songwriter"

Dick Whittinghill
11310 Valley Spring Lane
Toluca Lake, CA 91602
"Radio Personality"

The Who
533-579 Harrow Road
London W10 4RH ENGLAND
"Rock & Roll Group"

Tom Wicker
229 West 43rd Street
New York, NY 10036
"Columnist"

Kathleen Widdoes
200 West 57th Street #900
New York, NY 10019
"Actress"

Elie Wiesel
745 Common Wealth Avenue
Boston, MA 02115
"Author, Journalist"

Simon Wiesenthal
Salvtorgasse 6
1010 Vienna 1 AUSTRIA
"Jewish Leader"

Dianne Wiest
40 West 57th Street
New York, NY 10019
"Actress"

Mats Wilander
Vickersvagen 2
Vaxjo, SWEDEN
"Tennis Player"

The Wilburn Brothers
P.O. Box 50
Goodlettsville, TN 37072
"C&W Group"

Larry Wilcox
10 Appaloosa Lane
Canoga Park, CA 91307
"Actor, Director"

Shannon Wilcox
1264 N. Hayworth Avenue #17
Los Angeles, CA 90046
"Actress"

Jack Wild
68 Old Brompton Road
London SW7 3LQ ENGLAND
"Actor"

Kim Wilde
1 Stevenage Road
Nebrowth, Herts. ENGLAND
"Singer, Songwriter"

Billy Wilder
10375 Wilshire Blvd.
Los Angeles, CA 90024
"Writer, Producer"

Gene Wilder
1511 Sawtelle Blvd. #155
Los Angeles, CA 90025
"Actor, Writer, Director"

James Wilder
8601 Wilshire Blvd. #801
Beverly, Hills, CA 90211
"Actor"

Michael Wilding, Jr.
8428-C Melrose Place
Los Angeles, CA 90069
"Actor"

Hoyt Wilhelm
3102 North Himes Avenue
Tampa, FL 33607
"Ex-Baseball Player"

Donna Wilkes
16228 Maplegrove Street
La Puente, CA 91744
"Actress"

Jamaal Wilkes
7846 West 81st Street
Playa del Rey, CA 90291
"Ex-Basketball Player"

June Wilkinson
1025 N. Howard Street
Glendale, CA 91207
"Actress"

George Will
9 Grafton Street
Chevy Chase, MD 20815
"Columnist, Writer"

Jo Ann Willette
9300 Wilshire Blvd. #400
Beverly Hills, CA 90212
"Actress"

Kathleen Willey
2320 Castlebridge Road
Midlothian, VA 23113
"Ex-Unpaid White House Aid"

HRH Prince William
Highgrove House
Gloucestershire ENGLAND
"Royalty"

Williams & Ree
P.O. Box 163
Hendersonville, TN 37077
"Vocal Duo"

Andy Williams
2500 West Highway 76
Branson, MO 65616
"Singer, Actor"

Anson Williams
24615 Skyline View Drive
Malibu, CA 90265
"Actor"

Barry Williams
3646 Reina Court
Calabasas, CA 91302
"Actor"

Billy Williams
586 Prince Edward Road
Glen Ellyn, IL 60137
"Ex-Baseball Player"

Billy Dee Williams
18411 Hatteras Street #204
Tarzana, CA 91356
"Actor"

Bruce Williams
P.O. Box 547
Elfers, FL 34680
"Radio Personality"

Cara Willaims Dann
146 South Peck Drive
Beverly Hills, CA 90212
"Actress"

Cindy Williams
7023 Birdview Avenue
Malibu, CA 90265
"Actress"

Clarence Williams III
9057A Nemo Street
Los Angeles, CA 90069
"Actor"

Darnell Williams
1930 Century Park West #403
Los Angeles, CA 90067
"Actor"

Don Williams
207 Westport Road #202
Kansas City, MO 64111
"Singer, Songwriter"

Edy Williams
1638 Blue Jay Way
Los Angeles, CA 90069
"Actress, Model"

Esther Williams
9377 Readcrest Drive
Beverly Hills, CA 90210
"Actress"

Hal Williams
P.O. Box 14227
Palm Desert, CA 92255
"Actor"

Hank Williams, Jr.
Hwy. 79 East
Box 1350
Paris, TN 38242
"Singer, Guitarist"

Jobeth Williams
9911 W. Pico Blvd. #PH 1
Los Angeles, CA 90035
"Actress"

Joe Williams
2810 W. Charleston #G-72
Las Vegas, NV 89102
"Singer"

John Williams
333 Loring Avenue
Los Angeles, CA 90024
"Composer, Conductor"

Kelli Williams
1999 Avenue of the Stars #2850
Los Angeles, CA 90067
"Actress"

Kimberly Williams
151 El Camino Drive
Beverly Hills, CA 90212
"Actress"

Mary Alice Williams
30 Rockefeller Plaza #508
New York, NY 10020
"Broadcast Journalist"

Mason Williams
P.O. Box 5734
Santa Rosa, CA 94102
"Singer, Songwriter"

Montel Williams
435 W. 53rd Street
New York, NY 10019
"TV Show Host"

Paul Williams
8545 Franklin Avenue
Los Angeles, CA 90069
"Singer, Songwriter"

Robin Williams
3145 Geary Blvd. #524
San Francisco, CA 94118
"Actor, Comedian, Writer"

Roger Williams
16150 Clear Valley Place
Encino, CA 91436
"Pianist"

Stephanie Williams
1269 South Orange #1
Los Angeles, CA 90019
"Actress"

Ted Williams
2448 No. Essex Avenue
Hernando, FL 33441
"Ex-Baseball Player"

Treat Williams
1244 - 11th Street #A
Santa Monica, CA 90401
"Actor"

Van Williams
P.O. Box 6679
Ketchum, ID 83340
"Actor"

Vanessa Williams
P.O. Box 858
Chappaqua, NY 10514
"Singer"

Fred Williamson
10880 Wilshire Blvd. #1101
Los Angeles, CA 90024
"Actor"

Marianne Williamson
565 Valley Club Rd.
Montecito, CA 93108
"Singer"

Nicol Williamson
76 Oxford Street
London W1N OAX ENGLAND
"Actor"

Bruce Willis
1122 S. Robertson Blvd. #15
Los Angeles, CA 90035
"Actor, Singer"

Brian Wilson
14042 Aubrey Road
Beverly Hills, CA 90210
"Musician"

Carnie Wilson
13601 Ventura Blvd. #286
Sherman Oaks, CA 91423
"Actress"

Elizabeth Wilson
200 West 57th Street #900
New York, NY 10019
"Actress"

Flip Wilson
21970 Pacific Coast Hwy.
Malibu, CA 90265
"Comedian, Actor, Writer"

Jeannie Wilson
10358-A Riverside Drive
North Hollywood, CA 91602
"Actress"

Jennifer Wilson
1947 Lakeshore Drive
Branson, MO 65616
"Actress"

Lambert Wilson
91 rue Saint-Honore
75001 Paris FRANCE
"Actor"

Mara Wilson
3500 West Olive, #1400
Burbank, CA 91505
"Actress"

Mary Wilson
163 Amsterdam Avenue #125
New York, NY 10023
"Singer"

Melanie Wilson
12946 Dickens Street
Studio City, CA 91604
"Actress"

Nancy Wilson
2810 W. Charleston G-72
Las Vegas, NV 89102
"50's Singer"

Nancy Wilson
202 San Vicente Blvd. #4
Santa Monica, CA 90402
"Heart's Lead Singer"

Peta Wilson
12754 Sarah Street
Studio City, CA 91604
"Actress"

Gov. Pete Wilson (CA)
State Capitol
Sacramento, CA 95814
"Governor"

Wilson Phillips
1290 Ave. of the Americas #4200
New York, NY 10104
"Rock & Roll Group"

Rita Wilson
P.O. Box 900
Beverly Hills, CA 90213
"Actress"

Sheree J. Wilson
7218 South Jan Mar Drive
Dallas, TX 75230
"Actress"

Stuart Wilson
P.O. Box 5617
Beverly Hills, CA 90210
"Actor"

Brian Wimmer
3375 Creek Road
Salt Lake City, UT 84121
"Actor"

Paul Winchell
32262 Oakshore Drive
Westlake Village, CA 91361
"Actor"

Jeff Wincott
3880-B Fredonia Drive
Los Angeles, CA 90068
"Actor"

William Windom
P.O. Box 1067
Woodacre, CA 94973
"Actor"

Marie Windsor
9501 Cherokee Lane
Beverly Hills, CA 90210
"Actress"

Dave Winfield
11809 Gwynne Lane
Los Angeles, CA 90077
"Baseball Player"

Paul Winfield
5693 Holly Oak Drive
Los Angeles, CA 90068
"Actor"

Oprah Winfrey
P.O. Box 909715
Chicago, IL 60690
"TV Show Host, Actress"

Debra Winger
P.O. Box 9078
Van Nuys, CA 91409
"Actress"

Jason Wingreen
4224 Teesdale Avenue
North Hollywood, CA 91604
"Actor"

Henry Winkler
P.O. Box 49914
Los Angeles, CA 90049
"Actor, Producer"

Michael Winner
31 Melbury Road
London W14 8AB ENGLAND
"Writer, Producer"

Mare Winningham
9560 Topanga Canyon Blvd., #103
Chatsworth, CA 91311
"Actress"

Kate Winslet
503/504 Lotts Road
The Chambers, Chelsea Harbour
London, SWIO OXF ENGLAND
"Actress"

Alex Winter
107 West 25th Street #6B
New York, NY 10001
"Actor"

Edward Winter
4374 Ventura Canyon Avenue #3
Sherman Oaks, CA 91423
"Actor"

Johnny Winter
208 East 51st Street #151
New York, NY 10022
"Singer"

Judy Winter
Kaiserdamm 28
D-14057 Berlin GERMANY
"Singer"

Jonathan Winters
4310 Arcola Avenue
Toluca Lake, CA 91602
"Comedian, Actor"

Shelley Winters
457 N. Oakhurst Drive
Beverly Hills, CA 90210
"Actress"

Steve Winwood
9200 Sunset Blvd. PH 15
Los Angeles, CA 90069
"Singer, Songwriter"

Billy Wirth
9255 Sunset Blvd., #1010
Los Angeles, CA 90069
"Actor"

Norman Wisdom
The Lhen, Andreas
Ramsay 1M7 3EH Isle of Man UK
"Actor"

Ernie Wise
306-16 Euston Road
London NW13 ENGLAND
"Comedian"

Robert Wise
315 S. Beverly Drive, #214
Beverly Hills, CA 90212
Director, Producer"

Googie Withers
1740 Pittwater Road
Bay View NSW 2104 AUSTRALIA
"Actress"

Jane Withers
3676 Longridge Avenue
Sherman Oaks, CA 91423
"Actress"

Jimmy Witherspoon
223 1/2 E. 48th Street
New York, NY 10017
"Singer, Musician"

Reese Witherspoon
8912 Burton Way
Beverly Hills, CA 90211
"Actress"

Alicia Witt
11350 Ventura Blvd. #206
Studio City, CA 91604
"Actress"

Katarina Witt
Lindenstr. 8
16244 Altenhof GERMANY
"Ice Skater"

Paul Junger Witt
1438 North Gower Street
Los Angeles, CA 90028
"TV Producer"

Kevin Wixted
10100 Santa Monica Blvd.
Suite #700
Los Angeles, CA 90067
"Actor"

Mr. Wizard (Don Herbert)
P.O. Box 83
Canoga Park, CA 91305
"TV Personality"

Charles Wolcott
P.O. Box 155
Haifa, ISRAEL
"Composer

Dick Wolf
9560 Wilshire Blvd. #516
Beverly Hills, CA 90212
"Producer"

Scott Wolf
10390 Santa Monica Blvd. #300
Los Angeles, CA 90025
"Actor"

Michael Wolfe
41 Landowne Road
London W11 26Q ENGLAND
"Actor"

Tom Wolfe
21 East 79th Street
New York, NY 10021
"Writer"

David L. Wolper
1833 Rising Glen
Los Angeles, CA 90069
"Film Director"

Bobby Womack
1048 Tatnall Street
Macon, GA 31201
"Singer"

Stevie Wonder
4616 Magnolia Blvd.
Burbank, CA 91505
"Singer, Songwriter"

John Woo
450 N. Roxbury Dr. #800
Beverly Hills, CA 90210
"Film Director"

Elijah Wood
9150 Wilshire Blvd., #350
Beverly Hills, CA 90212
"Actor"

Judith Wood
1745 N. Gramercy Place #517
Los Angeles, CA 90028
"Actress"

Lana Wood
868 Masterson Drive
Thousand Oaks, CA 91360
"Actress"

Alfre Woodard
8942 Wilshire Blvd.
Beverly Hills, CA 90211
"Actress"

Bokeem Woodbine
19351 Ventura Blvd.
Tarzana, CA 91356
"Actor"

John Wooden
17711 Margate Street #102
Encino, CA 91316
"Ex-Basketball Coach"

Cynthia Woodhead
P.O. Box 1193
Riverside, CA 92501
"Swimmer"

Frank Woodruff
170 North Crescent Drive
Beverly Hills, CA 90210
"Director, Producer"

Judy Woodruff
P.O. Box 2626
Washington, DC 20013
"Broadcast Journalist"

Donald Woods
690 North Camino Real
Palm Springs, CA 92262
"Actor"

James Woods
760 N. La Cienega Blvd.
Los Angeles, CA 90069
"Actor, Director"

Michael Woods
1608 Courtney Avenue
Los Angeles, CA 90046
"Actor"

Robert S. Woods
227 Central Park W. #5-A
New York, NY 10024
"Actor"

Rosemary Woods
1194 West Cambridge Street
Alliance, OH 44601
"Secretary to President Nixon"

Tiger Woods
4281 Katella Avenue #111
Los Alamitos, CA 90720
"Golfer"

Bob Woodward
2907 "Q" Street NW
Washington, DC 20007
"News Corespondent"

Edward Woodward
Ravens Court, Calstock
Cornwall PL18 9ST ENGLAND
"Actor"

Joanne Woodward
1120 - 5th Avenue #1C
New York, NY 10128
"Actress, Director"

Marjorie Woodworth
807 North La Brea Avenue
Inglewood, CA 90301
"Actress"

Chuck Woolery
620 North Linden Drive
Beverly Hills, CA 90210
"TV Show Host"

Sheb Wooley
123 Walton Ferry Road #200
Hendersonville, TN 37075
"Singer"

Tom Wopat
2614 Woodlawn Drive
Nashville, TN 37212
"Actor, Director"

Joanne Worley
P.O. Box 2054
Toluca Lake, CA 91610
"Actress"

Cal Worthington
3815 Florin Road
Sacramento, CA 95823
"Car Dealer"

Irene Worty
333 West 56th Street
New York, NY 10018
"Actress"

Herman Wouk
303 Crestview
Palm Springs, CA 92264
"Author"

Steve Wozniak
475 Alberto Way
Los Gatos, CA 95030
"Computer Builder"

Clare Wren
5750 Wilshire Blvd. #512
Los Angeles, CA 90036
"Actress"

Cobina Wright, Jr.
1326 Dove Meadow Road
Solvang, CA 93463
"Actress"

Jenny Wright
245 West 104th Street
New York, NY 10025
"Actress"

Jim Wright
9A10 Lanham Federal Bldg.
819 Taylor Street
Fort Worth, TX 76102
"Former House Speaker"

Steven Wright
9000 Sunset Blvd. #1200
Los Angeles, CA 90069
"Comedian"

Teresa Wright
948 Rowayton Wood Drive
Norwalk, CT 06854
"Actress"

William Wrigley
410 North Michigan Avenue
Chicago, IL 60611
"Chewing Gum & Baseball Exec."

Robert Wuhl
10590 Holman Avenue
Los Angeles, CA 90024
"Comedian, Actor, Writer"

Jane Wyatt
651 Siena Way
Los Angeles, CA 90024
"Actress"

Shannon Wyatt
8949 Falling Creek Court
Annandale, VA 22003
"Actress"

Sharon Wyatt
24549 Park Grande
Calabasas, CA 91302
"Actress"

Andrew Wyeth
c/o General Delivery
Chadds Ford, PA 19317
"Artist"

Noah Wyle
P.O. Box 27278
Los Angeles, CA 90027
"Actor"

Gretchen Wyler
15215 Weddington Street
Van Nuys, CA 91411
"Actress"

George Wyner
3450 Laurie Place
Studio City, CA 91604
"Actor"

Early Wynn
P.O. Box 3969
Venice, FL 34293
"Ex-Baseball Player"

Steve Wynn
P.O. Box 610
Las Vegas, NV 89101
"Casino Owner"

Wynonna
325 Bridge Street
Franklin, TN 37064
"Singer"

Amanda Wyss
9229 Sunset Blvd., #311
Los Angeles, CA 90069
"Actress"

Frank Yablans
100 Bull Path
East Hampton, NY 11937
"Film Writer, Producer"

Andrea Yaeger
P.O. Box 10970
Aspen, CO 81612
"Tennis Player"

Jeff Yagher
15057 Sherview Place
Sherman Oaks, CA 91403
"Actor"

Kristi Yamaguchi
3650 Montecito Drive
Fremont, CA 94536
"Ice Skater"

Emily Yancey
247 South Beverly Drive #102
Beverly Hills, CA 90212
"Actress"

Wierd Al Yankovic
923 Westmount Drive
Los Angeles, CA 90069
"Singer, Songwriter"

Yanni
509 Harnell Street
Monterey, CA 93940
"Rock & Roll Group"

Cale Yarborough
9617 Dixie River Road
Charlotte, NC 28270
"Race Car Driver"

Mollie Yard
1000-16th Street N.W.
Washington, DC 20036
"Feminist Leader"

Claire Yarlett
9300 Wilshire Blvd. #410
Beverly Hills, CA 90212
"Actor"

Amy Yasbeck
151 El Camino Drive
Beverly Hills, CA 90212
"Actress"

Carl Yastrzemski
4621 S. Ocean Blvd.
Highland Beach, FL 33431
"Ex-Baseball Player"

Cassie Yates
260 S. Beverly Drive #210
Beverly Hills, CA 90212
"Actress"

Petet Yates
3340 Caroline Avenue
Culver City, CA 90230
"Film Director"

Chuck Yeager
P.O. Box 128
Cedar Ridge, CA 95924
"Ex-Military Test Pilot"

Jeana Yeager
Rt. #2
P.O. Box 47
Campbell, TX 75442
"Avaitrix"

Trisha Yearwood
4636-316 Lebanon Pike
Nashville, TN 37076
"Singer"

Yellowjackets
9220 Sunset Blvd., #320
Los Angeles, CA 90069
"Jazz Group"

Boris Yeltsin
Uliza Twerskaya
Jamskaya 2
Moscow, Russia
"President of Russia"

Michelle Yeoh
10301 W. Pico Blvd. #121
Los Angeles, CA 90064
"Actress"

David Yip
15 Golden Square #315
London W1R 3AG ENGLAND
"Actor"

Dwight Yoakam
1250 - 6th Street #401
Santa Monica, CA 90401
"Singer, Guitarist"

Philip Yordan
4894 Mt. Elbrus Drive
San Diego, CA 92117
"Screenwriter"

Francine York
14333 Addison Street #315
Sherman Oaks, CA 91423
"Actress"

Michael York
9100 Cordell Drive
Los Angeles, CA 90069
"Actor"

Susannah York
13 Shorts Garden
London WC2H 9AT ENGLAND
"Actress"

Bud Yorkin
250 North Delfern Drive
Los Angeles, CA 90077
"Writer, Producer"

Mayor Sam Yorty
12979 Blairwood Drive
Studio City, CA 91604
"Ex-Mayor"

Tina Yothers
280 S. Beverly Drive #400
Beverly Hills, CA 90212
"Actress"

Alan Young
24072 La Hermosa
Laguna Niguel, CA 92677
"Actor"

Andrew Young
1088 Veltrie Circle S.W.
Atlanta, GA 30311
"Ex-Mayor of Atlanta"

Burt Young
9300 Wilshire Blvd. #410
Beverly Hills, CA 90212
"Actor, Screenwriter"

Chris T. Young
5959 Triumph Street
Commerce, CA 90040
"Actor"

Jesse Colin Young
P.O. Box 31
Lancaster, NH 03584
"Singer, Songwriter"

Neil Young
8501 Wilshire Blvd. #220
Beverly Hills, CA 90211
"Singer, Songwriter"

Raymond Young
Hampton Cottage
7 Church Street
Littlehampton BN1Y ENGLAND
"Actor"

Richard Young
1275 Westwood Blvd.
Los Angeles, CA 90024
"Actor"

Sean Young
P.O. Box 20547
Sedona, AZ 86341
"Actress"

Steve Young
261 E. Broadway
Salt Lake City, UT 84111
"Football Player"

William Allen Young
1213 West 122nd Street
Los Angeles, CA 90044
"Actor"

Barrie Youngfellow
9255 Sunset Blvd. #515
Los Angeles, CA 90069
"Actress"

Malika Yuba
230 Park Avenue #550
New York, NY 10069
"Actor"

Harris Yulin
1630 Crescent Place
Venice, CA 90291
"Actor"

Grace Zabriskie
1800 S. Robertson Blvd. #426
Los Angeles, CA 90035
"Actress"

John Zaccaro
22 Deepdene Road
Forest Hills, NY 11375
"Businessman"

Pia Zadora
9560 Wilshire Blvd.
Beverly Hills, CA 90212
"Actress, Singer"

Paula Zahn
524 West 57th Street
New York, NY 10019
"TV Show Host"

Steve Zahn
2372 Veteran Avenue #102
Los Angeles, CA 90064
"Actor"

Steven Zaillan
1300 Marquesas Way "C" #83
Marina del Rey, CA 90292
"Screenwriter"

Roxanne Zal
1450 Belfast Drive
Los Angeles, CA 90069
"Actress"

Billy Zane
450 N. Rossmore Avenue #1001
Los Angeles, CA 90004
"Actor"

Lisa Zane
209 S. Orange Drive
Los Angeles, CA 90036
"Actress"

Carmen Zapata
6107 Ethel Avenue
Van Nuys, CA 91405
"Actress"

Dweezil Zappa
P.O. Box 5265
North Hollywood, CA 91616
"Singer"

Moon Zappa
P.O. Box 5265
North Hollywood, CA 91616
"Singer"

Franco Zefferelli
91 Regent Street
London W1R 7TB ENGLAND
"Film Director"

Heidi Zeigler
4444 Lankershim Blvd. #207
North Hollywood, CA 91602
"Actress"

Anthony Zerbe
1175 High Road
Santa Barbara, CA 93150
"Actor"

Ian Ziering
2700 Jalmia Drive
West Hollywood, CA 90046
"Actress"

Efrem Zimbalist, Jr.
1448 Holsted Drive
Solvang, CA 93463
"Actor"

Stephanie Zimbalist
16255 Ventura Blvd. #1011
Encino, CA 91436
"Actress"

Don Zimmer
10124 Yacht Club Drive
St. Petersberg, FL 33706
"Ex-Baseball Player"

Kim Zimmer
9255 Sunset Blvd. #710
Los Angeles, CA 90069
"Actress"

Adrian Zmed
4345 Freedom Dr. Unit E
Calabasas, CA 91302
"Actor"

"Fuzzy" Zoeller
418 Deer Run Terrace
Floyd's Knobs, IN 47119
"Golfer"

Louis Zorich
222 Upper Mountain Road
Montclair, NJ 07043
"Actor"

Pinchas Zuckerman
711 West End Avenue #5K-N
New York, NY 10025
"Violinist"

Adm. Elmo Zumwalt Jr.
1000 Wilson Blvd., #3105
Arlington, VA 22209
"Ex-Military Leader"

Daphne Zuniga
P.O. Box 1249
White River Junction, VT 05001
"Actress"

ZZ Top
P.O. Box 19744
Houston, TX 77024
"Singer"

Other Places to write Celebrities: Movie Studios, TV Networks and Record Companies

Major Movie Studios:

Columbia Pictures
(Sony Pictures Entertainment, Inc.)
10202 West Washington Blvd.
Culver City, CA 90232

Fox, Inc.
10201 West Pico Blvd.
Los Angeles, CA 90035

Home Box Office, Inc.
2049 Century Park East, Suite 4100
Los Angeles, CA 90067

MGM-Pathe Communications Co.
10000 West Washington Blvd.
Culver City, CA 90232

Orion Pictures Corporation
1888 Century Park East
Los Angeles, CA 90067

Paramount Communication, Inc.
New York (Home Office)
15 Columbus Circle
New York, NY 10023

Paramount Communication, Inc.
West Coast Office:
5555 Melrose Avenue
Los Angeles, CA 90038

Touchstone Pictures
500 South Buena Vista Street
Burbank, CA 91521

Twentieth Century Fox
P.O. Box 900
Beverly Hills, CA 90213

Universal Pictures
100 Universal City Plaza
Universal City, CA 91608

Warner Bros., Inc.
4000 Warner Blvd.
Burbank, CA 91522

Major Television Network:

ABC
77 West 66th Street
New York, NY 10023

ABC
West Coast Studio:
2040 Avenue of the Stars
Century City, CA 90067

CBS
51 West 52nd Street
New York, NY 10019

CNN
One CNN Center
P.O. Box 105366
Atlanta, GA 30348

Fox Broadcasting Company
10201 West Pico Blvd.
Los Angeles, CA 90035

NBC
New York (Home Office)
30 Rockefeller Plaza
New York, NY 10112

NBC
West Coast Studio:
3000 Alameda Avenue
Burbank, CA 91523

ESPN
935 Middle Street
Bristol, CT 06010

Black Entertainment Network
1232 31st Street N.W.
Washington, DC 20007

C-SPAN
400 N. Capitol Street NW#650
Washington, DC 20001

PBS
1320 Braddock Place
Alexandria, VA 22314

Major Record Companies:

CBS Records, Inc.
51 West 52nd Street
New York, NY 10019

EMI
810 Seventh Avenue
8th Floor
New York, NY 10019

Emeral Records
830 Glastonbury Road
Suite 614
Nashville, TN 37217

Erika Records, Inc.
9827 Oak Street
Bellflower, CA 90706

MCA Records
70 Universal City Plaza
Universal City, CA 91608

Motown Record Company
6255 Sunset Blvd.
17th Floor
Los Angeles, CA 90028

PolyGram Records, Inc.
825 Eighth Avenue
New York, NY 10019

PolyGram Records: Nashville
901 - 18th Avenue South
Nashville, TN 37212

RCA Records, Inc.
P.O. Box 126
405 Tarrytown Road
Suite 335
Elmsford, NY 10523

SBK Records
1290 Avenue of the Americas
New York, NY 10104

Warner Music International
75 Rockefeller Plaza
New York, NY 10019

Other Places to Write Sports Celebrities: Baseball, Basketball and Football Teams

Major League Baseball
350 Park Avenue
New York, NY 10022
Commissioner:
Fay Vincent

American League Teams:

Baltimore Orioles
333 West Camden Street
Baltimore, MD 21201

Boston Red Sox
Fenway Park
Boston, MA 02215

California Angeles
P.O. Box 2000
Anaheim, CA 92803

Chicago White Sox
333 West 35th Street
Chicago, IL 60016

Cleveland Indians
Cleveland Stadium
Cleveland, OH 44114

Detroit Tigers
2121 Trumbull Avenue
Detroit, MI 48216

Kansas City Royals
P.O. Box 419969
Kansas City, MO 64141

Milwaukee Brewers
Milwaukee County Stadium
Milwaukee, WI 53214

Minnesota Twins
501 Chicago Avenue South
Minneapolis, MN 55415

New York Yankees
Yankee Stadium
Bronx, NY 10451

Oakland Athletics
Oakland Alameda County Stadium
Oakland, CA 94621

Seattle Mariners
P.O. Box 4100
Seattle, WA 98104

Texas Rangers
P.O. Box 90111
Arlington, TX 76004

Toronto Blue Jays
1 Blue Jays Way #3200
Toronto, Ont. M5V 1J1 CANADA

National League Teams:

Atlanta Braves
P.O. Box 4064
Atlanta, GA 30302

Chicago Cubs
1060 West Addison
Chicago, IL 60613

Cincinnati Reds
100 Riverfront Stadium
Cinncinnati, OH 45202

Colorado Rockies
1700 Broadway
Suite #2100
Denver, CO 80290

Florida Marlins
2267 NW 199th Street
Miami, FL 33056

Houston Astros
P.O. Box 288
Houston, TX 77001

Los Angeles Dodgers
1000 Elysian Park Avenue
Los Angeles, CA 90012

Montreal Expos
P.O. Box 500, Station M
Montreal, Que. H1V 3P2 CANADA

New York Mets
Shea Stadium
Flushing, NY 11368

Philadelphia Phillies
P.O. Box 7575
Philadelphia, PA 19101

Pittsburgh Pirates
Three Rivers Stadium
Pittsburg, PA 15212

St. Louis Cardinals
250 Stadium Plaza
St. Louis, MO 63102

San Diego Padres
P.O. Box 2000
San Diego, CA 92120

San Francisco Giants
Candlestick Park
San Francisco, CA 94124

National Basketball Association:

Olympic Tower
645 Fifth Avenue
New York, NY 10022
Commissioner:
David Stern

Atlanta Hawks
One CNN Center
South Tower, Suite 405
Atlanta, GA 30303

Boston Celtics
151 Merrimac Street, 5th Floor
Boston, MA 02114

Charlotte Hornets
100 Hive Drive
Charlotte, NC 28217

Chicago Bulls
980 North Michigan Avenue
Suite #1600
Chicago, IL 60611

Cleveland Cavaliers
Gateway Arena
1 Center Court
Cleveland, OH 44115

Dallas Mavericks
Reunion Arena
777 Sports Street
Dallas, TX 75207

Denver Nuggets
1635 Clay Street
P.O. Box 4658
Denver, CO 80204

Detroit Pistons
The Palace
3777 Lapeer Road
Auburn Hills, MI 48057

Golden State Warriors
Oakland Coliseum Arena
7000 Coliseum Way
Oakland, CA 94621

Houston Rockets
The Summit
10 Greenway Plaza East
Houston, TX 77277

Indiana Pacers
300 East Market Street
Indianapolis, IN 46204

Los Angeles Clippers
3939 South Figueroa
Los Angeles, CA 90037

Los Angeles Lakers
Great Western Forum
3900 W. Manchester Blvd.
Inglewood, CA 90306

Miami Heat
Miami Arena
701 Areana Blvd.
Miami, FL 33136

Milwaukee Bucks
The Bradley Center
1001 North Fourth Street
Milwaukee, WI 53203

New Jersey Nets
405 Murray Hill Parkway
East Rutherford, NJ 07073

New York Knickerbockers
Madison Square Garden
Two Pennsylvania Plaza
New York, NY 10121

Orlando Magic
Orlando Arena
One Magic Place
Orlando, FL 32801

Philadelphia 76ers
P.O. Box 25040
Philadelphia, PA 19147

Phoenix Suns
201 East Jefferson
Phoenix, AZ 85001

Portland Trail Blazers
700 N.E. Multnomah Street
Suite #950 - Lloyd Building
Portland, OR 97232

Sacramento Kings
One Sports Parkway
Sacramento, CA 95834

San Antonio Spurs
100 Montana Street
San Antonio, TX 78205

Seattle Supersonics
190 Queen Anne Avenue North
Suite 200
Seattle, WA 98109

Toronto Raptors
150 York Street, Suite 1100
Toronto, Ontario
M5H 3S5 CANADA

Utah Jazz
Delta Center
301 West South Temple
Salt Lake City, UT 84101

National Football League:
410 Park Avenue
New York, NY 10022
Commissioner:
Paul Tagliabue

American Football Conference:
Buffalo Bills
One Bills Drive
Orchard Park, NY 14127

Cincinnati Bengals
200 Riverfront Stadium
Cinncinnati, OH 45202

Denver Broncos
1900 West Eliot
Denver, CO 80204

Indianapolis Colts
100 South Capitol Avenue
Indianapolis, IN 46225

Jacksonville Jaguars
1 Stadium Place
Jacksonville, FL 32202

Kansas City Chiefs
One Arrowhead Drive
Kansas City, MO 64129

Miami Dolphins
Joe Robbie Stadium
2269 N.W. 199th Street
Miami, FL 33056

New England Patriots
Sullivan Stadium-Route 1
Foxboro, MA 02035

New York Jets
Giants Stadium
East Rutherford, NJ 07073

Oakland Raiders
3911 South Figueroa Street
Los Angeles, CA 90037

Pittsburgh Steelers
Three Rivers Stadium
300 Stadium Circle
Pittsburgh, PA 15212

San Diego Chargers
9449 Friars Road
San Diego, CA 92120

Seattle Seahawks
201 South King Street
Seattle, WA 98033

Tennessee Oilers
Liberty Stadium
335 South Hollywood
Memphis, TN 38104

National Football Conference:
Atlanta Falcons
1 Georgia Drive
Atlanta, GA 30313

Baltimore Ravens
333 West Camden Street
Baltimore, MD 21201

Carolina Panters
227 West Trade Street #1600
Charlotte, NC 28202

Chicago Bears
425 McFetridge Place
Chicago, IL 60605

Dallas Cowboys
1 Cowboys Parkway
Irving, TX 75063

Detroit Lions
1200 Featherstone Road
Pontiac, MI 48057

Green Bay Packers
1265 Lombardi Avenue
Green Bay, WI 54303

St. Louis Rams
4245 North King Hwy
St. Louis, MO 63115

Minnesota Vikings
500 - 11th Avenue South
Minneapolis, MN 55415

New Orleans Saints
1500 Poydras Street
New Orleans, LA 70112

New York Giants
Giants Stadium
East Rutherford, NJ 07073

Philadelphia Eagles
Veterans Stadium
Broad Street & Pattison Avenue
Philadelphia, PA 19148

Phoenix Cardinals
Sun Devil Stadium
Fifth Street
Tempe, AZ 85287

San Francisco 49ers
Candlestick Park
San Francisco, CA 94124

Tampa Bay Buccaneers
Tampa Stadium
North Dale Mabry
Tampa, FL 33607

Washington Redskins
RFK Stadium
East Capitol Street
Washington, DC 20003

MAKE CONTACT WITH THE STARS!

The **Celebrity Directory**™ **(9th Edition)** covers the entire spectrum of of celebrities. If a person is famous or worth locating, it's almost certain that their address can be found in the Celebrity Directory. ISBN 0-943213-31-2 **$39.95+$2.95 postage & handling.**

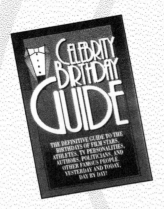

Use the **Celebrity Birthday Directory**™ **(4th Edition)** to find the birthdays of your favorite celebrities. Alphabetized for quick reference.
ISBN 0-943213-26-6
Only $10.95+$1.95 postage & handling

The **Celebrity Birthday Guide**™ **(4th Edition)** lists the birthdays of celebrities past and present. Thousands of entries by calendar date.
ISBN 0-943213-25-8
Only $10.95+$1.95 postage & handling.

The **1999-2000 Star Guide**™ is the most reliable and up-to-date guide available for over 3200 addresses of major stars from every field.
ISBN 0-943213-30-4
Only $12.95+$1.95 postage & handling.